Digital Humanities and Christianity

Introductions to
Digital Humanities – Religion

Edited by
Claire Clivaz, Charles M. Ess, Gregory Price Grieve,
Kristian Petersen and Sally Promey

Volume 4

Digital Humanities and Christianity

An Introduction

Edited by
Tim Hutchings and Claire Clivaz

DE GRUYTER

ISBN 978-3-11-055989-7
e-ISBN (PDF) 978-3-11-057404-3
e-ISBN (EPUB) 978-3-11-057188-2

Library of Congress Control Number: 2021937616

Bibliographic information published by the Deutsche Nationalbibliothek
The Deutsche Nationalbibliothek lists this publication in the Deutsche Nationalbibliografie;
detailed bibliographic data are available on the Internet at http://dnb.dnb.de.

© 2021 Walter de Gruyter GmbH, Berlin/Boston
Printing and binding: CPI books GmbH, Leck

www.degruyter.com

Table of Contents

Tim Hutchings and Claire Clivaz
Introduction —— 1

Part I: Canon, corpus and manuscript

Claire Clivaz
The Bible in the digital age: multimodal Scriptures in communities —— 21

Michael Stenskjær Christensen, Jeffrey C. Witt and Ueli Zahnd
Re-conceiving the Christian scholastic corpus with the scholastic commentaries and texts archive —— 47

Roman Bleier
Canonical structure and the referencing of digital resources for the study of ancient and medieval Christianity —— 77

Dan Batovici and Joseph Verheyden
Digitizing the ancient versions of the Apostolic Fathers: preliminary considerations —— 103

Part II: Words and meanings

Jeanne-Nicole Mellon Saint-Laurent
Languages, texts, and inscribed objects of early Christianity: a survey of digital resources for students —— 127

Mathias Coeckelbergs
Between statistics and hermeneutics: the interplay between digital and traditional methods in Hebrew linguistics as evidenced from the study of *hapax legomena* —— 151

Matthew Munson
Lexicography, the Louw–Nida Lexicon, and computational co-occurrence analysis —— 169

Part III: Digital Christian history

Delfi I. Nieto-Isabel and Carlos López-Arenillas
From inquisition to inquiry: inquisitorial records as a source for social network analysis —— 195

Katherine Faull
Visualizing religious networks, movements, and communities: building Moravian Lives —— 213

John N. Wall
The theology of relational practice: digital modeling and the historical study of Christianity —— 237

Louis Chevalier
Liturgical history in a digital world: principles and future developments —— 261

Part IV: Theology and pedagogy

Tim Hutchings and Karen O'Donnell
Digital pedagogy and spiritual formation: training for ministry and games for children —— 281

Gary Slater
Nested histories: digital humanities as pedagogical laboratory for early Christian studies —— 301

Alexander Chow
Public theology behind the Great Firewall of China —— 319

Index —— 339

Tim Hutchings and Claire Clivaz
Introduction

1 Introduction: What is Digital Humanities?

The relationship between Christianity and computers goes back to the very dawn of punched cards and magnetic tape. Christians and scholars of Christianity quickly recognised that computers offered a powerful new way to analyze the vast libraries of interconnected texts that make up the Bible and the libraries of Christian philosophy and theology. Christians also seized on the emerging forms of computer-mediated communication, just as they had embraced previous media revolutions like the telegraph, radio and television. New forms of communication promised new ways to coordinate, build networks, share ideas, and promote Christian messages to new audiences.[1]

The field of research, collaboration, teaching and communication now known as Digital Humanities (DH) emerged in the early 00s out of the older tradition of humanities computing, which focused particularly on the use of computational tools to analyze texts. DH promised a broader, more radically transformational approach, designed both to challenge the traditional humanities and to embed humanities thinking in the new digital industries.[2] DH encourages humanities scholars to learn from computational sciences in order to digitize the multimodal sources used in humanities research, to use digital tools to study those sources, and to share their data in open ways according to shared standards. Using these digital tools, methods and networks, DH searches for new insights into old humanities questions, new questions for the humanities to ask, and new opportunities to bring humanities perspectives to bear on the analysis of digital culture. DH challenges humanities scholars to rethink the forms in which academic knowledge is produced and published, to embrace interdisciplinary collaboration, and to communicate their ideas in new, digital ways to reach new audiences.

This volume is an introduction to the place now occupied by the study of Christianity within DH. The editors, Tim Hutchings and Claire Clivaz, have both worked in DH research centers, but in quite different disciplinary areas.

---

[1] Tim Hutchings, *Creating Church Online* (London/New York: Routledge, 2017); Claire Clivaz, *Ecritures digitales. Digital writing, digital Scriptures* (DBS 4, Leiden: Brill, 2019).
[2] Patrik Svensson and David Theo Goldberg, "Introduction", in *Between the Humanities and the Digital*, ed. P. Svensson and D. T. Goldberg (Cambridge: MIT Press, 2015), 5.

Dr. Clivaz is a biblical scholar with expertise in New Testament studies, while Dr. Hutchings is a sociologist of digital religion and religious media ethics. As our range of interests indicates, DH today is a broad landscape, united less by a single cohort of methods, sources or tools than by a shared fascination with the ways in which the digital is transforming the horizons of humanities scholarship.

Christianity and the Digital Humanities seeks to capture something of that breadth, including contributions by textual scholars, linguists, historians, theologians and teachers of religion. Essays in this volume explain the history of DH work in the study of Christianity, introduce some of the key tools and approaches now being used, and evaluate the impact of DH on different areas of Christian studies. Digital work outside the academy will also be explored, in recognition of the long and vibrant tradition of Christian digital innovation. Christian institutions and organizations have spent decades pioneering their own digital approaches to textual analysis, publishing and communication, and these endeavors often reach much larger audiences than academic DH projects.[3]

We hope that this volume will prove valuable for students and scholars looking for their first introduction to what DH might mean for research and teaching in their disciplines, but the case studies described here should also challenge DH scholars interested in the latest advances in their fields of research.

2 Christianity and the Digital Humanities

Creating a volume focused on Christianity and the Digital Humanities (DH) assumes that we can consider them together, as related subjects. A more fundamental question is whether one can speak of a digital way to do Christian studies, whether theological, historical or social-scientific. Can we talk about Christian Digital Humanities, or digital Christian studies? From a formal point of view, the question is the same for all fields in the humanities: is the digital revolution affecting a discipline to the point of transforming it drastically?

The impact of this digital revolution is often perceived as so important that it requires new or specific words to describe it. For example, Steven Jones has chosen the term "eversion" to illustrate the present state of the digital turn,[4]

---

[3] Tim Hutchings, "Digital Humanities and the Study of Religion", in *Between the Humanities and the Digital*, ed. P. Svensson and D. T. Goldberg (Cambridge: MIT Press, 2015), 283.

[4] Steven E. Jones, "The Emergence of the Digital Humanities (the Network Is Everting)", in *Debates in the Digital Humanities* 2, ed. Matthew K. Gold and Lauren Klein (Minneapolis: University Minnesota Press, 2016), http://dhdebates.gc.cuny.edu/debates/text/52.

whereas the French thinker Bernard Stiegler focuses on "disruption".[5] But as Clivaz proposed in 2019, we could also now argue that the revolution has progressed so far that it has become unnecessary to distinguish the digital as a subset or type of humanities. Instead, we could

> speak about the digitized humanities, or simply about humanities again, instead of digital humanities [...T]he expression 'digital computer', which was in common usage during the fifties [...] has been now replaced by the single latter word 'computer'[6]. When humanities finally become almost entirely digitized, perhaps it is safe to bet that we will once again speak simply about humanities.[7]

Even if this statement proves in part to be a bet, such a step will take time to be accomplished. Meanwhile, institutional marks of digital Christian theology, digital biblical studies or digital religious studies have begun to emerge. Scholars in these fields have founded dedicated journals,[8] special issues,[9] book series,[10] academic networks[11] and conference streams.[12] The Jesuit order founded the Centre for the Study of Communication and Culture in London (UK) in 1977, and the CSCC

---

[5] Bernard Stiegler, *Dans la disruption. Comment ne pas devenir fou?* (Paris: Les liens qui libèrent, 2016).
[6] Bernard O. Williams, *Computing with Electricity, 1935–1945* (PhD diss., Lawrence: University of Kansas, 1984), 310; Robert Dennhardt, *The Term Digital Computer (Stibitz 1942) and the Flip-Flop (Turner 1920)* (München, Grin Verlag, 2016).
[7] Clivaz, *Digital Writing, Digital Scriptures*, 85–6.
[8] *Heidelberg Journal of Religions on the Internet,* https://heiup.uni-heidelberg.de/journals/index.php/religions/index; *Religion, Media and Digital Culture,* https://brill.com/rmdc; *Gamevironments,* https://www.gamevironments.uni-bremen.de/.
[9] Claire Clivaz and Garrick Allen, "Digital Humanities in Biblical Studies and Theology", *Open Theology* 5 (2019).
[10] *Digital Biblical Studies* (Leiden: Brill); *Routledge Studies in Religion and Digital Culture* (Abingdon: Routledge).
[11] Network for New Media, Religion and Digital Culture Studies (https://digitalreligion.tamu.edu/); not accessible in July 21; Global Network for Digital Theology (https://www.dur.ac.uk/digitaltheology/gndt/).
[12] For example, an annual digital humanities session has been hosted by the Society for Biblical Literature since 2012 (Claire Clivaz and Sarah Bowen Savant, "Introduction: The Dissemination of the Digital Humanities within Research on Biblical, Early Jewish and Early Christian Studies", in *Ancient Manuscripts in Digital Culture,* ed. David Hamidovic, Claire Clivaz and Sarah Bowen Savant (Leiden: Brill, 2019), 1.) The American Academy of Religion hosted a five-year seminar on Video Gaming and Religion from 2015–2019 (https://papers2015.aarweb.org/content/video-gaming-and-religion-seminar). Regular conferences of digital theology include the European Christian Internet Conference, hosted annually since 1996 (https://ecic.mobi/), and TheoCom, hosted annually by the Centre for the Study of Communication and Culture at Santa Clara University (US) since 2012 (http://cscc.scu.edu/theocom19/about.html).

continues to publish the quarterly journal *Communication Research Trends*.[13] The Eep Talstra Centre for Bible and Computer at Vrije University (Amsterdam, NL) was founded as Wergroep Informatica VU in 1977 to promote computer-aided methods of biblical studies, and now offers a Master degree in Biblical Studies and Digital Humanities.[14] Much more recently, the CODEC research initiative in the UK became a Research Centre of Durham University in 2014, launched a degree of Master of Arts in Digital Theology in 2017 (now based at Spurgeon's College in London),[15] and was renamed the Centre for Digital Theology in 2018. In 2019, the Centre for Digital Theology founded the first worldwide network of digital theologians, the Global Network for Digital Theology.[16] From the religious studies side, a center like MAVCOR,[17] the Center for the Study of Material & Visual Cultures of Religion at Yale University, is deeply shaped by digital culture, even if its name does not mention DH as such. MAVCOR perhaps anticipates the step at which the Humanities, digitized, could simply go back to their shorter name.

Most of this institutional evolution is surprisingly recent, if we consider the fact that Christianity has been present since the very first DH projects. It is well known that the first ever computing tool built for the humanities was the *Index Thomisticus*, created in 1949 by the Jesuit Father Roberto Busa,[18] and this story will be analyzed in more detail by Claire Clivaz in Chapter 1 of this volume. This traditional starting point in the history of DH has often promoted Roberto Busa to the position of "father of the discipline", a preeminent role underlined by the enthusiasm he himself demonstrated for DH, going so far as to compare DH to the "finger of God".[19] Soon thereafter, the Reverend John W. Ellison used computers to produce a concordance of the English translation of the *Revised Standard Version* of the Bible, published in 1957.[20]

---

[13] *Communication Research Trends*, http://cscc.scu.edu/CSCC/history.html.
[14] *MA in Digital Theology*, Spurgeon's College, https://www.spurgeons.ac.uk/ma-in-digital-theology/; *MA in Biblical Studies and DH*, Vrije Amsterdam University, http://www.godgeleerdheid.vu.nl/nl/Images/BiblicalStudies_tcm238-829352.pdf.
[15] *Centre for Digital Theology*, Durham University, https://www.dur.ac.uk/digitaltheology/.
[16] Pete Phillips, Kyle Schiefelbein-Guerrero and Jonas Kurlberg, "Defining Digital Theology: Digital Humanities, Digital Religion and the Particular Work of the CODEC Research Centre and Network", *Open Theology* 5 (2019): 29–43.
[17] *MAVCOR*, https://mavcor.yale.edu/.
[18] https://www.corpusthomisticum.org/it/index.age.
[19] Roberto Busa, "Foreword: Perspectives on the Digital Humanities", in *A Companion to Digital Humanities*, ed. Susan Schreibman, Ray Siemens and John Unsworth (Hoboken, NJ: Wiley Blackwell, 2004), http://www.digitalhumanities.org/companion/.
[20] Steven E. Jones, *Roberto Busa, S.J., and the Emergence of Humanities Computing: The Priest and the Punched Cards*, (New York: Routledge, 2016), 100–1.

The close relationship between biblical studies and digital humanities has continued over subsequent decades. In the early 1990s, it has been argued, biblical studies relied on and advanced alongside DH to a greater extent than any other discipline in the humanities.[21] But academic publications demonstrating critical self-reflection on the relationship between DH and the Bible have been slow to emerge. Jeffrey Siker's *Liquid Scripture*, the first monograph devoted to the Bible in digital culture, was published only in 2017,[22] sixty years after the concordance built by Ellison. Siker's work has been followed in quick succession by Claire Clivaz's *Ecritures digitales: Digital Writing, Digital Scriptures* (2019) and Peter Phillips' *The Bible, Social Media and Digital Culture* (2019).[23]

This substantial six decade gap reflects the deep transformation of the status of the biblical text provoked by the advent of digital culture,[24] as well as the multimodal expression of the Bible and theological discourse in digital culture.[25] Software packages and tools like *Bibleworks*, *Accordance*, and *Logos* are now widely used in seminaries and churches. The free biblical app *YouVersion*,[26] created by a church in the United States, now hosts 1200 versions of the Bible in 900 languages and has been installed on almost 450 million devices worldwide.

Digital tools are now widely used to access and study the Bible by Christian ministers, churches and practitioners around the world. Products like *YouVersion*, developed outside the academy, show careful consideration of the impact of digital media on Christian thought and practice.[27] In other words, scholars of contemporary Christianity are studying a religion that is already rapidly digitizing.[28] This digital revolution within Christianity has been inspired at least in part by the same excitement that drives the academic Digital Humanities: a recognition that digital media can transform the study of texts, languages and cor-

---

[21] Juan Garcés and Jan Heilmann, "Digital Humanities und Exegese. Erträge, Potentiale, Grenzen und hochschuldidaktische Perspektiven", *Forum Exegese und Hochschuldidaktik: Verstehen von Anfang an, Digital Humanities* 2 (2017), 30.
[22] Jeffrey Siker, *Liquid Scripture: The Bible in a Digital World* (Minneapolis: Fortress Press, 2017).
[23] Claire Clivaz, *Ecritures digitales. Digital writing, digital Scriptures*, DBS 4 (Brill, Leiden, 2019) ; Peter M. Phillips, *The Bible, Social Media and Digital Culture* (Routledge, New York, 2019).
[24] Clivaz, *Ecritures digitales. Digital writing, digital Scriptures*, 173–81, 218–21.
[25] Peter M. Phillips, "The Power of Visual Culture and The Fragility of the Text", in *Ancient Manuscripts in Digital Culture*, ed. David Hamidović, Claire Clivaz and Sarah Bowen Savant, DBS 3 (Brill, Leiden, 2019): 10–21.
[26] *YouVersion*, https://www.bible.com.
[27] Tim Hutchings, "Design and the Digital Bible", *Journal of Contemporary Religion* 32 (2) (2017): 205–19.
[28] Tim Hutchings, "Christianity and Digital Media", in *The Changing World Religion Map*, ed. Stanley Brunn (Berlin: Springer, 2015): 3811–30.

pora, support new ways of analyzing and visualizing data, and enable the communication of ideas to new audiences.

In recognition of this reciprocal relationship between the academic digital humanities and the Christian digital revolution, this volume argues that the religious studies approaches to digital Christianity should also be considered within the DH conversation. The study of digital religion emerged in the 1990s[29] and is now located primarily within the larger field of media, religion and culture, bringing together the methods and theories of media studies, cultural studies and the study of religion, often in conversation with media philosophy and theology. Digital religion starts from the foundational position of media, religion and culture, the principle that religion and media cannot be separated.[30] Contemporary religion is enacted through the digital, transforming and being transformed by digital culture. Heidi Campbell's edited volume *Digital Religion*[31] offers a summary of many of the key issues explored by scholars over the previous two decades, including ritual, identity, community, authority, authenticity, and the definition of "religion". Campbell's work has also been foundational for the relationship between digital religious studies and digital theology, inviting dialogue and partnership between these disciplines, notably in her 2016 co-authored volume with Stephen Garner.[32]

In summary, Christian theology, religious studies and biblical studies have a long, rich and productive history of interaction with the academic digital humanities. There is no unique Christian way to do DH, but the numerous signs of academic institutionalization of DH, the rich libraries of academic DH publications and the extraordinary global Christian interest in digital theology and digital Bible study all demonstrate the value of an introductory book to Christianity and the digital humanities. The next section of this chapter identifies some features and trends in Christian DH today.

---

29 Heidi A. Campbell and Brian Altenhofen, "Methodological Challenges, Innovations and Growing Pains in Digital Religion Research", in *Digital Methodologies in the Sociology of Religion*, ed. Sariva Cheruvallil-Contractor and Suha Shakkour (Bloomsbury Publishing, 2015): 1–12.
30 Jeremy Stolow, "Religion and/as Media", *Theory, Culture and Society* 22(4) (2005): 119–45.
31 Heidi A. Campbell (ed.), *Digital Religion. Understanding Religious Practice in New Media Worlds* (Abingdon: Routledge, 2013).
32 Heidi A. Campbell and Stephen Garner, *Networked Theology. Negotiating Faith in Digital Culture* (London: Baker Academy, 2016).

3 Orientations and directions in Christianity and the Digital Humanities

As Carrie Schroeder has emphasized, quoting Bianco, "'digital and computational work' produces new worlds, 'both felt and real but multimodally layered worlds'.[33] Worlds of empowerment, engagement, interactivity."[34] This statement can be tested every day in the production and analysis of digital culture. Nothing about this is unique to Christianity, or even to religious studies. Religious studies are embedded, reshaped, transformed by the digital culture, as all the other humanities fields are – indeed, as all cultural areas are. Considering the ubiquity of digital transformation reinforces the idea that we will probably in the future speak simply about "humanities".

A recent debate has emerged in DH over the choice between "digitized" and "digitalized" humanities. Brennen and Kreiss distinguish digitization, the simple process of converting information into digital forms, from digitalization, defined as the social impact of digital communication.[35] Whereas DHers are just beginning to take account of this choice,[36] the word digitalization has been widely used for many years in business and marketing milieus to express "the adoption or increase in use of digital or computer technology by an organization, industry, country, etc",[37] one of the major "trends changing society and business."[38] Some

---

[33] Jamie "Skye" Bianco, "This Digital Humanities Which Is Not One", *Debates in the Digital Humanities*, ed. Matthew K. Gold (Minneapolis: University of Minnesota Press, 2012): 96–112, here 100 ; http://dhdebates.gc.cuny.edu/debates/text/9.
[34] Caroline T. Schroeder, "The Digital Humanities as Cultural Capital: Implications for Biblical and Religious Studies", *Journal of Religion, Media, and Digital Culture* 5(1) (2016): 21–49, here 43. http://doi.org/10.1163/21659214–90000069.
[35] J. Scott Brennen and Daniel Kreiss, "Digitalization", *International Encyclopedia of Communication Theory and Philosophy* (23.10.2016): 1–11, https://onlinelibrary.wiley.com/doi/abs/10.1002/9781118766804.wbiect111.
[36] Claire Clivaz, "Digitized and Digitalized Humanities: Words and Identity", in *Atti del IX Convegno Annuale dell'Associazione per l'Informatica Umanistica e la Cultura Digitale. La svolta inevitabile: sfide e prospettive per l'informatica umanistica*, ed. Cristina Marras, Marco Passarotti, Greta Franzini and Eleonora Litta, (Bologna: AIUCD, 2020) 67–73; https://umanisticadigitale.unibo.it; Simon Tanner, *Delivering Impact with Digital Resources: Planning Strategy in the Attention Economy* (London: Facet Publishing, 2020).
[37] Entry "digitalization n.2" in the *Oxford English Dictionary* online: https://www.oed.com/view/Entry/242061.
[38] Päivi Parvianien, Jukka Kääriäinen, Maarit Tihinen, and Susanna Teppola, "Tackling the digitalization challenge: how to benefit from digitalization in practice", *International Journal of In-*

humanist voices argue that DH should preserve a critical distance from this large-scale phenomenon of digitalization. Domenico Fiormonte argues that the world of research and education has been colonized by the digital: "Digitalization has become not only a vogue or an imperative, but a normality. In this sort of 'gold rush', the digital humanities perhaps have been losing their original openness and revolutionary potential."[39] Maja van der Velden argues that the standardization inherent in digitalization enacts the erasure of diversity: "the technology that produces digital connectivity also produces the non-existence of people and their stories, the fabric of the social nature of knowledge."[40] Her post-colonial analysis of an independent journalism network and an Aboriginal database demonstrates that technology can be designed sensitively to support different ways of knowing, instead of making them invisible.

DH approaches to religion, including Christianity, are still at the threshold of such awareness, like other humanities fields. Numerous projects are deeply reshaping points of view and methodologies in religious studies, but often without making explicit the impact of "digitalization" upon them. The project "Uncle Tom's Bibles: Bibles as Visual and Material Objects from Antebellum Abolitionism to Jim Crow Cinema",[41] led at the *MAVCOR* center, illustrates this phenomenon. The project describes its purpose and methodology as follows: it "examines biblical materiality in *Uncle Tom's Cabin*, its various illustrated editions, and its theatrical and cinematic afterlives. It argues that the various bibles addressed profound issues of the co-construction of race and religion from the middle of the nineteenth century to the first decades of the twentieth."[42] This project offers enlightening new perspectives on this historical period. But if it is based on a deep awareness of the influency of the materiality of the book, it apparently leaves aside the impact of the next materiality, digital culture, on the project itself, including possible distortion coming from the "digitalization effect".

---

formation Systems and Project Management 5 (2017/1): 63–76; here 63; http://doi.org/10.12821/ijispm050104.

39 Domenico Fiormonte, "Toward a Cultural Critique of Digital Humanities", in *Debates in the Digital Humanities* 2, ed. Matthew K. Gold and Lauren F. Klein, https://dhdebates.gc.cuny.edu/read/untitled/section/5cac8409-e521-4349-ab03-f341a5359a34#ch35.

40 Maja van der Velden, "Invisibility and the Ethics of the Digitalization: Designing so as Not to Hurt Others" in *Information Technology Ethics: Cultural Perspectives*, ed. Sonja Hongladarom and Charles Ess (Hershey, PA: Idea Group Reference Ed., 2007), 82.

41 Edward J. Blum, "Uncle Tom's Bibles: Bibles as Visual and Material Objects from Antebellum Abolitionism to Jim Crow Cinema", *MAVCOR Journal* 3 (2019/2), *Special Issue: Material and Visual Cultures of Religion in the American South*, https://mavcor.yale.edu/mavcor-journal/uncle-tom-s-bibles-bibles-visual-and-material-objects-antebellum-abolitionism-jim.

42 Ibid., §7.

In this sense, it illustrates features common today to numerous projects in religious studies: materiality, visualization and orality are raised to the top of the studied parameters in the multimodal digital culture. Scholars are consequently more conscious about what print culture has shaped or constrained in previous analysis, whereas they are often still ignoring the distinct but comparable effect of digital culture on their own research. Embedded in institutions in which digitalization is advancing every day, it will require a conscious effort for all scholars in theology and religious studies to develop a critical, scholarly awareness of digitalization, including its ethical aspects. From this perspective, one of the biggest challenges in the digital transformation of theology and religious studies is their relationship to textuality, like all humanities fields, and to religious texts in particular. As underlined by Sarah Mombert, the digital edition or collection has in itself a "decanonizing effect", beyond religious connotations:

> From the viewpoint of non-canonical texts (e.g., documents that until now had been deemed not worthy of reeditions with a critical apparatus and were kept out of the traditional circuit of learned books) [...] digital technology represents not only the opportunity of being salvaged from the ravage of time but also the end of a marginal editorial status.[43]

This ability to make available to the world texts and contents that were once hidden in the stomachs of libraries blurs the categories so well established in Modernity, for example between canonical and apocryphal texts in the Jewish and Christian traditions.[44] Such a blurring of categories, announced already in 2001 by Roger Chartier,[45] can be verified every day in scientific work. For example, as part of the SNSF-funded MARK16 project,[46] led by Claire Clivaz, with Mina Monier, Elisa Nury and Jonathan Barda (DH+ & Core-IT, SIB), has encoded material from a Patristic catena in the minuscule 304: non biblical material has been hold for the first time in the INTF New Testament Virtual Room of Manuscripts[47], partner of MARK16. This is New Testament textual criticism beyond the New Testa-

---

[43] Sarah Mombert, "From Books to Collections: Critical Editions of Heterogeneous Documents", in *Digital Critical Editions (Topics in the Digital Humanities)*, D. Apollon – C. Bélisle – P. Régnier (eds.) (Illinois: University of Illinois Press, 2014) Kindle edition: l. 5128.
[44] See Claire Clivaz, "Categories of Ancient Christian Texts and Writing Materials: 'Taking Once Again a Fresh StartingPpoint'", in *Ancient Worlds in Digital Culture*, DBS 1, ed. Claire Clivaz, Paul Dilley and David Hamidović, with Apolline Thromas (Leiden: Brill, 2016): 35–58.
[45] Roger Chartier, *Les métamorphoses du livre: Les rendez-vous de l'édition. Le livre et le numérique* (Paris: Bibliothèque du Centre Pompidou, 2001): 12–4.
[46] MARK16 Project, http://p3.snf.ch/project-179755; VRE website: https://mark16.sib.swiss.
[47] NTVRM, https://ntvmr.uni-muenster.de/manuscript-workspace?docID=30304&pageID=4900. On MARK16: https://mr-mark16.sib.swiss/show?id=R0EzMDQ=.

ment's canonical boundaries, because the digital research platform allows scholars to explore the content of this 12th century manuscript.[48] On a larger scale, Peter Gurry and Tommy Wasserman have cleverly demonstrated that the computing culture is leading scholars to give up on what were once the major schools of text theory in New Testament Textual Criticism.[49]

This reshaping of the textuality of the corpus that stands at the heart of Christianity is accompanied in the DH culture by the finest developments of the Text Encoding Initiative.[50] At the computing level, considering the fact that the Command-line Interface (CLI) will remain always more specific and efficient than the Graphical User Interface (GUI),[51] scholars will continue to wrestle with letters and textuality at all levels of digital research in religious studies, from the matter of the religious texts themselves to their digital encoding. That's the paradox of the multimodal digital culture: to push images and orality to the front of the stage, while shaping them entirely within digitally encoded letters and numbers.

4 Introducing the volume

As this survey has demonstrated, digital humanities scholarship can be found across the whole spectrum of the study of Christianity and Christian sources. To introduce this diversity, the volume is divided into four sections, each collecting a group of case studies around one theme: texts and manuscripts; languages and linguistics; Christian history; and Christian theology and pedagogy.

The first section, titled Canon, Corpus and Manuscript, brings together four essays on the contribution of DH methods to the analysis of Christian texts, from the Bible to the medieval period. In Chapter 1, titled "The Bible in the digital age", **Claire Clivaz** evaluates the digital turn in biblical studies. Both within and beyond the academy, she argues, the Bible is moving beyond the printed page into a new multimodal, networked culture of community engagement. Clivaz calls for biblical exegetes and theologians to pay attention to this transfor-

---

[48] Mina Monier, "GA 304, Theophylact's Commentary and the Ending of Mark", *Filología Neotestamentaria* 52 (2019): 94–106.
[49] Tommy Wasserman and Peter J. Gurry, *A New Approach to Textual Criticism: An Introduction to the Coherence-Based Genealogical Method* (Resources for Biblical Study 80) (Atlanta: SBL Press, 2017), 16.
[50] See for example the *Manual for Encoding Letters and Postcards in TEI-XML and DTABf demonstrates*, https://encoding-correspondence.bbaw.de/v1/index.html.
[51] See Clivaz, *Ecritures digitales. Digital writing, digital Scriptures*, 144–6, 165–6.

mation, contributing alongside humanists and philosophers to current debates over the future of teaching, scholarship and publishing in the unbound humanities.

In Chapter 2, "Re-conceiving the Christian scholastic corpus with the *Scholastic Commentaries and Texts Archive*", **Michael Stenskjær Christensen, Jeffrey C. Witt and Ueli Zahnd** present the scholastic method of theological work as "a huge network of thought". Scholastic reliance on textual interdependencies, explored through the creation of commentaries and compendia, means that scholasticism is only poorly represented in traditional scholarly print editions published under traditional forms of copyright. What is needed instead, they argue, is a new DH approach based on linked open data prepared according to open standards, to foster a new understanding of scholastic texts not as documents but as "first and foremost a network of connected data."

In Chapter 3, "Canonical structure and the referencing of digital resources for the study of ancient and medieval Christianity", **Roman Bleier** explores this theme of textual interdependence further by introducing the long history of citation systems. The system of dividing biblical books into chapters and verses with agreed titles emerged only in the medieval period, and was gradually applied to a diverse range of texts, growing into the system we use today – including the division of this book into chapters with titles and page numbers. Digital publishing raises new challenges, because online texts can vanish, move from one website to another, or their contents can be updated. Bleier argues that "in online publications a clear strategy is needed to generate sustainable identifiers and anchors", and outlines the options available to the producers of digital scholarly editions.

Chapter 4, "Digitizing the ancient versions of the Apostolic Fathers" by **Dan Batovici and Joseph Verheyden**, discusses a proposed project to study a corpus of early Christian texts originally written in Greek. While the Greek texts have received scholarly attention, the many ancient translations of these texts into other languages have been largely overlooked. Once again, we see here an example of the power of DH methods for enabling scholars to understand networks of textual interdependencies, including the opportunity to trace how texts are copied and interpreted across different centuries, languages and parts of the world. This proposed project will list and describe all the extant manuscripts, transcribe them, tag words, parts of speech and paratextual features to enable searches in any language, use these corpora to study the ancient languages themselves, and finally link data across languages to enable users to easily access an image of the original manuscript page.

The second section of this volume, titled Words and Meanings, presents three chapters focused on the study of language. In Chapter 5, "Languages, texts, and inscribed objects of early Christianity", **Jeanne-Nicole Mellon Saint-Laurent** reminds us that students of this period need to study "the languages in which the early Christians told their stories." A wide range of texts and objects have now been digitized, and this chapter promises to help students appreciate the range of resources at their disposal. Alongside an extensive list of projects and databases, explaining the strengths of each, Mellon Saint-Laurent also introduces some of the key terminology and concepts of DH, reinforcing once again the centrality of working collaboratively, publishing open data, and understanding the networks of relationships between texts and objects.

In Chapter 6, "Between statistics and hermeneutics", **Mathias Coeckelbergs** focuses our attention on the study of Hebrew. Coeckelbergs observes that the digitalization of linguistics has in some ways shifted the focus of the discipline, leading researchers to prioritize the study of countable entities over interpretation. To challenge this one-sided shift, Coeckelbergs introduces the medieval and modern history of the study of *hapax legomena*, words that appear only once in a corpus. Analysis of these rare words, he argues, requires both quantitative study of patterns and interpretative analysis of their significance and meaning. Computational analysis is now essential to understanding Hebrew texts, but only as part of the hermeneutical process.

In Chapter 7, "Lexicography, the *Louw–Nida Lexicon*, and computational co-occurrence analysis", **Matthew Munson** compares what can be learned from computational methods of studying New Testament words with the semantic information contained in the more traditional lexicon. A computer can build a profile of a particular word by analyzing what other words appear alongside it in a particular corpus. This kind of profile allows scholars to compare how that word is used in different texts, exploring the contextual meaning of the word rather than its inherent, lexical meaning.

The third section of the volume, "Digital Christian History", shares four case studies in the historical use of DH methods. In Chapter 8, "From Inquisition to inquiry", **Delfi Nieto-Isabel and Carlos López-Arenillas** remind us that the DH interest in networks and relationships is nothing new. The Inquisition investigated heresy through a form of social network analysis, determining who was connected to each suspected heretic. Inquisitorial archives detail thousands of individuals and their interrelations, and the computational methods of DH are ideal for tackling such a vast and complex source of data. Quantitative analysis of this data can be used to explore historical dissident religion, but this requires both careful appreciation of the representativeness of the limited surviving sources, and an understanding of the process through which the information was originally gathered.

Chapter 9, "Visualizing religious networks, movements, and communities", also uses archival sources to explore historical religious networks. **Katherine Faull** works with an American archive containing tens of thousands of memoirs representing 300 years of autobiographical Christian testimony, all designed to be read at funerals. Digitizing this archive allows scholars to gain access to this valuable historical resource, sharing previously untold life stories. Digital tools can be used to map the relationships between the people mentioned within the texts, as well as their authors. Visualizing these networks opens new possibilities for understanding gender, family and ethnicity in this Christian Pietist community.

Chapter 10, "The theology of relational practice", uses digital tools to explore a different kind of relationship: that between speaker and audience. **John Wall** studies public worship in the 17th century by recreating the experience of listening to a sermon in the churchyard of St Paul's Cathedral, London. Visitors to the project website can listen to an actor perform a sermon and hear how it might have sounded from different parts of the churchyard, including different background noises. This project uses visual and acoustic modelling to study how historical worship might have been organized and staged, while recentering the experience of hearing public worship in scholarly understanding of historical Christianity.

Chapter 11, "Liturgical history in a digital world", continues this exploration of historical worship. **Louis Chevalier** examines "the profound impact" of the digital revolution on liturgical history. Liturgy is a complex phenomenon with many components, and scholars study its development over time and trace connections between different liturgies. As in many other fields of DH, scholars have embarked on the production of new catalogues and databases of primary sources, and Chevalier explains exactly what is needed to ensure that a digital edition supports new kinds of search, analysis and comparison. Digital tools also allow for multimodal study, with the opportunity to include audio as well as textual resources, allowing scholars "to study liturgy in all its dimensions."

The fourth and final section of the volume, "Theology and Pedagogy", consists of three chapters showing how digital technology is transforming Christianity in the church and the classroom. In Chapter 12, "Digital pedagogy and spiritual formation", **Tim Hutchings and Karen O'Donnell** analyze the use of digital media in the teaching of Christian theology. If DH is about using technology to seek understanding, they argue, then teaching and pedagogy should be at its heart. This is certainly the case outside the secular universities. The educational potential of digital media is well understood among Christian churches, seminaries and ministries, where new digital projects are just the latest in many centuries of media initiatives. However, Christians have also expressed concern that digital learning might undermine the centrality of embodiment, context, collaboration, and physical co-presence in spiritual formation. Hutchings and O'Donnell explore how two very different Christian initiatives have addressed these criticisms: the Common Awards programme for training students to become clergy in the Church of England, and the children's videogame *Guardians of Ancora*.

Chapter 13, "Nested Histories", shifts focus back to the university classroom. **Gary Slater** shares a DH resource he developed to help students learn about the relationships between texts, ideas and actors in early Christian history. Students work together to develop models of worldviews, lists of definitions, and mind maps on which concepts are arranged in order from more local and concrete to more abstract and all-encompassing. These maps are then transposed onto a nested set of concentric circles, in which more concrete principles can be arranged to fit within more general principles. Once this outline has been created, students work to fill each circle with definitions, examples, images and videos. For Slater, this approach to teaching invites students to play an active role in uncovering their own assumptions and constructing new relationships between historical concepts.

Our final chapter turns to the use of digital communications in Christian churches. In Chapter 14, "Public theology behind the Great Firewall of China", **Alex Chow** explores digital Christianity in a context of both numerical growth and government suppression. The two Protestant churches he describes have tried to develop a new public theological discourse, using blogs and social media to share a Christian perspective on human rights and civil society even while government censors try to locate and shut down their online profiles. Digital magazines are easy to copy and distribute, but also easy to detect and delete. Understanding this complex situation requires an appreciation of the history of Chinese public discourse, print culture, and Christianity in China, and Chow shows that the digital revolution is just the latest twist in many centuries of mutual suspicion.

As a final word, we would like to thank warmly all the authors of this volume, and in particular Makenzi Ilse Crouch for her editing work. All the hyperlinks have been checked on the 22nd July 2021. Last but not least, our recognition goes to our publisher, De Gruyter, for its support during the birth of this book with the efficient and gracious collaboration of Matthias Wand and Katrin Mittmann, as well as of Sophie Wagenhofer, IDHR series publisher.

5 Bibliography

Bianco, Jamie 'Skye'. "This Digital Humanities Which Is Not One." In *Debates in the Digital Humanities*, edited by Matthew K. Gold, 96–112. Minneapolis: University of Minnesota Press, 2012. http://dhdebates.gc.cuny.edu/debates/text/9.

Blum, Edward J. "Uncle Tom's Bibles: Bibles as Visual and Material Objects from Antebellum Abolitionism to Jim Crow Cinema." *MAVCOR Journal* 3 (2019/2), *Special Issue: Material and Visual Cultures of Religion in the American South*, https://mavcor.yale.edu/mavcor-journal/uncle-tom-s-bibles-bibles-visual-and-material-objects-antebellum-abolitionism-jim.

Brennen, J. Scott and Kreiss, Daniel. "Digitalization", *International Encyclopedia of Communication Theory and Philosophy* (23 October 2016): 1–11, https://onlinelibrary.wiley.com/doi/abs/10.1002/9781118766804.wbiect111.

Busa, Roberto. "Foreword: Perspectives on the Digital Humanities." In *A Companion to Digital Humanities*, edited by Susan Schreibman, Ray Siemens and John Unsworth. Hoboken, NJ: Wiley Blackwell, 2004, http://www.digitalhumanities.org/companion/.

Campbell, Heidi A. (ed.). *Digital Religion. Understanding Religious Practice in New Media Worlds*. London/New York: Routledge, 2013.

Campbell, Heidi A. and Altenhofen, Brian. "Methodological Challenges, Innovations and Growing Pains in Digital Religion Research." In *Digital Methodologies in the Sociology of Religion*, edited by Sariva Cheruvallil-Contractor and Suha Shakkour, 1–12. London: Bloomsbury, 2015.

Campbell, Heidi A. and Garner, Stephen. *Networked Theology. Negotiating Faith in Digital Culture*. London: Baker Academy, 2016.

Chartier, Roger. *Les métamorphoses du livre: Les rendez-vous de l'édition. Le livre et le numérique*. Paris: Bibliothèque du Centre Pompidou, 2001.

Clivaz, Claire. "Categories of Ancient Christian Texts and Writing Materials: 'Taking Once Again a Fresh Starting Point'." In *Ancient Worlds in Digital Culture*, DBS 1, edited by Claire Clivaz, Paul Dilley and David Hamidović, with Apolline Thromas, 35–58. Leiden: Brill, 2016.

Clivaz, Claire. *Ecritures digitales. Digital writing, digital Scriptures* (DBS 4), Leiden: Brill, 2019, https://brill.com/view/title/54748.

Clivaz, Claire. "Digitized and Digitalized Humanities: Words and Identity." In *Atti del IX Convegno Annuale dell'Associazione per l'Informatica Umanistica e la Cultura Digitale. La svolta inevitabile: sfide e prospettive per l'informatica umanistica*, edited by Cristina Marras, Marco Passarotti, Greta Franzini and Eleonora Litta, 67–73. Bologna: AIUCD, 2020.

Clivaz, Claire and Garrick V. Allen. "The Digital Humanities in Biblical Studies and Theology." *Open Theology* 5 (2019/1): 461–5, https://doi.org/10.1515/opth-2019–0035.

Dennhardt, Robert. *The Term Digital Computer (Stibitz 1942) and the Flip-Flop (Turner 1920)*. München: Grin Verlag, 2016.

Fiormonte, Domenico. "Toward a Cultural Critique of Digital Humanities." In *Debates in the Digital Humanities* 2, edited by Matthew K. Gold and Lauren F. Klein, Ch. 35. Minneapolis: University of Minnesota Press, 2016. https://dhdebates.gc.cuny.edu/read/untitled/section/5cac8409-e521–4349-ab03-f341a5359a34#ch35.

Garcés, Juan and Heilmann, Jan. "Digital Humanities und Exegese. Erträge, Potentiale, Grenzen und hochschuldidaktische Perspektiven." *Forum Exegese und Hochschuldidaktik: Verstehen von Anfang an, Digital Humanities* 2 (2017): 29–52.

Hutchings, Tim. "Digital Humanities and the Study of Religion." In *Between the Humanities and the Digital*, edited by Patrik Svensson and David Theo Goldberg, 283–94. Cambridge: MIT Press, 2015.

Hutchings, Tim. "Christianity and Digital Media." In *The Changing World Religion Map*, edited by Stanley Brunn, 3811–3830. Berlin: Springer, 2015.

Hutchings, Tim. "Design and the Digital Bible". *Journal of Contemporary Religion* 32(2) (2017): 205–19.

Hutchings, Tim. *Creating Church Online*. London/New York: Routledge, 2017.

Jones, Steven E. "The Emergence of the Digital Humanities (the Network Is Everting)." In *Debates in the Digital Humanities* 2, edited by Matthew K. Gold and Lauren Klein. Minneapolis: University Minnesota Press, 2016. http://dhdebates.gc.cuny.edu/debates/text/52.

Jones, Steven E. *Roberto Busa, S.J., and the Emergence of Humanities Computing: The Priest and the Punched Cards*. London/New York: Routledge, 2016.

Krüger, Olivier. *Die mediale Religion. Probleme und Perspektiven religionswissenschaftlicher und wissenssoziologischer Medienforschung, Reihe Religion und Medien* (Bd.1). Freiburg: Transcript Verlag, 2012.

Mombert, Sarah. "From Books to Collections. Critical Editions of Heterogeneous Documents." In *Digital Critical Editions* (*Topics in the Digital Humanities*), edited by Daniel Apollon, Claire Bélisle and Paul Régnier. Champaign: University of Illinois Press, 2014.

Monier, Mina. "GA 304, Theophylact's Commentary and the Ending of Mark", *Filología Neotestamentaria* 52 (2019): 94–106.

Parvianien, Päivi, Jukka Kääriäinen, Maarit Tihinen, and Susanna Teppola. "Tackling the Digitalization Challenge: How to Benefit from Digitalization in Practice", *International Journal of Information Systems and Project Management* 5/1 (2017): 63–76. https://doi.org/10.12821/ijispm050104.

Phillips, Peter M. *The Bible, Social Media and Digital Culture*. London/New York: Routledge, 2019.

Phillips, Peter M. "The Power of Visual Culture and The Fragility of the Text." In *Ancient Manuscripts in Digital Culture*, DBS3, edited by David Hamidović, Claire Clivaz, Sarah Bowen Savant, 10–21. Leiden: Brill, 2019.

Phillips, Peter M., Kyle Schiefelbein-Guerrero and Jonas Kurlberg, "Defining Digital Theology: Digital Humanities, Digital Religion and the Particular Work of the CODEC Research Centre and Network", *Open Theology* 5 (2019): 29–43. https://doi.org/10.1515/opth-2019-0003.

Schroeder, Caroline T. "The Digital Humanities as Cultural Capital: Implications for Biblical and Religious Studies." *Journal of Religion, Media, and Digital Culture* 5(1) (2016): 21–49. https://doi.org/10.1163/21659214-90000069.

Siker, Jeffrey. *Liquid Scripture: The Bible in a Digital World*. Minneapolis: Fortress Press, 2017.

Stiegler, Bernard. *Dans la disruption. Comment ne pas devenir fou?* Paris: Les liens qui libèrent, 2016.

Stolow, Jeremy. "Religion and/as Media". *Theory, Culture and Society* 22(4) (2005): 119–45.

Svensson, Patrik and David Theo Goldberg. "Introduction", in *Between the Humanities and the Digital*, edited by Patrik Svensson and David Theo Goldberg, 1–8. Cambridge: MIT Press, 2015.

Tanner, Simon. *Delivering Impact with Digital Resources: Planning Strategy in the Attention Economy*. London: Facet Publishing, 2020.

van der Velden, Maja. "Invisibility and the Ethics of the Digitalization: Designing so as not to Hurt Others." In *Information Technology Ethics: Cultural Perspectives*, edited by Sonja Hongladarom and Charles Ess , 81–93. Hershey, PA: Idea Group Reference Ed., 2007.

Wasserman, Tommy and Gurry, Peter J. *A New Approach to Textual Criticism: An Introduction to the Coherence-Based Genealogical Method* (*Resources for Biblical Study* 80). Atlanta: SBL Press, 2017.

Williams, Bernard O. *Computing with Electricity, 1935–1945*. PhD diss., Lawrence: University of Kansas, 1984.

Part I: **Canon, corpus and manuscript**

Claire Clivaz
The Bible in the digital age: multimodal Scriptures in communities

1 Introduction: the interface between printed and digital biblical worlds

The entrance of the 2017 International Reformation Exposition in Wittenberg was described on the exhibition website as a "huge book" (*riesiges Buch*): a 27-meter-high Bible.[1] Within Protestant Church life, one could hardly find a clearer physical manifestation of the statement by reformed theologian Pierre Gisel, which he believed to be valid for the whole of Christianity: "Scripture *fills the place of the origin*, while it is a *historically secondary* phenomenon."[2] The visitors to the 2017 Exposition were indeed invited to enter at the point of "origin," through the gate consisting of a Bible. In the face of such a clear theological and cultural proclamation in the form of a giant Bible, it is a challenge to evaluate the impact of the digital turn on biblical studies.

But all Christian movements are currently engaging in the rise of digital biblical culture, and we can see its effects in academic institutions, qualifications, networks, meetings, and publications. The first research center of digital theology opened in 2014 at Durham University and awarded its first master's degree in digital theology in 2017. Likewise, Vrije University Amsterdam has offered a master's degree in biblical studies and digital humanities since 2015.[3] Brill has also

---

Note: This chapter is an English translation of an article originally published in German, with the kind authorization of Narr publisher: Claire Clivaz, "Die Bibel im digitalen Zeitalter: Multimodale Schrift in Gemeinschaften," *Zeitschrift für Neues Testament* 20, no. 39/40 (2017): 35–57. It presents an overview regarding the Bible and digital humanities in Christianity. Minor details, like publication dates, have been adapted. These arguments were developed in a 2019 book, Claire Clivaz, *Ecritures digitales: Digital Writing, Digital Scriptures*, Digital Biblical Studies 4 (Leiden: Brill, 2019). Thank you to Andrea Stevens for her English proofreading.

1 "Torraum Welcome," reformation2017, https://r2017.org/weltausstellung/welcome/.
2 Pierre Gisel, "Apocryphes et canon: leurs rapports et leur statut respectif. Un questionnement théologique," *Apocrypha* 7 (1996), 230.
3 "MA in Digital Theology," Durham University, https://www.dur.ac.uk/codec/courses/; "New MA Programme 'Biblical Studies and Digital Humanities'," Faculty of Religion and Theology, Vrije Universiteit Amsterdam, http://www.godgeleerdheid.vu.nl/en/news-agenda/news-archive/2015/okt-dec/151023-new-ma-programme-biblical-studies-and-digital-humanities.aspx.

https://doi.org/10.1515/9783110574043-002

begun a new series, *Digital Biblical Studies*, and the present volume is part of De Gruyter's series *Introductions to Digital Humanities and Religion*.[4] The annual international SBL (Society for Biblical Literature) and EABS (European Association of Biblical Studies) meetings have organized digital humanities (DH) sections since 2012 and 2013 respectively.

A number of scholars have also already written overview articles on the relationship between biblical studies and the digital turn. For example, in 2010, Wido van Peursen highlighted the turn from texts to documents;[5] in 2012, Ulrich Schmid drafted a general outline of the evolution of the New Testament editions;[6] in 2014, the question was raised whether the New Testament would become a *biblaridion*, lost in the web, a topic I have developed further in other articles and collected essays.[7] In 2016, Carrie Schroeder demonstrated that the expansion of digital textual studies would include "'multimodal layered worlds', worlds of empowerment, engagement, and interactivity," a feature not specific to biblical studies but present in religious studies and beyond.[8] Religious studies

---

4 "Digital Biblical Studies," Brill, www.brill.com/dbs; "Introductions to Digital Humanities – Religion," De Gruyter, https://www.degruyter.com/serial/IDHR-B/html.
5 Wido van Peursen, "Text Comparison and Digital Creativity: An Introduction," in *Text Comparison and Digital Creativity: The Production of Presence and Meaning in Digital Text Scholarship*, ed. Wido van Peursen, Ernst D. Thoutenhoofd, and Adrian Van der Weel, Scholarly Communication 1 (Leiden: Brill, 2010): 1–27.
6 Ulrich Schmid, "Thoughts on a Digital Edition of the New Testament," in *Reading Tomorrow: From Ancient Manuscripts to the Digital Era / Lire Demain. Des manuscrits antiques à l'ère digitale*, ed. Claire Clivaz et al., in coll. with Benjamin Bertho (Lausanne: PPUR, 2012): 299–306. Previously see especially David C. Parker, "Through a Screen Darkly: Digital Texts and the New Testament," *Journal for the Study of the New Testament* 25, no. 4 (2003): 395–411.
7 Claire Clivaz, "New Testament in a Digital Culture: A *Biblaridion* (Little Book) Lost in the Web?", *Journal of Religion, Media and Digital Culture* 3, no. 3 (2014): 20–38. See also Claire Clivaz, "Homer and the New Testament as 'Multitexts' in the Digital Age?", *Scholarly and Research Communication* 3, no. 3 (2012): 1–15, http://src-online.ca/index.php/src/article/view/97; Claire Clivaz, "Jamais deux sans trois! Théologie, exégèse et culture," in *Entre exégètes et théologiens: la Bible. 24ᵉ congrès de l'ACFEB (Toulouse 2011)*, ed. Elian Cuvillier and Bernadette Escaffre (Paris: Cerf, 2014): 253–69; Claire Clivaz, "Introduction: Digital Humanities in Jewish, Christian and Arabic Traditions," *Journal of Religion, Media and Digital Culture* 5 (2016): 1–20. Collected essays: Claire Clivaz, Andrew Gregory, and David Hamidović, eds., *Digital Humanities in Biblical, Early Jewish and Early Christian Studies*, in coll. with Sarah Schulthess, Scholarly Communication 2 (Leiden: Brill, 2013); Claire Clivaz, Paul Dilley, and David Hamidović, eds., *Ancient Worlds in Digital Culture*, in coll. with Apolline Thromas, Digital Biblical Studies 1 (Leiden: Brill, 2016); Claire Clivaz et al., eds., "Digital Humanities in Jewish, Christian and Arabic Traditions," special issue, *Journal of Religion, Media and Digital Culture* 5, no. 1 (2016).
8 Caroline T. Schroeder, "The Digital Humanities as Cultural Capital: Implications for Biblical and Religious Studies," *Journal of Religion, Media and Digital Culture* 5, no. 1 (2016), 43.

have also been prolific with regards to the digital turn, notably the work of Heidi Campbell, who published an overview of the topic in *Digital Religion: Understanding Religious Practice in New Media Worlds*. She developed these topics further in publications in 2015 and 2016.[9] In 2017, Jeffrey Siker published the first monograph about the Bible in a digital age.[10]

However, on its own, this rigorous digital research does not engage with the fact that an important epistemological turn is at stake, nor does it explore this turn's impact on the theological and cultural attachments to the Bible as a printed book. Despite many years of study dedicated to the digital turn in the humanities and biblical studies, such a question can only be studied in increments. Embedded in a quickly evolving cultural context, considerable effort must be made to reorient our minds, which are so accustomed to printed culture. A renewed attention to the famous adage *sola scriptura* and the theological impact of the digital turn in New Testament studies is necessary. A possible model or starting point is the Swiss Federation of Protestant Churches (SEK) publication of a Reformation commemoration study on the topic, entitled *Sola lectura*.

Written by a group of Swiss theologians, the text clearly states that the transition from the "Gutenberg-Galaxie" to the world of electronic media challenges the reading culture of Christianity based on the Bible. This turning point will then be relativized by the long-term perspective. In the history of Christian media, one can indeed observe several affinities between the Christian message and the book as medium. But this relationship is not related by essence to Christianity; it does not reach the identity of the Christian faith. [...] Christianity is not a religion of the book.[11]

---

9 Heidi A. Campbell, ed., *Digital Religion: Understanding Religious Practice in New Media Worlds* (Oxford: Routledge, 2013); Heidi A. Campbell and Brian Altenhofen, "Methodological Challenges, Innovations and Growing Pains in Digital Religion Research," in *Digital Methodologies in the Sociology of Religion*, ed. Sariva Cheruvallil-Contractor and Suha Shakkour (London: Bloomsbury Publishing, 2015): 1–12; including theology: Heidi A. Campbell and Stephen Garner, *Networked Theology: Negotiating Faith in Digital Culture* (Buffalo, NY: Baker Academy, 2016). See also notably Olivier Krüger, *Die mediale Religion. Probleme und Perspektiven religionswissenschaftlicher und wissenssoziologischer Medienforschung*, Reihe Religion und Medien 1 (Bielfeld: Transcript Verlag, 2012); Tim Hutchings, *Creating Church Online* (Oxford: Routledge, 2017).
10 Jeffrey S. Siker, *Liquid Scripture: The Bible in a Digital World* (Minneapolis: Fortress Press, 2017); Claire Clivaz, "Review of Jeffrey S. Siker, *Liquid Scripture: The Bible in a Digital World*," *Review of Biblical Literature* 5 (2018): 1–6, https://www.sblcentral.org/home/bookDetails/11851.
11 SEK, *Sola lectura? Aktuelle Herausforderungen des Lesens aus protestantischer Sicht* (Bern: Stämpfli AG, 2016), https://www.evref.ch/wp-content/uploads/2019/08/18_sola_lectura_de.pdf. My English translation.

Arguing for "the emancipation of the writing from the book," this SEK document also underlines "that 'Scripture' in the electronic format will become more interactive and so less canonical: it won't be a pre-existent, printed holy Scripture, but a part of an ongoing process of communication."[12] Consequently, moving beyond *sola scriptura*, the focus is placed on *sola lectura*, reminding one that "to read is a core competence of Protestantism. From the beginning, the Reformation was related to the reading experiment, based on the Bible and developing from it."[13] The SEK document does not claim to make all people enter through "the welcome gate of the book," in contrast to the Wittenberg Reformation Exposition.[14] Instead, it attempts to understand the challenge of the emancipation of the writing from the book[15] and writing's participation in the communication process.

Well before the rise of the digital turn, Karl Barth insisted on considering writing as a communication process with an "invisible community." In a short video recording now available on Vimeo,[16] Barth comments on his process of writing his commentary on the epistle to the Romans. He was looking for interpretive comrades during the early 1920s:

> What I was trying to reach with that? Initially not a book that I wanted to publish. But a collection of manuscripts, which I read to my friends. But then, step by step, it was supposed to become a book anyway. And so it resulted in a book. But if I get asked what I tried to reach with it, I can only say I was looking for comrades, for fellow men and fellow Christians, who possibly, out of the same confusion that I found myself in, were also about to reach out for the Bible, and the New Testament and the Epistle to the Romans, in a very different way. And with them together, sort of in an invisible community, to read this old text.

Keeping in mind the SEK document and this statement in the Barth video, it is worth testing this emancipation of the biblical text from the book and exploring how emancipation would – for better or worse – reconnect the biblical text to diverse communities while pointing to processes of communication. The first section of this article claims that the "the emancipation of the writing from the book" is a challenge for the entire academic humanities community. The symbolic dimensions of the Bible as a particular book have had backward effects on the

---

[12] Ibid., 10. My English translation.
[13] Ibid., 31. My English translation.
[14] See p. 21 above.
[15] Ibid., 10.
[16] The Center for Barth Studies, "Karl Barth & the Epistle to the Romans," Vimeo, uploaded 28 March 2014, https://vimeo.com/90346827; no year or place are indicated for the video itself on Vimeo.

constitution of digital humanities research in which religious representations are often present but not always assumed or criticized as such.

The second section below presents an update on the latest steps of the production of Greek New Testament critical editions. Their recent multiplication points to the diversification of the academic communities that are studying it. This section raises the question of the canon and whether the digital Bible tends to be "less canonical"[17] and also more multicultural and multilingual, as shown for example by PAVONe, the Platform of the Arabic Versions of the New Testament.[18]

Finally, the third section analyzes the challenge of the digital Bible, which is becoming increasingly multimodal on a daily basis, its text associated with images, sounds, and music. Diverse Christian communities are already spreading biblical content in multimodal ways, such as the successful application YouVersion[19] or the Facebook page *Pain de ce jour*.[20] Every day it becomes more difficult to avoid considering what these evolutions could mean for the future of biblical studies. As a theological horizon, this analysis of a few challenges related to the Bible in a digital age will lead to the enlightenment of an adage that was promoted in one of my earliest research articles: *sola scriptura in koinonia*.[21]

2 The text out of the book: a turning-point for the entire humanities

In 1998, the philosopher Jacques Derrida described in a radio interview the depth of the epistemological change he saw coming: "What is in the making, at a rhythm still not calculable, in a way at the same time very slow and very fast, is of course a new human, a new human body, a new relationship between

---

[17] I fully developed this topic in Claire Clivaz, "Categories of Ancient Christian Texts and Writing Materials: 'Taking Once Again a Fresh Starting Point'," in *Ancient Worlds in Digital Culture*, ed. Claire Clivaz, Paul Dilley, and David Hamidović, in coll. with Apolline Thromas, Digital Biblical Studies 1 (Leiden: Brill, 2016): 35–58.
[18] PAVONe: Platform of the Arabic Versions of the New Testament, University of Balamand – Digital Humanities Center, http://pavone.uob-dh.org/.
[19] YouVersion, https://www.youversion.com.
[20] "Pain de ce jour," Facebook page, https://www.facebook.com/paindecejour/.
[21] Claire Clivaz, "La troisième quête du Jésus historique et le canon: le défi de la réception communautaire. Un essai de relecture historique," in *Jésus de Nazareth: Nouvelles approches d'une énigme* (*MBo* 38), ed. Daniel Marguerat, Enrico Norelli, and Jean-Michel Poffet (Genève: Labor et Fides, 1998), 558.

the human body and the machines, and we can already perceive this transformation."[22] Within this transformation he considers the future of the book, recognizing at the same time the attachment to this writing form without hindering the development of the numerous means of communication depending on it.

The transformation of writing via digital support must consequently be understood against this general hermeneutical background: it is a deeply ambiguous phenomenon, in the face of which we have the full right to feel uncertain. This feeling is clearly illustrated by the translation gap between the German word *Emanzipation* and the French word chosen in the translated SEK document, "dissociation." "Die Emanzipation der Schrift vom Buch" – "the emancipation of the writing from the Book"– is indeed translated by "la dissociation entre l'écrit et le livre," "the dissociation between the written text and the book," in the French version.[23] "Emancipation" contains a potential liberating and positive element that is not included in the term "dissociation." This discrepancy reflects the mixed feelings of the entire humanities community in the face of the departure – exodus? – of the written text from the book. Scholars have diverse reactions when confronting the digital turn: I often emphasize the fear expressed by Robert Darnton himself, as well as his great enthusiasm with digital culture,[24] or the complete disapprobation of Umberto Eco before the "Mother of all Lists," the World Wide Web, that blurs "any distinction between truth and error."[25]

Recognizing with Jacques Derrida that the exodus from paper media is nothing less than a seism,[26] I stay nevertheless convinced that humanities beyond the book – or unbound humanities[27] – can find fresh developments in the digital adventure. Not bound by covers, pages, and paper, the humanities must explore new digital boundaries that promise not a "better world," but instead new research and thinking conditions, established under the sign of the "capture." Digital humanist scholar Johanna Drucker cleverly proposed in 2011 a switch from the notion of "data" to "capta":

---

22 Radio interview in December 1998, and published in Jacques Derrida, *Sur parole. Instantanés philosophiques* (Paris: Editions de l'Aube, 2000), 484.
23 FEPS, *Sola lectura? Enjeux actuels de la lecture dans une perspective protestante* (Bern: Stämpfli AG, 2016), 10, http://www.kirchenbund.ch/fr/publications/tudes/sola-lectura.
24 Robert Darnton, *The Case for Books: Past, Present, Future* (New York: Public Affairs, 2009), 53 and XIII.
25 Umberto Eco, *The Infinity of Lists*, trans. Alastair McEwen (New York: Rizzoli, 2009), 327.
26 Jacques Derrida, "Paper or Myself, You Know… (New Speculations on a Luxury of the Poor)," in *Paper Machine*, trans. Board of Trustees (Stanford: Stanford University Press, 2005), 42.
27 Claire Clivaz and Dominique Vinck, eds., "Les humanités délivrées," *Les Cahiers du Numériques* 10, no. 3 (2014): 9–16; Dominique Vinck and Claire Clivaz, eds., "Les humanités délivrées," *La Revue d'Anthropologie des Connaissances* 8, no. 4 (2014): 681–704.

Differences in the etymological roots of the terms data and capta make the distinction between constructivist and realist approaches clear. Capta is "taken" actively while data is assumed to be a "given" able to be recorded and observed. From this distinction, a world of differences arises. Humanistic inquiry acknowledges the situated, partial, and constitutive character of knowledge production, the recognition that knowledge is constructed, taken, not simply given as a natural representation of pre-existing fact.[28]

To understand the vastness of the unbound humanities, one must consider the epistemological conditions of the 17th century, according to the French theologian Olivier Abel:

> The time of the buccaneers was particularly flourishing in the Caribbean between 1630 and 1670. In the new worlds, everything is offered with profusion by the divine Providence. [...] We are not in a gift and exchange economy anymore, but in an economy of the "capture", that stands even in the title of the Dutch philosopher Grotius *On the Right of Capture*.[29] This "capture culture" implies that "the right to depart is the condition of the capacity to be bound. The political question will thus gradually become: 'How can we stay together?' when we can always become unbound?"[30]

The humanities are facing this same question today in the expanse of the data age: how will scholars make links and define boundaries, how will they record information, sailing over the unbound humanities? To be bound/unbound exposes the topic of communities as particularly important in digital culture. In her precursor 2009 text, digital humanist scholar – or "DHer" – Kathleen Fitzpatrick pointed to the importance of building a community and developing a new kind of peer-review in the digital academic circles: "[to build a community] is key to the scholarly publishing network of the future, and in particular to its implementation of peer-to-peer review," a peer-review process that she envisioned becoming filtered post-publication and on a community basis.[31] Twelve years later, the peer-review process has not substantively changed, but the (re)configuration of academic communities remains a strategy point that is beginning to impact the production of edition(s) of the New Testament, as we will see in section 2.

---

[28] Johanna Drucker, "Humanities Approaches to Graphical Display," *Digital Humanities Quarterly* 5, no. 1 (2011): 3, http://www.digitalhumanities.org/dhq/vol/5/1/000091/000091.html.
[29] Olivier Abel, "L'océan, le puritain, le pirate," *Esprit* 356 (2009): 107.
[30] Olivier Abel, "Essai sur la prise. Anthropologie de la flibuste et théologie radicale protestante," *Esprit* 356 (2009): 115.
[31] Kathleen Fitzpatrick, *Planned Obsolescence: Publishing, Technology, and the Future of the Academy* (Norfolk: MediaCommons Press, 2009), 16, http://mcpress.media-commons.org/plannedobsolescence/.

The dialogue between humanities and the so-called hard sciences is also at stake in this time of community reconfiguration.[32] If humanist scholars are able to leave old boundaries and to test new ones, their centuries-old knowledge will be as useful as ever. As DHer Domenico Fiormonte underlines, "each act of encoding, or rather each act of representation of the specific 'object' via a formal language involves a selection from a set of possibilities and is therefore an interpretative act."[33] Computing languages – such as Unix[34] – remain languages, and will continue to require interpretation, a core task of humanities.[35]

In such a context, several humanist scholars, including Jean-Claude Carrière, Umberto Eco,[36] and more recently Maurice Olender, have considered our relationship to the symbolism of the book, or even the Book, often speaking explicitly of the Bible's symbolic impact. Whereas the SEK report underlines that the relationship between Christianity and the book is not essential,[37] Olender, coming from a Jewish cultural background, belongs to a strand of humanist scholars who continue to emphasize strongly both archives and Christianity as fundamental to Western civilization.[38] His fear is that digital writing material prevents forgetting, preserving all our traces in a hyperbolic way.[39] His monograph concludes with a kind of parable, with a man performing an "analphabetic reading," a reading devoid of cultural information and context:[40] readers can consider if an automated computer reading would also produce such an analphabetic reading.

Whereas writers, philosophers, and thinkers from diverse fields continue to meditate on the exodus out of the book in diverse ways, exegetes are quite ab-

---

32 For further developments on this topic, see Claire Clivaz, "Lost in Translation? The Odyssey of the 'Digital Humanities' in French," *Studia UBB Digitalia* 62, no. 1 (2017): 26–41, http://digihubb.centre.ubbcluj.ro/journal/index.php/digitalia/article/view/4/18.
33 Fiormonte, Domenico. "The Digital Humanities from Father Busa to Edward Snowden." *Media Development* 64, no. 2 (2017): 30. Fiormonte refers here notably to the work of the Italian scholars Tito Orlandi, Raul Mordenti, and Giuseppe Gigliozzi.
34 "Unix," Wikipedia, last updated 24 Feb 2021, https://en.wikipedia.org/wiki/Unix.
35 See Yves Citton, *L'Avenir des Humanités. Économie de la connaissance ou culture de l'interprétation?* (Paris: La Découverte, 2010), 21.
36 Jean-Claude Carrière and Umberto Eco, *N'espérez pas vous débarrasser des livres* (Paris: Seuil, 2009), 294: "with the religions of the Book, the book has served not just as a container, as a receptacle, but also as a 'wide angle' from which it has been possible for everything to be observed, everything related, maybe even for everything to be decided" (quotation translated for this chapter).
37 SEK, *Sola lectura*, 7.
38 Maurice Olender, *Un fantôme dans la bibliothèque* (Paris: Seuil, 2017), 78–80.
39 Ibid., 65.
40 Ibid., 190–2.

sent from this general debate: their preferred object of study, the Bible, is thus at the center of the issue, as well as their core skills of reading and interpreting. I consider it an urgent task to see our field involved in this general cultural debate, and to take part in at least the two following issues. First, a religious vocabulary often haunts digital culture and should be questioned, beginning with the French word "ordinateur" (computer). In 1953, the IBM president requested that Sorbonne professor Jacques Perret choose a French word to translate the English "computer." Perret explains in a letter why he chose to translate "computer" with the French word "ordinateur," referring to the order of creation and even to the Catholic priestly ceremony of "ordination" to justify his choice.[41] Another example is the choice of the word "cloud,"[42] used to designate digital material moving "in the air," and remembering – *nolens*, *volens* – the cloud symbolizing the presence of God in the desert. Such a vocabulary should be analyzed and probably demystified: we might stop wrongly assimilating the digital world to something that is "dematerialized."[43]

Second, theologians and exegetes should participate in the debate regarding the early history of the digital humanities, so often placed under the patronage of Jesuit Father Roberto Busa, as Julianne Nyhan and Andrew Flinn remind us.[44] Busa's visit in 1949 to the IBM president is often seen as emblematic, and for Fiormonte, there is no doubt that "Busa's undertaking founded the discipline of the humanities computing (although years later it was renamed digital humanities), but above all it laid the groundwork for a profound epistemological and cultural transformation."[45]

---

[41] Jacques Perret, Lettre du 16 avril 1955 de J. Perret, professeur à l'université de Paris, à C. de Waldner, président d'IBM France. Archives IBM France. The letter has been digitalized by Alain Pesson (CIGREF) and made available in this blog post: Loïc Depecker, "Que diriez-vous d' 'ordinateur' ?", *Bibnum, Calcul et informatique*, published on the 1st June 2015; consulted on the 1st June 2021. http://journals.openedition.org/bibnum/534.
[42] Sydney J. Shep, "Digital Materiality," in *A New Companion to Digital Humanities*, ed. Susan Schreibman, Ray Siemens and, John Unsworth (Hoboken, NJ: Wiley Blackwell, 2016): 322–30.
[43] Claire Clivaz, "Vous avez dit 'dématerialisation'? Diagnostic d'une panne culturelle," *Le Temps* (blog), 2 July 2016, https://blogs.letemps.ch/claire-clivaz/2016/07/02/vous-avez-dit-dematerialisation-diagnostic-dune-panne-culturelle/.
[44] Julianne Nyhan and Andrew Flinn, *Computation and the Humanities: Towards an Oral History of Digital Humanities*, Springer Series on Cultural Computing (Washington, DC: Springer, 2016), 1.
[45] Fiormonte, "Digital Humanities," 30.

I fully agree with Milad Doueihi that such a foundational historical reading must also include other major figures such as Alan Turing.[46] Steven E. Jones' clever monograph about Busa has instigated a useful inquiry that allows us to better understand what is at stake around this Jesuit figure. Jones does not pretend to have achieved a religious or theological analysis of Busa,[47] but he enlightens several points that invite theologians and exegetes from the diverse Christian confessions to think also from their own position on these facts. Jones underlines that "IBM's interests in 1949–1952 surely included shoring up post-war diplomatic relations with the Vatican, Italy, and Europe as a whole just at the advent of its World Trade Corporation."[48] Conscious of this commercial context, Busa asks in a private 1960 letter if this cooperation between a businessman and a priest is blessed by God. He concludes affirmatively, referring to an unidentified biblical verse.[49] His spiritual enthusiasm for humanities computing can even be read in his 2004 introduction to the first edition of the *Companion to Digital Humanities*: "*Digitus Dei est hic!* The finger of God is here!"[50]

Busa never applied his computational philology to the Bible, but rather to the Dead Sea Scrolls and Thomas Aquinas,[51] the latter of which is a text sixteen times longer than the Bible.[52] In fact, the first scholar to cross the Bible and a computational approach is an Episcopalian minister, Reverend John W. Ellison, who prepared an index of the English Revised Standard Version of the Bible in parallel to Busa's Thomas Aquinas Index.[53] Nobody remembers his name today, whereas the name of Roberto Busa is honored by a regular award in the digital humanities milieu.[54] Regarding the theological, political, economic, and confessional implications of this story, it would be interesting to include the competences of biblical scholars in the inquiry. Whether one rejoices or deplores it, *sola*

---

46 Milad Doueihi, "Préface. Quête et enquête," in *Le temps des humanités digitales*, ed. Olivier Le Deuff (Limoges: FyP editions, 2014): 8–9. For an application of this suggestion, see chapter 2 in Clivaz, *Ecritures digitales*.
47 Steven E. Jones, *Roberto Busa, S.J., and the Emergence of Humanities Computing: The Priest and the Punched Cards* (London: Routledge, 2016), 14.
48 Ibid., 97.
49 Ibid., 97.
50 Roberto Busa, "Foreword: Perspectives on the Digital Humanities," in *A Companion to Digital Humanities*, ed. Susan Schreibman, Ray Siemens and, John Unsworth (Hoboken, NJ: Wiley Blackwell, 2004): xvi–xi, http://www.digitalhumanities.org/companion/.
51 Jones, *Roberto Busa*, 13.
52 Ibid., 126.
53 Ibid., 100–10.
54 "Roberto Busa Prize," ADHO, http://adho.org/awards/roberto-busa-prize.

scriptura became part of the digital scenes with the work of John W. Ellison in the 1950s, and the biblical research milieu must engage in the analysis of this new writing support, the most important since the transition from the scrolls to the codices, according to Roger Chartier and Christian Vandendorpe.[55] Let's now turn to see how this new medium has impacted the production of editions of the Greek New Testament.

3 Textuality at stake: editing the New Testament in a digital culture

Teaching the New Testament in its original language can provoke surprises for the most attentive professor. Students are indeed more and more used to searching online for a Greek New Testament version, instead of opening a 28th Nestle Aland paper edition (NA28).[56] When the professor is listening to a student reading a Greek text other than the NA28, he/she is forced to interrupt the teaching, and to check with the students what kind of Greek New Testament they have found online. If one googles in French "Nouveau" + "Testament" + "Grec," the first ranked site is an anonymous homemade Greek New Testament edition,[57] published by the so-called TheoTeX edition.[58] Only after a patient search can one locate a statement about the principles of the TheoTeX edition: this edition wishes to "reedit books about protestant evangelical theology, in the PDF, ePUB formats, using LaTeX and Perl."[59] The anonymous Greek New Testament edition

---

[55] Roger Chartier, *Les métamorphoses du livre: Les rendez-vous de l'édition. Le livre et le numérique* (Paris: Bibliothèque du Centre Pompidou, 2001): 8; Christian Vandendorpe, *From Papyrus to Hypertext: Toward the Universal Digital Library*, trans. Phyllis Aronoff and Howard Scott, Topics in the Digital Humanities (Champaign, IL: University of Illinois Press, 2009): 127; for a comment, see Claire Clivaz, "The New Testament at the Time of the Egyptian Papyri: Reflections Based on P[12], P[75] and P[126] (P. Amh. 3b, P. Bod. XIV–XV and PSI 1497)," in *Reading New Testament Papyri in Context – Lire les papyrus du Nouveau Testament dans leur context*, ed. Claire Clivaz and Jean Zumstein, in coll. with Jenny Read–Heimerdinger and Julie Paik, BETL 242 (Leuven: Peeters, 2011): 20 – 3.
[56] Barbara Aland, ed., *Nestle Aland 28th Edition of the Greek New Testament* (Münster: German Bible Society, 2013); Greek text without apparatus online: www.nestle-aland.com/en/read-na28-online/.
[57] Last googled on 22 July 2021.
[58] "Η ΚΑΙΝΗ ΔΙΑΘΗΚΗ / Le Nouveau Testament," ThéoTeX, https://theotex.org/ntgf/cover.html.
[59] "About Éditions ThéoTeX," Lulu (Lulu Press, 2020), http://www.lulu.com/spotlight/TheoTeX.

TheoTeX explains in its introduction,⁶⁰ signed simply "Phoenix, 12ᵗʰ September 2014," that it is an adaptation of the Robinson–Pierpont Byzantine Greek New Testament edition, with changes and modifications executed according to a personal system.⁶¹ The anonymous author rejoices that the digital age has made it so easy to read the New Testament in its original language, but does not confirm if he/she has obtained the copyright to reuse the Robinson–Pierpont edition.⁶² There is no word about the financial and/or institutional resources used to establish this homemade edition.

When a student in the classroom finds such a resource, the first reflex of the professor could be to complain, along with Umberto Eco, that the World Wide Web blurs "any distinction between truth and error" (section 1). But this homemade TheoTeX edition, even as a specific, awkward case, belongs to the seismic situation that has begun to be felt in the field of Greek New Testament editions and New Testament textual criticism (NTTC). David Parker qualified the NTTC digital turn as "dramatic change" in 2008,⁶³ in an area in which the Institute for the New Testament Textual Research (INTF) and the International Greek New Testament Project (IGNTP) were charged to maintain and develop Greek NT editions for many decades. In 2012, I drafted the general outlines of this "dramatic change" by describing notably the "bombshell" that occurred in 2010:

> At the *Society of Biblical Literature* (SBL) annual meeting in November 2010 in Atlanta – a new, independent edition of the Greek NT was presented and offered to all participants, published by a respected scholar in the field, Michael Holmes, with the support of *Logos Software* and the *Society of Biblical Literature:*⁶⁴ neither the INTF nor the IGNTP had been informed of the project. This edition came as a shock for scholars working in the field.⁶⁵

---

60 "Notice ThéoTeX," ThéoTeX, https://theotex.org/ntgf/notice_theotex.html.
61 Maurice A. Robinson and William G. Pierpont, eds., *The New Testament in the Original Greek: Byzantine Textform 2005* (Washington, DC: Chilton Book Publishing, 2005).
62 "Notice ThéoTeX": "Jamais acquérir les ouvrages nécessaires pour pouvoir lire le Nouveau Testament dans sa langue originale n'aura été aussi aisé qu'à notre époque du numérique" (anonymous author).
63 David C. Parker, *An Introduction to the New Testament Manuscripts and Their Texts* (Cambridge: Cambridge University Press, 2008): 1.
64 Michael W. Holmes, ed., *The SBL Greek New Testament* (Atlanta: SBL/Logos Bible Software, 2010), http://www.sblgnt.com.
65 Clivaz, "Homer," 2.

Even if this SBL edition is based on the 19th edition of Westcott and Hort[66] and omits all of the information provided by the papyri, it has generated enthusiasm, notably because of its apparatus in open access (OA), whereas the NA28 presents in OA only the Greek text, without apparatus.[67] The auto-didact chemist Wieland Willker, moderator of the NTTC Yahoo forum,[68] wished in 2010 to see textual critics produce more new Greek NT texts like Michael Holmes.[69] This call has been heeded in places, for example the Tyndale House Edition of the Greek New Testament (THGNT) edited by Dirk Jongkind, Peter Head, and Peter Williams. Their edition is based on the 19th century Tregelles edition,[70] with the collaboration of Dan Wallace and his team at the Center for the Study of the New Testament Manuscripts in Texas.[71] Apparently, the phenomenon I referred to in 2012 as "institutional deregulation" in the scholarly Greek edition of the NT[72] has been expanded even further in the intervening years. I would be inclined today to speak rather about an institutional diversification or transformation: a more neutral word is required here, since, on the one hand, it has become evident that we will not come back to the institutionalized situation, and, on the other hand, NTTC as a field needs to analyze the entire picture of this quite complex evolution to understand what is at stake. What follows are some remarks that will surely continue to evolve in coming years.

First, I strongly underline that the INTF and the IGNTP have to continue their patient work with tenacity to maintain a critical reference edition of the Greek New Testament, to which all New Testament students should look in the first instance. In particular, I hope that public academic funds will continue to support this work intensively. The emergence of non-academic initiatives such as the TheoTeX Greek NT edition is an ambiguous fact: only a detailed sociological inquiry

---

66 Brooke F. Westcott and Fenton J. A. Hort, eds., *The Greek New Testament* (Peabody, MA: Hendrickson Publishers, 2007 [1881]).
67 See note 57.
68 For an analysis of the NTTC evolution in the social networks, see Claire Clivaz, "Internet Networks and Academic Research: The Example of the New Testament Textual Criticism," in *Digital Humanities in Biblical, Early Jewish and Early Christian Studies*, ed. Claire Clivaz, Andrew Gregory, and David Hamidović, in coll. with Sara Schulthess, Scholarly Communication 2 (Leiden: Brill, 2013): 151–73.
69 Wieland Willker, "Analysis of the SBL GNT in the Gospels," unpublished manuscript, November 2010, PDF file, https://tinyurl.com/y2loqydp.
70 "Greek New Testament," Tyndale House, http://www.tyndale.cam.ac.uk/thegnt; Samuel P. Tregelles, *Hē kainē diathēkē = The Greek New Testament* (London: Samuel Bagster & Sons, 1887).
71 "Home," Center for the Study of New Testament Manuscripts, http://www.csntm.org.
72 Clivaz, "Homer," 3.

could make the author team or group public and show what strategic intentions lie behind such a project. We simply have no answer to these questions. Ancient NT manuscripts are able today to spark interest in the most unexpected circles, even in some Salafist circles, with the production of an entire Arabic transliteration of the Codex Vaticanus in OA.[73] A sociological inquiry would also help to understand all the implications of such an initiative. Last but not least, the INTF and IGNTP are also securing an etic, rather than emic, approach to the study and edition of Greek New Testament manuscripts. For example, when Robinson and Pierpont invoke God and explicitly pray for their work in the introduction of their Greek NT Byzantine edition,[74] it represents a clear barrier for secularized students and scholars.

Second, the digital turn is rapidly transforming the NTTC field, creating huge challenges for the NA28 – and the next NA29 edition. The German *Bibelgesellschaft* should urgently consider putting in OA the apparatus criticus of the NA28. As long as this is not the case, some will use a more approximate critical apparatus simply because it is in OA. Another urgent question for the NA editing team to consider is the question raised by Olivier Abel, commenting on the new freedom of the 17th century (section 1): "the political question will thus gradually become: 'How can we stay together?' when we can always become unbound?"[75] The innovation of the New Testament Virtual Room of Manuscripts (NTVMR) has created potential new habits for direct collaboration between scholars in the transcription of the manuscripts.[76] But at the same time, it is illusory to think, if we follow Fitzpatrick's analysis regarding the importance of communities in digital culture, that one day all concerned scholars will work in the same virtual research environment (VRE) in editing the Greek New Testament.[77]

---

73 The address of the webpage was http://ww38.sheekh-3arb.net/vb/showthread.php?t=2127; the website has now been archived on https://web.archive.org/web/20140703080949/http://www.sheekh-3arb.net/vb/showthread.php?t=2127&page=3. A screenshot of a page of the transliterated Codex Vaticanus in Arabic can be found in Sara Schulthess, "The Role of the Internet in New Testament Textual Criticism: The Example of the Arabic Manuscripts of the New Testament," in *Digital Humanities in Biblical, Early Jewish and Early Christian Studies*, ed. Claire Clivaz, Andrew Gregory, and David Hamidović, in coll. with Sara Schulthess, Scholarly Communication 2 (Leiden: Brill, 2013): 76.
74 See, for example, Robinson–Pierpont, *New Testament*, ii: "Our prayer and fervent hope is that the Lord Jesus Christ will prosper the work of our hands and use our labors for the benefit of his kingdom."
75 Abel, "Essai sur la prise," 115.
76 "New Testament Virtual Manuscript Room," Institut für Neutestamentliche Textforschung, WWU Münster, http://ntvmr.uni-muenster.de/.
77 See Fitzpatrick, *Planned Obsolescence*.

The importance of specific, close, and diverse research communities – or research community social networks – becomes more evident every day. An impressive example is the recent OA project PAVONe[78] at the University of Balamand, Lebanon, designed to be a Platform for the Arabic Versions of the New Testament, including manuscript images. It is clear that such a project is rightly located in a Middle Eastern country, and is surely of highest interest and importance for Arabic-speaking scholars in these countries. The linguistic aspect seems to naturally distinguish PAVONe from the NTVMR, but the question of PAVONe's interaction with and relationship to the German tool should be raised.

Other online New Testament manuscript editing projects are in preparation or currently running, such as HumaReC, a Swiss National Foundation project on which Sara Schulthess, Anastasia Chasapi, and Martial Sankar have been working under my direction.[79] Its object of study is the only trilingual Arabic–Greek–Latin NT manuscript we know, the Marc. Gr. Z. 11 (379), GA 460. In scrutinizing its content, this project also has another purpose, to test new models of data publication in a continuous way,[80] and this VRE has just received an ISSN by the Swiss National Library. Thanks to the support of the Marciana Library, all of the concerned folios are progressively posted online.[81] In dialogue with the publisher Brill, our team is also preparing a new model of hyperlinked monograph, the web book.[82] A collaboration with an Austrian team allows us to test *Transkribus* on this manuscript, a handwritten text recognition tool.[83] Such a project requires the development of a specific VRE, and the question of interaction with the Münster NTVMR has been established in the next SNSF project, MARK16.[84]

---

[78] PAVONe, http://pavone.uob-dh.org/.
[79] HumaReC, DH+, SIB | Swiss Institute of Bioinformatics 2016–2019, https://humarec.org; "HumaReC – Humanities Research and Continuous Publishing: A Digital New Testament Test-Case," P³, http://p3.snf.ch/project-169869.
[80] "Launching HumaReC: The Project," HumaReC Blog, 20 January 2017, https://humarec.org/index.php/continuous-publications-blog/12-announcements/18-launching.
[81] "Humarec Manuscript Viewer," HumaReC, 2016–2017, http://humarec-viewer.vital-it.ch.
[82] Claire Clivaz, "Web Book," HumaReC Blog, 20 January 2017, https://humarec.org/index.php/continuous-publications-blog/11-articles/15-webbook.
[83] Sara Schulthess, "Collaboration with Transkribus," HumaRec Blog, 1 February 2017, https://humarec.org/index.php/continuous-publications-blog/19-transkribus; Claire Clivaz, "HumaReC mentioned by the H2020 project READ (Transkribus)," HumaRec Blog, 7 April 2017, https://humarec.org/index.php/continuous-publications-blog/24-humarec-mentioned-by-the-h2020-project-red-transkribus.
[84] MARK16 (2020), ISSN 2673-9836, https://mark16.sib.swiss.

These two examples show how much the question "how can we stay together, when we can always become unbound" matters in the digital NTTC research field. New ideas should be developed to foster the most efficient interactions between the NTVMR and other online platforms with NT manuscripts. This overview fits exactly with the shift from the text to the document announced in 2010 by van Peursen,[85] a shift also assumed by the project Homer Multitext, which works on each specific manuscript, instead of proposing a critical edition.[86] This shift from text to document explains a certain fear among NT scholars: the SBL and Tyndale House Greek New Testament editions, going back to 19th-century printed editions, are understandable reactions to a situation that threatens the idea of having a common Greek NT. Consequently, the need for a "majority text" or a *textus receptus* has returned. At the same time, the simple fact that the Tyndale House team produced its own edition shows that a certain Pandora's box has been too far opened to be closed again. We now see the majority of NT manuscripts online, and more are added every day: to see the manuscripts so easily is progressively transforming the depth of scholarly text critical practices. Will the digital Bible therefore become "less canonical," following the reasoning of the SEK document (section 1)?

Looking at this situation, it is striking for me to read again what I was writing in 1998 – at a pre-digital age period of my career.[87] I was pleading for the *sola scriptura in koinonia*, afraid to see the canon lose its meaning in the framework of the third quest for the historical Jesus, asking if the cover of the book would not be lost.[88] Twenty-two years later, it is the Scripture itself that has been emancipated from the book, and *sola scriptura* is now looking for new expressions, either as *sola lectura* (SEK document), or as *sola scriptura in koinonia*, as I have proposed. But I absolutely missed in 1998 the link between material writing and our perception of the texts themselves. By including the digital turn on the

---

85 See van Peursen, "Text Comparison and Digital Creativity."
86 Casey Dué and Mary Ebbott, eds., *The Homer Multitext Project*, 2014, http://www.homermultitext.org/about.html: "Unlike printed editions, which offer a reconstruction of an original text as it supposedly existed at the time and place of its origin, the Homer Multitext offers the tools for reconstructing a variety of texts as they existed in a variety of times and places."
87 Clivaz, "Categories": 35–9.
88 Clivaz, "La troisième quête," 557: "On peut se demander si la recomposition canonique à laquelle conduisent certaines retombées de la troisième quête, ne révèle pas l'apothéose de l'autonomisation du *sola scriptura*: l'adage ne va-t-il pas ici éclater du fait même de son isolement? La couverture du livre ne va-t-elle pas sauter, laissant s'en aller au vent les feuillets qui composaient l'ouvrage?"

issue, it becomes possible to demonstrate the ways in which categories of ancient Christian texts are shaped at different times by the writing material itself.[89]

At a time where we can see so many NT manuscripts and evaluate them as they are, the need to keep not only one but multiple types of critical NT editions seems highly related to the question of community, whether it is the larger academic community (for the NA28) or more specific communities (for the SBL or Tyndale House NT editions). In other words, we face issues with some common points in the "important codices period" (Sinaiticus, Vaticanus, Alexandrinus, etc.) of the 4th–5th century: the Codex Sinaiticus presents a Greek New Testament *according to* the people who produced Sinaiticus; in a similar way, the Tyndale House Greek NT edition presents a Greek NT *according to* Tregelles and the Tyndale House scholars. Consequently, it is useful to listen to Karl Barth's short and striking video, in which he explains, in his own voice and accent, that his writing is related to people, to an "invisible community."[90] It is surely a different experience to listen to Barth, instead of reading his sentences (section 1). Let's think in the last section about the emergence of a multimodal digital culture…and Scripture.

4 A digital multimodal Scripture in communities

In a way typical of the present conditions of digital culture, the Barth video is accessible online in open access, downloadable from the Center for Barth Studies, but without mention of its place, date, and circumstances of production. Humanist scholars working at this Barth center have surely been trained in the proper way to quote texts and make references with great exactitude. Textual scholars are not used to considering 60 seconds of oral discourse in the same way that they regard a nicely written text; the latter has greater gravitas. This anecdote points to the substantial digital wave that is deeply transforming the humanities: the possibility to create multimodal knowledge and multimodal expressions, integrating text, images, and sounds. For two generations (1945– 2000), humanities considered computational resources essentially as a way to "list" knowledge, to create every kind of catalogue and classification according to a logic of association. The "humanities" AND "computing" were essentially based on texts and textuality.

---

89 Clivaz, "Categories": 48–55.
90 The Center for Barth Studies, "Karl Barth & the Epistle to the Romans," Vimeo, uploaded 28 March 2014, https://vimeo.com/90346827; no year or place are indicated for the video itself on Vimeo.

At the end of the Second World War, the ingenious Vannevar Bush described a hypothetical proto-hypertext system called the "memex" (memory extender), "in which an individual stores all these books, records and communications" and could create "wholly new forms of encyclopedia."[91] A list of "Literary Works in Machine-Readable Form" was published in 1966.[92] The period from the 1960s to the 1980s saw the extensive development of document markup systems, and the Text Encoding Initiative consortium was created in 1987 to coordinate the efforts of electronic editions in the humanities. Dozens of scholars collaborated in creating common guidelines, which were fully published for the first time in 2002.[93] This central relationship between the humanities, computing, and textuality cannot be underestimated: in 2004, when Busa wrote his foreword to the first edition of the *Companion to Digital Humanities*, he affirmed that "humanities computing is precisely the automation of every possible analysis of human expression (therefore, it is exquisitely a 'humanistic' activity), in the widest sense of the word, from music to the theater, from design and painting to phonetics, but whose nucleus remains the discourse of written texts."[94] But a quick look at the projections of the kind of data present on the internet in the intervening years shows that the humanities digitized "out of the paper" are becoming multimodal in digital formats that *are not printable any more:* in the 2020s, three-fourths of the data will be composed of audiovisual material (videos, images, and audio material), according to IBM projections.[95]

Humanist scholars do not have much time to adapt themselves and their specialized skills to this dominant new material. In 2009, Fitzpatrick said that "if we have the ability to respond to video with video, if we can move seamlessly from audio files to images to text as means of representing music, it may behove us to think about exactly what it is we're producing when we write, how it is that these different modes of communication come together in complex document forms."[96] Interesting projects are now emerging at the crossroad of texts and

---

[91] Vannevar Bush, "As We May Think," *Atlantic Magazine*, 9 July 1945, http://www.theatlantic.com/magazine/print/1945/07/as-we-may-think/303881/.
[92] Gary Carlson, "Literary Works in Machine-Readable Form: Computers and the Humanities 1," *Computer and the Humanities* 1, no. 3 (1967): 75–102.
[93] Claire Clivaz and David Hamidović, "Critical Editions in the Digital Age," in *The Johns Hopkins Guide to Digital Media and Textuality*, ed. Marie-Laure Ryan, Lori Emerson, and Benjamin J. Robertson (Baltimore: JHU Press, 2014): 94–8.
[94] Busa, "Foreword."
[95] Representation of expected waves of data showing the growth of audiovisual data (video, images, audio), in IBM Market Insights 2013, ("Background," AVinDH SIG, https://avindhsig.wordpress.com/background/).
[96] Fitzpatrick, *Planned Obsolescence*, 27.

sounds, such as the Baudelaire Song project.[97] Multimodal editing tools such as Scalar or the Etalks are in development,[98] and the topic of data visualization is crucial in DH.[99] The revolution of a multimodal knowledge is arriving even in biblical exegesis with the emergence of performance criticism[100] and in Vernon K. Robbins and Walter S. Melion's 2017 *Art Visual Exegesis: Rhetoric, Texts, Images*.[101]

It is still very hard to predict, of course, how the New Testament exegesis will evolve in a multimodal culture, but uses of the Bible are already in transformation, as one can observe with the first biblical applications on the market. As Tim Hutchings observes, "in many churches and Bible study groups, at least in Britain and the United States, it is now common to see mobile phones and tablets used during services instead of printed Bibles. [...] Publishers have begun to augment the Bible with multi-media resources, promising to help the user achieve a deeper and more frequent engagement with the text."[102] In two articles, Hutchings analyzes two of the most successful biblical applications, YouVersion and GloBible,[103] promoted by evangelical Christian movements.[104] YouVersion was founded by Life.Church, which is not "an independent online community but the online ministry of a single large church founded in the United States in 1996," with 13 different physical locations as of 2009.[105]

Hutchings' main point is to demonstrate that, contrary to the opinion of several evangelical theologians, the Bible is not "vanishing" or becoming "liquid" in these applications. They maintain a strong evangelical interpretation framework, using all the multi-media possibilities; Hutchings concludes that

---

97 The Baudelaire Song Project, https://www.baudelairesong.org/.
98 The Alliance for Networking Visual Culture, 2020, http://scalar.usc.edu/; Claire Clivaz, The eTalks, SIB | Swiss Institute of Bioinformatics, https://etalk.sib.swiss/. See Claire Clivaz, Marion Rivoal, and Martial Sankar, "A New Platform for Editing Digital Multimedia: The eTalks," in *New Avenues for Electronic Publishing*, ed. Birgit Schmidt and Milena Dobreva (Amsterdam: IOS Press, 2015): 156–9.
99 See for example Taylor Arnold and Emily Tilton, *Humanities Data in R. Exploring Networks, Geospatial Data, Images, and Text* (Heidelberg: Springer, 2015).
100 Bernhard Oestreich and Glenn S. Holland, *Performance Criticism of the Pauline Letters* (Eugene, OR: Cascade Books, 2016).
101 Vernon K. Robbins and Walter S. Melion, *The Art of Visual Exegesis: Rhetoric, Texts, Images*, Emory Studies in Early Christianity 19 (Atlanta: SLB Press, 2017).
102 Tim Hutchings, "Design and the Digital Bible: Persuasive Technology and Religious Reading," *Journal of Contemporary Religion* 32, no. 2 (2017): 205–19.
103 YouVersion, https://www.youversion.com; gloBIBLE, 2020, https://globible.com/.
104 See Tim Hutchings, "E-reading and the Christian Bible", *Studies in Religion/Sciences Religieuses* 44, no. 4 (2015): 423–40.
105 Tim Hutchings, *Creating Church Online* (London/NY: Routledge, 2017).

these products offer extensive libraries, with audio and multi-media options and thousands of texts to choose from, but their portfolios are not infinite. Contents are carefully chosen, as are the user's options for navigation through the library. At times, as indicated above, the digital product can even go against the user's independence, offering advice, reprimanding the wayward, and using the techniques of persuasive technology to form new habits of textual engagement. [...] My evidence demonstrates that the funders, designers, and marketers of some digital Bibles are trying hard to promote a traditional Evangelical attitude to the Bible, but further research will be needed to evaluate the consequences of widespread adoption of digital text within religious communities.[106]

Common research projects with interdisciplinary teams of theologians should examine the topic. These applications are in any case a rich laboratory for observing the diverse uses of multimodality to represent biblical content. Notably, orality has made a comeback. On 15 April 2017, YouVersion users shared 166 written verses in India; in Egypt, 3,525 audio chapters were listened to, and 94 in Ukraine. On the same day, in Sweden, 25 written biblical verses were shared, but 2,532 Bible chapters have been listened in this same country. These observations are joining more general observations about the comeback of orality generally in Western culture, with the emergence of cinemas for the ears, festivals of literary performances, or sound studies as an academic field.[107] "Word" and "Scripture," the old theological words facing one another, have begun again to claim our close attention.

In such a context, the quotation in the introduction to this article, claiming that "Scripture *fills the place of the origin*," even if considered as a "*historically secondary* phenomenon,"[108] becomes less obvious. By stating that "das Christentum ist keine Buchreligion,"[109] the SEK document seems to be more in line with our present cultural situation. "Die Emanzipation der Schrift vom Buch" clearly points to a question that has remained unsolved since the 17th century: "How can we stay together when we can always become unbound?" The issue of community is raised when the *sola lectura* is defined as a core Protestant skill.[110] Are the diverse Protestant churches ready to consider that *sola scriptura* as a *lectura* be done in *koinonia*? In digital culture, it is not so much a theological or conceptual question: it is very concrete, since the words of Scripture itself are now emancipated from the book. Unbound digital humanities will create new boundaries for the 500-year-old doctrine of *sola scriptura*.

---

106 Hutchings, "Design," 215–6.
107 Clivaz et al., "A New Platform," 156–7.
108 Gisel, "Apocryphes et canon," 230.
109 SEK, *Sola lectura*, 7.
110 Ibid., 31.

With such conclusive remarks, one can rightly orient[111] this discussion towards the following question: in which specific ways does the digital transformation influence the discussion regarding *sola scriptura*? After all, Barth's video, claiming that he desired to reach a community rather than to write a book, is expressed entirely in the midst of a culture totally embedded in printed material. The diversification of Greek NT editions, as striking as it is, has already happened in previous times, and the shift from text to document underlined by Wido van Peursen can be considered as a shift back towards previous aspects.

But in 1998, by scrutinizing the issue of the canon and the *sola scriptura*, I missed at that time the importance of writing support in the development of ideas and concepts. Here we are: when we interrogate the digital turn in theology or Christian studies, we are not speaking particularly about a transformation per se in this field. We are analyzing something that happens to all fields in the humanities, to the entire Western epistemology: the impact of a totally new material of writing, and consequently of thinking, with words embedded in images and sounds, in cultural productions no longer printable. To the contrary of theological disputes about canonicity or Christology or other internal topics, emerging digital culture offers an incredibly powerful opportunity for scholars in Christian studies to be involved in an epistemological discussion currently occurring in all fields in the humanities. They have only to consider lucidly that *sola scriptura* must now be considered in relationship to digital writing in general, and not only as evolving towards digital Scriptures.

5 Bibliography

Abel, Olivier. "Essai sur la prise. Anthropologie de la flibuste et théologie radicale protestante." *Esprit* 356 (2009): 114–5.

Abel, Olivier. "L'océan, le puritain, le pirate." *Esprit* 356 (2009): 104–10.

Aland, Barbara, ed. *Nestle Aland 28th Edition of the Greek New Testament*. Münster: German Bible Society, 2012.

Arnold, Taylor, and Emily Tilton. *Humanities Data in R. Exploring Networks, Geospatial Data, Images, and Text*. Heidelberg: Springer, 2015.

Busa, Roberto. "Foreword: Perspectives on the Digital Humanities." In *A Companion to Digital Humanities*, edited by Susan Schreibman, Ray Siemens, and John Unsworth, xvi–xi. Hoboken, NJ: Wiley Blackwell, 2004. http://www.digitalhumanities.org/companion/.

Bush, Vannevar. "As We May Think." *Atlantic Magazine*, 9 July 1945. http://www.theatlantic.com/magazine/print/1945/07/as-we-may-think/303881/.

---

[111] Thank you to the reviewer of the English translation of this article for having pointed out this question.

Campbell, Heidi A., ed. *Digital Religion: Understanding Religious Practice in New Media Worlds*. Oxford: Routledge, 2013.
Campbell, Heidi A., and Brian Altenhofen. "Methodological Challenges, Innovations and Growing Pains in Digital Religion Research." In *Digital Methodologies in the Sociology of Religion*, edited by Sariva Cheruvallil-Contractor and Suha Shakkour, 1–12. London: Bloomsbury Publishing, 2015.
Campbell, Heidi A., and Stephen Garner. *Networked Theology: Negotiating Faith in Digital Culture*. Buffalo, NY: Baker Academy, 2016.
Carlson, Gary. "Literary Works in Machine-Readable Form: Computers and the Humanities 1." *Computer and the Humanities* 1, no. 3 (1967): 75–102.
Carrière, Jean-Claude, and Umberto Eco. *N'espérez pas vous débarrasser des livres*. Paris: Seuil, 2009.
Chartier, Roger. *Les métamorphoses du livre: Les rendez-vous de l'édition. Le livre et le numérique*. Paris: Bibliothèque du Centre Pompidou, 2001.
Citton, Yves. *L'Avenir des Humanités. Économie de la connaissance ou culture de l'interprétation?* Paris: La Découverte, 2010.
Clivaz, Claire. "La troisième quête du Jésus historique et le canon: le défi de la réception communautaire. Un essai de relecture historique." In *Jésus de Nazareth: Nouvelles approches d'une énigme* (MBo 38), edited by Daniel Marguerat, Enrico Norelli, and Jean-Michel Poffet, 541–58. Genève: Labor et Fides, 1998.
Clivaz, Claire. "The New Testament at the Time of the Egyptian Papyri: Reflections Based on P^{12}, P^{75} and P^{126} (P. Amh. 3b, P. Bod. XIV–XV and PSI 1497)." In *Reading New Testament Papyri in Context – Lire les papyrus du Nouveau Testament dans leur context*, edited by Claire Clivaz and Jean Zumstein and in collaboration with Jenny Read-Heimerdinger and Julie Paik, 15–55. BETL 242. Leuven: Peeters, 2011.
Clivaz, Claire. "Homer and the New Testament as 'Multitexts' in the Digital Age?" *Scholarly and Research Communication* 3, no. 3 (2012): 1–15. http://src-online.ca/index.php/src/article/view/97.
Clivaz, Claire. "Internet Networks and Academic Research: The Example of the New Testament Textual Criticism." In *Digital Humanities in Biblical, Early Jewish and Early Christian Studies*, edited by Claire Clivaz, Andrew Gregory, and David Hamidović and in collaboration with Sara Schulthess, 151–73. Scholarly Communication 2. Leiden: Brill, 2013.
Clivaz, Claire. "Jamais deux sans trois! Théologie, exégèse et culture." In *Entre exégètes et théologiens: la Bible. 24ᵉ congrès de l'ACFEB (Toulouse 2011)*, edited by Elian Cuvillier and Bernadette Escaffre, 253–69. Paris: Cerf, 2014.
Clivaz, Claire. "New Testament in a Digital Culture: A *Biblaridion* (Little Book) Lost in the Web?" *Journal of Religion, Media and Digital Culture* 3, no. 3 (2014): 20–38.
Clivaz, Claire. "Categories of Ancient Christian Texts and Writing Materials: 'Taking Once Again a Fresh Starting Point'." In *Ancient Worlds in Digital Culture*, edited by Claire Clivaz, Paul Dilley, and David Hamidović and in collaboration with Apolline Thromas, 35–58. Digital Biblical Studies 1. Leiden: Brill, 2016.
Clivaz, Claire. "Vous avez dit 'dématérialisation'? Diagnostic d'une panne culturelle." *Le Temps* (blog), 2 July 2016. https://blogs.letemps.ch/claire-clivaz/2016/07/02/vous-avez-dit-dematerialisation-diagnostic-dune-panne-culturelle/.

Clivaz, Claire. "Introduction: Digital Humanities in Jewish, Christian and Arabic Traditions." *Journal of Religion, Media and Digital Culture* 5 (2016): 1–20.
Clivaz, Claire. "Die Bibel im digitalen Zeitalter: Multimodale Schrift in Gemeinschaften." *Zeitschrift für Neues Testament* 20, no. 39/40 (2017): 35–57.
Clivaz, Claire. "Lost in Translation? The Odyssey of the 'Digital Humanities' in French." *Studia UBB Digitalia* 62, no. 1 (2017): 26–41. http://digihubb.centre.ubbcluj.ro/journal/index.php/digitalia/article/view/4/18.
Clivaz, Claire. "Review of Jeffrey S. Siker, *Liquid Scripture: The Bible in a Digital World*." *Review of Biblical Literature* 5 (2018): 1–6. https://www.sblcentral.org/home/bookDetails/11851.
Clivaz, Claire. *Ecritures digitales: Digital Writing, Digital Scriptures*. Digital Biblical Studies 4. Leiden: Brill, 2019.
Clivaz, Claire, Paul Dilley, and David Hamidović, eds. *Ancient Worlds in Digital Culture*. In collaboration with Apolline Thromas. Digital Biblical Studies 1. Leiden: Brill, 2016.
Clivaz, Claire, Paul Dilley, David Hamidović, Mladen Popović, Caroline T. Schroeder, and Joseph Verheyden, eds. "Digital Humanities in Jewish, Christian and Arabic Traditions." Special issue, *Journal of Religion, Media and Digital Culture* 5, no. 1 (2016).
Clivaz, Claire, Andrew Gregory, and David Hamidović, eds. *Digital Humanities in Biblical, Early Jewish and Early Christian Studies*. In collaboration with Sarah Schulthess. Scholarly Communication 2. Leiden: Brill, 2013.
Clivaz, Claire, and David Hamidović. "Critical Editions in the Digital Age." In *The Johns Hopkins Guide to Digital Media and Textuality*, edited by Marie-Laure Ryan, Lori Emerson, and Benjamin J. Robertson, 94–98. Baltimore: JHU Press, 2014.
Clivaz, Claire, Marion Rivoal, and Martial Sankar. "A New Platform for Editing Digital Multimedia: The eTalks." In *New Avenues for Electronic Publishing*, edited by Birgit Schmidt and Milena Dobreva, 156–59. Amsterdam: IOS Press, 2015.
Clivaz, Claire, and Dominique Vinck, eds. "Les humanités délivrées." *Les Cahiers du Numériques* 10, no. 3 (2014): 9–16.
Darnton, Robert. *The Case for Books: Past, Present, Future*. New York: Public Affairs, 2009.
Depecker, Loïc. "Que diriez-vous d' 'ordinateur' ?", *Bibnum, Calcul et informatique*, published on the 1st June 2015; consulted on the 1st June 2021. http://journals.openedition.org/bibnum/534.
Derrida, Jacques. *Sur parole. Instantanés philosophiques*. Paris: Editions de l'Aube, 2000.
Derrida, Jacques. "Paper or Myself, You Know... (New Speculations on a Luxury of the Poor)." In *Paper Machine*, translated by Board of Trustees, 41–65. Stanford: Stanford University Press, 2005.
Doueihi, Milad. "Préface. Quête et enquête." In *Le temps des humanités digitales*, edited by Olivier Le Deuff, 7–10. Limoges: FyP editions, 2014.
Drucker, Johanna. "Humanities Approaches to Graphical Display." *Digital Humanities Quarterly* 5, no. 1 (2011): 1–52. http://www.digitalhumanities.org/dhq/vol/5/1/000091/000091.html.
Eco, Umberto. *The Infinity of Lists*, trans. Alastair McEwen. New York: Rizzoli, 2009.
FEPS. *Sola lectura? Enjeux actuels de la lecture dans une perspective protestante*. Bern: Stämpfli AG, 2016. http://www.kirchenbund.ch/fr/publications/tudes/sola-lectura.
Fiormonte, Domenico. "The Digital Humanities from Father Busa to Edward Snowden." *Media Development* 64, no. 2 (2017): 29–33.

Fitzpatrick, Kathleen. *Planned Obsolescence: Publishing, Technology, and the Future of the Academy.* Norfolk: MediaCommons Press, 2009. http://mcpress.media-commons.org/plannedobsolescence/.
Gisel, Pierre. "Apocryphes et canon: leurs rapports et leur statut respectif. Un questionnement théologique." *Apocrypha* 7 (1996): 225–34.
Holmes, Michael W., ed. *The SBL Greek New Testament.* Atlanta: SBL/Logos Bible Software, 2010.
Hutchings, Tim. "E-reading and the Christian Bible." *Studies in Religion/Sciences Religieuses* 44, no. 4 (2015): 423–40.
Hutchings, Tim. *Creating Church Online: Ritual, Community and New Media.* Abingdon: Routledge, 2017.
Hutchings, Tim. "Design and the Digital Bible: Persuasive Technology and Religious Reading." *Journal of Contemporary Religion* 32, no. 2 (2017): 205–19. https://doi.org/10.1080/13537903.2017.1298903.
Jones, Steven E. *Roberto Busa, S.J., and the Emergence of Humanities Computing: The Priest and the Punched Cards.* London: Routledge, 2016.
Krüger, Olivier. *Die mediale Religion. Probleme und Perspektiven religionswissenschaftlicher und wissenssoziologischer Medienforschung.* Reihe Religion und Medien 1. Bielfeld: Transcript Verlag, 2012.
Nyhan, Julianne, and Andrew Flinn. *Computation and the Humanities: Towards an Oral History of Digital Humanities.* Springer Series on Cultural Computing. Washington, DC: Springer, 2016.
Olender, Maurice. *Un fantôme dans la bibliothèque.* Paris: Seuil, 2017.
Oestreich, Bernhard, and Glenn S. Holland. *Performance Criticism of the Pauline Letters.* Eugene, OR: Cascade Books, 2016.
Parker, David C. "Through a Screen Darkly: Digital Texts and the New Testament." *Journal for the Study of the New Testament* 25, no. 4 (2003): 395–411.
Parker, David C. *An Introduction to the New Testament Manuscripts and Their Texts.* Cambridge: Cambridge University Press, 2008.
van Peursen, Wido. "Text Comparison and Digital Creativity: An Introduction." In *Text Comparison and Digital Creativity: The Production of Presence and Meaning in Digital Text Scholarship*, edited by Wido van Peursen, Ernst D. Thoutenhoofd, and Adrian Van der Weel, 1–27. Scholarly Communication 1. Leiden: Brill, 2010.
Robbins, Vernon K., and Walter S. Melion. *The Art of Visual Exegesis: Rhetoric, Texts, Images.* Emory Studies in Early Christianity 19. Atlanta: SLB Press, 2017.
Robinson, Maurice A., and William G. Pierpont, eds. *The New Testament in the Original Greek: Byzantine Textform 2005.* Washington, DC: Chilton Book Publishing, 2005.
Schmid, Ulrich. "Thoughts on a Digital Edition of the New Testament." In *Reading Tomorrow: From Ancient Manuscripts to the Digital Era / Lire Demain. Des manuscrits antiques à l'ère digitale*, edited by Claire Clivaz, Jérôme Meizoz, François Vallotton, and Joseph Verheyden and in collaboration with Benjamin Bertho, 299–306. Lausanne: PPUR, 2012.
Schroeder, Caroline T. "The Digital Humanities as Cultural Capital: Implications for Biblical and Religious Studies." *Journal of Religion, Media and Digital Culture* 5, no. 1 (2016): 21–49. https://doi.org/10.1163/21659214-90000069.
Schulthess, Sara. "The Role of the Internet in New Testament Textual Criticism: The Example of the Arabic Manuscripts of the New Testament." In *Digital Humanities in Biblical, Early*

Jewish and Early Christian Studies, edited by Claire Clivaz, Andrew Gregory, and David Hamidović and in collaboration with Sara Schulthess, 71–81. Scholarly Communication 2. Leiden: Brill, 2013.

SEK. *Sola lectura? Aktuelle Herausforderungen des Lesens aus protestantischer Sicht*. Bern: Stämpfli AG, 2016. https://www.evref.ch/wp-content/uploads/2019/08/18_sola_lectura_de.pdf.

Shep, Sydney J. "Digital Materiality." In *A New Companion to Digital Humanities*, edited by Susan Schreibman, Ray Siemens and, John Unsworth, 322–330. Hoboken, NJ: Wiley Blackwell, 2016.

Siker, Jeffrey S. *Liquid Scripture: The Bible in a Digital World*. Minneapolis: Fortress Press, 2017.

Tregelles, Samuel P. *Hē kainē diathēkē = The Greek New Testament*. London: Samuel Bagster & Sons, 1887.

Vandendorpe, Christian. *From Papyrus to Hypertext: Toward the Universal Digital Library*, trans. Phyllis Aronoff and Howard Scott. Topics in the Digital Humanities. Champaign, IL: University of Illinois Press, 2009.

Vinck, Dominique, and Claire Clivaz, eds. "Les humanités délivrées." *La Revue d'Anthropologie des Connaissances* 8, no. 4 (2014): 681–704.

Westcott, Brooke F., and Fenton J. A. Hort, eds. *The Greek New Testament*. Peabody, MA: Hendrickson Publishers, 2007 [1881].

Willker, Wieland. "Analysis of the SBL GNT in the Gospels." Unpublished manuscript, November 2010. PDF file. https://tinyurl.com/y2loqydp

Michael Stenskjær Christensen, Jeffrey C. Witt and Ueli Zahnd

Re-conceiving the Christian scholastic corpus with the scholastic commentaries and texts archive

1 Introduction

The Western Christian tradition was and is critically shaped by the methodological paradigm known today as scholasticism, a paradigm that prevailed in crucial periods of both Catholic and Protestant Christian traditions. Scholasticism was marked by literary genres (such as commentaries and compendia) that fostered textual interdependencies to the point that the scholastic corpus can be understood as a huge network of thought. It is our belief that emerging approaches within the digital humanities, and the open semantic web in particular, allow us, for the first time in modern research, to understand the full depth and fundamental interwovenness of scholastic thought. However, the current mechanisms of publishing scholarly editions, be it in traditional book form or as digital presentations, do not help to advance scholarship in this direction. The ongoing fragmentation of editions with different publishers, who prepare data according to proprietary and incompatible data standards, means not only that the creation of an edition requires wasteful redundancy but also that the aggregation and analysis of connected content, which are so essential to scholastic thought, are impossible.

In this article, we would like to present an alternative founded on open community data standards and linked open data; an alternative that promotes the shift from seeing a text as a document, page, or file (the "text-as-document" paradigm) to seeing the text as first and foremost a network of connected data (a "text-as-network" paradigm). We look first more closely at the nature of scholasticism and its interwovenness, arguing why existing publishing paradigms are limiting our potential exploration of this tradition. Secondly, we offer an overview of what a promising shift in publishing could look like, and how the Scholastic Commentaries and Texts Archive (scta.info)[1] and its supporting community

---

[1] All hyperlinks cited in this volume were retrieved on 30 May 2021. As things are constantly improving, this means that we are constantly improving workflows, documentation, and consuming apps. This also means that links listed here may be changed or reorganized. We provide links accessible at time of publication; these links have been archived using Archive.org's Way-

are attempting to provide the foundation to actualize this shift. Finally, we offer an example of how a connected corpus of scholastic data, the likes of which the SCTA aims to make possible, will open new avenues of research and exploration on a scale that would be impossible without the aid of digital technology.

2 Scholasticism and the Christian tradition

Scholasticism was a paradigm that shaped academic traditions of Western Christianity for almost 700 years. From the beginnings in the 11th century to the remnants in the late 18th century, the scholastic approach was characterized by a common intellectual tradition reflected in the vocabulary, methods, and framing of traditional academic disciplines.[2] Neither the Renaissance nor the Reformation led to an enduring displacement of scholasticism; in fact, as early as the late 16th century, even in Protestant milieus, a second scholasticism emerged. While complemented by some new tools such as philological studies, it nevertheless presented the traditional features of medieval scholasticism, chief among them the use of compendia and commentaries.[3]

It is this fundamental commitment to compendia and commentaries that makes scholasticism a complex intellectual tradition to study, a tradition that is best understood as a community project (instead of a loose conglomerate of individual contributions). The genre of commentaries epitomizes the scholastics' commitment to other texts and authors.[4] Since these commentaries were used in a scholarly context for the training of the next generation of scholastics, and

---

back Machine and can be accessed there. But as pages and information get re-routed, readers should consult scta.info for up to date links.

2 See Ulrich G. Leinsle, *Introduction to Scholastic Theology*, trans. Michael J. Miller (Washington, DC: The Catholic University of America Press, 2010); and Herman J. Selderhuis, ed., *A Companion to Reformed Orthodoxy* (Leiden: Brill, 2013).

3 See Willem J. van Asselt, *Introduction to Reformed Scholasticism*, trans. Albert Gootjes, Reformed Historical–Theological Studies (Grand Rapids, MI: Reformation Heritage Books, 2011); and Ueli Zahnd, "Das trojanische Pferd der Scholastik. Antoine de Chandieu († 1591) über Sophistereien, Syllogistik – und Rhetorik," in *Language and Method: Historical and Historiographical Reflections on Medieval Thought*, ed. idem (Freiburg: Rombach, 2017): 247–79.

4 Cf. Francesco del Punta, "The Genre of Commentaries in the Middle Ages and Its Relation to the Nature and Originality of Medieval Thought," in *Was ist Philosophie des Mittelalters?*, ed. Andreas Speer and Jan A. Aertsen (Berlin: De Gruyter, 1998): 138–51; and Jan-Hendryk de Boer, "Kommentar," in *Universitäre Gelehrtenkultur vom 13.–16. Jahrhundert. Ein interdisziplinäres Quellen- und Methodenhandbuch*, ed. Jan-Hendryk de Boer, Marian Füssel, and Maximilian Schuh (Stuttgart: Franz Steiner, 2018): 265–318.

since this institutionalized scholarly context narrowed down the number of works commented on to a manageable set of base texts, it was natural that scholastic commentators not only dealt with these base texts but also discussed the commentaries of their peers.[5] After all, students were repeatedly trained and encouraged to engage in rigorous debate through the prevalent scholastic exercise of disputation (*disputatio*), and this environment of perpetual scholarly debate resulted in a complex network of arguments and counter-arguments brought up by peer scholastics on problems emerging in their collective discussion of texts. This "communitarian" approach was condensed in the most basic literary device of medieval scholasticism: the *quaestio*, which, in its essence, consisted of the confrontation of arguments and counter-arguments traditionally brought forward by a problem.[6] Yet, given that a *quaestio* focused on a problem rather than on textual exegesis, scholastic commentaries soon underwent a kind of emancipation from their base texts, and the later we get in time, the more we find them replaced by compendia collecting the relevant material on a topic, such as the huge collections of *loci communes* we find in Protestant orthodoxy.[7] The basic outline of these compendia, however, remained the same: they were inscribed into a huge network of problems, arguments, positions, and well-defined terms that had been developed in the scholastic community. Thus, they represent only a node within the rich complexity and interconnectedness of the entire scholastic tradition.

Despite the deep connectedness of scholastic texts, they have been and continue to be mostly studied by means of the traditional and somewhat romantic paradigm of "individual works." This has resulted in several problems. With regards to the traditional printed editions of works, it is true that scholars have and continue to do their best to account for the scholastic network of ideas by means of a comprehensive *apparatus fontium* or scholarly *scholion*.[8] But the possibilities have remained restricted to what a publisher is willing to print and to what an editorial team is able to take into account. Among other things, this has restric-

---

5 As an example, see the developments in the *Sentences* tradition as described in the three volumes of *Mediaeval Commentaries on the Sentences of Peter Lombard:* Gillian R. Evans, ed., *Mediaeval Commentaries on the Sentences of Peter Lombard*, vol. 1 (Leiden: Brill, 2002); Philipp W. Rosemann, ed., *Mediaeval Commentaries on the Sentences of Peter Lombard*, Vols. 2–3 (Leiden: Brill, 2010–2015).
6 Cf. Chris Schabel, ed., *Theological Quodlibeta in the Middle Ages*, 2 vols. (Leiden: Brill, 2006–2007).
7 See Günter Frank, "Topische Dogmatik im Zeitalter der Reformation," in *Topik als Methode der Dogmatik. Antike – Mittelalter – Neuzeit*, ed. idem (Berlin: de Gruyter, 2016): 172–210.
8 See, for example, the richly commented edition of Bonaventure, *Opera Omnia*, ed. the Collegium S. Bonaventurae (Quaracchi: Typographia Collegii S. Bonaventurae, 1882–1902).

ted the detection of unnamed references, hidden citations, and concealed sources: a problem that affects the whole scholastic network but is particularly virulent in the study of Protestant scholasticism. Most Protestant scholastics had an astonishingly good knowledge of medieval scholastic theology and did not hesitate to draw upon it, but they rarely named their sources.[9] This makes the task of connecting the corpus, in such a way that encourages networked connections of sources and influences, all the more urgent.

Moreover, just as paper editions have had difficulties in providing us with a sense of the scholastic network, most of the digital editions that have appeared in the last few years have not fared much better, largely because they persist within the paradigm of the older medium. Rather than shifting to a new paradigm, they are recreating the book (along with its limitations) within the new medium.[10] There are several problems with this, but let us for the moment name two of the most important ones:

First, the current publication system, whether print or online, is fragmenting the corpus and isolating one text from another. Proprietary publication systems receive returns on their investment only if they retain exclusive control over their content. In retaining an exclusive monopoly over data, publishers have little incentive to share their data with other publications, nor do they have much incentive to create innovative or groundbreaking displays of this connected data.[11] Because they are aware that they are the exclusive silo in which this data can be found, there is no need to improve the quality of the end user viewing and research experience to retain an audience. In an insightful piece, Ruben Verborgh notes that this problem plagues all centralizing tendencies of the web and argues that in order to counteract these tendencies, data must be separated from presentation in a way that frees data to be repeatedly used in a plurality of presentation environments. Verborgh writes:

> The key to a healthy ecosystem is the independence of these two markets, realized through a noncommittal relationship between apps and data. Since there currently exists no such separation, new innovative application platforms have trouble emerging because they

---

9 Cf. Richard A. Muller, "Scholasticism Protestant and Catholic: Francis Turretin on the Object and Principles of Theology," *Church History* 55, no. 2 (1986), 197 and 205.
10 Joris van Zundert, "Barely Beyond the Book?" in *Digital Scholarly Editing: Theories and Practices*, ed. Matthew J. Driscoll and Elena Pierazzo (Cambridge: OpenBook Publishers, 2016): 83–106.
11 For research on scholasticism, *Library of Latin Texts* published by Brepols (http://www.brepols.net) is a prime example of a proprietary database that purposely prevents these texts from being linked to larger open datasets, while producing rather mediocre results in the quality of data presentation.

don't have the data – and existing platforms lack incentives to innovate adequately because they already possess data anyway.[12]

The rich complexity and interconnectedness of the scholastic ecosystem suggests that the texts within this tradition must be read within their context. Each text, each paragraph is a thread within a larger tapestry, and the significance and importance of each thread cannot be understood in isolation but only in the context of its connected threads, and ultimately in light of the entire whole. Unfortunately, the desire to retain exclusive control over texts that represent a common cultural inheritance and to profit from this monopoly is incompatible with the goal of bringing these threads together.

Second, even if we succeeded in making every text open access and freely available to all, whether in print or on the web, we would not yet have solved the problem. The current proprietary publication workflow (which is partly a consequence of its interest in publishing siloed presentations of data) is still rooted in the belief that a published text is inseparable from the presentation of that text, namely, the typeset display of that text, either on printed page or webpage. We call this the text-as-document paradigm, inherited from book culture where the separation of text data from its visual presentation in a document was impossible.[13] This paradigm perpetuates the belief that an edited text is something found on a page, whether in print or on a screen, formatted to facilitate a particular kind of visual experience for a human reader. The welding of meaning and presentation together means that a text is locked or siloed in this presentation.

The fact that this kind of coupling occurred prior to the digital revolution is understandable. Prior to the digital revolution, it was not possible to separate presentational form from the function of a text segment. This meant that the data recorded through its visual appearance could only be used and preserved as long as that visual appearance was preserved.

But what is more surprising is that this paradigm of welding meaning to presentation continues today on the web, through HTML and presentational mark-

---

12 Ruben Verborgh, "Paradigm Shifts for the Decentralized Web," *Ruben Verborgh* (blog), 20 December 2017, https://ruben.verborgh.org/blog/2017/12/20/paradigm-shifts-for-the-decentralized-web.
13 Cf. Peter Robinson, "Towards a Theory of Digital Editions," *Variants* 10 (2013): 105–31; van Zundert, "Barely Beyond the Book?"; and Jeffrey C. Witt, "DSE's and API Consuming Applications," in *Digital Scholarly Editions as Interfaces*, ed. Roman Bleier et al. (Norderstedt: Books on Demand, 2018): 219–47.

up. Given that publishers of digital texts typically continue to view the web*page* as if it were an actual "page," van Zundert observes:

> Indeed, it is far easier to point to examples of digital scholarly editions that are in essence metaphors of the book, or in other words: translations of a print text to the digital medium, apparently for no other reason than to fulfil the same role as the print text.[14]

Mimicking the printed book and text-as-document paradigm in one digital project after another tightly couples the data of that project to its display on a particular webpage. The consequence is that the data underlying this presentation is encoded only to foster this presentation, and hence is not machine actionable and not reusable. This means that loads of information about the larger corpus to which a given text belongs is simply lost.

To give an example of this, suppose editor A records in her project that author X cites author Z, and editor B records in a different siloed project that author Y cites author Z. Now we have to leave it to Google (if the texts are freely available), or to the random efforts of a well-off researcher, to find out that author Z is cited by both author Y and X. Such discoveries usually occur haphazardly, over coffee or the chance discovery of an article, and can hardly be considered scientific. But scholastic texts consist essentially of such cross-references, such that by pulling the texts out of that network, and treating it in isolation, we do not simply lose this or that interesting footnote, but rather misrepresent the fundamental way a scholastic text works, how it is cross-linked into its context, and to what broader network of concepts and ideas it belongs to.[15]

In sum, the current publication workflow of scholastic texts, its fragmentation and isolation of individual texts (whether in print or digital form), hinders our understanding of scholasticism as a connected corpus. The saying that premodern thinkers considered themselves dwarfs standing on the shoulders of giants is well known,[16] but our persistence with the text-as-document paradigm,

---

14 van Zundert, "Barely Beyond the Book?," 103–4.
15 Scholasticism is, of course, not the only intellectual tradition that builds on a high level of intertextuality. One could mention Patristic literature, with its rich borrowings from classical literature, or the huge network of correspondences in the Republic of Letters. In these and similar cases, we assume that our identification of problems (as well as the solutions we propose below) would also apply. One could even imagine that the model we develop here could stand as an example case for other similar text corpora and offer a powerful example of the benefits of hypertextuality. On intertextuality in general, see Graham Allen, *Intertextuality*, 2nd ed. (London: Routledge, 2011).
16 David Sytsma, "'As a Dwarfe set upon a Gyants shoulders': John Weemes (ca. 1579–1636) on the Place of Philosophy and Scholasticism in Reformed Theology," in *Philosophie der Reformier-*

despite the presence of revolutionary media, actively works against our ability to see and appreciate this fact.

3 The text-as-network paradigm and the SCTA

In order to be able to represent and study the interconnectedness of scholastic texts (and consequently enrich our understanding of the Christian tradition), we need a different publication paradigm and workflow. We therefore propose to shift from a text-as-document to a text-as-network paradigm.

This entails first and foremost a commitment to publishing textual data as semantically structured, machine-actionable data. Consequently, this also means making sure this data is freely accessible for reuse and that the standards used to structure this data are well documented and maintained by the community. Finally, it means developing a workflow that clearly describes, in practical detail, how this data, created in distributed environments, can be aggregated and disseminated as a connected corpus.

The Scholastic Commentaries and Texts Archive is a community that is trying to provide the requisite service to affect this shift. Concretely, the work of the SCTA revolves around the following three aims: 1) to maintain a set of domain-specific standards for the publication of distributed textual data *as data*; 2) to help connect this decentralized data by aggregating it and organizing it with detailed metadata; and 3) to disseminate and publish this newly aggregated data through various APIs that enable the proliferation of a variety of data presentation clients.

3.1 SCTA standards and distributed data creation

The dream of being able to access the entire scholastic network of thought, of being able to exploit the computer's inferential power and make discoveries beyond the capability of any individual alone, starts with creating data according to data standards. System independent data standards, far from limiting how data is created or used, creates freedom and flexibility while preserving the possibility of coordination and interoperability. An important example is the freedom that data standards provide for creating data in diverse environments, for

---

ten, ed. Günter Frank and Herman Selderhuis (Stuttgart-Bad Cannstatt: frommann-holzboog, 2012): 299–321.

diverse purposes, while nevertheless still allowing us to merge that data seamlessly into a connected network. In this way, rather than being locked in a particular content management system (like WordPress, Omeka, etc.), individual editors and groups can pick the tools and media that work best for them. At the same time, because the SCTA maintains a data standard independent of any system, all systems can write export functions that convert their data to standards expected by the community.

The contribution of distributed data to the SCTA raw data layer might look something like the illustration in Figure 1 below, where data is created in a particular system, maintained internally, but then exported according to the community standard and announced for inclusion in the SCTA raw data layer, for example via a pull request in GitHub.

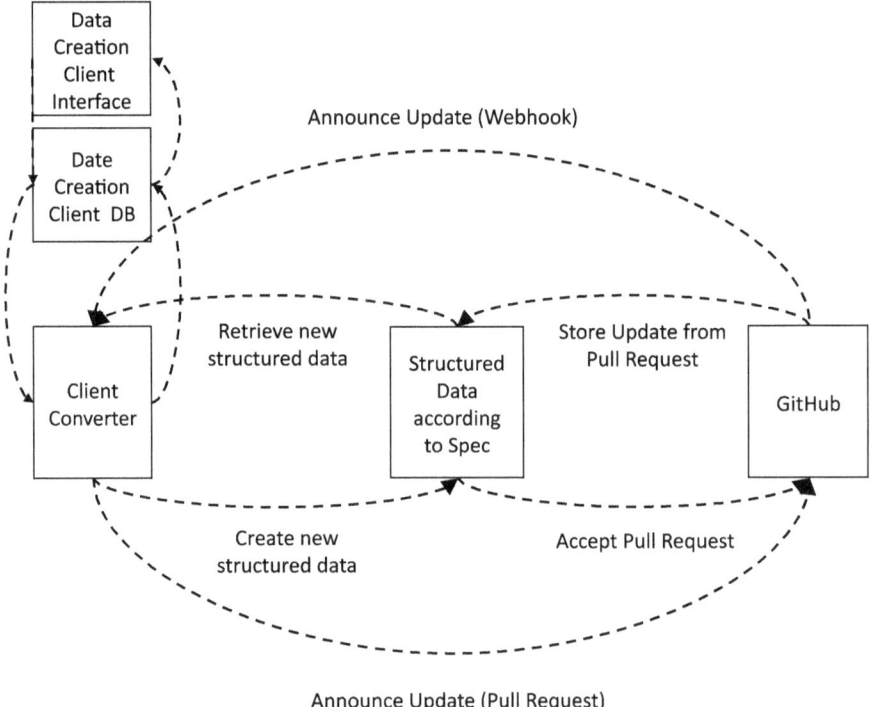

Figure 1: Data synchronization across data creation clients with independent databases.

At the heart of this workflow and automation is a fundamental commitment on the part of the community and data contributors to creating data according to the community standards. By way of example, two of the most important data standards currently used in the SCTA aggregation process are described below.

3.1.1 Expression Description File (EDF)

The Expression Description File derives its name from a privileged layer within a data model that will be familiar to librarians as the "Functional Requirements for Bibliographic Reference" or FRBR.[17] Briefly, FRBR models a fourfold relationship between works, expressions, manifestations, and items. A work refers to a very abstract notion of a text, for example the idea of Moby Dick: an idea that can be expressed as a novel or a screenplay but by itself indicates no particular expression of this idea or work. Each expression, novel or screenplay, can be further manifested in various forms. The novel expression could be printed (or manifested) in one edition, say the 1959 edition, but then be re-typeset (re-manifested) into an entirely new edition, say the 1980 edition, though manifesting the same expression as the 1959 edition. Finally, each of these editions (manifestations) can be printed thousands of times as items, finding a physical home in public and personal libraries all around the world. To this model, we also add the concept of a transcription, which is meant to identify the digital surrogate of any manifestation, for example a TEI (Textual Encoding Initiative) XML file.[18]

Listing a catalogue of expressions of scholastic works is a central goal for the SCTA. However, one might point out that, to varying degrees, this is also the aim of many world libraries and digital repositories. However, what may be less obvious to the non-specialist of scholastic texts is that simply identifying top level expressions will yield a quite limited and fairly uninformative network or graph. For example, a graph that records that the scholastic author Henry of Ghent quotes a passage from somewhere in Aquinas' *Commentary on the Sentences of Peter Lombard*, somewhere in his seminal work, the *Summa quaestionum or-*

---

[17] For more on FRBR see Peter Noerr et al., "User Benefits from a New Bibliographic Model: Follow-up of the IFLA Functional Requirements Study," paper presented at 64th IFLA General Conference, Amsterdam, Netherlands, 16–21 August 1998, http://www.ifla.org/IV/ifla64/084-126e.htm; Edward T. O'Neill, "FRBR: Functional Requirements for Bibliographic Records," *Library Resources and Technical Services* 46, no. 4 (2002): 150–59, https://journals.ala.org/index.php/lrts/article/view/5272; Rick Bennett, Brian F. Lavoie, and Edward T. O'Neill, "The Concept of a Work in WorldCat: An Application of FRBR," *Library Collections, Acquisitions and Technical Services* 27, no. 1 (2003): 45–59, https://doi.org/10.1080/14649055.2003.10765895.

[18] For a discussion of how to understand these concepts, see Jeffrey C. Witt, "A SCTA Modeling Proposal," *Jeffrey C. Witt* (blog), 12 June 2016, http://jeffreycwitt.com/2016/06/12/scta-modeling-proposal; and *idem*, "DSE's and API Consuming Applications."

dinariarum, is about as general as saying Shakespeare quotes the Bible. In both cases, this is so general as to be both obvious and useless. We would rather like to know in which verse, scene, and act of which play Shakespeare quoted which book and verse of the Bible. From that we could ask how often Shakespeare quoted which verses from which books in which plays. Similarly, we do not simply want to know that Henry of Ghent quoted Aquinas; we want to know which precise passages of Aquinas' corpus Henry quoted, in which passages of his own work he quoted Aquinas, whether other scholastic authors mention or quote this precise passage, and whether they do so in similar or different contexts as Henry of Ghent. A catalogue that only records top level expressions is woefully insufficient for these kinds of queries.

Thus, the Expression Description File is a specification that begins the process of cataloguing every level of the text hierarchy from the top level down to a specific level (called the "Structure Item" level), a level determined as the desired division of transcription files. From here, an aggregator can link to individual transcriptions representing the rest of the hierarchy within a text. The hierarchy within this transcription file can then be used to populate the rest of the expression hierarchy to which all further information about manifestations and transcriptions will be mapped. In this way, each level within the hierarchy will *eventually* be catalogued first and foremost as an expression. This means that we mint an ID not only for a specific transcription of a part of a text, but also for the abstract idea of this text part.

Using this hierarchy and the Expression Description File, an aggregator can then begin to generate IDs for every manifestation (and every digital transcription of every manifestation) that corresponds to every chapter, paragraph, and quotation, eventually enabling links from these manifestations back to the corresponding expression IDs. In this way, we model FRBR relationships across all levels of the expression hierarchy, treating the text as an Ordered Hierarchy of Content Objects or OHCO.[19] This is the kind of networking that allows client presentation applications to offer users a choice between the various manifestations of any quote, paragraph, or division, and likewise for every transcription of every manifestation. Figure 2 below illustrates this kind of mapping at multiple levels of the text hierarchy.

It is important here to reiterate the social change that is required alongside the practical technical requirements in order to enable that change. It is rather common for researchers and editors to create and publish question lists of little

---

19 For more on OHCO, see Steven J. DeRose, "What Is Text, Really?" *Journal of Computing in Higher Education* 1, no. 2 (1990): 3–26.

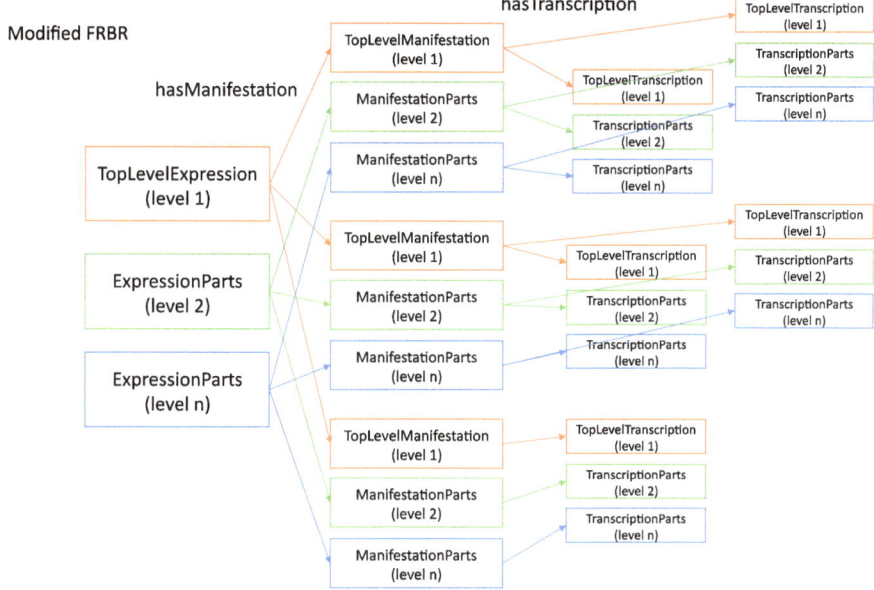

Figure 2: Illustration of expression, manifestation, and transcription relationships between distinct levels of the text hierarchy.

known or newly discovered items.[20] But these question lists are usually visually formatted in a Word document and then printed by a publisher in a proprietary format, where the sole expected use of this data is for it to be read by a human reader. The Expression Description File is an attempt to offer an alternative format: a format that can give us everything that the old workflow gave us (including a nicely formatted list of questions, that if desired can be presented in a PDF, on a static website, or in a printed article). However, because it is thoughtfully structured data according to a community standard, that same data can be aggregated by a machine to begin the process of building a connected corpus. As exemplified here, a large part of what the SCTA is trying to do is to provide a new and better workflow and data structure for the data collection that we,

---

20 See e.g. Paul M. Bakker, "Natural Philosophy and Metaphysics in Late Fifteenth-Century Paris. I: The Commentaries on Aristotle by Johannes Hennon," *Bulletin de philosophie médiévale* 47 (2005): 125–55; *idem*, "Natural Philosophy and Metaphysics in Late Fifteenth-Century Paris. II: The Commentaries on Aristotle by Johannes le Damoisiau," *Bulletin de philosophie médiévale* 48 (2006): 209–28; *idem*, "Natural Philosophy and Metaphysics in Late Fifteenth-Century Paris. III: The Commentaries on Aristotle by Johannes de Caulaincourt," *Bulletin de philosophie médiévale* 49 (2007): 195–237.

as scholars, already do collect. But because this data is prepared only for visual presentation and we usually have little concern for the underlying data, the community is prevented from taking full advantage of our collective work.

As we will see below, when it comes to the preparation of text editions and transcriptions, we aim to provide similar pathways for doing what we already do in better ways.

3.1.2 LombardPress TEI Schema

As noted above, the Expression Description File is not the only specification needed to allow aggregators to build a complete graph. To build a list of expressions down to the paragraph, quotation, and reference level, we also need to create transcriptions of the actual texts.

The SCTA aggregator, for example, begins by crawling an Expression Description File. At each "Structure Item," the crawler begins to look for a transcription file. We then use this default transcription file to populate the rest of the expression text hierarchy, to which individual manifestation resources can be mapped, and to which individual transcription text fragments can be mapped in turn (see Figure 4 for reference).

The ability to crawl millions and millions of words and thousands and thousands of paragraphs and to reliably organize this data requires data integrity. When it comes to establishing data integrity of text transcriptions, the Textual Encoding Initiative (TEI) is the right starting place. But what is not always obvious to those starting out, and often neglected by those trying to convince others of the merits of TEI, is that TEI itself is not a guarantee of data interoperability. Hugh Cayless, former chair of the TEI Technical Council, writes:

> Just because two documents are marked up in TEI, that does not mean they are interoperable. This is because each document represents the editor's *model* of that text. Compatibility is certainly achievable if both documents follow the same set of conventions, but we shouldn't *expect* it any more than we'd expect to be able to merge any two models that follow different ground rules.[21]

---

21 Hugh Cayless, "TEI is a text modelling language," *Scriptio Continua* (blog), 11 January 2011, http://philomousos.blogspot.com/2011/01/tei-is-text-modelling-language.html.

TEI is a base standard designed for further customization and refinement. By itself, TEI offers an editor a wide variety of acceptable encoding practices.[22] In order to build the kind of network described above, tighter restrictions need to be enforced. In this respect, the SCTA, by demanding that corpus texts follow supported schema customizations, has chosen to privilege a particular way of modeling texts in order to create an interoperable corpus.

The SCTA community works hard to maintain such a standard. While it is possible for more than one such standard to exist and to be supported by the community, the current supported standard is the LombardPress Schema for critical and diplomatic transcriptions which was developed by the SCTA community.[23]

With this standard, we are looking to affect a social change within the field. We are asking editors, who in their preparation of print editions are already collecting the kind of data we need, to make corpus connections. Every time a name is capitalized, a title is italicized, or a quotation is surrounded in quotation marks, valuable data is being created. Unfortunately, this data is being recorded visually and therefore in an imprecise and non-machine-actionable way. The LombardPress standard exists to alert editors to the fact that there is a better way to do what you are already doing. Recording (or exporting) one's data according to this schema rather than preserving it in Microsoft Word's proprietary format allows us to both continue producing beautiful print layouts (see Figure 9), but also to exploit the data encoded in these editions to construct a connected corpus.

3.2 Connecting decentralized data / the SCTA aggregation and SCTA RDF Schema

Through exporting to a common standard, independent services can then index and re-index the diverse data created by distributed groups in different ways depending on the service provided. One such example is the SCTA RDF Triple Store

---

[22] See Syd Bauman, "Interchange vs. Interoperability," paper presented at Balisage: The Markup Conference 2011, Montréal, Canada, 2–5 August 2011, in *Proceedings of Balisage: The Markup Conference 2011*, Balisage Series on Markup Technologies 7, http://doi.org/10.4242/BalisageVol7.Bauman01; and Desmond Schmidt, "Towards an Interoperable Digital Scholarly Edition," *Journal of the Text Encoding Initiative* 7 (2014), https://doi.org/10.4000/jtei.979.
[23] Jeffrey C. Witt, Michael S. Christensen, and Nick Vaughan, "The LombardPress Schema," LombardPress, 2017, http://lombardpress.org/schema/docs .

(Resource Description Framework),[24] a graph database connecting diverse data points into a connected, queryable data structure.

The construction of this graph is the task of the SCTA–RDF Builder application.[25] The builder nightly crawls new data and adds this to the existing graph. Using the raw data, structured according to the specifications described above, the SCTA–RDF Builder first crawls Expression Description Files, then crawls out to individual transcriptions (encoded according to the LombardPress Schema), as well as other data files (e.g. People Description Files and Codex Description Files), and other linked open data repositories (e.g. Wikidata, etc.). Using this information, it transforms this information into an RDF graph that adheres to another community-maintained data standard, the SCTA RDF Schema.[26] The SCTA RDF Schema is a higher order specification describing the logic and rules of the aggregated dataset. This schema itself can be versioned, so that client applications can rely on the logic of the 0.x.x network, even as the SCTA works to fine tune this schema and ultimately release a 1.0.0 specification.[27] The resulting RDF data can then be ingested into any RDF Triple Store and served over HTTP as a public SPARQL endpoint (SPARQL Protocol and RDF Query Language).[28] Further, multiple independent instances of this SPARQL endpoint can be easily run, preventing any single point of failure. At the same time, all instances can stay in sync without consultation with any other instance because no one writes to these databases directly. Instead, each instance responds to updates in the raw data layer and builds the appropriate triples according to the community-established RDF Schema.

Aggregation of this distributed data, along with computational inferences gleaned from combining this information (for example, the discovery that author Z is cited by both author X and Y) is visualized at the center of Figure 3.

---

24 "RDF," W3C, 25 February 2014, https://www.w3.org/RDF.
25 "scta / scta-rdf," Github, https://github.com/scta/scta-rdf.
26 "scta / scta-rdf-schema," Github, https://github.com/scta/scta-rdf-schema.
27 See Witt, "A SCTA Modeling Proposal."
28 "SPARQL Query Language for RDF," W3C, 15 January 2008, https://www.w3.org/TR/rdf-sparql-query.

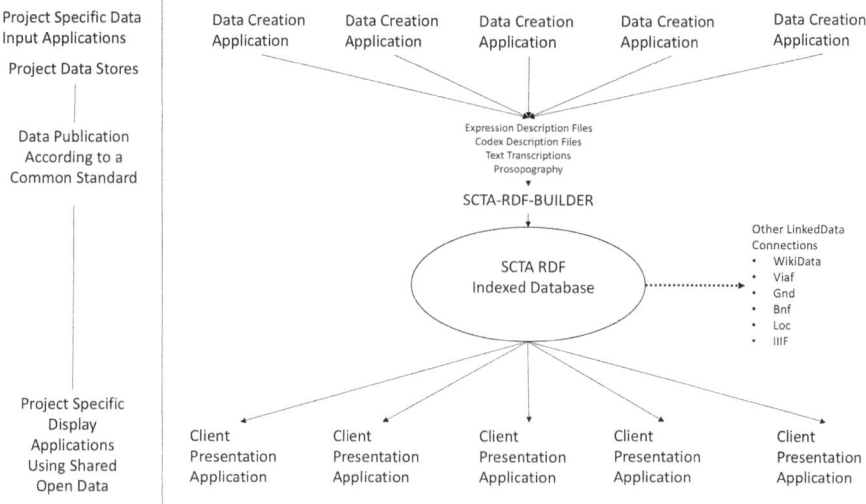

Figure 3: Illustration of data aggregation of the SCTA raw data layer and exposure via public SPARQL endpoint for use by client presentation applications.

3.3 Disseminate and publish through APIs / decentralized data presentations

Finally, aggregators, in turn, can offer a new set of APIs tailored to different presentation applications that can make use of the connected graph in a variety of ways.

Figure 4 offers a simple visualization of how an independent data standard enables data reuse by presentation clients. Data can be created by diverse groups and diverse projects, but once aggregated by the SCTA, the created data, along with the additional information inferred by the computer, becomes available according to documented standards and APIs. Presentation clients can then be written to understand these APIs, agnostic to where and how the data was originally created.

The public SPARQL endpoint constitutes the first and most flexible API (Application Programming Interface) that client applications use. Client applications can then send SPARQL queries directly to this endpoint, receive back JSON data, and begin to display this data however they desire. The SPARQL endpoint likewise is also the point from which more specialized APIs can be created. For

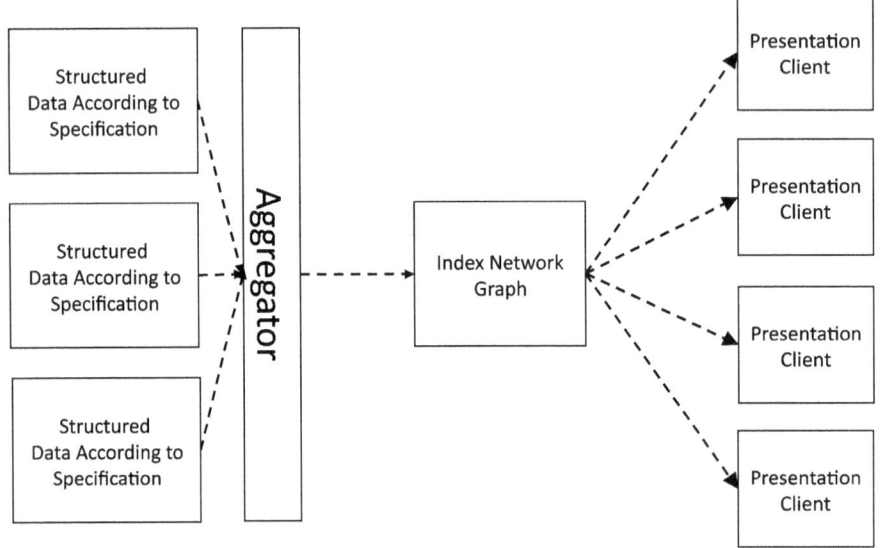

Figure 4: Data reuse by data presentation clients.

example, for digital images of manuscripts, the SCTA offers a IIIF API,[29] which offers IIIF collections, manifests, annotation lists, and ranges, which can be used directly by IIIF compliant viewers.[30] This API is built on the back of SPARQL queries and then translates this information to comply with IIIF specifications. Other APIs might include, for example, an OAI–PMH API to integrate with library discovery layers and WorldCat,[31] or a CTS/DTS API to allow SCTA texts to be viewed by clients designed for these more generic text APIs.[32] In addition to these restful APIs, there are code libraries designed to facilitate interaction with the SPARQL database, including the Lbp.rb Ruby library, the Lbppy python library, and the lbp.js library.[33] Other experimental APIs are also under development. For example, the community is working on a GraphQL API layer[34] to facil-

---

[29] International Image Interoperability Framework, http://iiif.io.
[30] Jeffrey C. Witt, "Forscher und Institutionen via IIIF verbinden," *Jeffrey C. Witt* (blog), 15 October 2018, http://jeffreycwitt.com/2018/10/15/leipzig-iiif-scta.
[31] https://scta.info. NdE: Project description: https://forschdb2.unibas.ch/inf2/rm_projects/object_edit.php?r=3963280.
[32] For CTS: http://cite-architecture.org/; for DTS: https://distributed-text-services.github.io/specifications/.
[33] All these libraries can be found https://github.com/lombardpress.
[34] See GraphQL, 2020, https://graphql.org/.

itate application queries without requiring raw SPARQL queries and simple CSV API designed for experts in corpus linguistics to easily subject the corpus to different forms of linguistic analysis.[35] While we are only just beginning to realize the potential latent in this kind of connected data, we are already starting to see a number of client applications make use of the data.

A flagship client is the LombardPress–Web application. This is a Ruby on Rails application that underlies the SCTA Reading Room.[36] This application itself is information agnostic and could be used to display any corpus that structures its data according to the SCTA–RDF Schema. On the server of this application, there is no text and there are no images. Rather, as seen in Figure 5, the application understands how to request information from the SCTA–RDF database, to use information in this database to request texts and images from distributed sources, and finally to display those resources to the end user.

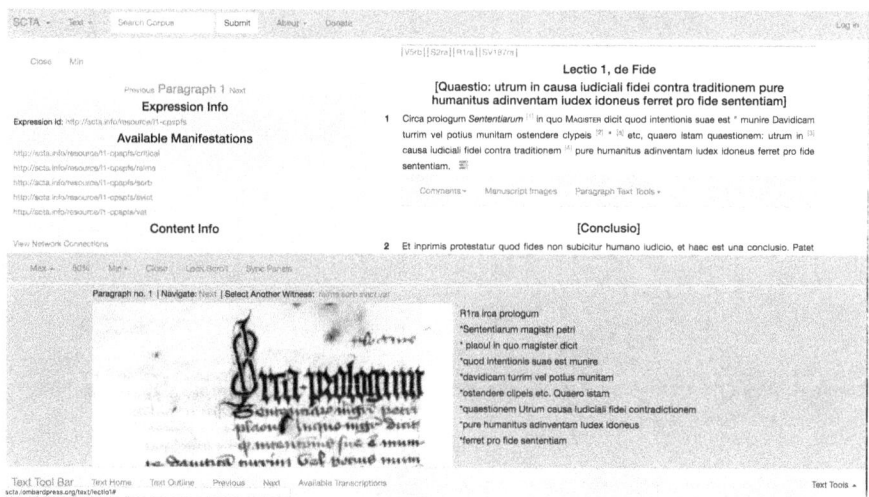

Figure 5: LombardPress–Web, showing text and images retrieved from the SCTA for end user presentation (http://scta.info/resource/lectio1).

Another example, shown in Figure 6, illustrates how this data reuse allows existing applications to enhance their own catalogue. This application offers a

---

35 http://community.scta.info/pages/technical-overview.html.
36 LombardPress, The SCTA Reading Room, http://scta.lombardpress.org.

web-based updated version of the Stegmüller *Sentences* commentary catalogue.[37] Rather than having to regenerate question lists, this client now easily pulls in question lists from the SCTA aggregation for each text within its catalogue.

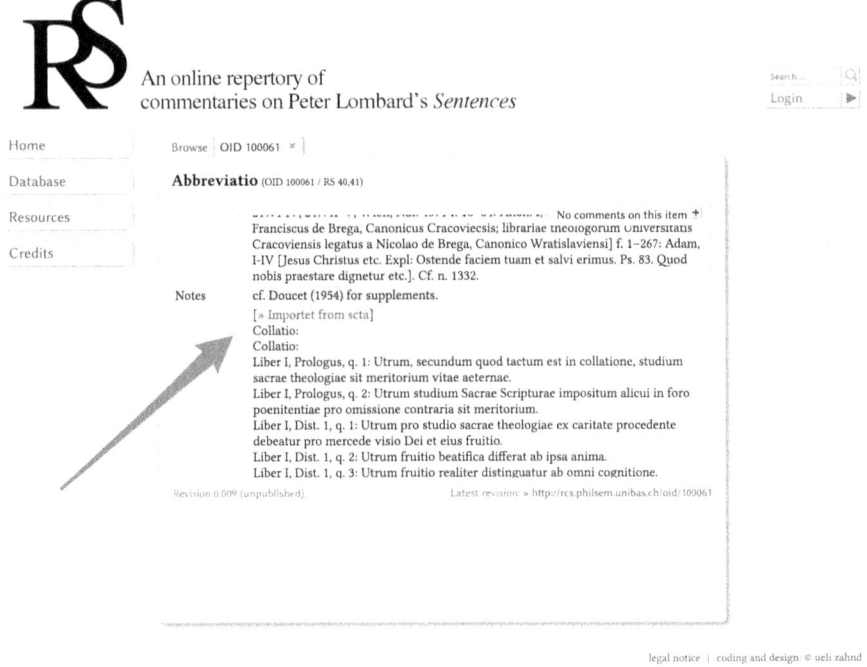

Figure 6: RCS Client showing question list retrieved from the SCTA (see https://drcs.zahnd.be/oid/100061).

Other existing client applications work in a similar fashion. The Ad fontes site (see Figure 7)[38] allows users to navigate the sources, quotations, and references of various texts as though moving through a global index, bi-directionally in time.

Such relations can also easily be visualized in another application designed to emphasize the connections between paragraphs from a bird's-eye view, as shown in Figure 8.

---

37 Friedrich Stegmüller, *Repertorium Commentariorum in Sententias Petri Lombardi*, 2 vols. (Würzburg: Schöningh, 1947–1948).
38 LombardPress, Ad fontes: A Scholastic Quotation Explorer, http://lombardpress.org/ad fontes.

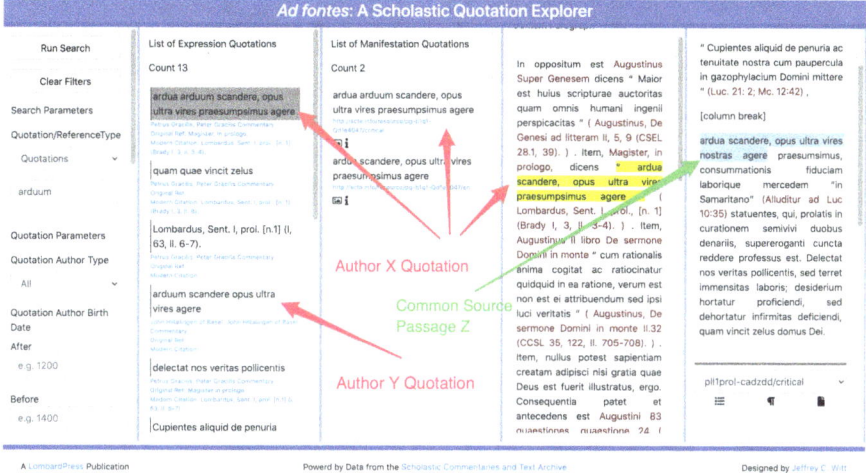

Figure 7: Ad fontes, an exploration of quotations and sources throughout the scholastic corpus.

The LombardPress–Print application[39] uses the SCTA–RDF database to locate the appropriate TEI transcription files and then produces nicely typeset PDF files (see Figure 9). Here we can see clearly that through a commitment to preparing textual data divorced from presentation, we expose the false binary between making a print or digital edition, as if one must choose one over the other. With well-prepared data, we can easily have the best of both worlds.

Figure 10 shows the SCTA Mirador site,[40] which uses the IIIF API to request transcriptions as IIIF Annotation Lists and then loads the text as annotations alongside images of corresponding manuscript pages delivered by world libraries via IIIF image servers.

It is important to emphasize that in each of these applications, users can experience the text and images of the scholastic corpus in different ways, but none of them contain the text or images as part of the application. None of them were required to create redundant data or to figure how to store and index that data within their applications. Nor do any of them silo away data, preventing other applications from using this data. Instead, each application was written with the ability to send queries to the SCTA RDF Triple Store based on the SCTA RDF specification or to consume and appropriate API tailored to the uses intend-

---

39 https://lombardpress.org/print/.
40 Scholastic Commentaries and Text Archive Image Viewer, http://mirador.scta.info.

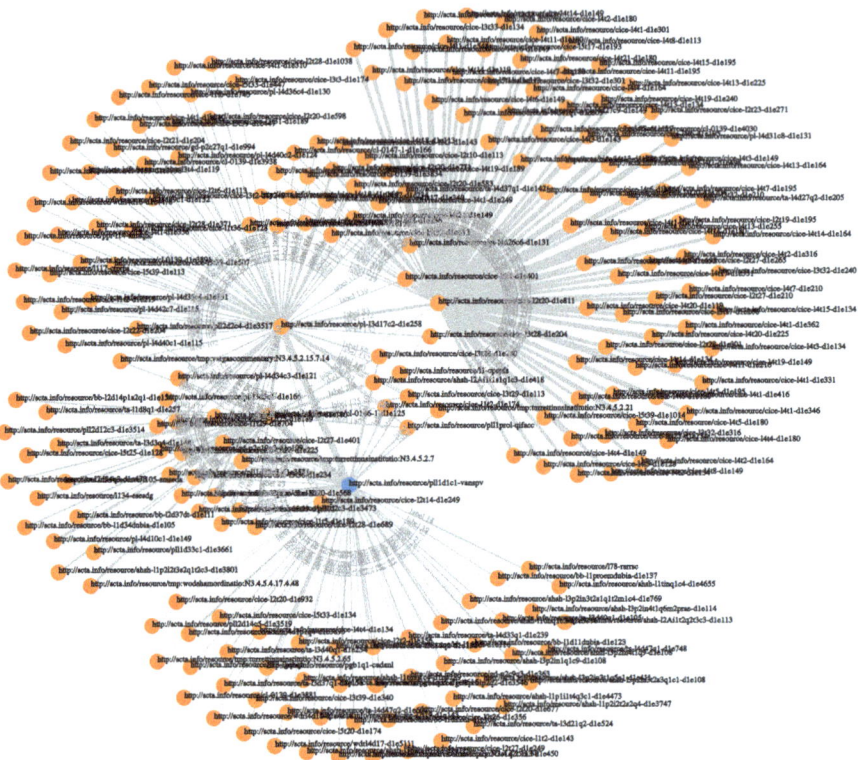

Figure 8: Text relations visualized as a networked graph.

ed by the client. Following the rules of this specification, each application is able to request the information it needs to create its desired presentation. Before the SCTA brought this data together, each application would have been responsible for re-collecting and re-indexing this data. This is an incredibly laborious task that generally prohibits people from investing time in the creation of such applications. But now that we have separated this data from any particular presentation layer, we have dramatically reduced the time it takes to create such applications.

4 Case study: the immortality of the soul

The above overview of the SCTA decentralized workflow, while technical, represents the necessary practical steps that have to be taken in order to realize the theoretical possibilities enabled by the digital medium. These practical steps

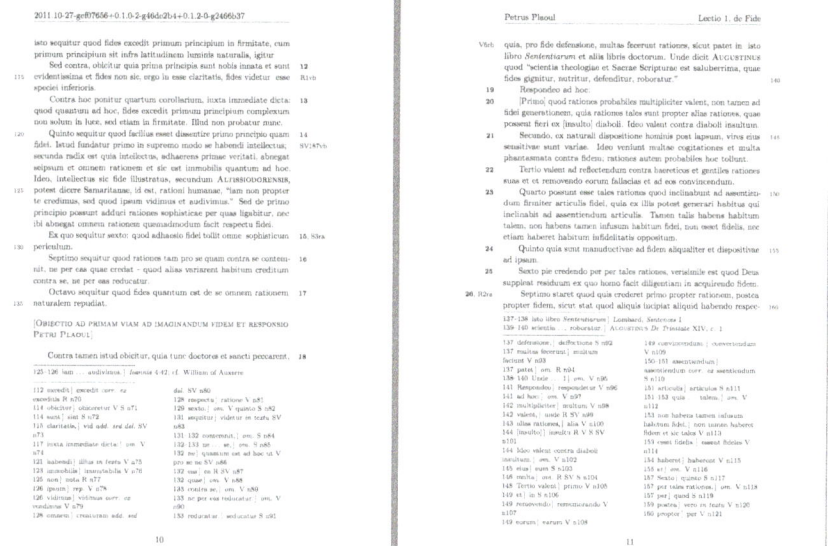

Figure 9: LombardPress–Print: SCTA data, presented in a traditional print format.

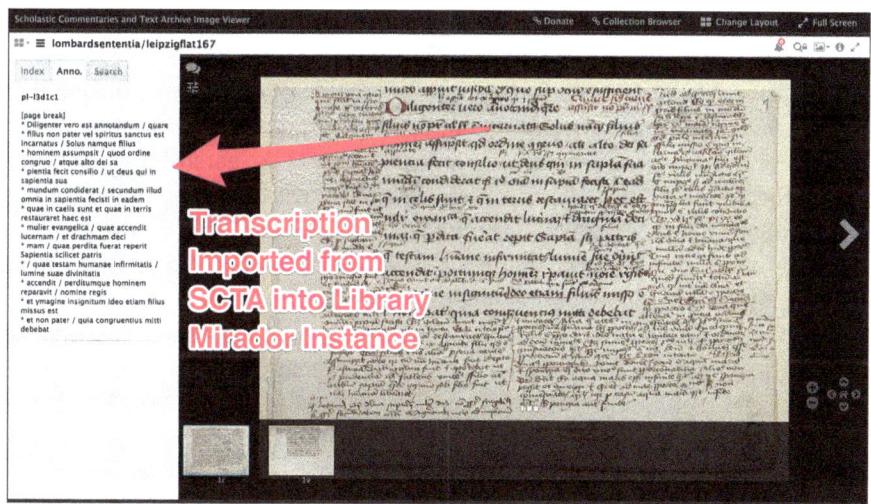

Figure 10: Mirador, displaying IIIF images alongside SCTA aggregated text content.

have already been taken by the SCTA community, and the size and connected nature of the archive grows with each passing day, enabling ever deeper insights into the connected corpus.

To illustrate the kinds of discoveries and perspectives that the resulting networked graph and accompanying client applications can present to end users, we will take up the example of the immortality of the human soul. This is a topic at the intersection between theology and philosophy, treated between 1200 and 1800 by scholastics of any provenance, and thus particularly representative of the "interwoven" of the scholastic tradition.

There are several ways a global graph could enhance research and enable new discoveries. Below we describe two ways this could happen. The first case simply shows the power of breaking down data silos and bringing together question lists from different genres in the scholastic tradition. The second case shows the power of more fine-grained connections through connecting information that is usually confined to an *apparatus fontium*. In this case, the computer's ability to index granular information and make inferences based on existing data helps us build a graph of passages connected through common quotations, references, and reused ideas.

First, discovering related material in a world where content lists are easily available to the scholar, preferably online, would mean obtaining these lists manually, wherever they may be spread across the web and physical publications. This could yield some results, but the haphazard and possibly anecdotal approach would limit the generality and reproducibility of the results. This whole feat becomes simpler with a fully indexed list of questions aggregated in one place. The main terms relevant to the problem of the soul's immortality will be *immortalis, (in)corruptibilis, aeternus,* and *perpetuus* with related cognates (e.g. forms of *corrumpere* for *[in]corruptibilis*). A search on these terms across the whole corpus yields no less than 448 text headings, but if we use the advanced filtering possibilities of the SCTA system to focus on the Aristotelian side of the corpus, this insurmountable material is reduced to 19 different texts on Aristotle's *De anima* treating this problem.

An interested scholar could then create a subscription to a specific query like the one above so that every time a change occurs relevant to her subject somewhere in the graph, she would be notified. This would mean that once other scholars register new question lists of texts containing information on this material, the results of such a search would be enhanced in a way it cannot be when the question lists are published in disparate places across the internet or in academic journals.

Second, with an extensive scholastic corpus of complete texts where all references and names mentioned are annotated systematically, the next step is to dig into this treasure trove. A good working hypothesis for such an analysis will be that if two different texts make reference to a particular passage in a textual authority, there is good reason to assume that those two texts deal with some of the same problems. Based on that assumption, we can establish connections between texts that make no reference to each other, where the authors may not even be aware of their existence, and which may be very far from each other in space and time. Such connections can of course be curated in order of relevance of passage, amount of contained references, combination of references, etc. Seen from the perspective of graph analysis, what we do here is to discover all the (unknown) nodes that contain a reference to a passage to which one of our (known) nodes refers (see Figure 11).

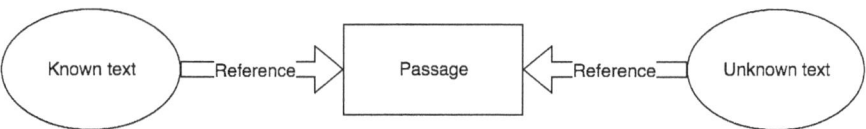

Figure 11: Connection between known and unknown text through shared passage.

A survey of the already discovered section of the Aristotelian material mentioned above would reveal to us all the passages quoted in this context.[41] Based on the working hypothesis just described, we can discover other texts which refer to the same passages and may therefore also be relevant for the analysis. The graph representation of the texts is ideally suited for these types of queries. We would thus find that on the question of immortality, two passages from Aristotle's *De anima* are central to the Aristotelian tradition (i.e. *De anima*, II.2 413b26–27 and II.5 430a23). Almost all of the relevant *De anima* commentaries would therefore be connected to Thomas Aquinas' *Quaestiones disputatae de anima* through their shared references to the same passages in the work. At the same time, Aquinas' work is an example of the type of text which incorporates much Aristotelian material as well as theological authorities. This composition of references on the same subject means that from Aquinas' discussion of immortality, the whole domain of theological material also opens up. For example, he refers to Augustine's *De civitate Dei* XIX, 26, which is also included in another discussion of immortality presented by Alexander of Hales.[42] In the SCTA

---

41 Among others, *De anima* I.1 403a10–13; II.2 413b26–27; III.4 429a10–b5 and III.5 430a17–24 in whole or in part; *Metaphysics* XII.3 1070a24–27.
42 It needs to be noted that the prevalence of examples from Alexander Hales is due to the large quantity of Alexander of Hales material made available through funding from Lydia Schumacher's ERC Project 714427: Authority and Innovation in Early Franciscan Thought, https://www.earlyfranciscans.com/. Her project's financial investment and commitment to the semantic encoding of the *Summa Halensis* according to the SCTA community data standards is what has made these kinds of computational inferences possible. We will see more results of this kind as more

RDF database, the expression of this passage by Hales is referred to with the unique RDF ID <https://scta.info/resource/ahsh-l2Ai4t3q1t2d2c2-d1e377/>. This ID can be given to any client application, which can then render a graphical presentation to help the user navigate and traverse the graph as far as the user wishes to pursue it. This is illustrated with a few of the connections in the graph in Figure 12.

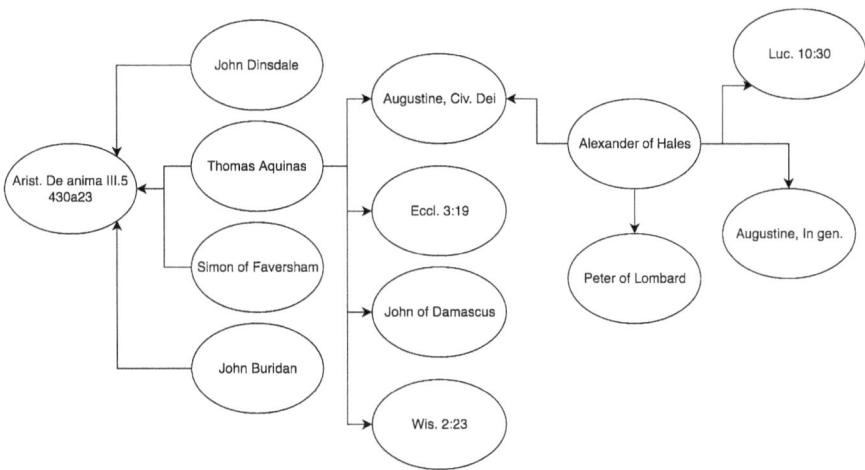

Figure 12: Excerpt of graph starting from *De anima* III.5 430a23.

Remember that this illustration only draws out a few steps in a very narrow selection of the large graph that these quotations constitute. In such a scenario, the challenge for the scholar will probably not be the *discovery* of data, but rather to find ways of *limiting* the results according to her research objectives. Such a curation of raw search results requires detailed metadata, precisely the kind of metadata that SCTA aims to organize. The connections and material discovered through such a procedure would outmatch even the most well-read scholar in its span across genres, text types, geographical areas, and periods.

If we approach the immortality question from the other end of the spectrum, we can look at it from the side of Scripture. In the second part of the second question of his *Summa universae theologiae* (or *Summa Halensis*), Alexander of Hales asks "whether indebted love is hate" (*utrum amor indebitus sit odium*). One of the objections to this claim invokes Augustine's gloss on John 12:25,

---

projects realize the importance of this kind of data preparation and begin making it a priority in their grant proposal.

"whoever loves his soul shall lose it." Augustine interprets this passage to mean that the "love of the soul is its destruction."[43] In his response to this objection, Hales glosses Augustine's own statement. He says that the term love of soul here means "the carnal and animal love of desire which tends toward destruction and hate of divine reformation."[44] It so happens that this quotation, John 12:25, which is used in a theological discussion of indebted love, is also used as a proof in a 17th-century *De anima* commentary for the immortality of the soul by Placidus Aegidius Melander. As far as we know, this commentary survives in only one manuscript, embedded in a codex with other printed works of similar type (UPenn Ms. Codex 855). This text stands as an example of the kind of text that one would rarely encounter or stumble across when researching arguments for the immortality of the soul. Its profile is simply not large enough to attract attention. But because the SCTA is able to connect this text to other known texts, we make it possible for it to be serendipitously discovered. In this case, Melander is concerned with the second half of the Bible verse, namely that the person who "hates his soul will save it for eternity." Thus, the argument for the immortality of the soul is based on the belief that the hate of the carnal self is rewarded with everlasting life.

Similar patterns could be followed for other verses quoted by both Hales and Melander. In his commentary, Melander argues for the immortality of the soul using the text of Matthew 10:28 and 1 Corinthians 15:19. Alexander of Hales, in turn, quotes Matthew 10:28 in at least two places. One discussion is about the nature of fear, which connects Matthew 10:28 to a quotation by Bede, Isaiah 51:12, and the ordinary gloss on Isaiah 51:12. A second use occurs in a discussion of oaths where Hales uses Matthew 10:28 as a response to an objection supported by a passage from civil law.[45] In this case, a corpus connected at the paragraph and quotation level allows us to crawl from a passage in Alexander of Hales to the uses of the same verse in Melander's *De anima* commentary, to discover other Bible verses used in support of the same premise, which again leads us back to Hales, and finally all the way out to a passage in civil law. This excerpt of the graph is illustrated in Figure 13.

As should be apparent from these two examples, this only illustrates the beginning of the kinds of connections and routes that could be taken through such a multi-dimensional network.

---

43 Alexander of Hales, *Summa Halensis*, IIa–IIae, Inq. 3, Tract. 6, Q. 2, T. 2, C. 6, [n. 6]: https://scta.info/resource/ahsh-l2Bi3t6q2t2c6-d1e179.
44 Alexander of Hales, *Summa Halensis*, IIa–IIae, Inq. 3, Tract. 6, Q. 2, T. 2, C. 6, [n. 18]: https://scta.info/resource/ahsh-l2Bi3t6q2t2c6-d1e415.
45 In the Justinian Digest: http://scta.info/resource/ahsh-l3p2in3t2s1q2t2d2 m8c4-d1e474.

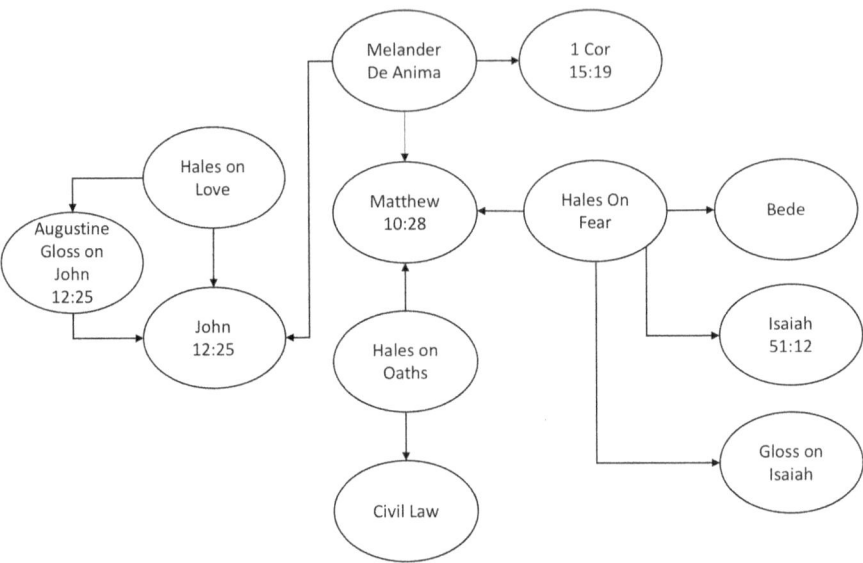

Figure 13: Excerpt of graph of references starting from Augustine's gloss of John 12:25.

5 Conclusion: the SCTA and the SCTA community

It is a curious fact that while technological advances are responsible for creating the possibility of the modern internet, the actualization of these possibilities is due in large part to social and political achievements. The HTTP protocol was not the only proposed protocol for data sharing across a network, nor is its technological achievement of earth-shattering complexity. On the contrary, it is more than likely its simplicity that made the HTTP protocol a social success. The mass adoption of this protocol is, in the end, what makes the internet possible. In a similar way, the achievement of a connected scholastic corpus is already possible from a technological point of view. The greatest hurdles to further progress are therefore social. Long-term success requires a core of committed scholars and technologists who see the long-term payoff of developing and maintaining these standards, and beyond that are willing to change ingrained habits that have been learned through years of training in a paradigm that, rather than advancing the cause, is now beginning to work against progress. A willingness to decouple textual data from presentation will always require a community of people that are committed to a long-term vision for which they are willing to sacrifice the immediacy and convenience of short term pay-offs. This decoupling of data and presentation creates an extra layer of work before one can arrive at the first presentation. For those only interested in the immediate presentation of this work, this decoupling appears needless and burdensome. But the extra work is also what is required for our work to be reusable for the long term, by generations not yet born and in contexts not yet imagined. The SCTA is already in the midst of forming such a community,[46] and we invite those with passion for the scholastic tradition to join us.

6 Bibliography

Allen, Graham. *Intertextuality*. 2nd ed. London: Routledge, 2011.
Bakker, Paul M. "Natural Philosophy and Metaphysics in Late Fifteenth-Century Paris. I: The Commentaries on Aristotle by Johannes Hennon." *Bulletin de philosophie médiévale* 47 (2005): 125–55.
Bakker, Paul M. "Natural Philosophy and Metaphysics in Late Fifteenth-Century Paris. II: The Commentaries on Aristotle by Johannes le Damoisiau." *Bulletin de philosophie médiévale* 48 (2006): 209–28.
Bakker, Paul M. "Natural Philosophy and Metaphysics in Late Fifteenth-Century Paris. III: The Commentaries on Aristotle by Johannes de Caulaincourt." *Bulletin de philosophie médiévale* 49 (2007): 195–237.
Bauman, Syd. "Interchange vs. Interoperability." Paper presented at Balisage: The Markup Conference 2011, Montréal, Canada, 2–5 August 2011. In *Proceedings of Balisage: The Markup Conference 2011*. Balisage Series on Markup Technologies 7. https://doi.org/10.4242/BalisageVol7.Bauman01.
Bennett, Rick, Brian F. Lavoie, and Edward T. O'Neill. "The Concept of a Work in WorldCat: An Application of FRBR." *Library Collections, Acquisitions and Technical Services* 27, no. 1 (2003): 45–59. https://doi.org/10.1080/14649055.2003.10765895.
Bonaventure. *Opera Omnia*, edited by the Collegium S. Bonaventurae. Quaracchi: Typographia Collegii S. Bonaventurae, 1882–1902.
Cayless, Hugh. "TEI is a text modelling language." *Scriptio Continua* (blog), 11 January 2011. http://philomousos.blogspot.com/2011/01/tei-is-text-modelling-language.html.

---

[46] The community already has a number of active and interested contributors from partner projects in Europe and North America. For a list of participating editors and acknowledgment of contributing projects and individuals, see http://community.scta.info/. This burgeoning collaboration represents the first step in the breaking down of silos, given that without the coordination of the SCTA each project would have resorted to creating redundant websites with each project's data locked inside. Moreover, the aggregation of this data by the SCTA does not amount to simply the creation of a larger, regional silo because the SCTA has prioritized the separation of data from presentation and the making of data openly accessible and reusable according to documented standards. As mentioned above, and as Witt has shown elsewhere (e.g. Witt, "Forscher und Institutionen"), this data is available for re-incorporation and reuse in other datasets via linked data standards, such as linked data notifications and a public SPARQL endpoint.

de Boer, Jan-Hendryk. "Kommentar." In *Universitäre Gelehrtenkultur vom 13.–16. Jahrhundert. Ein interdisziplinäres Quellen- und Methodenhandbuch*, edited by Jan-Hendryk de Boer, Marian Füssel, and Maximilian Schuh, 265–318. Stuttgart: Franz Steiner, 2018.

del Punta, Francesco. "The Genre of Commentaries in the Middle Ages and Its Relation to the Nature and Originality of Medieval Thought." In *Was ist Philosophie des Mittelalters?*, edited by Andreas Speer and Jan A. Aertsen, 138–51. Berlin: De Gruyter, 1998.

DeRose, Steven J. "What Is Text, Really?" *Journal of Computing in Higher Education* 1, no. 2 (1990): 3–26.

Evans, Gillian R., ed. *Mediaeval Commentaries on the Sentences of Peter Lombard*. Vol. 1. Leiden: Brill, 2002.

Frank, Günter. "Topische Dogmatik im Zeitalter der Reformation." In *Topik als Methode der Dogmatik. Antike – Mittelalter – Neuzeit*, edited by Günter Frank, 172–210. Berlin: De Gruyter, 2016.

Leinsle, Ulrich G. *Introduction to Scholastic Theology*, trans. Michael J. Miller. Washington, DC: The Catholic University of America Press, 2010.

Muller, Richard A. "Scholasticism Protestant and Catholic: Francis Turretin on the Object and Principles of Theology." *Church History* 55, no. 2 (1986): 193–205.

Noerr, Peter, Paula Goossens, Dan Matei, Petra Otten, Susanna Peruginelli, and Maria Witt. "User Benefits from a New Bibliographic Model: Follow-up of the IFLA Functional Requirements Study." Paper presented at 64th IFLA General Conference, Amsterdam, Netherlands, 16–21 August 1998. http://www.ifla.org/IV/ifla64/084-126e.htm.

O'Neill, Edward T. "FRBR: Functional Requirements for Bibliographic Records." *Library Resources and Technical Services* 46, no. 4 (2002): 150–59. http://dx.doi.org/10.5860/lrts.46n4.150.

Robinson, Peter. "Towards a Theory of Digital Editions." *Variants* 10 (2013): 105–31.

Rosemann, Philipp W., ed. *Mediaeval Commentaries on the Sentences of Peter Lombard*. Vols. 2–3. Leiden: Brill, 2010–2015.

Schabel, Chris, ed. *Theological Quodlibeta in the Middle Ages*. 2 vols. Leiden: Brill, 2006–2007.

Schmidt, Desmond. "Towards an Interoperable Digital Scholarly Edition." *Journal of the Text Encoding Initiative* 7 (2014). https://doi.org/10.4000/jtei.979.

Selderhuis, Herman J., ed. *A Companion to Reformed Orthodoxy*. Leiden: Brill, 2013.

Stegmüller, Friedrich. *Repertorium Commentariorum in Sententias Petri Lombardi*. 2 vols. Würzburg: Schöningh, 1947–1948.

Sytsma, David. "'As a Dwarfe Set upon a Gyants Shoulders': John Weemes (ca. 1579–1636) on the Place of Philosophy and Scholasticism in Reformed Theology." In *Philosophie der Reformierten*, edited by Günter Frank and Herman Selderhuis, 299–321. Stuttgart-Bad Cannstatt: frommann-holzboog, 2012.

van Asselt, Willem J. *Introduction to Reformed Scholasticism*, trans. Albert Gootjes. With contributions by T. Theo J. Pleizier, Pieter L. Rouwendal, and Maarten Wisse, and with a foreword by Richard A. Muller. Reformed Historical–Theological Studies. Grand Rapids, MI: Reformation Heritage Books, 2011.

van Zundert, Joris. "Barely Beyond the Book?" In *Digital Scholarly Editing: Theories and Practices*, edited by Matthew J. Driscoll and Elena Pierazzo, 83–106. Cambridge: OpenBook Publishers, 2016.

Verborgh, Ruben. "Paradigm Shifts for the Decentralized Web." *Ruben Verborgh* (blog), 20 December 2017. https://ruben.verborgh.org/blog/2017/12/20/paradigm-shifts-for-the-decentralized-web.
Witt, Jeffrey C. "A SCTA Modeling Proposal." *Jeffrey C. Witt* (blog), 12 June 2016. http://jeffreycwitt.com/2016/06/12/scta-modeling-proposal.
Witt, Jeffrey C. "DSE's and API Consuming Applications." In *Digital Scholarly Editions as Interfaces*, edited by Roman Bleier, Martina Bürgermeister, Helmut W. Klug, Frederike Neuber, Gerlinde Schneider, 219–47. Norderstedt: Books on Demand, 2018.
Witt, Jeffrey C. "Forscher und Institutionen via IIIF verbinden." *Jeffrey C. Witt* (blog), 15 October 2018. http://jeffreycwitt.com/2018/10/15/leipzig-iiif-scta.
Witt, Jeffrey C., Michael S. Christensen, and Nick Vaughan. "The LombardPress Schema." LombardPress, 2017. http://lombardpress.org/schema/docs.
Zahnd, Ueli. "Das trojanische Pferd der Scholastik. Antoine de Chandieu († 1591) über Sophistereien, Syllogistik – und Rhetorik." In *Language and Method: Historical and Historiographical Reflections on Medieval Thought*, edited by Ueli Zahnd, 247–79. Freiburg: Rombach, 2018.

Roman Bleier
Canonical structure and the referencing of digital resources for the study of ancient and medieval Christianity

1 Introduction

References and citations are central to scholarship and scholarly publications to verify one's research process and to underpin subsequently drawn research findings. For print publication, citation styles have evolved that allow for the citation of a wide range of resources. Additionally, for some texts, canonical numbers and special citation rules have been introduced that provide a means of citing a text or parts of a text across editions and translations. With the emergence of the internet, a new publication space was created that has become highly important for academic communities. In the humanities, as academics increasingly engage with online content and digital media, more and more resources are being produced for or on the internet. However, experience of the first three decades of online publication has shown that publications online tend to be less persistent than print publications, and issues of citability and persistent accessibility are yet to be fully resolved. Furthermore, scholarly online resources are produced for a community of researchers that has certain needs regarding citation and established practices.

This chapter discusses canonical numbers in the context of scholarly online publications with a focus on ongoing work in the digital humanities. Special attention will be given to digital editing projects of ancient and medieval Christian texts. St Patrick's epistles will be presented as a case study throughout the chapter to discuss citation needs and issues related to these texts and scholars working with them. The epistles have been a research focus of the author, as he previously worked on the Saint Patrick's *Confessio* Hypertext Stack Project[1] and is currently compiling a new edition of St Patrick's epistles at the University of

---

Note: This chapter was finalized and revised in summer 2018. A number of web resources are mentioned here that were under development while this chapter was written. Some web resources have been saved in Archive.org's WaybackMachine in order to preserve their current state.

[1] Franz Fischer and Anthony Harvey, eds., Saint Patrick's *Confessio* Hypertext Stack (Dublin: Royal Irish Academy, 2011), http://www.confessio.ie.

https://doi.org/10.1515/9783110574043-004

Graz.[2] It is hoped that the examples will illustrate some of the points and issues that are being discussed. The author is aware that the examples provided in this chapter are not representative for all kinds of texts, editions, or scholarly citation requirements. No generalization is attempted, but it is hoped that the general discussions and examples may serve as a gentle introduction to the topic and issues related to it.

2 Citation and canonical numbers

Citations and references can be described as signs pointing from one document to another, and the terms citation and reference have been explained as forward-looking or backward-looking acknowledgements.[3] However, when looking closer at the use of these two terms in literature, one finds that there are no clear-cut boarders: they are often used interchangeably.

In this chapter, the focus is primarily on citation of canonical numbers and titles. Such numbers or titles are used for works that are central to a group of people, for instance, editions of primary sources or religious texts such as the Bible for people quoting from it.[4] A canonical citation would point to a canonical

---

[2] The research leading to these results has received funding from the People Programme (Marie Curie Actions) of the European Union's Seventh Framework Programme FP7/2007–2013/ under REA grant agreement n° 317436 and was carried out during a fellowship at the University of Graz which focused on "Canonical reference & sustainability of digital editions." I would like to express my thanks to my supervisor, Georg Vogeler, and my colleagues at the Center for Information Modelling at the University of Graz for their suggestions and many interesting discussions around this topic. Many thanks also to Franz Fischer, who read a draft of this paper and gave valuable advice. DiXiT Blog, https://dixit.hypotheses.org/. Roman Bleier, ed., St. Patrick's Epistles: Transcriptions of the Seven Medieval Manuscript Witnesses, Graz: University of Graz, 2019, http://gams.uni-graz.at/context:epistles.
[3] Leo Egghe and Ronald Rousseau, *Introduction to Informetrics: Quantitative Methods in Library, Documentation and Information Science* (Amsterdam: Elsevier, 1990), 204.
[4] The use of canonical numbers and titles might differ between disciplines, and they are also used outside of textual scholarship, but as the focus of this chapter is on textual editing, this aspect will primarily be discussed. For a general introduction to the topic, see the relevant passages in Joel Kalvesmaki. "Canonical References in Electronic Texts: Rationale and Best Practices," *Digital Humanities Quarterly* 8, no. 2 (2014): par. 1–14, http://www.digitalhumanities.org/dhq/vol/8/2/000181/000181.html; and Bernhard Assmann, *Sind die kanonischen Zitierweisen der Geisteswissenschaften als nachhaltige Komponenten digitaler Repositorien geeignet? Unveröffentlichte Magisterarbeit* (Cologne: University of Cologne, 2005): 5–7, http://www.cei.lmu.de/pub/MagArbAssmann.pdf. Neel Smith discusses the special requirements of classicist scholars: "Ci-

number or title in a text. The advantage of canonical numbers is that they can be used to discuss sections of a text without referring to a specific text version, edition, or translation. A frequently used example are the chapters and verses of the Bible. No matter what edition or translation of the Bible one consults, a reference following the canonical book–chapter–verse citation should always lead to the same book, chapter, and verse. Therefore, a reference to Mark 2:14–15 could be easily found and compared in the English New International Version and Standard Version and the German *Einheitsübersetzung*.

2.1 Canonical numbers

The earliest examples of forms of citation go back to antiquity. Ancient and medieval authors used quotations, citations, and allusions, too. However, no consistent citation rules were applied. Occasionally the name of an author, a work, a law text, or a chapter of the Bible would have been quoted directly, but often an author used a well-known expression from another work as an allusion, or indirect reference, to make a connection and remind the reader of the intellectual context of the work.[5] It was of minor importance to point an audience to the exact place in the source text where the cited information can be found, or even to get a quote or citation right. This was even the case for citation of Gospel texts. For instance, a recent study found that Clement of Alexandria sometimes confuses the words of Jesus with the words of Paul.[6] Another example that highlights how little relevance exact citations had for ancient authors are

---

tation in Classical Studies," *Digital Humanities Quarterly* 3, no. 1 (2009), http://www.digital humanities.org/dhq/vol/3/1/000028/000028.html.

5 In the context of Pauline literature, issues of identifying and categorizing ancient citation methods are discussed by Christopher Stanley, *Paul and the Language of Scripture: Citation Technique in the Pauline Epistles and Contemporary Literature* (Cambridge: Cambridge University Press, 1992), 31–6 and 65–82; for a general introduction to the early Christian attitude towards quoting, see Michael J. Kruger, "Early Christian Attitudes towards the Reproduction of Texts," in *The Early Text of the New Testament*, ed. Charles E. Hill and Michael J. Kruger (Oxford: Oxford University Press, 2012): 63–80; and Charles E. Hill, "'In These Very Words': Methods and Standards of Literary Borrowing in the Second Century," in *The Early Text of the New Testament*, ed. Charles E. Hill and Michael J. Kruger (Oxford: Oxford University Press, 2012): 261–80.

6 Carl P. Cosaert, "Clement of Alexandria's Gospel Citations," in *The Early Text of the New Testament*, ed. Charles E. Hill and Michael J. Kruger (Oxford: Oxford University Press, 2012), 396.

so-called composite citations, which is the fusion of quotations from to different works into one without reference to the individual works.⁷

The way ancient citations work has something in common with canonical citations: it is not a page in a manuscript being cited, but rather a text or book or chapter within a text. The main difference is that no established canonical numbers and titles for smaller entities in a text exist yet, such as canonical chapter, line, or verse numbers. The Eusebian canons, and also the Eusebian apparatus, is often credited as one of the first attempts to try something like this for the Gospel texts; the Eusebian canons were widely used in medieval Europe.⁸ The book, chapter, and verse division of the Bible and Gospels we use today was a much later development and is traditionally attributed to the English cleric Stephen Langton (around 1200) and Rabbi Isaac Nathan (around 1440). The canonical verse numbers that we use today first appeared in 16th-century print editions.⁹ Other texts, such as legal texts, developed canonical titles and numbers during the medieval and early modern period.¹⁰ In the modern period, the concept of canonical numbers and titles became applied to a wide range of diverse texts, and editions of ancient and medieval authors were at the core of this development.¹¹ Canonical numbers and titles developed into a powerful research tool for scholars in general. Later we will see how online services such as bibleserver.com or protocols like Canonical Text Services (CTS) make use of them to align editions and translations and to facilitate research online.

Two aspects of canonical numbers are important and must be discussed briefly before we proceed. The first is that canonical citation systems usually fol-

---

7 Sean A. Adams and Seth M. Ehorn, "What Is a Composite Citation? An Introduction," in *Composite Citations in Antiquity: Volume One: Jewish, Graeco–Roman, and Early Christian Uses*, ed. Sean A. Adams and Seth M. Ehorn (London: Bloomsbury, 2016): 1–16.
8 The earliest example is the Codex Sinaiticus. Thomas O'Loughlin lists a number of Insular Latin manuscripts as examples, such as the *Lindisfarne Gospels*, the *Book of Durrow*, and the *Book of Kells*, in "Harmonizing the Truth: Eusebius and the Problem of the Four Gospels," *Traditio* 65 (2010), 26, www.jstor.org/stable/41417988.
9 Hugh A. G. Houghton, "Chapter Divisions, Capitula Lists, and the Old Latin Versions of John," *Revue Bénédictine* 121, no. 2 (2011), 316; Hugh A. G. Houghton, *The Latin New Testament* (Oxford: Oxford University Press, 2016), 106.
10 Hermann Ulrich Kantorowicz, "Die Allegationen im späteren Mittelalter," *Archiv für Urkundenforschung* 13 (1935): 15–29; Eltjo J. H. Schrage, *Utrumque Ius (=Schriften zur Europäischen Rechts- und Verfassungsgeschichte Band 8)* (Berlin: Duncker and Humbolt, 1992).
11 An example are the so-called Stephaus numbers, which are used as canonical numbers to cite parts of Plato's works. They go back to a 1578 edition by Henri II Estienne. The canonical numbers used in editions of St Patrick's texts will be discussed in detail later in this chapter. John M. Cooper and D. S. Hutchinson, eds., *Plato: Complete Works* (Indianapolis, IN: Hackett Publishing Company, 1997), xxvii.

low a hierarchical structure. Using the above example of citing parts of the Bible, this means that a book of the Bible can be referenced using the title of the book; within a book one or more paragraphs can be cited using the number(s) of the paragraph(s); and within a paragraph one or more verses can be cited using the verse numbers.[12] The second important aspect of canonical numbers is that they might refer either to "semantic" or "visual" structures of a text.[13] Semantic numbers would be chapter numbers in a book, such as the first chapter of J.R.R. Tolkien's book *The Hobbit*, or the already mentioned canonical book and chapter numbers of the Bible. Visual numbers are related to a "text-bearing object" such as page numbers in a book or folio and column numbers in a manuscript. It must be emphasized that semantic and visual numbers are equally important; the preference depends on the discipline or research focus. For instance, even though passages of the Bible are usually cited using the canonical book, chapter, and verse numbers, if a manuscript is the focus of a paleographical or art historical discussion, a reference to a particular folio in a manuscript might be relevant.

Another example is the pagination of the *Patrologia Latina* (PL). The history of the PL illustrates a major issue when using visual numbers for citation. A citation to a passage in the PL usually refers to the established canonical column numbers of Jacques-Paul Migne's first edition. If this is not the case, it needs to be stated explicitly. The reason why knowledge about the version used is crucial is that in 1865 Migne sold the rights to the printing house Garnier, who started reprinting the PL using different plates than Migne had used originally. Therefore, the column numbering of reprints of the PL after 1865 differs from Migne's first edition, sometimes for several pages. The main online resource about the PL, the Patrologia Latina Database (PLD), uses only Migne's original edition in order to avoid confusion.[14] Other examples of publications that gained canonical status would be the *Patrologia Graeca*, *Corpus Christianorum: Continuatio Mediaevalis* (CCCM) and *Series Latina* (CCSL), and the *Monumenta Germaniae Historica* (MGH).[15]

---

[12] Smith discusses this aspect of citation in a classicist context using Homer's *Iliad* as an example. The CTS protocol, which will be discussed later in this chapter, is an attempt to translate the hierarchical logic of canonical citation into persistent identifiers. Smith, "Citation," par. 16–34.
[13] Kalvesmaki, "Canonical References," par. 1–6.
[14] See the About section of the Patrologia Latina Database, http://pld.chadwyck.co.uk/help/about2.htm.
[15] For instance, the style guide of the American Academy lists how canonical collections such as the MGH should be cited: http://www.medievalacademy.org/page/StyleSheet.

2.2 A case study: canonical numbers used for St Patrick's epistles

To exemplify how canonical numbers are used in research, St Patrick's epistles will briefly be discussed. St Patrick, also known as St Patrick of Ireland or St Patrick of Armagh, was a missionary and bishop in 5th-century Ireland. He was also a writer of epistles, and two of his epistles, the *Confessio* and the *Epistola ad milites Corotici*, have survived until today and are the main source for his life and mission. At the core of a digital editing project currently under development at the University of Graz are transcriptions of the seven surviving manuscript witnesses, marked up using the TEI. The manuscript witnesses are quite diverse. They are visually different and also have a different text structure that differs from that used by modern editors. One of the goals of the project is to connect the diplomatic transcriptions and use canonical numbers from 20th-century editions to make the transcriptions more accessible for research.

The canonical numbers widely used in Patrician scholarship today go back to the early 20th-century text-critical edition by Newport White.[16] White introduced a new chapter structure: 62 short chapters for the *Confessio* and 21 for the *Epistola ad milites Corotici*. When White published his edition, it soon became the measure for future text-critical work, and his chapter structure was later adopted by editors and translators such as Ludwig Bieler, A.B.E. Hood, and Thomas O'Loughlin. One example to illustrate the importance of White's numbers is that David Howlett, who in 1994 published an edition *per cola et commata* with a totally new chapter structure, still included White's chapter numbers in brackets in the margin of his edition.[17]

White's chapter numbers are semantic numbers. However, it can also be argued that the line and page numbers (visual numbers) of White's edition somehow have canonical status as they were later used by other editors. Bieler made extensive use of White's work when compiling his own edition. He adopted White's chapter numbers and, additionally, prefixed White's page and line numbers to his own edited text. Furthermore, Bieler's apparatus refers to White's page and line numbers and not to the pages and lines in Bieler's own edition (see Figure 1). White's page and line numbers are used as identifiers in the recently published online edition by the Royal Irish Academy.[18] This edition is

---

[16] Newport J. D. White, "Libri Sancti Patricii: The Latin Writings of Saint Patrick," *Proceedings of the Royal Irish Academy (PRIA) 25 (Section C)* (1905): 201–326.
[17] David R. Howlett, ed., *Liber Epistolarum Sancti Patricii Episcopi = The Book of Letters of Saint Patrick the Bishop* (Blackrock, Dublin: Four Courts Press, 1994).
[18] Fischer and Harvey, Saint Patrick's *Confessio* Hypertext Stack.

> LIBRI EPISTOLARUM SANCTI PATRICII EPISCOPI.
> LIBER PRIMUS: CONFESSIO.
>
> N. White
> 235,2   1. Ego Patricius peccator rusticissimus et minimus omnium
> fidelium et contemptibilissimus apud plurimos
> patrem habui Calpornium diaconum filium quendam Potiti pres-
> 5 byteri, qui fuit uico †bannauem taburniae†; uillulam enim prope
> habuit, ubi ego capturam dedi.
> Annorum eram tunc fere sedecim. Deum enim uerum ignorabam et
> Hiberione in captiuitate adductus sum cum tot milia hominum —
>
> ---
>
> 4—5 MUIR I. 1 (494,7; cf. Codices Patriciani Latini 54; Proc R. I. A. 52 C 5, p 185)
> Calfurnio (N: Cualfarni B) diacono (-i B) ortus, filio, ut ipse ait, Potiti presbyteri;
> cf IOCEL. 1 et GUILELMUM MALMESBURIENSEM De uita s. Patricii, lib I (LELANDI
> Collectanea II. 236).   5—6 MUIR^B I. 1 (494,8; Prob I. 1) qui fuit uico bannauem
> thaburniae; cf in campo Taburniae W (V$_{2,4}$, c. 1), in pago Taburnia uocabulo IOCEL. 1,
> sed Banauen uicus in Taberniae campo GUILELMUS MALMESBURIENSIS 1 c; Banauona
> ... uiculus littoralis campi Tabernarii LELANDUS IV. 30.
>
> ---
>
> ω   Incipiunt libri sci patricii epis D.   Libri (liber) epistolarum uel episcopi saepius
> laudantur in Ψ.   Incipit uita Beati patricij V.   INCIPIT CONFESIO SCI PA-
> TRICI EPISCOPI Q.—.XVI.KL.- APL-. F.   INCIPIT CONFESSIO SCI PATRI-
> CII EPISCOPI ⟨.XVI.KL-. APRILI G⟩ Δ$_2$.   Inscriptio deest in PR.   3 con-
> temptibilissimus: contemptibilis sum D.   4 calpornum D. calpurnium RF. Calpur-
> nius, Calphurnius, Calfurnius, Kalfurnius Ψ; cf specimina uariae scripturae in ThLL

Figure 1: Part of the first page of St Patrick's *Confessio* in Bieler's edition. The numbers on the left side of the edited text correspond to the line numbers in White's 1905 edition (screenshot); © 1993 & 2011, Royal Irish Academy, CC BY-NC 3.0. Screenshot from: "The Edition by Ludwig Bieler (1950/51)," Saint Patrick's *Confessio* (Dublin: Royal Irish Academy, 1993), https://www.confessio.ie/manuscripts/bieler#1.

part of a thematic research collection about the historical St Patrick, the Saint Patrick's *Confessio* Hypertext Stack, which includes digital facsimile images of all manuscript witnesses, several print editions, translations, and many other resources. At the core of this research environment is a digital edition of Bieler's *Libri epistolarum Sancti Patricii*. Bieler's Latin text with apparatus and commentary were converted to TEI and enriched with metadata. An ID was assigned to each word of Bieler's text in order to interlink the Latin text with entries in the apparatus and commentary. An example for a word ID would be: W.238.01.01.[19] Each ID contains four positions separated by a dot. The first posi-

---

[19] The TEI encoded transcriptions can be viewed under: https://www.confessio.ie/sites/confessio.ie/files/downloads/confessio_latin.xml.

tion simply indicates that this is an ID for a word. The second position refers to a page number, the third position to a line number, and the final position indicates the position of the word in White's edition. In the above example, the ID refers to the first word in the first line of page 238 of White's edition. As both Bieler and the online edition adopted not only White's chapters, but also his page and line numbers for more granular addressing, it can be argued that White's publication has received canonical status and that both semantic and visual numbers are used by the scholarly community as identifiers.

Besides referring to the semantic or visual numbers of White's edition, one might want to cite an individual manuscript witness. This form of citation is important for many digital editing projects, as transcriptions and facsimile images of manuscripts are increasingly being put online. In text-critical editing, manuscript witnesses are referred to by sigla, which are identifiers resolved somewhere within an edition. Sigla of important editions might again be reused by other editors and the research community as canonical identifiers for a manuscript witness. This happens also in the context of St Patrick's writings. Bieler did not use all of White's sigla but created new ones for some witnesses. In the online edition by Fischer and Harvey, on the other hand, Bieler's sigla are reproduced.[20] The sigla are linked to the image of the corresponding folio of the manuscript witnesses and can be used to jump to the image viewer showing the relevant manuscript folio. Within the manuscript witnesses, visual numbers can again be used to reference folio, column, and line numbers that might be relevant for paleographical research, such as Sharpe's analysis of the manuscript witness in the Book of Armagh.[21]

This brief case study of St Patrick's epistles and White's edition has shown how complex and varied canonical numbers can be and how semantic and visual numbers are relevant. For a more detailed discussion about canonical numbers of St Patrick's epistles, one would need to consider the historical perspective and look at editions that were used before White's time. This, however, is a topic that goes beyond the scope of this chapter.[22]

To conclude, visual and semantic numbers may both be relevant for citation, depending on what a researcher is trying to achieve using an edition. Therefore,

---

20 See the apparatus criticus of the Latin text as example: "I. Confessio," Saint Patrick's *Confessio* (Dublin: Royal Irish Academy, 1993), https://www.confessio.ie/etexts/confessio_latin#01.
21 Richard Sharpe, "Palaeographical Considerations in the Study of the Patrician Documents in the Book of Armagh," *Scriptorium* 36 (1982): 3–28.
22 On the topic, see chapter 3 of the author's dissertation: Roman Bleier, "Encoding St Patrick's Epistles: History and Electronic Editing of the Manuscript Witnesses," (Diss., Trinity College Dublin, 2015).

it is difficult to give an editor general advice on when to use what system. It certainly makes sense to use visual numbers when the editorial focus is on a close representation of the text as it is presented in the "text-bearing object" (e.g. diplomatic/hyper-diplomatic editions, genetic editions, text-facsimile views) and semantic numbers when the focus is on the content of a text. However, it also should be kept in mind that (digital) editions are complex objects and that for different parts of the edition a user may require different citation options.[23] Consequently, a subject and user study is important before implementing any citation system.

3 Citation of online resources and canonical numbers

The first part of this chapter focused on canonical numbers and titles in a print publishing context. Now the discussion will turn to citation in digital media. It can be argued that due to the great amount of texts being published in digital format, canonical numbers are more important than ever, as they provide a means to align and compare versions of a text.[24] Furthermore, canonical numbers are a vital topic for digital scholarly editing as most scholarly texts published online have a rich editorial history and established canonical numbers. St Patrick's epistles is one example. The second half of this chapter will discuss challenges of the citation of resources on the internet and possible solutions to provide stable and persistent identifier for citation. The final section of this chapter will than look at attempts to combine the idea of stable and persistent identifier with established canonical naming schemes from the humanities.

---

[23] Using Sahle's text wheel model, visual numbers could be associated with "text as sign" or "text as document" and semantic numbers with "text as content," "text as work," or "text as linguistic code." Patrick Sahle, *Digitale Editionsformen. Teil 3: Textbegriffe und Recodierung*, Schriften des Instituts für Dokumentologie und Editorik 9 (Norderstedt: Books on Demand, 2013): 45–49, https://kups.ub.uni-koeln.de/5353/1/DigEditionen_3.pdf . However, as Fischer shows, digital editions are complex, and different parts of an edition may be placed in different areas of Sahle's text wheel. Consequently, it is likely that for some editions it is advisable to use both kinds of numbers, visual and semantic, for citation. Franz Fischer, "The Pluralistic Approach: The First Scholarly Edition of William of Auxerre's Treatise on Liturgy," *Computerphilologie* 10 (2010): 151–68.
[24] Kalvesmaki, "Canonical References," par. 1–4.

3.1 Permalinks and persistent identifiers

For the citation of websites, blogs, and similar digital objects, it has become common practice[25] to include a Uniform Resource Locator (URL) with an access date or Digital Object Identifier (DOI). The reason why an access date is required is that URLs have proven not to be a reliable and persistent means for citation. The most prominent issue is that of broken links, which means that a digital resource becomes unavailable via the original URL because it has been moved, replaced, or deleted. In a famous paper, Tim Berners-Lee pointed out that URLs could be a persistent means to address content, and he demanded that webmasters should not change URLs or move or remove content in order to avoid broken links.[26] And indeed, URLs can be an effective means for the citation of online resources with the additional benefit that they lead to the content directly. However, institutional commitment is required to guarantee the persistent relationship between a URL and an online resource. If this is ensured, a URL can be called a *permalink*. Ideally, the commitment would be declared in a publicly available permalink policy. In addition to permalinks, persistent identifiers (PIDs), such as Handle, DOI, or Uniform Resource Name (URN), are used by some institutions.[27] A main difference between permalinks and PIDs is that a permalink is an http URI that can be used in the browser directly – also called *actionable* – while PIDs need a resolver to match a PID to the actual location of a resource. In regard to long-term sustainability, there is no point in arguing for one system over another. Service is the key to success, and permalink and PID infrastructures will fail if not properly maintained.[28]

---

[25] This is documented be a number of citation style guidelines recently used by the author, such as the MLA 8th and Chicago style 17th editions.
[26] Tim Berners-Lee, "Cool URIs Don't Change," WC3, 1998, https://www.w3.org/Provider/Style/URI .
[27] For addressing and naming online resources, Uniform Resource Identifiers (URI) are used. A URI can be used either to identify the location of a resource as a URL (sometimes also "http URI") or as a globally unique name or identifier for a resource itself, a URN. URI Planning Interest Group, "URIs, URLs, and URNs: Clarifications and Recommendations 1.0," W3C/IETF, 2001, https://www.w3.org/TR/uri-clarification.
[28] Hans-Werner Hilse and Jochen Kothe, *Implementing Persistent Identifiers* (London: Consortium of European Research Libraries, 2006), https://www.ica.org/sites/default/files/WG_2006_PAAG-implementing-persistent-identifiers_EN.pdf; Herbert Van de Sompel et. al., "Persistent Identifiers for Scholarly Assets and the Web: The Need for an Unambiguous Mapping," *International Journal of Digital Curation* 9, no. 1 (2014): 331–42; Eckhart Arnold and Stefan Müller, "Wie permanent sind Permalinks?" *Informationspraxis* 3, no. 1 (2017), https://doi.org/10.11588/ip.2016.2.33483. For an overview over the different PID systems available and an in-depth discussion of DOI and URN, see chapter 9 of the nestor handbook. Rachael Neuroth et al., eds., *nestor Hand-*

A further point to discuss about identifiers, URLs, permalinks, and PIDs in digital scholarly editions is if they should be semantic, human-understandable identifiers, or not. Non-human-understandable identifiers are unique identifiers randomly generated or based on day- and timestamps or an incremental number. Examples would be DOIs and Handles frequently used in editing projects.[29] Another approach would be to use semantic identifiers that are created following a logic that can be understood by a human reader. These kinds of identifiers can be divided into semantic identifiers that do not follow existing citation practices and identifiers that follow a logic that reflects already established citation practices of a discipline. An example of the latter would be URNs used by the CTS, which will be discussed later.[30] Both approaches have benefits and downsides. The human-understandable semantic identifier conveys meaning, and from the identifier name a human reader may infer the content of the resource. For instance, the URL of the Codex Sinaiticus project can be used to add human-understandable search parameters. An example would be a reference to verse 27 of chapter 21 of the second book (Leviticus) of the Bible:[31]

http://www.codexsinaiticus.org/en/manuscript.aspx?book=2&chapter=21&verse=27.

The biggest issue with semantic identifiers is that the principles used to make them need to be persistent. For instance, if the name of an archive is part of an identifier, this may cause problems in the future, as names of archives change, and a persistent identifier should not be changed. Another example would be a digital edition with growing content or an edited text that is not yet finished. If new content is added or the editor decides to change the chapter or paragraph numbers of an edited text, semantic identifiers may cause problems. Therefore, if there is any chance that the structure, names, and numbers

---

buch: Eine kleine Enzyklopädie der digitalen Langzeitarchivierung. Version 2.3 (Göttingen: nestor, 2010), http://nestor.sub.uni-goettingen.de/handbuch/nestor-handbuch_23.pdf.
29 An example would be the DOIs used by the edition *Welsche Gast – Digital:* https://doi.org/10.11588/diglit.192#0017. The Handle PIDs used by the *GAMS* are another example; this is a digital asset management system at the University of Graz which hosts a number of digital editions: http://hdl.handle.net/11471/1010.2.1.
30 Another example would be Peter Robinson's DET system. This will not be discussed in this chapter. How DET works is described in Robinson, "Some Principles for Making Collaborative Scholarly Editions in Digital Form," *Digital Humanities Quarterly* 11, no. 2 (2017): par. 14–33, http://www.digitalhumanities.org/dhq/vol/11/2/000293/000293.html.
31 The Codex Sinaiticus project does not promote its URLs as permalinks; however, this simple example may illustrate what a human-readable URL might look like.

used for the construction of an identifier might change in the future, it is advised to use non-human-understandable identifiers.

3.2 Versioning scholarly resources

Another issue is the citation of different versions or releases of online publications. It is very common that online resources are first published in an unfinished state and are updated and revised later. In the context of digital scholarly editing, this is known as *fluid publication*.[32] As was already mentioned, URLs are addresses and do not guarantee that the online resource at the URL does not change. This can be problematic if one tries to gain access to an older version of a website by following the URL used in the citation, but the URL now leads to a new version with significant differences. For digital scholarly editions, this is a serious issue. Editions should provide stable texts that can be cited clearly in order to provide a basis for discussion within a scholarly community. Digital scholarly editions should present the same degree of stability as print editions. This includes that all changes made to its resources have to be transparent and the individual versions addressable. Therefore, in digital scholarly editions, access to older versions of its resources should be possible, and it should be clearly stated which version is the latest one. Ideally, all version of a resource should be citable with their own permalink or PID.[33]

Wikipedia is an example of a website with constantly changing content, and every edit of an article results in a new version with a permalink. The most recent authorized revision of an article can be accessed via a *canonical URL* that usually points to the newest accepted version of an article. However, older versions can still be accessed using their permalink, and Wikipedia recommends using these permalinks for citation.[34] Therefore, there is a difference between canonical URLs and the before-mentioned canonical numbers and titles used to cited a part of a text across different versions. Canonical URLs were introduced out of a practical need to optimize search engine results. They are implemented using a HTML *canonical tag*, and its purpose is to specify what URL should be

---

[32] Patrick Sahle, "What is a Scholarly Digital Edition?," in *Digital Scholarly Editing: Theories and Practices*, ed. Matthew James Driscoll and Elena Pierazzo (Cambridge: Open Book Publishers, 2016): 28–33, https://dx.doi.org/10.11647/OBP.0095.02.
[33] Elena Pierazzo, *Digital Scholarly Editing: Theories, Models and Methods* (London: Routledge, 2016), 184–87.
[34] For more details, see Wikipedia's permalink strategy: "Permalink," Wikipedia, https://en.wikipedia.org/w/index.php?title=Permalink&oldid=877394616.

listed in search results.³⁵ Instead of having all existing versions of a Wikipedia article listed in a search result, only the canonical URL is listed, which will point to the latest version this article.³⁶ The way Wikipedia generates versions is similar to *versioning control systems* (VCS) used in software development, such as Git. Every little change is recorded and generates a new version. There is a difference between this approach and the traditional print publishing approach. In print publishing, the creation of new versions is controlled by the author or editor, who decides if a revised publication is necessary. Also, in digital scholarly editing this might be a suitable strategy and alternative to the VCS method, which generates a huge number of unnecessary versions.

3.3 Granular citation strategies

The citation of subsections or parts of an online resource is also a central topic. While it is straightforward to cite a digital resource using a permalink or PID, the citation of a subset of a webpage, a subset of a digital datasets or individual components of a multi-media webpage is often not clear to the user.³⁷ Let's start with a simple example: the citation of pages or paragraphs of an online article. If the article is published as PDF or a similar format, the approach is like citing a printed article, as pages and page numbers would be available. However, if the article is published as a webpage, a different approach may be necessary. A webpage can fit the text of the entire article (even of an entire book) and the user would "scroll" up and down the webpage to read the text. In such a scenario, a user can cite the entire webpage using its URL. An electronic way to refer to subsection of the webpage would be to use HTML IDs and HTML anchors. For instance, the journal *Digital Humanities Quarterly* (DHQ) provides IDs for para-

---

35 "Canonicalization," Moz, https://moz.com/learn/seo/canonicalization.
36 In a digital scholarly editing context, this approach is also used. For instance, by the project *Edition Humboldt Digital*. Stefan Dumont, "Interfaces in Digital Scholarly Editions of Letters," in *Digital Scholarly Editions as Interfaces*, ed. Roman Bleier et al., Schriften des Instituts für Dokumentologie und Editorik 12 (Norderstedt: Books on Demand, 2018): 219–47, https://kups.ub.uni-koeln.de/9118; Stefan Dumont, "Digitale Methodik. Ein Überblick über Datenmodellierung und verwendete Technologien. Version 3 vom 14.09.2018," in *edition humboldt digital*, ed. Ottmar Ette (Berlin: Berlin-Brandenburgische Akademie der Wissenschaften, 2018), https://edition-humboldt.de/v3/H0016212 .
37 Michael Sperberg-McQueen, "Data Citation in the Humanities: What's the Problem?," in *For Attribution: Developing Data Attribution and Citation Practices and Standards: Summary of an International Workshop*, ed. National Research Council (Washington, DC: The National Academies Press, 2012), https://dx.doi.org/10.17226/13564.

graphs of each article. Articles are published on a separate webpage with their own URL and next to each paragraph is a hyperlink with the paragraph number, which points to the HTML ID of the paragraph next to the number. By clicking on the hyperlink, a fragment identifier is added to the URL of the webpage. The following URL is a reference to paragraph 45 of the article "Canonical References in Electronic Texts: Rationale and Best Practices":

> http://www.digitalhumanities.org/dhq/vol/8/2/000181/000181.html#p45

The string after the # mark in the URL above is called a *fragment identifier* and it is a means to address HTML IDs and anchors in an HTML document. If a valid fragment identifier is added to a URL, the default behavior of a web browser is to move its view to the HTML element with the corresponding ID.

Other online resources need a different approach to granular addressing: examples are zones or regions within images and frames of videos. The International Image Interoperability Framework (IIIF) standard is currently state-of-the-art for addressing regions within images. The community is increasingly acknowledging IIIF, which has been developed since 2011, and its practicality for digital collections and digital editions. Projects such as Europeana, e-codices (www.e-codices.unifr.ch/en), or Fragmentarium (https://fragmentarium.ms/) and some of libraries[38] already make use of IIIF, and a small number of digital editions show the great potentials of IIIF.[39] An example shall illustrate how IIIF URIs can be used for granular addressing of an image region. The French theologian Peter of Poitier, ca. 1125/1130 – 1205, wrote a diagrammatic synopsis of biblical history known as the *Compendium historiae in genealogia Christi*.[40] A 13th-

---

[38] The IIIF Collections search for *Manuscripts and Rare Books* contains several collections, including the *Bibliothèque nationale de France (Gallica)*, *Digital.Bodleian*, Europeana Regia, Parker Library On the Web, e-codices, BVMM, etc. Duba and Widmer provide an overview of the projects, e-codices, and Fragmentarium, including a brief discussion on its resources. William O. Duba, "Fragmentarium," *Das Mittelalter* 24, no. 1 (2019): 221–23, https://doi.org/10.1515/mial-2019–0015; Maria Widmer, "e-codices," *Das Mittelalter* 24, no. 1 (2019): 253–55, https://doi.org/10.1515/mial-2019–0023.

[39] How to use this in a digital editing context is discussed in a recent publication by Jeffrey C. Witt, "Digital Scholarly Editions and API Consuming Applications," in *Digital Scholarly Editions as Interfaces*, ed. Roman Bleier et al., Schriften des Instituts für Dokumentologie und Editorik 12 (Norderstedt: Books on Demand, 2018): 229–33, https://kups.ub.uni-koeln.de/9118.

[40] Andrea Worm, "'Ista est Jerusalem': Intertextuality and Visual Exegesis in Peter of Poitiers' *Compendium historiae in genealogia Christi* and Werner Rolevinck's *Fasciculus temporum*," in *Imagining Jerusalem in the Medieval West*, ed. Lucy Donkin and Hanna Vorholt, Proceedings

century scroll containing the *Compendium historiae* is made available through the Harvard Library IIIF service.[41] Making images available using the IIIF standard means that the full image can be accessed using a IIIF conform URI (Figure 2):[42]

> https://ids.lib.harvard.edu/ids/iiif/12438384/full/full/0/native.jpg

Additionally, regions of the image can be uniquely addressed and accessed. For instance, the following URI retrieves the region corresponding to the depiction of Adam in the manuscript:

> https://ids.lib.harvard.edu/ids/iiif/12438384/2700,1700,800,800/full/0/native.jpg

Figure 3 shows the result of the above URI request to the Harvard Library IIIF service. The URI can be used to identify this specific region of the image and include it in websites and image viewers, which is an important step forward into the direction of *distributed editions*.[43] Within the IIIF community, there are also developments to extend the IIIF principles to video and audio content (IIIF A/V), which would be an interesting opportunity for digital editions and collections dealing with these kinds of content.[44]

3.4 Digital identifiers and the traditional workflow in TEI editions

The use of fragment identifiers is very common in digital scholarly editing projects. However, digital scholarly editions are usually not written directly in HTML, as the HTML standard primarily describes the structure of webpages and is not a

---

of the British Academy 175 (London: British Academy Scholarship Online, 2012): 123–61, http://dx.doi.org/10.5871/bacad/9780197265048.003.0006.

41 MS Typ 216, Houghton Library, Harvard University, Cambridge, MA, https://iiif.lib.harvard.edu/manifests/view/drs:12438364$1i.

42 For a detailed description of the IIIF region parameters see the IIIF Image API documentation, https://iiif.io/api/image/2.0/#region.

43 Joris J. van Zundert, "On Not Writing a Review about Mirador: Mirador, IIIF, and the Epistemological Gains of Distributed Digital Scholarly Resources," *Digital Medievalist* 11, no. 1 (2018), http://dx.doi.org/10.16995/dm.78; Peter Boot and Joris van Zundert, "The Digital Edition 2.0 and the Digital Library: Services, Not Resources," in *Digitale Edition und Forschungsbibliothek*, ed. Christiane Fritze et al., Bibliothek und Wissenschaft 44 (Wiesbaden: Harrassowitz, 2011): 141–52.

44 IIIF A/V Technical Specification Group, https://iiif.io/community/groups/av/ .

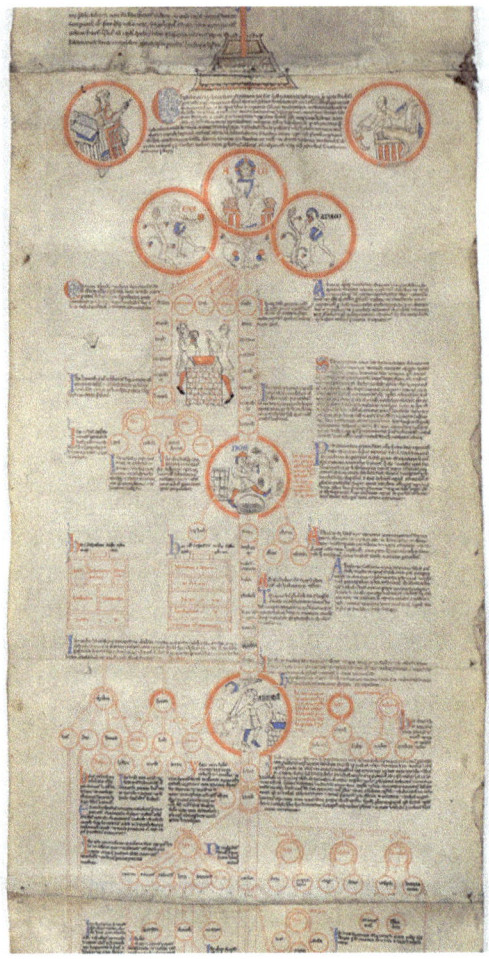

Figure 2: Full view of the second image of MS Typ 216 as provided by the Harvard Library IIIF service (Screenshot); © US fair use. MS Typ 216, Houghton Library.

suitable standard for the preservation of humanities research data. Instead, the Text Encoding for Interchange (TEI) standard was developed for that purpose, and therefore TEI is preferred. The HTML website displays selections or views on the TEI-encoded research data. Consequently, the scholarly research data underlying the edition and the web presentation are not the same.

Figure 3: Detail image of MS Typ 216 retrieved using the IIIF service. The detail image corresponds to the coordinates 2700,1700,800,800 of the full image. The coordinates were passed as parameter in the IIIF request (Screenshot); © US fair use. MS Typ 216, Houghton Library.

The established workflow for publishing digital scholarly editions using TEI/XML[45] is that the primary document for long-term storage and sharing is an XML document and from this document various outputs are generated using XSLT or XQuery. In this transformation process, the original XML document is called the *source document* and the output *result document*. In digital scholarly editions, the result document is usually a HTML document, and it is the fundamental building block for the user interface of the edition and for many users the main access point to the research data.

From a citation perspective, the main issue with the TEI–HTML transformation workflow is that the structure of the TEI source document and the HTML result document can be fundamentally different. During the transformation process, certain data is selected and included in the result document, element and attribute names are changed, and new elements, attributes, and content are added.[46] Furthermore, HTML IDs are often generated during the transforma-

---

[45] The current TEI standard is defined in XML (eXtensible Markup Language).
[46] Julia Flanders, Syd Bauman, and Sarah Connell, "XSLT: Transforming Our XML Data," in *Doing Digital Humanities: Practice, Training, Research*, ed. Constance Crompton, Richard J. Lane, and Ray Siemens (Abingdon, Oxon: Routledge, 2017), 264.

tion process, and they do not necessarily correspond to IDs in the original TEI source document.

The difference between a TEI document and its HTML presentation is irrelevant for the common user, but might cause confusion. However, serious problems may arise if HTML IDs are generated during the transformation process. This is not a persistent procedure, because such IDs are frequently based on the position of an element in the TEI document and the addition or removal of an element preceding it would result in a change to its HTML ID. Consequently, as the TEI is the format for long-term preservation of the research data, a citation should point to identifiers that already exist in the TEI. An attempt to solve the problem caused by the TEI–HTML workflow is the CETEIcean project. The strategy used by CETEIcean is to convert all elements of the TEI source to custom HTML elements with the result that the web presentation is a complete mirror document of the original TEI.[47]

Another option is to use the TEI mechanisms to document foreseeable citation options in the TEI document itself. The TEI as the main standard for the encoding of humanities data and long-term preservation has strategies to record information about how canonical numbers for a text are formed and to what parts of the text they refer. The benefit is that in that citation, information is stored together with the edited text in the same document. In a TEI document, the *header* (teiHeader) section is the place where metadata about the primary source and the electronic representation is stored. A child element of the header, the *encoding description* (encodingDesc), contains the element *references declaration* (refsDecl), which "specifies how canonical references for the encoded text can be constructed." There are three methods outlined in the TEI guidelines: the *prose method*, the *milestone method*, and the *search-and-replace method*.[48]

The first method requires that the information about how canonical references to the text can be constructed should be written in prose text within TEI elements for paragraphs (p element). The second method, the milestone method, uses so-called milestone elements such as the element for page breaks (pb) or line breaks (lb) within the encoded texts. Using a range of attributes, such as those for numbers or labels (@n), editions (@ed), and text units (@unit), these elements provide the necessary information for where in a text canonical

---

[47] Hugh A. Cayless, "Critical Editions and the Data Model as Interface," in *Digital Scholarly Editions as Interfaces*, ed. Roman Bleier et al., Schriften des Instituts für Dokumentologie und Editorik 12 (Norderstedt: Books on Demand, 2018): 249–63, https://kups.ub.uni-koeln.de/9118 .
[48] TEI Consortium, eds., "2.3.6 The Reference System Declaration," TEI P5: Guidelines for Electronic Text Encoding and Interchange 3.3.0. 2018–01–31, https://tei-c.org/Vault/P5/3.3.0/doc/tei-p5-doc/en/html/HD.html#HD54 .

numbers should be set. The information about what these numbers should look like is encoded within the TEI element for the declaration of references (refsDecl). It includes a child element (which is a subordinated element) *reference statement* (refState), which indicates how the data from the milestone elements should be combined to form canonical numbers. The third method, the search-and-replace method, uses the TEI element *canonical reference pattern* (cRefPattern) to specify rules for canonical references and URI requests. The value of the attribute *matchPattern* defines the rules to which a reference must conform as a regular expression pattern, and the value of the attribute *replacementPattern* defines how the reference should be turned into a URI. The matchPattern can be used to define any combination of possible references to a TEI document and what part of the document should be returned. How this could be used in practice is demonstrated by Robinson's Documents, Entities, and Texts (DET) system. The system uses a semantic and flexible URN naming strategy comparable to CTS. In a recent article, Robinson describes how DET uses the cRefPattern element to resolve URN requests.[49]

To conclude, the TEI provides different solutions to store information about canonical citation that could/should be applied to a text in the header section of a TEI document. However, as so often is the case, the TEI leaves it to the user to decide what level of complexity is necessary and appropriate for a project to record citation information. The advantage of the more complex matchPattern approach is that in an abstract way, using patterns and the standardized XPath notation, a set of citation rules can be expressed and both the citation requests that a user may submit and the parts of the text that should be returned are clearly defined for future use.

3.5 Turning canonical numbers into permalinks and PIDs

Several prominent projects will now be discussed to illustrate how semantic permalinks or PIDs may be constructed based on canonical numbers and titles. The first example is the permalink strategy of the website bibleserver.com. The project uses the canonical titles and numbers of books, chapters, and verses of the Bible for addressing and cross-version navigation. The primary way to cite texts on this website would be to use the canonical numbers and the name of the Bible version that should be cited. What most users might not know is that bibleserver.com has a permalink strategy and uses sematic URLs that follow the logic

---

[49] Robinson, "Some principles."

of canonical citations to the Bible. The following example is a link to the second verse of the first chapter of the First Epistle to the Corinthians in the New International Version of the Bible:

> https://www.bibleserver.com/text/NIV/1 Corinthians1.2

The benefit of this human-readable URL syntax is that it does not introduce a new identifier but instead uses a combination of already existing identifiers that were in use long before the internet. Additionally, the project website provides instructions for web developers on how to correctly include links for bibleserver.com into other projects.[50] Bibleserver.com has become successful and it is used e.g. as a default target for links of biblical citation in the German Wikipedia. Furthermore, WordPress plugins such as *Link to Bible* allow links to bibleserver.com to be automatically generated for all biblical citations on a blog. An example for integration of links to the references to bibleserver.com is the digital edition Saint Patrick's *Confessio* Hypertext Stack, which has been online since 2011 and uses links to bibleserver.com in their *apparatus biblicus*.[51]

The citation of pages of print publications is specific to the print culture; however, its tradition continues in the digital age. A great number of online resources are digitized from print, and the established way to cite these resources is by page or column number. The *Patrologia Latina Database* (PLD) was already mentioned; another example is the digital *Monumenta Germaniae Historica* (dMGH). For the dMGH, page numbers are crucial, as its image viewer shows the digitized pages. Furthermore, page numbers can be used in the URL address for citation of the online reproduction. The human-understandable URL of the dMGH resembles the way the MGH is traditionally cited:

> http://www.mgh.de/dmgh/resolving/MGH_Capit._episc._1_S._55

However, there are two issues: one is that the syntax of the dMGH URL cannot be used to address page ranges; the other issue is that the URL cannot be used to address semantic entities of the texts. This is a shortcoming that has already been mentioned by Assmann and Sahle.[52]

---

[50] "BibleServer for Webmasters," BibleServer, https://www.bibleserver.com/webmasters/.
[51] "I. Confessio," Saint Patrick's *Confessio*. Available on bibleserver.com in 2018.
[52] Bernhard Assmann and Patrick Sahle, *Digital ist besser: Die Monumenta Germaniae Historica mit den dMGH auf dem Weg in die Zukunft – eine Momentaufnahme*, Schriften des Instituts für Dokumentologie und Editorik 1 (Norderstedt: Books on Demand, 2008), http://kups.ub.uni-koeln.de/2317.

A third example is the already mentioned Canonical Text Services (CTS) protocol, which translate canonical citations into URNs. CTS is part of the CITE architecture, which provides a framework for the citation of "discrete objects of any kind" using CITE URNs.[53] This protocol was originally developed in the context of the Homer Multitext project but has gained wider interest in the digital humanities community in recent years. One reason for this is that it is being used and promoted by *Perseus*.[54] CTS is based on the idea that texts can be cited using canonical numbers following a hierarchical nesting down to the word level. Smith exemplifies this using the FRBR and OHCO model.[55] Therefore, within a book various chapters can be cited; within a chapter paragraphs can be cited; within the paragraphs sentences; and within a sentence words can be cited. CTS uses URNs with a specific syntax to make the different levels of a canonical citation persistently citable. An important aspect of CTS URNs is that the syntax is human-understandable and follows established citation practices in the classics. Accordingly, citations to text groups, individual works, specific editions, chapters, sections, and paragraphs of a work can be formed, and even citations to individual words and word ranges can be expressed.[56]

Perseus uses CTS URNs as identifiers for texts and CITE URNs as identifiers for authors. In the Perseus environment, stable identifiers for citation are provided with each text. These identifiers make use of the CTS URN, as the following example of a URI identifying an epistle of St Augustine shows:

http://data.perseus.org/citations/urn:cts:latinLit:stoa0040.stoa0011.perseus-lat1:1

The first part of this URL is the address of the Perseus resolver. The actual CTS URN starts with the string "urn:cts" followed by the CTS namespace (latinLit), the textgroup (stoa0040), work (stoa0011), and edition/version (perseus-lat1:1) identifiers. Depending on a text's original language, a different namespace is assigned by Perseus (other options would be greekLit or ancJewLit). Textgroup and work identifiers start with the string "stoa," which means that they are based on the Stoa Consortium for Electronic Publication's Latin Text Inventory and main-

---

[53] Christopher Blackwell, Christine Roughan, and Neel Smith Blackwell, "Citation and Alignment: Scholarship Outside and Inside the Codex," *Manuscript Studies* 1, no. 1 (2017): 5–27, https://repository.upenn.edu/mss_sims/vol1/iss1/2.
[54] "Perseus CTS API," *Perseus Digital Library Updates*, 5 January 2013, http://sites.tufts.edu/perseusupdates/beta-features/perseus-cts-api/.
[55] Smith, "Citation," par. 31.
[56] Ibid., par. 35–8.

tained and extended by Perseus.⁵⁷ The edition/version identifier perseus-lat1 indicates that this is the Perseus edition – Latin – file 1. The potential of working with the CITE architecture is well demonstrated by the recently launched collaboration platform, Perseus Digital Library's CapiTainS environment. Requests for texts or text fragments can be submitted via the URL to the CTS service. The syntax of the URL contains all the elements necessary for a CTS URN.⁵⁸ CTS is an innovative approach to express citations; however, the use of CTS URNs as PIDs is problematic as the CTS namespace has not yet been registered with the Internet Assigned Numbers Authority. This is a requirement for all URN namespaces in order to ensure they are globally unique.⁵⁹

4 Conclusion

This chapter explored topics related to the citation of digital resources with an emphasis on canonical numbers and long-term availability. As has been shown, traditional citation strategies are still relevant in the digital publication space, and the citation of online resources is strongly inspired by the print paradigm. Nevertheless, it is augmented by the possibilities of digital technology, which allow the use of URIs to clearly identify and address digital resources. It has been shown by the example of bibleserver.com and CTS that URIs can be used to identify text fragments corresponding to canonical numbers. Furthermore, the URIs used in these two projects are semantic persistent identifiers containing canonical numbers in the URI in a similar form as they are used in traditional citations by the scholarly community. This highlights that traditional canonical citation systems persist beyond the printed book, and, as has been pointed out, they have great value for the alignment of multiple electronic versions of a text when one builds a text collection and digital scholarly edition.

It has been mentioned that the use of URIs for citation, canonical or not, is not without issues. Therefore, a clear permalink or PID strategy and policy is crucial for all scholarly resources that are created for and published on the web in order to eliminate major doubts about their long-term availability. This includes a strategy for preserving versions of a digital object. However, it has also been

---

57 Alison Babeu, "Regarding the Perseus Catalog's Data and How It Is Created," The Perseus Catalog Blog, 27 August 2015, https://sites.tufts.edu/perseuscatalog/documentation/user-guide/definitions-of-terms/#defs_stoa.
58 "Welcome to the Perseus Digital Library's CapiTainS Environment," *Perseids Project*, https://www.perseids.org/.
59 Kalvesmaki, "Canonical References," p. 20.

pointed out that persistence cannot be achieved by technical means alone; it is first a question of institutional service and continuous maintenance. It is desirable that the permalink and PID policy of an online publication is clearly communicated on the website and that it is stated who guarantees the permalinks and PIDs will work in the future. Furthermore, it has been shown that in online publications a clear strategy is needed to generate sustainable identifiers and anchors. In a digital scholarly editing context, this could be done by documenting and defining the canonical numbers and possible citation options for an electronic text as metadata in the TEI document's header section. Such documentation is also necessary as different canonical systems, both semantic and visual, may be in use for an edited text. This matter has been demonstrated by discussing the canonical numbers used in different editions of St Patrick's epistles. Different research communities might require or prefer one system over another, and an editor should make it clear and document to the user what citation strategy (or strategies) a digital edition supports.

5 Bibliography

Adams, Sean A., and Seth M. Ehorn. "What Is a Composite Citation? An Introduction." In *Composite Citations in Antiquity: Volume One: Jewish, Graeco-Roman, and Early Christian Uses*, edited by Sean A. Adams and Seth M. Ehorn, 1–16. London: Bloomsbury, 2016.
Arnold, Eckhart, and Stefan Müller. "Wie permanent sind Permalinks?" *Informationspraxis* 3, no. 1 (2017). https://doi.org/10.11588/ip.2016.2.33483.
Assmann, Bernhard. *Sind die kanonischen Zitierweisen der Geisteswissenschaften als nachhaltige Komponenten digitaler Repositorien geeignet? Unveröffentlichte Magisterarbeit.* Cologne: University of Cologne, 2005. http://www.cei.lmu.de/pub/MagArbAssmann.pdf.
Assmann, Bernhard, and Patrick Sahle. *Digital ist besser: Die Monumenta Germaniae Historica mit den dMGH auf dem Weg in die Zukunft – eine Momentaufnahme.* Schriften des Instituts für Dokumentologie und Editorik 1. Norderstedt: Books on Demand, 2008. http://kups.ub.uni-koeln.de/2317.
Berners-Lee, Tim. "Cool URIs Don't Change." WC3, 1998. https://www.w3.org/Provider/Style/URI.
Bieler, Ludwig, ed. *Libri epistolarum sancti Patricii episcopi: Part I. Introduction and Text.* Dublin: Irish Manuscripts Commission, 1952.
Blackwell, Christopher, Christine Roughan, and Neel Smith Blackwell. "Citation and Alignment: Scholarship Outside and Inside the Codex." *Manuscript Studies* 1, no. 1 (2017): 5–27. https://repository.upenn.edu/mss_sims/vol1/iss1/2.
Blaney, Jonathan, and Judith Siefring. "A Culture of Non-citation: Assessing the Digital Impact of British History Online and the Early English Books Online Text Creation Partnership."

Digital Humanities Quarterly 11, no. 1 (2017). http://www.digitalhumanities.org/dhq/vol/11/1/000282/000282.html.

Bleier, Roman. "Digital Documentary Editing of St Patrick's Epistles." *Studia Universitatis Babes-Bolyai Digitalia* 62, no. 1 (2017): 9–25. http://dx.doi.org/10.24193/subbdigitalia.2017.1.01.

Bleier, Roman. "Encoding St Patrick's Epistles: History and Electronic Editing of the Manuscript Witnesses." PhD diss., Trinity College Dublin, 2015.

Bleier, Roman, ed. St. Patrick's Epistles: Transcriptions of the Seven Medieval Manuscript Witnesses. Graz: University of Graz, 2019. http://gams.uni-graz.at/context:epistles.

Boot, Peter, and Joris van Zundert. "The Digital Edition 2.0 and the Digital Library: Services, Not Resources." In *Digitale Edition und Forschungsbibliothek*, edited by Christiane Fritze, Franz Fischer, Patrick Sahle, and Malte Rehbein, 141–52. Bibliothek und Wissenschaft 44. Wiesbaden: Harrassowitz, 2011.

Cayless, Hugh A. "Critical Editions and the Data Model as Interface." In *Digital Scholarly Editions as Interfaces*, edited by Roman Bleier, Martina Bürgermeister, Helmut W. Klug, Frederike Neuber, Gerlinde Schneider, 249–63. Schriften des Instituts für Dokumentologie und Editorik 12. Norderstedt: Books on Demand, 2018. https://kups.ub.uni-koeln.de/9118.

Codex Sinaiticus Online. The Codex Sinaiticus Project, 2009. http://www.codexsinaiticus.org/en/codex.

Cooper, John M., and D. S. Hutchinson, eds. *Plato: Complete Works.* Indianapolis, IN: Hackett Publishing Company, 1997.

Cosaert, Carl P. "Clement of Alexandria's Gospel Citations." In *The Early Text of the New Testament*, edited by Charles E. Hill and Michael J. Kruger, 393–413. Oxford: Oxford University Press, 2012.

Crane, Gregory, ed. Perseus Digital Library. Tufts University, 2019. http://www.perseus.tufts.edu.

Duba, William O. "Fragmentarium." *Das Mittelalter* 24, no. 1 (2019): 221–23. https://doi.org/10.1515/mial-2019-0015.

Dumont, Stefan. "Digitale Methodik. Ein Überblick über Datenmodellierung und verwendete Technologien. Version 3 vom 14.09.2018." In *edition humboldt digital*, edited by Ottmar Ette. Berlin: Berlin-Brandenburgische Akademie der Wissenschaften, 2018. https://edition-humboldt.de/v3/H0016212.

Dumont, Stefan. "Interfaces in Digital Scholarly Editions of Letters." In *Digital Scholarly Editions as Interfaces*, edited by Roman Bleier, Martina Bürgermeister, Helmut W. Klug, Frederike Neuber, Gerlinde Schneider, 219–47. Schriften des Instituts für Dokumentologie und Editorik 12. Norderstedt: Books on Demand, 2018. https://kups.ub.uni-koeln.de/9118.

Egghe, Leo, and Ronald Rousseau. *Introduction to Informetrics: Quantitative Methods in Library, Documentation and Information Science.* Amsterdam: Elsevier, 1990.

Fischer, Franz. "The Pluralistic Approach: The First Scholarly Edition of William of Auxerre's Treatise on Liturgy." *Computerphilologie* 10 (2010): 151–68.

Fischer, Franz, and Anthony Harvey, eds. Saint Patrick's *Confessio* Hypertext Stack. Dublin: Royal Irish Academy, 2011. http://www.confessio.ie.

Flanders, Julia, Syd Bauman, and Sarah Connell. "XSLT: Transforming Our XML Data." In *Doing Digital Humanities: Practice, Training, Research*, edited by Constance Crompton, Richard J. Lane, and Ray Siemens, 255–72. Abingdon, Oxon: Routledge, 2017.

Hill, Charles E. "'In These Very Words': Methods and Standards of Literary Borrowing in the Second Century." In *The Early Text of the New Testament*, edited by Charles E. Hill and Michael J. Kruger, 261–80. Oxford: Oxford University Press, 2012.

Hilse, Hans-Werner, and Jochen Kothe. *Implementing Persistent Identifiers*. London: Consortium of European Research Libraries, 2006. https://www.ica.org/sites/default/files/WG_2006_PAAG-implementing-persistent-identifiers_EN.pdf.

Houghton, Hugh A. G. "Chapter Divisions, Capitula Lists, and the Old Latin Versions of John." *Revue Bénédictine* 121, no. 2 (2011): 316–56.

Houghton, Hugh A. G. *The Latin New Testament*. Oxford: Oxford University Press, 2016.

Howlett, David R., ed. *Liber Epistolarum Sancti Patricii Episcopi = The Book of Letters of Saint Patrick the Bishop*. Blackrock, Dublin: Four Courts Press, 1994.

Inowlocki, Sabrina. *Eusebius and the Jewish Authors: His Citation Technique in an Apologetic Context*. Leiden: Brill, 2006.

Kalvesmaki, Joel. "Canonical References in Electronic Texts: Rationale and Best Practices." *Digital Humanities Quarterly* 8, no. 2 (2014). http://www.digitalhumanities.org/dhq/vol/8/2/000181/000181.html.

Kantorowicz, Hermann Ulrich. "Die Allegationen im späteren Mittelalter." *Archiv für Urkundenforschung* 13 (1935): 15–29.

Kruger, Michael J. "Early Christian Attitudes towards the Reproduction of Texts." In *The Early Text of the New Testament*, edited by Charles E. Hill and Michael J. Kruger, 63–80. Oxford: Oxford University Press, 2012.

Lammey, Rachael. "How to Apply CrossMark and FundRef via CrossRef Extensible Markup Language." *Science Editing* 1, no. 2 (2014): 84–90. https://doi.org/10.6087/kcse.2014.1.84.

Neuroth, Heike, Achim Oßwald, Regine Scheffel, Stefan Strathmann, and Karsten Huth, eds. *nestor Handbuch: Eine kleine Enzyklopädie der digitalen Langzeitarchivierung. Version 2.3*. Göttingen: nestor, 2010. http://nestor.sub.uni-goettingen.de/handbuch/nestor-handbuch_23.pdf.

O'Loughlin, Thomas. "Harmonizing the Truth: Eusebius and the Problem of the Four Gospels." *Traditio* 65 (2010): 1–29. https://www.jstor.org/stable/41417988?seq=1

Pierazzo, Elena. *Digital Scholarly Editing: Theories, Models and Methods*. London: Routledge, 2016.

Robinson, Peter. "Some Principles for Making Collaborative Scholarly Editions in Digital Form," *Digital Humanities Quarterly* 11, no. 2 (2017). http://www.digitalhumanities.org/dhq/vol/11/2/000293/000293.html.

Sahle, Patrick. "What Is a Scholarly Digital Edition?" In *Digital Scholarly Editing: Theories and Practices*, edited by Matthew James Driscoll and Elena Pierazzo, 19–39. Cambridge: Open Book Publishers, 2016. https://dx.doi.org/10.11647/OBP.0095.02.

Sahle, Patrick. *Digitale Editionsformen. Teil 3: Textbegriffe und Recodierung*. Schriften des Instituts für Dokumentologie und Editorik 9. Norderstedt: Books on Demand, 2013. https://kups.ub.uni-koeln.de/5353/1/DigEditionen_3.pdf.

Schrage, Eltjo J. H. *Utrumque Ius (=Schriften zur Europäischen Rechts- und Verfassungsgeschichte Band 8)*. Berlin: Duncker and Humblot, 1992.

Sharpe, Richard. "Palaeographical Considerations in the Study of the Patrician Documents in the Book of Armagh." *Scriptorium* 36 (1982): 3–28.
Smith, Neel. "Citation in Classical Studies." *Digital Humanities Quarterly* 3, no. 1 (2009). http://www.digitalhumanities.org/dhq/vol/3/1/000028/000028.html.
Stanley, Christopher. *Paul and the Language of Scripture: Citation Technique in the Pauline Epistles and Contemporary Literature*. Cambridge: Cambridge University Press, 1992.
Sperberg-McQueen, Michael. "Data Citation in the Humanities: What's the Problem?" In *For Attribution: Developing Data Attribution and Citation Practices and Standards: Summary of an International Workshop*, edited by National Research Council. Washington, DC: The National Academies Press, 2012. https://dx.doi.org/10.17226/13564.
TEI Consortium, eds. "TEI P5: Guidelines for Electronic Text Encoding and Interchange 3.3.0. 2018–01–31." TEI Consortium, 2018. http://www.tei-c.org/Guidelines/P5/.
URI Planning Interest Group. "URIs, URLs, and URNs: Clarifications and Recommendations 1.0." W3C/IETF, 2001. https://www.w3.org/TR/uri-clarification.
Van de Sompel, Herbert. "Data Citation – Technical Issues – Identification." In *For Attribution: Developing Data Attribution and Citation Practices and Standards: Summary of an International Workshop*, edited by the National Research Council. Washington, DC: The National Academies Press, 2012. http://dx.doi.org/10.17226/13564.
Van de Sompel, Herbert, Robert Sanderson, Harihar Shankar, and Martin Klein. "Persistent Identifiers for Scholarly Assets and the Web: The Need for an Unambiguous Mapping." *International Journal of Digital Curation* 9, no. 1 (2014): 331–42.
White, Newport J. D. "Libri Sancti Patricii: The Latin Writings of Saint Patrick." *Proceedings of the Royal Irish Academy (PRIA) 25 (Section C)* (1905): 201–326.
Widmer, Maria. "e-codices." *Das Mittelalter* 24, no. 1 (2019): 253–55. https://doi.org/10.1515/mial-2019–0023.
Witt, Jeffrey C. "Digital Scholarly Editions and API Consuming Applications." In *Digital Scholarly Editions as Interfaces*, edited by Roman Bleier, Martina Bürgermeister, Helmut W. Klug, Frederike Neuber, and Gerlinde Schneider, 219–47. Schriften des Instituts für Dokumentologie und Editorik 12. Norderstedt: Books on Demand, 2018. https://kups.ub.uni-koeln.de/9118.
Worm, Andrea. "'Ista est Jerusalem': Intertextuality and Visual Exegesis in Peter of Poitiers' *Compendium historiae in genealogia Christi* and Werner Rolevinck's *Fasciculus temporum*." In *Imagining Jerusalem in the Medieval West*, edited by Lucy Donkin and Hanna Vorholt, 123–61. Proceedings of the British Academy 175. London: British Academy Scholarship Online, 2012. http://dx.doi.org/10.5871/bacad/9780197265048.003.0006.
Zundert, Joris J. van. "On Not Writing a Review about Mirador: Mirador, IIIF, and the Epistemological Gains of Distributed Digital Scholarly Resources." *Digital Medievalist* 11, no. 1 (2018). http://dx.doi.org/10.16995/dm.78.

Dan Batovici and Joseph Verheyden
Digitizing the ancient versions of the Apostolic Fathers: preliminary considerations

1 Introduction

This is a programmatic essay, which means that several issues raised here – e.g. with regard to compatibility and licenses and data standards – depend on the outcome of a number of pending project applications, on the one hand, and on the data standards employed by a number of projects with which we hope to be able to collaborate, on the other. The object of our reflection has to do with digitizing the *Ancient Translations of the Apostolic Fathers* (AnTrAF). This corpus contains an interesting sample of early Christian texts, originally written in Greek, which is most relevant for our understanding of Early Christianity. The Greek text of the Apostolic Fathers has been edited twice in the past twenty years.[1] In addition, new critical editions and commentaries are being produced for each of the texts in the ongoing series of Oxford Apostolic Fathers.[2]

By contrast, interesting and varied as they may be, the versions seem to fall through the cracks and have received considerably less attention. These translations display quite a complex picture that deserves a treatment of its own and opens venues for a digitizing project. The versions are witnesses to the separate reception of these writings in new language spaces, including Latin, Syriac, Coptic, Ethiopic, Arabic, Armenian, Georgian, Old Church Slavonic, and Middle Persian. With one notable exception – the Latin versions of the Shepherd of Hermas[3]

---

[1] Bart D. Ehrman, ed., *The Apostolic Fathers I* and *II*, Loeb Classical Library 25 (Cambridge, MA: Harvard University Press, 2003); Michael W. Holmes, ed., *The Apostolic Fathers: Greek Texts and English Translations*, 3rd ed. (Grand Rapids, MI: Baker Academic, 2007).
[2] So far Christopher Tuckett, ed., *2 Clement: Introduction, Text, and Commentary*, Oxford Apostolic Fathers (Oxford: Oxford University Press, 2012); Paul Hartog, ed., *Polycarp's* Epistle to the Philippians *and the* Martyrdom *of Polycarp: Introduction, Text, and Commentary*, Oxford Apostolic Fathers (Oxford: Oxford University Press, 2013), and Clayton N. Jefford, ed., *The* Epistle to Diognetus *(With the* Fragment of Quadratus), Oxford Apostolic Fathers (Oxford: Oxford University Press, 2013).
[3] Anna Vezzoni, ed., *Il Pastore di Erma: Versione Palatina*, Introduzione di Antonio Carlini, Il nuovo melograno 13 (Firenze: Le Lettere, 1994); and Christian Tornau and Paolo Cecconi,

– critical editions of these versions are either still lacking or at least half a century old. The latter have not been systematically updated, despite the fact that new manuscripts have been discovered. The following offers some programmatic reflections on the possibilities, difficulties, and challenges of developing a digital environment for accessing the AnTrAF, in view of other ongoing digital projects on early Christian literature.

2 The versions of the Apostolic Fathers: an overview

This section briefly presents the state of the art of the known versions for each text of the corpus.

1 Clement has been preserved in Latin, Syriac, and Coptic.[4] The Latin translation is complete and found in only one manuscript.[5] It was first edited in 1894, then more recently in 1941.[6] The Syriac version, based on University Library, Cambridge, Add. MSS 1700, has long been published,[7] though at least two more witnesses are now known that are modern and seem to be connected: Birmingham Mingana Syr 4 and Houghton Library, Harvard, MS Syr 91 [99].[8] Of the two Coptic manuscripts, both in Akhmimic, one is almost complete, omitting only 34.6–42.2 (Staatsbibliothek zu Berlin, Ms. or. fol. 3065), while the other is more fragmentary and contains 1 Clem 1–26.2 (Strasbourg Université copte

---

eds., *The Shepherd of Hermas in Latin: Critical Edition of the Oldest Translation* Vulgata, Texte und Untersuchungen 173 (Berlin: De Gruyter, 2014).
4 Horacio E. Lona, *Der erste Clemensbrief*, Kommentar zu den Apostolischen Vätern 2 (Göttingen: Vandenhoeck & Ruprecht, 1998), 14–16.
5 Benjamin Gleede, Parabiblica Latina: *Studien zu den griechisch-lateinischen Übersetzungen parabiblischer Literatur unter besonderer Berücksichtigung der apostolischen Väter*, Supplements to Vigiliae Christianae 137 (Leiden / Boston: Brill, 2016): 186–98.
6 Germanus Morin, *Sancti Clementis Romani ad Corinthios epistulae versio latina antiquissima*, Anecdota Maredsolana 2 (Maredosus: The Editors / Oxford: J. Parker, 1894); Karl T. Schaefer, *S. Clementis Romani Epistula ad Corinthios quae vocatur prima graece et latine* (Bonn: Hanstein, 1941).
7 R. L. Bensly, *The Epistles of S. Clement to the Corinthians in Syriac: Edited from the Manuscript with Notes* (Cambridge: Cambridge University Press, 1899).
8 S. P. Brock, "Notes on Some Texts in the Mingana Collection," *Journal of Semitic Studies* 14, no. 2 (1969): 207–208.

362–385).⁹ 2 Clement is extant in Syriac in complete form in only one manuscript – University Library, Cambridge, Add. MSS 1700 – following 1 Clement.¹⁰

The Didache (or material close to what is also found in the Didache) exists in Latin, Coptic, and Ethiopic.¹¹ In Latin, the *Doctrina apostolorum* preserves the Two-Ways tractate found in the Didache (1.1–6.1), or rather a tradition that is also used in the Didache.¹² The one Coptic papyrus of the Didache, British Library Oriental Manuscript 9271, preserves about a fifth of the Greek text (10.3b–12.2a) and has been discussed and edited fairly recently.¹³ The Ethiopic *Ancient Church Orders* contains translations of material similar to several sections of the Didache, 11.3–13.7 and 8.1–2, and was edited a century ago.¹⁴ An updated edition is now available, based on a newly found witness.¹⁵ Almost a century ago a description (but no edition) of a Georgian translation of the Didache was published,¹⁶ but this is now generally dismissed as inauthentic.¹⁷

The Epistle of Barnabas is preserved partially in Latin and Syriac. The Latin translation is found in a single manuscript and does not contain the last sec-

---

9 These are edited respectively in Carl Schmidt, *Erste Clemensbrief in altkoptischer Übersetzung*, Texte und Untersuchungen 32, no. 1 (Leipzig: J.C. Hinrichs, 1908); and Friedrich Rösch, *Bruchstücke des ersten Clemensbriefes nach dem achmimischen Papyrus der Strassburger Universitäts- und Landesbibliothek mit biblischen Texten derselben Handschrift* (Strassburg: Schlesier & Schweikhardt, 1910).
10 See Wilhelm Pratscher, *Der zweite Clemensbrief*, Kommentar zu den Apostolischen Vätern 3 (Göttingen: Vandenhoeck & Ruprecht, 2007), 10–11; Tuckett, *2 Clement*, 5–6; It was edited together with 1 Clement in Bensly, *S. Clement in Syriac*.
11 Kurt Niederwimmer, *Die Didache*, Kommentar zu den Apostolischen Vätern 1 (Göttingen: Vandenhoeck & Ruprecht, 1993), 39–48.
12 Niederwimmer, *Die Didache*, 48–64; Gleede, *Parabiblica Latina*, 181–6.
13 F. Stanley Jones and Paul A. Mirecki, "Considerations on the Coptic Papyrus of the *Didache* (British Library Oriental Manuscript 9271)," in *The* Didache *in Context: Essays on Its Text, History and Transmission*, ed. C. N. Jefford, Supplements to Novum Testamentum 77 (Leiden/New York/Köln: Brill, 1995): 47–87.
14 G. Horner, *The Statutes of the Apostles or Canones Ecclesiastici: Edited with Translation and Collation from Ethiopic and Arabic MSS. Also a Translation of the Saidic and Collation of the Bohairic Versions, and Saidic Fragments* (London: Williams & Norgate, 1904), 54–5.
15 Alessandro Bausi, "La 'nuova' versione etiopica della Traditio apostolica: edizione e traduzione preliminare," in *Christianity in Egypt: Literary Production and Intellectual Trends. Studies in Honour of Tito Orlandi*, ed. Paola Buzi and Alberto Camplani, Studia Ephemeridis Augustinianum 125 (Rome: Augustinianum, 2011): 64–7.
16 Gregor Peradse, "Die 'Lehre der zwölf Apostel' in der georgischen Überlieferung," *Zeitschrift für die neutestamentliche Wissenschaft* 31 (1932): 111–16.
17 Niederwimmer, *Die Didache*, 44–45.

tions, 18–21; it was edited over a century ago.[18] In addition, a few lines from Barnabas (19.1–2.8 and 20.1) appear in a Syriac manuscript in University Library, Cambridge, Add. MSS 2023. The manuscript includes several ecclesiastical canons, followed by a collection of biblical and patristic quotations. In the latter group, these lines, counting 49 words, are explicitly introduced as an excerpt from the Epistle of Barnabas.[19] The text is transcribed in the standard catalogue of Syriac manuscripts in Cambridge, published over a century ago.[20]

The Letters of Ignatius have survived in Latin, Syriac, Coptic, Armenian, Ethiopic, and Arabic. The Ignatian corpus has been transmitted in three recensions: long, middle, and short.[21] The Latin preserves both the long recension in 14 manuscripts[22] and the middle one in two manuscripts, of which one is apparently lost.[23] The Syriac preserves the middle recension in three series of fragments found in seven manuscripts, the short recension in three manuscripts.[24] Furthermore, the letter to the Romans, included in the Acts of Martyr Ignatius, was translated into the Syriac, Coptic, Armenian, and Arabic versions of this text. The middle recension is further attested in Coptic and Armenian.[25] The two fragmentary Coptic manuscripts preserve sections of the letters to the Smyrnaeans, Polycarp, Ephesians, Trallians, Philadelphians, and Romans (as well as of the epistle to Hero, which is considered pseudepigraphical) and have been

---

18 Joseph Michael Heer, *Die versio latina des Barnabasbrief und ihr Verhältnis zur lateinischen Bibel, erstmals untersucht, nebst Ausgabe und Glossar des griechischen und lateinischen Textes* (Freiburg im Breisgau: Herder, 1908). See Gleede, *Parabiblica Latina*, 198–203.

19 Ferdinand R. Prostmeier, *Der Barnabasbrief*, Kommentar zu den Apostolischen Vätern 8 (Göttingen: Vandenhoeck & Ruprecht, 1999), 32–34.

20 William Wright, *A Catalogue of the Syriac Manuscripts Preserved in the Library of the University of Cambridge*, Vol. 2 (Cambridge: The University Press, 1901), 611–12.

21 William R. Schoedel, *Ignatius of Antioch: A Commentary* (Hermeneia; Philadelphia, PA: Fortress Press, 1985), 3–4.

22 J. B. Lightfoot, *The Apostolic Fathers, Part II: St. Ignatius, S. Polycarp*, Vol. 1 (London: Macmillan, 1889), 125–34; Gleede, *Parabiblica Latina*, 319–50; edited in Theodor Zahn, "Ignatii et Polycarpi epistolae martyria fragmenta," in *Patrum apostolicorum opera*, f. 2, ed. O. von Gebhardt, Adolf Harnack, and Theodor Zahn (Leipzig: Hinrichs, 1876): 127–73.

23 Schoedel, *Ignatius of Antioch*, 3; edited in J. B. Lightfoot, *The Apostolic Fathers, Part II: St. Ignatius, S. Polycarp*, Vol. 3 (London: Macmillan, 1889), 13–68.For the other four see now Dan Batovici, "Four New Syriac Witnesses to the Middle Recension of the Ignatian Corpus," in *Caught in Translation: Studies on Versions of Late Antique Christian Literature*, edited by Madalina Toca and Dan Batovici (Texts and Studies in Eastern Christianity 17. Leiden/Boston: Brill, 2020), 122–37.

24 Three are edited in William Wright, "The Syriac Remains of S. Ignatius," in *The Apostolic Fathers, Part II: St. Ignatius, S. Polycarp*, Vol. 3 (London: Macmillan, 1889): 73–124.

25 Schoedel, *Ignatius of Antioch*, 4.

edited most recently in 1952.[26] The Armenian is still in need of a critical edition.[27] There are two short extracts from pseudepigraphical Ignatian letters of the long recension in Ethiopic, found in two manuscripts, which have both been edited.[28] The same passages exist in Arabic, yet the most recent edition is more than a century old and is based on one manuscript collated with the previous edition of another Arabic witness and with the Ethiopic.[29] Fifty years ago, an important edition of several Arabic witnesses to the middle recension was published, followed by the publication of an additional Arabic witness to Ignatius' letter to the Romans.[30]

The Epistle of Polycarp has survived completely in Latin and in fragmentary form in Coptic, Armenian, and Syriac. The Latin version is preserved in 14 manuscripts and was re-edited some twenty-five years ago, in fact reproducing an edition of 1883, based on four witnesses.[31] It is of particular interest because the Greek original is incomplete, as in all its manuscripts the letter is interrupted mid-sentence at 9.2 and continues immediately with Barnabas 5.7, also mid-sentence.[32] Two quotations from the Epistle are included in the *Martyrium Ignatii Romanum*, which itself was translated into Coptic, Armenian,[33] and Old Slavonic. Several quotations survive in Syriac translations of various patristic works.[34]

---

[26] L.-Th. Lefort, *Les Pères apostoliques en copte*, CSCO 135/SC 17 (Louvain: L. Durbecq, 1952), 44–66.

[27] Schoedel, *Ignatius of Antioch*, 3–4, and especially Riccardo Pane, "Un'antica traduzione dimenticata: la versione armena delle lettere di S. Ignazio di Antiochia." *Le Muséon* 112 (1999): 47–63.

[28] William Cureton, *Corpus Ignatianum: A Complete Collection of the Ignatian Epistles, Genuine, Interpolated, and Spurious* (London: Francis & John Rivington, 1849), 256–61; see also 363.

[29] William Wright, "Arabic Extracts from Ignatian Letters," in J. B. Lightfoot, *The Apostolic Fathers, Part II: St. Ignatius, S. Polycarp*, Vol. 3 (London: Macmillan, 1889): 299–306.

[30] Basile Basile, "Un ancien témoin arabe des lettres d'Ignace d'Antioche," *Parole de l'Orient* 4, no. 2 (1968): 107–91; and Basile Basile, "Une autre version arabe de la lettre aux romains de St. Ignace d'Antioche," *Parole de l'Orient* 5, no. 2 (1969): 269–87.

[31] See Hartog, *Polycarp's* Epistle to the Philippians, 27. The edition is available in Johannes B. Bauer, *Die Polykarpbriefe*, Kommentar zu den Apostolischen Vätern 5 (Göttingen: Vandenhoeck & Ruprecht, 1995), 87–93, which reproduces that of F. X. Funk, *Die Echtheit der Ignatianischen Briefe aufs Neue vertheidigt* (Tübingen: Verlag der H. Laupp'schen Buchhandlung, 1883), 205–12.

[32] Gleede, *Parabiblica Latina*, 186–98.

[33] Edited respectively in Lefort, *Les Pères apostoliques en copte*, 102–104, and Julius Heinrich Petermann, *S. Ignatii Patris apostolici quae feruntur Epistolae una cum eiusdem Martyrio* (Leipzig: C.G. Vogelius, 1849), 544–48.

[34] Hartog, *Polycarp's* Epistle to the Philippians, 27. See T. B. Sailors, "Quotations of Polycarp's Letter to the Philippians Preserved in Syriac," *The Harp* 27 (2011): 335–42.

The Martyrdom of Polycarp is partially preserved in Latin, Syriac, Coptic, Armenian, and Old Slavonic. The Latin version is incomplete, paraphrastic, and abbreviated; it seems to be an independent recension.[35] There is now a preliminary critical edition, after the text of one manuscript was recently published.[36] Eusebius of Caesarea quotes most of the Martyrdom, paraphrasing 2.2–7.3 and omitting 19.2–22.3 in *Historia Ecclesiastica* 4.15,[37] which was itself translated into Latin and Syriac. There are also Coptic and Armenian versions of the Martyrdom that follow Eusebius' recension.[38] The Slavonic translation has received some scholarly attention, but so far, no edition has been published, although it seems to be independent of both the Latin and the Eusebian recension.[39]

Papias' *Expositions of the Sayings of the Lord* is now lost. Several fragments from or associated with this work have been identified, though the history of their identification is complicated and editions differ with regard to the number of fragments included.[40] Some of these fragments have only survived in Latin, Syriac, Armenian, and Arabic, whereas others have been translated together with the patristic works that contain them into Latin, Syriac, and Armenian (especially but not only Eusebius, *Historia Ecclesiastica* 3.39). The one fragment of Quadratus cited in the *Historia Ecclesiastica* 4.3.1–2 of Eusebius of Caesarea sur-

---

35 Hartog, *Polycarp's* Epistle to the Philippians, 170; Gleede, *Parabiblica Latina*, 213–45.
36 Benjamin Gleede, "Epistula ecclesiae Smyrnensis de passione Polycarpi (BHL 6870): Kritische Präliminaredition," *Sacris Erudiri* 59 (2020): 7–35, respectively, Gleede, *Parabiblica Latina*, 359–63.
37 Ehrman, *The Apostolic Fathers*, 363.
38 Hartog, *Polycarp's* Epistle to the Philippians, 169. The Coptic was edited from two manuscripts, Vatican MS Copt. 58 and 66, in I. Balestri and H. Hyvernat. *Acta Martyrum II*, CSCO 86/SC 6 (Paris: E Typographeo reipublicae, 1924), 62–89. The Armenian was recently republished in Otto Zwierlein, ed., *Die Urfassungen der Martyria Polycarpi et Pionii und das Corpus Polycarpianum*. Vol. 1, *Editiones criticae*. Vol. 2, *Textgeschichte und Rekonstruktion. Polykarp, Ignatius und der Redaktor Ps.-Pionius*, Untersuchungen zur antiken Literatur und Geschichte 116, no. 1 and 2 (Berlin: Walter de Gruyter, 2014), 46–64, but even that is based on two previous editions from 1874 and 1881, rather than on manuscripts, as mentionned on page 12; see vol. 2, 109. See also Armenuhi Drost-Abgarjan, "Die armenische Version des Polykarp-Martyriums," in *Orientalia Christiana. Festschrift für Hubert Kaufhold zum 70. Geburtstag*, ed. Peter Bruns and Heinz Otto Luthe, Eichstätter Beiträge zum Christlichen Orient 3 (Wiesbaden: Harrassowitz, 2013): 155–67.
39 Taras Khomych, "'An Early Church Slavonic Translation of the Martyrdom of St. Polycarp': Three Decades Later," *Analecta Bollandiana* 130 (2012): 294–302.
40 There are 16 fragments in Ehrman, *The Apostolic Fathers*; 26 in Enrico Norelli, *Papia di Hierapolis: Esposizione degli oracoli del signore. I frammenti. Introduzione, testo, traduzione e note*, Letture cristiane del primo millennio 36 (Milan: Paoline, 2005); and 28 in Holmes, *The Apostolic Fathers*.

vives in the Latin and Syriac translation of that work. So far, no surviving translation of the Epistle to Diognetus has been found.

Finally, the Shepherd of Hermas was translated into Latin (twice), Coptic, Ethiopic, Georgian, and Middle Persian. The two Latin translations and the Ethiopic one are complete, including the ending, which is missing in the Greek witnesses. The Latin translations have been edited recently.[41] The available Ethiopic edition is old and based on only one witness;[42] three more manuscripts are now known that are genetically different from the one published by d'Abbadie,[43] and a new edition is needed.[44] But even in the case of the Vulgata, more work needs to be done, since the 2014 edition is in fact based on only 14 of its 28 known manuscripts. The Coptic translations, in Akhmimic and Sahidic, cover about a third of the Shepherd. They were edited in the middle of the last century but need updating.[45] A Georgian manuscript, containing about one-quarter of the whole book, is known to exist, but a critical edition is still wanting.[46] An excerpt from the Ninth Similitude in Middle Persian, preserved in an abbreviated form, is probably of Manichaean origin. This fragment has received some attention and has been edited several times.[47] Notably, so far no traces of the Shepherd in Syriac have been found.

---

41 The Palatina of the 5th century in Vezzoni, *Il Pastore di Erma*, and the Vulgata of the 2nd or 3rd century in Tornau and Cecconi, *Shepherd of Hermas in Latin*. See above n. 3.

42 Antoine D'Abbadie, *Hermae Pastor: Aethiopice Primum Edidit et Aethiopica Latine Vertit Antonius de Abbadie*, Abhandlungen für die Kunde des Morgenlandes 2, no. 1 (Leipzig: Brockhaus, 1860).

43 Ted Erho, "A Third Ethiopic Witness to the Shepherd of Hermas," *La parola del passato* 67, no. 5 (2012 [2014]): 363–70, and more recently Ted Erho, "A Fourth Ethiopic Witness to the Shepherd of Hermas," in *Caught in Translation: Studies on Versions of Late Antique Christian Literature*, edited by Madalina Toca and Dan Batovici (Texts and Studies in Eastern Christianity 17; Leiden: Brill, 2020), 241–66.

44 Massimo Villa, "La versione etiopica del Pastore di Erma. Riedizione critica del testo (Visioni e Precetti)," *Comparative Oriental Manuscript Studies Bulletin* 1, no. 2 (2015): 115–18, and especially Massimo Villa, *Filologia e linguistica dei testi ge'ez di età aksumita. Il Pastore di Erma* (Studi Africanistici/Series Etiopica 10; Napoli: Unior Press, 2019).

45 See Enzo Lucchesi, "Compléments aux Pères apostoliques en copte," *Analecta Bollandiana* 99 (1981): 395–408; and Dan Batovici, "Two Lost Lines of the Coptic Hermas in BnF Copte 130 (2) f. 127," *Journal of Theological Studies* 68, no. 2 (2017): 572–75. Latest edition in Lefort, *Les Pères apostoliques en copte*.

46 Bernard Outtier, "La version géorgienne du Pasteur d'Hermas," *Revue des études géorgiennes et caucasiennes* 6/7 (1990–1991): 211–16.

47 Werner Sundermann, "The Shepherd of Hermas," *Encyclopaedia Iranica* (2004): 232–34, http://www.iranicaonline.org/articles/hermas-the-shepherd-of. The latest edition is available in Bogdan Burtea, "Interpretatio manichaica am Beispiel des mittelpersischen Turfan-Fragments M 97," *Annals of the Sergiu Al-George Institute* 4/5 (1995–1996 [2002]): 47–67.

The AnTrAF offers a fairly complex and rather mixed picture. The material is diverse and largely understudied as a witness to the reception history of the Apostolic Fathers. An integrative digital project focused on these versions will therefore have to go a long way towards elucidating these issues.

However, as far as the type of digital data gathered in this project is concerned, an apparent problem is the fact that the manuscripts involved are of different texts, written in different languages, belonging to different periods. For instance, whereas most AF appear in Latin, Coptic, and Syriac – which allows for some degree of cohesiveness – this project will also gather the Old Slavonic manuscripts of the Martyrdom of Polycarp, or the isolated Middle Persian fragment with the Shepherd of Hermas. The AF form a heterogeneous and, in a sense, an artificial corpus. This is all the more so for the AnTrAF, which collects different documents that were translated separately in different languages, at different times, resulting in reception artefacts found in different cultures that were not always in contact with one another. For this reason, if the AF are regarded as a corpus in modern scholarship, the project focused on the AnTrAF gathers, as far as digital models go, a "collection of heterogenous documents" that is best defined as "a potentially evolutionary set of interlinked digital objects" that "can be composed of strongly heterogenous documents or…documents of various nature and origin."[48] Indeed, this project will put together early translations extant in relatively early manuscripts (Coptic), early translations extant in medieval manuscripts (Latin), and comparatively late translations surviving in medieval (Ethiopic) or even modern manuscripts (Syriac).

3 DH venues for AnTrAF

Several interlinked approaches of the material are envisaged: compiling a Clavis, a comprehensive online list of manuscripts and an online bibliography, digitizing the available manuscripts, producing digital transcriptions for performing part-of-speech tagging and correlating these with existing lexical databases, and data mining for big data projects in each language. In the following, several directions for digitizing AnTrAF will be sketched, mainly by discussing how extant digital projects, focused on other text corpora, have dealt with similar issues and by indicating ways in which this works best for this corpus.

---

48 Sarah Mombert, "From Books to Collections: Critical Editions of Heterogeneous Documents," in *Digital Critical Editions*, ed. Daniel Apollon, Claire Bélisle, and Philippe Régnier, Topics in the Digital Humanities (Urbana, IL: University of Illinois Press, 2014).

3.1 Online Clavis and bibliography

The first step is to produce an online Clavis of AnTrAF with an exhaustive bibliography. A parallel in this regard is *e-Clavis: Christian Apocrypha*,[49] which is an ongoing project developed by members of the North American Society for the Study of the Christian Apocryphal Literature (NASSCAL), which aims at offering a comprehensive bibliography on Christian Apocrypha. The entries in *e-Clavis: Christian Apocrypha* are arranged per writing. For each of them, the names under which the work is known are listed, as are the inventory numbers in other Claves, the type of work, related apocryphal texts, a summary of the contents, and various online resources, such as translations and TV documentaries that mention it. These are then followed by a structured bibliography that lists manuscripts and editions by language, modern translations, and scholarly publications. A link is offered for items that are available online. This is a useful tool for a constant updating of literature on the apocryphal texts.

In the AnTrAF digitization project, the Clavis entries will be geared more towards the study of versions, rather than offering general information about a text. Therefore, each Clavis entry will be focused on one writing and will contain references to 1) the critical editions of the Greek text; 2) the main commentaries; and 3) each extant version with the list of a) manuscripts, b) editions, and c) bibliography. A series of *notae* will contain brief clarifications about the relationships between the various editions. These data are collected and processed within the project.[50]

In the case of 2 Clement, where only one Syriac manuscript is extant, the entry will list the Greek critical editions up to that by Tuckett of 2012, the main commentaries, then the heading of the only version – "Syriac" – under which University Library, Cambridge, Add. MSS 1700 is listed (giving also the folios on which 2 Clement is copied), followed by the full reference of the available edition[51] and a bibliography of scholarly contributions which meaningfully deal with this version of 2 Clement. The entry for 1 Clement, however, will be more complex, in that it will have more language headings – "Latin," "Syriac," "Coptic" – each with multiple manuscript entries and corresponding bibliographies.

---

[49] Available at "e-Clavis, Christian Apocrypha," North American Society for the Study of Christian Apocryphal Literature, http://www.nasscal.com/e-clavis-christian-apocrypha/.
[50] We are currently exploring ways to develop this part in collaboration with Trismegistos [TM] (https://www.trismegistos.org), in which case the Clavis and Bibliography part of DAnTrAF (the digital project around AnTrAF), as well as the Manuscript Platform described in the following section, will follow TM's data standards.
[51] Bensly, *S. Clement in Syriac*.

Additionally, the information will be arranged so that it is retrievable not only by individual text (as it is in each Clavis entry), but also by language. This means that it will be possible to visualize on one page all AF titles that appear in a selected language, with manuscripts, and links to editions and further bibliography. Finally, for each version, the bibliographical entries – which will be developed, updated, and synchronized in Zotero – are to be enhanced with hyperlinks to all publications that are either in the public domain due to their age, or have otherwise been made available as more recent open-access publications. This would involve a limited amount of work with an immediate application, given that such a tool would be useful for studying both the Apostolic Fathers in general and AnTrAF in particular.

3.2 Online manuscript platform

This involves producing a tool that contains descriptive entries of all known AnTrAF manuscripts. These data are also collected and processed within the project. It will be linked to the manuscript lists in AnTrAF Clavis and will also provide links to all manuscripts with AnTrAF that are already available online. A parallel project that collects in one place information and, where available, links to manuscripts that are already accessible online, mostly by their host institution, is *Manuscripta apocryphorum*, another tool devised by the members of NASSCAL.[52] The manuscripts are listed by city, collection, and various languages. This means that the upfront list is searchable by place of inventory and shelf number, not by title of the work. On the next level, however, each manuscript page on the site has a link to the website of the library with digitized images if extant, or the label "Images: not available online" in the opposite case. This is followed by a brief codicological description, information on the language and date, comments on its provenance, a list of apocryphal works and the folios they cover, a description of the contents of the whole manuscript, a reference to catalogues that mention the work (with links when the catalogue is available online), links to other online databases such as Pinakes, and even relevant Wikipedia entries.

Within the AnTrAF manuscript platform, each entry will similarly offer a general description of the manuscript, listing the host institution, inventory

---

[52] Available at North American Society for the Study of Christian Apocryphal Literature, *Manuscripta apocryphorum*, http://www.nasscal.com/manuscripta-apocryphorum/.

number, publication name, codicological and paleographical description,[53] provenance and dating, contents, catalogues that list them, and links to already digitized manuscripts when that is the case. In addition, it will also offer more specific data on the text it contains: the language, titles and colophons when extant, and the manner in which the work is identified in the introduction or prologue, if present.[54] The case of British Library Oriental Manuscript 9271 is straightforward in that it is a single-leaf manuscript, containing only a fragment of the Didache in Coptic. It can therefore be simply described along these lines. University Library, Cambridge, Add. MSS 1700, however, is a more complex artifact, in that it is a multiple-text as well as a composite codex[55] since it contains not only 1 and 2 Clement in Syriac but also several New Testament writings in that language (the Gospels, Acts, the Catholic Epistles and after 1 and 2 Clement the Pauline epistles, including Hebrews), and leaves with tables of readings were added at the beginning. In terms of content, all layers of text with their components will have to be described. The case of the Akhmimic and Sahidic codices of the Shepherd of Hermas, whose fragmentary leaves are kept in different institutions and countries, is also complex, albeit in a different way.[56] Such codices will receive one identifier and will be described as a whole, whereas each fragment is also given its corresponding data in terms of content, size, and location.

Finally, the manuscript platform is meant as a dynamic tool in which manuscript entries can be retrieved and visualized by a number of set parameters such as individual work, language, location (country, city, and host institution), the material used (papyrus, parchment, paper), or a combination of these (e. g. all AF Syriac manuscripts in London, or all AF Latin manuscripts in Italy). The

---

[53] The basis for treating together, in a comparative and consistent manner, manuscripts from different languages is now Alessandro Bausi et al., eds., *Comparative Oriental Manuscript Studies: An Introduction* (Hamburg: Tredition, 2015).
[54] For instance, in the only Georgian witness of the Shepherd, the text is introduced as if written by one Ephrem, instead of Hermas: "Here are the Commandments and the Similitudes ordered by the angel of God to Saint Ephrem" (Outtier, "La version géorgienne du Pasteur d'Hermas," 215).
[55] A multiple-text manuscript is now defined as "a codicological unit 'worked in a single operation' [...] with two or more texts or a 'production unit' resulting from one production process delimited in time and space," and a composite one as "a codicological unit which is made up of formerly independent units"; in Michael Friedrich and Cosima Schwarke, "Introduction: Manuscripts as Evolving Entities," in *One-Volume Libraries: Composite and Multiple-Text Manuscripts*, ed. Michael Friedrich and Cosima Schwarke, Studies in Manuscript Cultures 9 (Berlin: De Gruyter, 2016): 15–16.
[56] Dan Batovici, "Some Observations on the Coptic Reception of the Shepherd," *Comparative Oriental Manuscript Studies Bulletin* 3, no. 2 (2017). esp. 82–3 and 85–6.

manuscript entries will be correlated with the relevant bibliography in the Clavis.[57]

3.3 Digital transcriptions

The next logical step will be to produce transcriptions for each manuscript in view of producing digital critical editions of the corpus that allow for flexible searches and cross-referencing.

The tool used for producing digital transcriptions is the Virtual Manuscript Room Collaborative Research Environment (VMR CRE), therefore following their data standards.[58] It provides an open-access set of tools for cataloguing, indexing, tagging, transcribing, and collating manuscripts, as well as for producing critical apparatuses in view of digital or print editions. It has been applied already for several major corpus-based projects in different languages: Greek (the New Testament Virtual Manuscript Room in Münster[59]), Coptic (the Coptic–Sahidic Old Testament Project in Göttingen[60]), and Syriac (Syriac Climacus' Ladder of Divine Ascent Project in Washington[61]). Moreover, a VMR based project focused on 1 Clement coordinated by Dan Batovici and David Downs, producing transcriptions for all Greek, Syriac, Latin, and Coptic witnesses, is already on its way.[62]

In a digital environment such as the VMR, which supports the cataloguing of the witnesses by category,[63] it is possible to catalogue all AnTrAF witnesses by version. When an AnTrAF digitized manuscript is added to the VMR environ-

---

[57] A difficulty is that some manuscripts are now lost, or are in places with no access for academics, in which case the manuscript entries should nonetheless gather the available descriptions. For instance, in the case of the Sahidic bifolium of the Shepherd in the University Library in Leuven, which was lost to the fire in May 1940 (LDAB 107957), the entry will contain the information offered in the critical edition: Lefort, *Les Pères apostoliques en copte*, viii–ix.
[58] For this see Virtual Manuscript Room Collaborative Research Environment (VMR CRE), http://vmrcre.org.
[59] For which see "New Testament Virtual Manuscript Room," Institut für Neutestamentliche Textforschung, WWU Münster, http://ntvmr.uni-muenster.de/.
[60] For which see Digital Edition of the Coptic Old Testament, Göttingen Academy of Sciences and Humanities, 2020, http://coptot.manuscriptroom.com.
[61] For which see MOTB Syriac CCR Project, Institut für Neutestamentliche Textforschung, WWU Münster, http://ntvmr.uni-muenster.de/web/motb-syriac-ccr-project.
[62] For which now see https://ntvmr.uni-muenster.de/web/1Clement/home.
[63] In the NT VMR of the Münster project the papyri, majuscule manuscripts, minuscule manuscripts, and lectionaries each have different series of identifiers. The same system can be used in the AnTrAF project for categorizing manuscripts by language.

ment, it can be indexed folio by folio according to its contents, using the continuous numbering of a modern critical edition. What is more, the VMR CRE supports feature tagging for storing metadata, about the manuscript as a whole as well as for each page. Such predefined features can record other catalogue identifiers and external image repositories, as well as codicological and paleographical information about the whole manuscript. Moreover, feature tagging supports the recording of illuminations and marginalia, as well as the tagging of script samples for individual pages.[64] Specifically for transcriptions, the VMR CRE includes a web-based editor that makes it possible for collaborators from different places to transcribe online as registered users. This is a complete tool that allows a user not only to transcribe the text but also to mark all or most paratextual features present in the manuscript, from the disposition in columns and lines to enlarged initials, punctuation, decorative features, abbreviations, blank spaces, and lacunae. And in the case of corrections, for instance, each alteration to the text can be recorded separately, in a layered manner.[65]

The diplomatic transcriptions of each AnTrAF manuscript should eventually lead to the production of new critical editions. They can also be used for complex searches in each language and for compiling lexicons of the Apostolic Fathers corpus in any language for which enough material has survived to produce a relevant sample.[66] By working in such an environment, the text is correlated with the digital images of the manuscripts through indexing and tagging, which makes it easy both to check and to correct a reading in a manuscript. Finally, the way in which VMR CRE supports feature tagging makes the recorded features searchable as well, which would make these transcriptions relevant for codicological and paleographical studies in each language beyond the corpus.

Digital transcriptions realized in this manner will be readily available for various other DH purposes, even before new digital editions would reach completion. For instance, applying part-of-speech tagging and lemmatization would result in data that can then be correlated with lexical databases. More-

---

64 "VMR CRE Brief Introduction," Google Docs, https://docs.google.com/document/d/1vUFWN5R6_sLaMj2Qc7Se2_Dkpgfr6jjFDWThKqyeoeo/edit?usp=sharing.
65 A full description is available at "INTF Documentation for the use of the Transcription Editor and Instructions for the Transcription of New Testament Manuscripts," WWU Münster, trans. H. A. G. Houghton, 2 October 2013, http://ntvmr.uni-muenster.de/community/modules/transcript/edit/wce-ote/plugin/docu_en.htm.
66 There is, for instance, a Greek lexicon dedicated to the Apostolic Fathers: Daniel B. Wallace, Brittany C. Burnette, and Terry Darby Moore, *A Reader's Lexicon of the Apostolic Fathers* (Grand Rapids: Kregel Academic, 2013).

over, a grammatically tagged text can then be delivered for linguistic studies in each language.

3.4 Part-of-speech (POS) tagging and lemmatization

A transcription produced in VMR CRE can then be used on a different platform for POS tagging. A number of such platforms are available that are devoted to the main languages in which the Apostolic Fathers have been translated. The benefits of having a text enhanced with POS tagging are multiple. If a simple digital transcription has the advantage of being more searchable than a printed edition of that text, a POS-tagged text allows for far more complex searches, with a higher degree of retrievability, not only by text sequence but also by grammatical category.

In the case of Coptic it is possible, for instance, to import the XML of a VMR CRE transcription into the Coptic NLP (Natural Language Processing) Service of the Coptic Scriptorium (Sahidic Corpus Research: Internet Platform for Interdisciplinary Multilayer Methods), which is an open-source, open-access digital platform that provides a number of tools for linguistically processing Coptic literary texts.[67] This platform supports various annotations, e. g. POS tagging, lemmatization of lexically meaningful morphemes, and tokenization of Coptic words. Coptic Scriptorium already contains a corpus of texts that are fully annotated and can be visualized, for instance in a diplomatic, normalized, and analytic manner. While the diplomatic HTML visualization displays the text as it appears in the manuscript (i. e. preserving its spelling, columns, and lines and featuring annotations about various features in the manuscript), the normalized HTML visualization offers a text that has been normalized for spelling, punctuation, and word segmentation. Finally, the analytic HTML visualization displays a normalized text with its POS annotations and a correlated English translation.[68]

Another example would be the <TraCES/> project (From Translation to Creation: Changes in Ethiopic Style and Lexicon from Late Antiquity to the Middle Ages), which develops an "annotated digital corpus of [Ethiopic] texts from different periods with the aim of using it for language study" and also constructs a

---

[67] Available at Coptic Scriptorium: Digital Research in Coptic Language and Literature, last updated 16 June 2020, http://copticscriptorium.org. A description of the project is available in Caroline T. Schroeder and Amir Zeldes, "Raiders of the Lost Corpus," *Digital Humanities Quarterly* 10, no. 2 (2016), http://www.digitalhumanities.org/dhq/vol/10/2/000247/000247.html, and a description of the tools it offers can be found at http://copticscriptorium.org/tools.
[68] Bridget Almas and Caroline T. Schroeder, "Applying the Canonical Text Services Model to the Coptic SCRIPTORIUM," *Data Science Journal* 15 (2016), 13, http://doi.org/10.5334/dsj-2016–013.

Clavis of Ethiopic literature and a digital lexicon of Gəʿəz.⁶⁹ A digital environment was created that is devised for multi-layered linguistic annotation of Ethiopic texts. The input for this environment is plain digital transcriptions (mostly digitized though OCR) of Ethiopic texts, which then go first through an initial automatic transliteration, tokenization, and linguistic annotation based mainly on morphological criteria, followed by a manual correction of the transliteration and an updating of the tokenization. For the manual process of correction, the project has developed a complex tool that allows the user to select various levels of tagging features in order to achieve the disambiguation of morphologically identical forms.⁷⁰ The data mined in this manner can then be used for the creation of the projected digital lexicon of Gəʿəz and exported to established tools for complex analysis of the language.

These two examples may suffice to show that a POS-tagged AnTrAF corpus would constitute an important resource for each language in which enough text has survived to be significant (e.g. the Latin, or Ignatius and 1–2 Clement in Syriac, or the Shepherd in Ethiopic, or the cumulated texts in Coptic). It would lend itself to various types of research as well as didactic purposes. For instance, a POS-annotated Coptic digital text of the Apostolic Fathers would offer a more dynamic learning and teaching tool than a printed chrestomathy. Such an enhanced text will be invaluable not only for studying AnTrAF, but also for studies on translation technique in each target language in comparison with the Greek text, as well as for broader studies on stylistic and lexical developments in each of these languages.

3.5 Data mining for linguistic projects

One of the aims of the data mined through text annotation in Coptic Scriptorium and TraCES is to produce material that can then be used for linguistic analysis of Sahidic Coptic and Ethiopic. The tool used for this is ANNIS (ANNotation of Information Structure), which is "a web browser and visualization architecture for complex multi-layer linguistic corpora with diverse types of annotation," an

---

69 A description of the project can be found at TraCES Project, Universität Hamburg, last updated 9 May 2017, https://www.traces.uni-hamburg.de/en/texts.html.
70 These considerations summarize the material presented at the workshop "Linking Manuscripts from the Coptic, Ethiopian and Syriac Domain: Present and Future Synergy Strategies," (Hamburg, February 2018, https://www.aai.uni-hamburg.de/en/comst/pdf/bulletin4-1/05-10.pdf), especially the paper now published as Susanne Hummel, Vitagrazia Pisani, and Cristina Vertan, "Multi-level Digital Annotation of Ethiopic Texts," COMSt Bulletin 4.1 (2018): 97-106.

open access tool that can be installed on a personal computer or used online.[71] It allows simple and complex searches in digitized literary corpora, according to the categories of annotations encoded with the texts that compose it. One can search not only for all instances of a word in a corpus, but also for all words that include a particular lemma. One can search for all uses of a grammatical category, or indeed for any marker for which an annotation exists in the transcription, whether a toponym, the original language of a loanword, or any linguistically relevant morpheme.[72] The rather robust interface allows the researcher to select the corpus to analyze, the option to define complex queries, and the possibility to configure the visualization of the results and adapt it according to the needs of specific research.[73]

The annotated digital text of the Coptic and Ethiopic Apostolic Fathers not only will be useful for the study of translation techniques but will also add up to the corpus of digitized Coptic and Ethiopic texts for more complex linguistic queries in each of these languages. The same would also apply for the remaining versions when similar projects are started for texts in those languages.

3.6 Data correlation and visualization

Finally, a digital project focused on the versions of the Apostolic Fathers will have to deal with various problems concerning data linking both in each language component and across languages.

For each language, there should be a digital correlation between transcriptions, manuscripts, and extant lexical databases at the level of each language in which the corpus was translated. This means that for each lexically tagged word in transcription, it would be possible to retrieve and visualize the digital image of the manuscript page on which it is written, as well as the relevant lexicon entry, whenever a dictionary is available digitally. There are several digital pro-

---

[71] "About ANNIS," ANNIS, Humboldt-Universität zu Berlin, 2016, http://corpus-tools.org/annis/. A description of the project is available in Thomas Krause and Amir Zeldes. "ANNIS3: A New Architecture for Generic Corpus Query and Visualization," *Digital Scholarship in the Humanities* 31, no. 1 (2016): 118–39. Other corpus-based projects which employ ANNIS, including Perseus Latin and Ancient Greek Treebank (https://perseusdl.github.io/treebank_data/), are listed at http://corpus-tools.org/annis/cooperations.html.

[72] A friendly User Guide is available at http://corpus-tools.org/annis/resources/ANNIS_User_Guide_3.4.3.pdf.

[73] Examples of possible searches in ANNIS are presented at http://copticscriptorium.org/ANNIS-tips.html.

jects that link in various ways a transcription to the digital images of a manuscript and are then visualized together. In VMR CRE, a transcription of a manuscript page is by design linked to the relevant digital image, yet through their inbuilt Feature Tagger it is possible to link a text sequence to the relevant line of the manuscript. An even more relevant example is the Codex Sinaiticus project.[74] Its manuscript visualization presents the user with both the transcription and the manuscript image on the same page, and more importantly, a click on a word in the transcription highlights the area in which the corresponding word is written in the manuscript.

The question of linking data across languages, however, will probably prove to be the most complicated, as each version would be treated in the digital environment of, or in a manner that is consistent with, existing projects in each language. However, on the level of the whole corpus, the aim is to develop and make available the option to retrieve all versions of a verse, paragraph, or other manageable unit of the Apostolic Fathers, and to visualize them simultaneously. This is possible in VMR CRE, where a display can be added in which users navigate by verse reference and visualize its versions in a Synoptic format.

4 Concluding remarks

By way of conclusion, a digital project focused on AnTrAF developed along the lines described in this contribution will impact future research on the textual transmission of the corpus as well as the study of the versions as discrete strands of reception and, more generally, the study of late antique translations from Greek into other languages. The Clavis and the manuscript digital platform will systematize and classify the intricate histories of AnTrAF manuscripts in modern times and the scholarship devoted to them over the last two centuries. The digital transcriptions will make the text more accessible to research of various kinds, from textual studies on the Apostolic Fathers to translation studies from Greek to the target language, once the corpus is POS annotated.

The project will first and foremost facilitate the production of new or updated critical editions of AnTrAF. However, due to the composite nature of the corpus and the fragmentary state of the evidence, one will not have to wait for the completion of the whole project to see results, since it is possible to produce editions in a segmented manner, as the project progresses. As it were, the digital edition of the Latin version of the Epistle of Barnabas can be completed as soon as its single manuscript is

---

74 Codex Sinaiticus, http://codexsinaiticus.org/en/.

processed and does not have to wait, for instance, for the completion of the digitization of all 28 Latin manuscripts of the Shepherd of Hermas; this means that the project can produce results as it goes rather than only at the end. Importantly, due to the correlation with the digital images, each manuscript becomes readily available for textual research as soon as it has been transcribed. If an entry in a critical apparatus is a scholarly claim rather than the evidence itself, online transcription linked to and visualized with the corresponding digital images of the manuscript will facilitate the necessary verification, and therefore can readily be used for textual as well as reception–historical purposes.

5 Bibliography

Almas, Bridget, and Caroline T. Schroeder. "Applying the Canonical Text Services Model to the Coptic SCRIPTORIUM." *Data Science Journal* 15 (2016): 13. http://doi.org/10.5334/dsj-2016–013.

Balestri, I., and H. Hyvernat. *Acta Martyrum II*. CSCO 86/SC 6. Paris: E Typographeo reipublicae, 1924.

Basile, Basile. "Un ancien témoin arabe des lettres d'Ignace d'Antioche." *Parole de l'Orient* 4, no. 2 (1968): 107–91.

Basile, Basile. "Une autre version arabe de la lettre aux romains de St. Ignace d'Antioche." *Parole de l'Orient* 5, no. 2 (1969): 269–87.

Batovici, Dan. "Some Observations on the Coptic Reception of the Shepherd." *Comparative Oriental Manuscript Studies Bulletin* 3, no. 2 (2017): 81–96.

Batovici, Dan. "Two Lost Lines of the Coptic Hermas in BnF Copte 130 (2) f. 127." *Journal of Theological Studies* 68, no. 2 (2017): 572–5.

Batovici, Dan. "Four New Syriac Witnesses to the Middle Recension of the Ignatian Corpus." In Toca and Batovici, *Caught in Translation*, 122–37.

Bauer, Johannes B. *Die Polykarpbriefe*. Kommentar zu den Apostolischen Vätern 5. Göttingen: Vandenhoeck & Ruprecht, 1995.

Bausi, Alessandro. "La 'nuova' versione etiopica della Traditio apostolica: edizione e traduzione preliminare." In *Christianity in Egypt: Literary Production and Intellectual Trends. Studies in Honour of Tito Orlandi*, edited by Paola Buzi and Alberto Camplani, 19–69. Studia Ephemeridis Augustinianum 125. Rome: Augustinianum, 2011.

Bausi, Alessandro, Pier Giorgio Borbone, Françoise Briquel-Chatonnet, Paola Buzi, Jost Gippert, Caroline Macé, Marilena Maniaci, Zisis Melissakis, Laura E. Parodi, and Witold Witakowski, eds. *Comparative Oriental Manuscript Studies: An Introduction*. Hamburg: Tredition, 2015.

Bensly, R. L. *The Epistles of S. Clement to the Corinthians in Syriac: Edited from the Manuscript with Notes*. Cambridge: Cambridge University Press, 1899.

Brock, S. P. "Notes on Some Texts in the Mingana Collection." *Journal of Semitic Studies* 14, no. 2 (1969): 205–16.

Brox, Norbert. *Der Hirt des Hermas*. Kommentar zu den Apostolischen Vätern 7. Göttingen: Vandenhoeck & Ruprecht, 1991.

Burtea, Bogdan. "Interpretatio manichaica am Beispiel des mittelpersischen Turfan-Fragments M 97." *Annals of the Sergiu Al-George Institute* 4/5 (1995–1996 [2002]): 47–67.
Buschmann, Gerd. *Das Martyrium des Polykarp*. Kommentar zu den Apostolischen Vätern 6. Göttingen: Vandenhoeck & Ruprecht, 1998.
Cureton, William. *Corpus Ignatianum: A Complete Collection of the Ignatian Epistles, Genuine, Interpolated, and Spurious*. London: Francis & John Rivington, 1849.
D'Abbadie, Antoine. *Hermae Pastor: Aethiopice Primum Edidit et Aethiopica Latine Vertit Antonius de Abbadie*. Abhandlungen für die Kunde des Morgenlandes 2, no. 1. Leipzig: Brockhaus, 1860.
Drost-Abgarjan, Armenuhi. "Die armenische Version des Polykarp-Martyriums." In *Orientalia Christiana. Festschrift für Hubert Kaufhold zum 70. Geburtstag*, edited by Peter Bruns and Heinz Otto Luthe, 155–67. Eichstätter Beiträge zum Christlichen Orient 3. Wiesbaden: Harrassowitz, 2013.
Ehrman, Bart D., ed. *The Apostolic Fathers I* and *II*. Loeb Classical Library 25. Cambridge, MA: Harvard University Press, 2003.
Erho, Ted. "A Third Ethiopic Witness to the Shepherd of Hermas." *La parola del passato* 67, no. 5 (2012 [2014]): 363–70.
Erho, Ted. "A Fourth Ethiopic Witness to the *Shepherd of Hermas*." In Toca and Batovici, *Caught in Translation*, 241–66.
Friedrich, Michael, and Cosima Schwarke. "Introduction: Manuscripts as Evolving Entities." In *One-Volume Libraries: Composite and Multiple-Text Manuscripts*, edited by Michael Friedrich and Cosima Schwarke, 1–26. Studies in Manuscript Cultures 9. Berlin: De Gruyter, 2016.
Funk, F. X. *Die Echtheit der Ignatianischen Briefe aufs Neue vertheidigt*, 205–12 Tübingen: Verlag der H. Laupp'schen Buchhandlung, 1883.
Gleede, Benjamin. "Epistula ecclesiae Smyrnensis de passione Polycarpi (BHL 6870): Kritische Präliminaredition." *Sacris Erudiri* 59 (2020): 7–35.
Gleede, Benjamin. Parabiblica Latina: *Studien zu den griechisch-lateinischen Übersetzungen parabiblischer Literatur unter besonderer Berücksichtigung der apostolischen Väter*. Supplements to Vigiliae Christianae 137. Leiden/Boston: Brill, 2016.
Hartog, Paul, ed. *Polycarp's* Epistle to the Philippians *and the* Martyrdom of Polycarp: *Introduction, Text, and Commentary*. Oxford Apostolic Fathers. Oxford: Oxford University Press, 2013.
Heer, Joseph Michael. *Die Versio latina des Barnabasbriefes und ihr Verhältnis zur lateinischen Bibel, erstmals untersucht, nebst Ausgabe und Glossar des griechischen und lateinischen Textes*. Freiburg im Breisgau: Herder, 1908.
Holmes, Michael W., ed. *The Apostolic Fathers: Greek Texts and English Translations*. 3rd ed. Grand Rapids, MI: Baker Academic, 2007.
Horner, G. *The Statutes of the Apostles or Canones Ecclesiastici: Edited with Translation and Collation from Ethiopic and Arabic MSS. Also a Translation of the Saidic and Collation of the Bohairic Versions, and Saidic Fragments*. London: Williams & Norgate, 1904.
Hummel, Susanne, Vitagrazia Pisani, and Cristina Vertan. "Multi-level Digital Annotation of Ethiopic Texts." *Comparative Oriental Manuscript Studies Bulletin* 4, no. 1 (2018): 97–106.
Jefford, Clayton N., ed. *The* Epistle to Diognetus *(With the* Fragment of Quadratus*)*. Oxford Apostolic Fathers. Oxford: Oxford University Press, 2013.

Jones, F. Stanley, and Paul A. Mirecki. "Considerations on the Coptic Papyrus of the *Didache* (British Library Oriental Manuscript 9271)." In *The* Didache *in Context: Essays on Its Text, History and Transmission*, edited by C. N. Jefford, 47–87. Supplements to Novum Testamentum 77. Leiden: Brill, 1995.
Khomych, Taras. "'An Early Church Slavonic Translation of the Martyrdom of St. Polycarp': Three Decades Later." *Analecta Bollandiana* 130 (2012): 294–302.
Krause, Thomas, and Amir Zeldes. "ANNIS3: A New Architecture for Generic Corpus Query and Visualization." *Digital Scholarship in the Humanities* 31, no. 1 (2016): 118–39.
Lefort, L.-Th. *Les Pères apostoliques en copte*. CSCO 135/SC 17. Louvain: L. Durbecq, 1952.
Lightfoot, J. B. *The Apostolic Fathers, Part II: S. Ignatius, S. Polycarp*. Vols. 1–3. London: Macmillan, 1889.
Lona, Horacio E. *Der erste Clemensbrief*. Kommentar zu den Apostolischen Vätern 2. Göttingen: Vandenhoeck & Ruprecht, 1998.
Lucchesi, Enzo. "Compléments aux Pères apostoliques en copte." *Analecta Bollandiana* 99 (1981): 395–408.
Mombert, Sarah. "From Books to Collections: Critical Editions of Heterogeneous Documents." In *Digital Critical Editions*, edited by Daniel Apollon, Claire Bélisle, and Philippe Régnier. Topics in the Digital Humanities. Urbana, IL: University of Illinois Press, 2014.
Morin, Germanus. *Sancti Clementis Romani ad Corinthios epistulae versio latina antiquissima*. Anecdota Maredsolana 2. Maredsous: The Editors / Oxford: J. Parker, 1894.
Niederwimmer, Kurt. *Die Didache*. Kommentar zu den Apostolischen Vätern 1. Göttingen: Vandenhoeck & Ruprecht, 1993.
Norelli, Enrico. *Papia di Hierapolis: Esposizione degli oracoli del signore. I frammenti. Introduzione, testo, traduzione e note*. Letture cristiane del primo millennio 36. Milan: Paoline, 2005.
Osiek, Carolyn. *Shepherd of Hermas: A Commentary*. Hermeneia, PA: Fortress Press, 1999.
Outtier, Bernard. "La version géorgienne du Pasteur d'Hermas." *Revue des études géorgiennes et caucasiennes* 6/7 (1990–1991): 211–6.
Pane, Riccardo. "Un'antica traduzione dimenticata: la versione armena delle lettere di S. Ignazio di Antiochia." *Le Muséon* 112 (1999): 47–63.
Peradse, Gregor. "Die 'Lehre der zwölf Apostel' in der georgischen Überlieferung." *Zeitschrift für die neutestamentliche Wissenschaft* 31 (1932): 111–6.
Petermann, Julius Heinrich. *S. Ignatii Patris apostolici quae feruntur Epistolae una cum eiusdem Martyrio: Collatis edd. graecis versionibusque syriaca, armeniaca, latinis*. Leipzig: C.G. Vogelius, 1849.
Pratscher, Wilhelm. *Der zweite Clemensbrief*. Kommentar zu den Apostolischen Vätern 3. Göttingen: Vandenhoeck & Ruprecht, 2007.
Prostmeier, Ferdinand R. *Der Barnabasbrief*, Kommentar zu den Apostolischen Vätern 8. Göttingen: Vandenhoeck & Ruprecht, 1999.
Prostmeier, Ferdinand R. "The Epistle of Barnabas." In *The Apostolic Fathers: An Introduction*, edited by Wilhelm Pratscher, 27–45. Waco, TX: Baylor University Press, 2010.
Rösch, Friedrich. *Bruchstücke des ersten Clemensbriefes nach dem achmimischen Papyrus der Strassburger Universitäts- und Landesbibliothek mit biblischen Texten derselben Handschrift*. Strassburg: Schlesier & Schweikhardt, 1910.
Sailors, T. B. "Quotations of Polycarp's Letter to the Philippians Preserved in Syriac." *The Harp* 27 (2011): 335–42.

Schaefer, Karl T. *S. Clementis Romani Epistula ad Corinthios quae vocatur prima graece et latine*. Bonn: Hanstein, 1941.
Schmidt, Carl. *Erste Clemensbrief in altkoptischer Übersetzung*. Texte und Untersuchungen 32, no. 1. Leipzig: J.C. Hinrichs, 1908.
Schoedel, William R. *Ignatius of Antioch: A Commentary*. Hermeneia; Philadelphia, PA. Fortress Press, 1985.
Schroeder, Caroline T., and Amir Zeldes. Coptic Scriptorium: Digital Research in Coptic Language and Literature, 2013–2017. http://copticscriptorium.org.
Schroeder, Caroline T., and Amir Zeldes. "Raiders of the Lost Corpus." *Digital Humanities Quarterly* 10, no. 2 (2016). http://www.digitalhumanities.org/dhq/vol/10/2/000247/000247.html.
Sundermann, Werner. "The Shepherd of Hermas." *Encyclopaedia Iranica* (2004): 232–34. http://www.iranicaonline.org/articles/hermas-the-shepherd-of.
Toca, Madalina, and Dan Batovici, eds. *Caught in Translation: Studies on Versions of Late Antique Christian Literature*. Texts and Studies in Eastern Christianity 17; Leiden/Boston: Brill, 2020.
Tornau, Christian, and Paolo Cecconi, eds. The Shepherd of Hermas *in Latin: Critical Edition of the Oldest Translation* Vulgata. Texte und Untersuchungen 173. Berlin: De Gruyter, 2014.
Tuckett, Christopher, ed. *2 Clement: Introduction, Text, and Commentary*. Oxford Apostolic Fathers. Oxford: Oxford University Press, 2012.
Vezzoni, Anna, ed. *Il Pastore di Erma: Versione Palatina*. Introduzione di Antonio Carlini. Il nuovo melograno 13. Firenze: Le Lettere, 1994.
Villa, Massimo. "La versione etiopica del Pastore di Erma. Riedizione critica del testo (Visioni e Precetti)." *Comparative Oriental Manuscript Studies Bulletin* 1, no. 2 (2015): 115–18.
Villa, Massimo. *Filologia e linguistica dei testi geʿez di età aksumita. Il Pastore di Erma*. Studi Africanistici/Series Etiopica 10; Napoli: Unior Press, 2019.
Wallace, Daniel B., Brittany C. Burnette, and Terry Darby Moore. *A Reader's Lexicon of the Apostolic Fathers*. Grand Rapids: Kregel Academic, 2013.
Wright, William. "Arabic Extracts from Ignatian Letters." In J. B. Lightfoot, *The Apostolic Fathers, Part II: St. Ignatius, S. Polycarp*, Vol. 3, 299–306. London: Macmillan, 1889.
Wright, William. "The Syriac Remains of S. Ignatius." In *The Apostolic Fathers, Part II: St. Ignatius, S. Polycarp*, Vol. 3, 73–124. London: Macmillan, 1889.
Wright, William. *A Catalogue of the Syriac Manuscripts Preserved in the Library of the University of Cambridge*. Vol. 2. Cambridge: The University Press, 1901.
Zahn, Theodor. "Ignatii et Polycarpi epistolae martyria fragmenta." In *Patrum apostolicorum opera*, f. 2, edited by O. von Gebhardt, Adolf Harnack, and Theodor Zahn, 127–296. Leipzig: Hinrichs, 1876.
Zwierlein, Otto, ed. *Die Urfassungen der Martyria Polycarpi et Pionii und das Corpus Polycarpianum*. Vol 1, *Editiones criticae*. Vol 2, *Textgeschichte und Rekonstruktion. Polykarp, Ignatius und der Redaktor Ps.-Pionius*. Untersuchungen zur antiken Literatur und Geschichte 116, n. 1 and 2. Berlin: Walter de Gruyter, 2014.

Part II: **Words and meanings**

Jeanne-Nicole Mellon Saint-Laurent
Languages, texts, and inscribed objects of early Christianity: a survey of digital resources for students

1 Introduction

To appreciate the idioms and nuances of ancient Christian literature, one must learn the languages in which the early Christians told their stories, wrote their texts, celebrated their liturgies, and inscribed their objects and buildings. Early Christians articulated their theology, narrative, art, biblical commentary, and epigraphic poetry in the languages of Greek, Latin, Syriac, Coptic, Arabic, Armenian, Ethiopic, and Georgian. Thus, studying these tongues is an essential requirement for a student wishing to advance in the field of early Christian studies.

In the past 20 years, scholars have developed databases and digital projects that grant access to a wide range of texts, manuscripts, and inscribed objects from the ancient Christian world. Some of these projects have focused on a single linguistic tradition; others have included several languages; and others still have acted as repositories or hubs for bringing the work of multiple linguistic traditions into a single portal. Students and scholars can use these tools to learn the languages themselves. Scholars of ancient Christianity also have access to digital infrastructures for understanding textual corpora across linguistic traditions. The digital scholarship addressed here is meant to help students recognize the size of different ancient Christian textual corpora in the various languages of the ancient world. It discusses the complexity of the transmission, transcription, translation, and circulation of late ancient Christian stories and treatises onto manuscripts, papyri, and inscriptions. This aim of this article is to familiarize students or beginners with digital humanities resources for their scholarship and research.

2 Clarification of terminology

It is appropriate to clarify some basic terminologies of the digital humanities.
1. Computer languages: A programming language is "a set of instruction or code which tells a computer what it needs to do."[1] Programming languages, however, must be converted into a language that a machine can read (binary language, using 1 and 0). A programmer writes the programming language at a high level; then, that language is converted into something that a machine can read, and the computer performs a task. When the computer must perform more detailed or specific tasks, the programmer writes a script. Scripting languages are therefore a subset of programming languages that (as the name suggests) gives the computer a script to perform. Some examples of programming languages are Java or C++. Some examples of scripting languages are Python and JavaScript.[2]
2. A markup language, however, is distinct from a programming language. Markup languages do not give instructions to a computer. Digital humanists do not need to be fluent in programming languages (although it is useful to have some understanding of how they work). But an understanding of how markup languages work is essential because these are the languages in which data is presented. Indeed, markup languages are presentational languages that "prepare a structure for the data or prepare the look or design of the page."[3] Markup languages put data in the proper format so that a web browser can present them. An example of a markup language would be HTML.
3. XML: XML (eXtensible Markup Language) is a framework for defining markup language that gives rules for encoding documents. It is both human-readable and machine-readable.[4] XML carries data and, more specifically, it shows what kind of data it is (as opposed to HTML, which presents or displays data).[5]
4. Database schema: Since many projects in the digital humanities involve creating databases for scholarly use, it is also appropriate to address what a

---

[1] Anu Upadhyay, "Difference Between Programming, Scripting, and Markup Languages," *GeeksforGeeks*, 6 January 2020, https://www.geeksforgeeks.org/difference-between-programming-scripting-and-markup-languages/.
[2] Ibid.
[3] Ibid.
[4] Shubrodeep Banerjee, "XML: Basics," *GeeksforGeeks*, 6.11.17, https://www.geeksforgeeks.org/xml-basics/.
[5] Ibid.

schema is. A database schema is a visual representation of a database or a set of rules that governs a database.
5. TEI: TEI stands for Text Encoding Initiative. It is a "consortium which collectively develops and maintains a standard for the representation of texts in digital form."[6] The TEI consortium establishes "specify encoding methods for machine-readable texts, chiefly in the humanities, social sciences and linguistics."[7]
6. API: API stands for Application Program Interface. It is the part of a server that receives requests and sends responses.[8]
7. URI: URI stands for Uniform Resource Identifier. It is a string of characters to identify and disambiguate a resource. In a database, each entity has its own URI to identify it as what it is.
8. RDF: RDF (Resource Description Framework) describes resources on the web. It is an infrastructure that "enables the encoding, exchange, and reuse of structured metadata. It is an application of XML that imposes needed structural constraints to provide unambiguous methods of expressing semantics."[9] RDF allows you to describe data in a three-part statement (subject/predicate/object or entity identifier/attribute name/attribute value).
9. SPARQL: SPARQL is the standard query language of the *semantic web*. It is the protocol for linked open data on the web that "enables users to query information from databases or any data source that can be mapped to RDF." It helps users to focus on "what they would like to know instead of how a database is organized."[10]

The projects of the digital humanities that use open access, linked data, and linked open data are beneficial for visualizing relationships among persons, texts, and places from different linguistic heritages, because this scholarly data, when published under an open license, can be accessed and reused in productive ways. Open access involves "the free, immediate, online access to the results of scholarly research, and the right to use and re-use those results as [one]

---

[6] TEI Text Encoding Initiative, https://tei-c.org/.
[7] Ibid.
[8] Petr Gazarov, "What Is an API? In English, Please," *freeCodeCamp.org*, 26 March 2020, https://www.freecodecamp.org/news/what-is-an-api-in-english-please-b880a3214a82/.
[9] Eric Miller, "An Introduction to the Resource Description Framework," *Association for Information Science & Technology* (John Wiley & Sons, 31 January 2005), https://asistdl.onlinelibrary.wiley.com/doi/pdf/10.1002/bult.105.
[10] "What Is SPARQL – Semantic Search Query Language," *Ontotext*, https://www.ontotext.com/knowledgehub/fundamentals/what-is-sparql/.

need[s]."[11] Open access allows scholars to "maximize research investments, increase the exposure and use of published research, facilitate the ability to conduct research across available literature, and enhance the overall advancement of scholarship."[12] Linked data is a crucial pillar of the *web of data* or semantic web, which entails "making links between datasets understandable not only to humans but also to machines."[13] Sir Tim Berners-Lee, an inventor of the World Wide Web, noted in 2006 that building linkable data rests on four principles,[14] and these are found in several of the projects discussed in this article:
1. Use of URIs to identify entities and disambiguate these entities from others
2. Use of HTTP URIs so that the users can look up URIs
3. Use of semantic standard models (like RDF) for data publishing and interchange on the web
4. Inclusion of links to other URIs

Linked open data is a principle that comes from combining the ideas of open access and linked data. It provides for the free and open sharing of data published under an open license. With linked open data, libraries or museums can exchange collections of data and metadata.

Many of the projects discussed in this article are reference hubs that link research together, compiling and classifying core data for texts and inscriptions in languages like Latin, Greek, Syriac, Coptic, and Arabic. Linked open data allows for the free dissemination of data. The creation of linked open digital tools and infrastructure facilitates further research. Scholars who have constructed reference hubs discussed below according to the best practices of linked open data, like Syriaca.org and the Coptic Scriptorium, have identified core entities (people, names, places, and works) and have minted them with stable URIs. Through inserting these URIs into an architecture of linked open data, resources and users are connected to the data that they need.[15]

---

[11] Nick Shockey, "Open Access Week," *International Open Access Week*, http://www.openaccessweek.org/page/about.
[12] Shockey, "Open Access Week."
[13] Ontotext, "What Are Linked Data and Linked Open Data?" https://ontotext.com/knowledgehub/fundamentals/linked-data-linked-open-data/.
[14] Tim Berners-Lee, "Linked Data," *Linked Data – Design Issues*, 2006, https://www.w3.org/DesignIssues/LinkedData.html.
[15] Nathan P. Gibson, "Challenges of Polyvalent Infrastructures: The Case of Syriac Studies and Syriaca.org," Lecture presented at the *Global Philology Open Conference*, Leipzig, Germany, 22 February 2017.

Students today are acclimated to a world of visualized data, and instructors have learned to use digital scholarship in their teaching to enhance student learning. The projects listed below use digital technology to visualize the linguistic maps of the first Christians in stimulating ways, showing relationships among textual literary traditions, performing linguistic analyses of texts, and producing side-by-side translations of ancient texts into modern languages. Such scholarship brings the colors, textures, graffiti, inscriptions, manuscripts, colophons, and even scribes of Christian manuscripts to life.

Familiarity with these projects and facility of how to use them are necessary skills for specialists in ancient Christianity. Yet, the sheer number of databases and reference portals can be daunting. In a blog post from 17 August 2017, digital humanist and classicist Gregory Crane wrote about the challenges facing the next generation of digital humanists who are working to create resources that help students and scholars to internalize an understanding of the languages they study:

> The goal is not to replace learning but to provide a scaffolding whereby we can go from no knowledge to as much internalized understanding as we have the time and determination to acquire. If I were to pick one challenge for the coming ten years, it would be to create the framework to foster such learning. ... There is no greater topic for research in historical languages – a question that is technical, social, and profoundly intellectual, for it challenges us to understand why we care about the past as much as we do – and why we should care even more.[16]

3 Learning the languages and lexicographical tools

Digital technologies and computing linguistics help scholars to hone, improve, and perfect their knowledge of languages of the ancient world. The development of online tutorials in languages like Latin, Greek, Hebrew, Syriac, and Arabic facilitate reading, writing, and even speaking these languages.[17] Lexicographical

---

16 Gregory Crane, "Why We Need User Profiles and a New Perseus," *Perseus Digital Library Updates* (blog), 17.08.17, https://sites.tufts.edu/perseusupdates/2017/08/18/why-we-need-user-profiles-and-a-new-perseus/.
17 See, for example, the Surayt–Aramaic Online program for teaching Syriac managed by an interdisciplinary consortium: Freie Universität Berlin (coordinator), Stockholm's Universitet St Ephrem Syriac Orthodox Monastery (NL), Beth Mardutho Syriac Institute (USA), and Midyat Süryani Cultural Association (Turkey) (http://www.surayt.com/).

aids and analytic tools make the process of translating and interpreting texts more efficient for scholars and students.

The team at Perseids, whose goal is to help students and scholars to create and edit digital projects, provides innovative ways to improve the instruction of Latin and Greek to students. It also gives tutorials on how to train students to encode texts from the ancient world.[18] Perseids (an offshoot of the Perseus Digital Library, discussed below) "provides a platform for creating, publishing, and sharing research data, in the form of textual transcriptions, annotations and analyses."[19] The Perseids project is at the forefront of digital pedagogy for ancient languages. Perseids has lesson plans for introducing students to Greek and Latin and makes these materials available online for free.[20]

For the study of Latin, a good starting point is Latinitium, a repository with links to resources for learning Latin.[21] Latinitium includes links to PDFs of books and grammars as well as links to online libraries of Latin texts, including the Bibliotheca Augustana.[22] The National Archives of the United Kingdom has a website with drills and lessons in beginning[23] and advanced medieval Latin.[24] Digital lexicographical tools make word searches more efficient, like the site entitled glossa: [a Latin dictionary]. Glossa is founded upon the 1879 edition of the Lewis and Short Latin dictionary.[25] Finally, the Latin Lexicon – Numen is a su-

---

[18] Timothy Buckingham, "Teach the Teachers Summer 2017", *Perseids* (blog), 17.03.17, http://sites.tufts.edu/perseids/2017/03/17/teach-the-teachers-summer-2017/.
[19] Bridget Almas, "Perseids: Experimenting with Infrastructure for Creating and Sharing Research Data in the Digital Humanities," *Data Science Journal* 16 (2017), http://dx.doi.org/10.5334/dsj-2017–019.
[20] Gregory Crane and Anna Krohn, eds., "Breaking the Language Barrier," *Perseids*, Tufts University, and the *Perseus Digital Library*, n.d., https://sites.tufts.edu/perseids/breaking-the-language-barrier/.
[21] "Learn Latin: Resources. Subsidia Latine Discentibus," *Latinitium*, https://www.latinitium.com/learn-latin-links/.
[22] *Bibliotheca Augustana*, http://www.hs-augsburg.de/~harsch/augustana.html.
[23] The National Archives, "Latin 1086–1733: An Advanced Practical Online Tutorial," *Beginners' Latin, The National Archives*, 31 March 2007, http://www.nationalarchives.gov.uk/latin/.
[24] The National Archives, "Latin 1086–1733: An Advanced Practical Online Tutorial," *Advanced Latin, The National Archives*, 31 March 2007, http://www.nationalarchives.gov.uk/latin/.
[25] "*Glossa* is a Latin dictionary based on *A Latin Dictionary: Founded on Andrews' Edition of Freund's Latin Dictionary: Revised, Enlarged, and in Great Part Rewritten by Charlton T. Lewis, PhD and Charles Short, LL.D* (commonly referred to as *Lewis and Short*). This work, published in 1879, is now in the public domain. *A Third Way Technologies, Glossa: A Latin Dictionary*, https://orbilius.org/glossa/.

perb site with a dictionary and grammatical tools based upon many different sources.²⁶

Donald Mastronarde has published a first-rate site for the study of ancient Greek entitled AtticGreek.org.²⁷ This site contains free tutorials in Attic Greek that teach the user pronunciation, accentuation, vocabulary, and principal parts.

Classicists at the University of Chicago have constructed Logeion, a lexicographical resource that allows users to look up entries simultaneously in all the dictionaries included in the Perseus Classical collection.²⁸ The scholars and students who constructed Logeion were able to build their site since Perseus shared its data with the creators of Logeion.²⁹

Syriac studies has led the field for innovations of linguistic pedagogy and the computer. Dr George Kiraz, the founder of Beth Mardutho: the Syriac Institute, has spearheaded many of these efforts. He launched Beth Mardutho for the promotion of the study and preservation of Syriac heritage.³⁰ The projects and efforts to bring the Syriac studies community together through digital technology have resulted in several serendipitous projects, most recently the creation of SEDRA, Syriac Electronic Data Research Archive.³¹ SEDRA allows a user to enter a word in Syriac, and then the user can see the definition of that word as it appears in up to five dictionaries. It is an outstanding tool for both word study and linguistic research.

4 Philological and textual projects – corpora

The Perseus Digital Library of Greek and Latin texts,³² housed at Tufts University and edited by Gregory R. Crane, has several modules pertinent for scholars of Christianity. Perseus' Greek and Roman Materials contain Greek and Latin texts with morphological analyses as well as English translations of classical and late antique texts. The collection includes Christian texts by Eusebius of Cae-

---

26 Keith Alexander Woodell, *Numen: The Latin Lexicon*, http://latinlexicon.org/index.php.
27 Donald Mastronarde, "Ancient Greek Tutorials @ AtticGreek.org," *AtticGreek.org*, University of California Press, 2013, http://atticgreek.org/.
28 Gregory Crane, ed., "Perseus Collection Greek and Roman Materials,": *Perseus Digital Library*, n.d., http://www.perseus.tufts.edu/hopper/collection?collection=Perseus%3Acollection%3AGreco-Roman.
29 Helma Dik, *About ΛΟΓΕΙΟΝ*, http://logeion.uchicago.edu/about.html.
30 Beth Mardutho, *The Syriac Institute*, 2018, http://www.bethmardutho.org.
31 "Sedra," *Beth Mardutho: the Syriac Institute*, 2018, http://www.bethmardutho.org.
32 Crane, "Perseus Collection."

sarea, Minucius Felix, Prudentius, and Tertullian, as well as the Latin Vulgate and the Greek New Testament. It is an open-source database. It is arranged in a useful manner with the URIs readily available so that users know how to cite the information accurately and so that other databases can incorporate their data. Also noteworthy is the word study tool. A user can click on any word in the Greek or Latin text, leading the user to a new window with definitions and word morphologies. Perseus has developed the Perseus Catalog "to integrate two complementary kinds of resources. The first is a bibliography of authors and editions produced by and for classicists. The second contains metadata about Greek and Latin authors as they are generally organized in library catalogues."[33]

Corpus Corporum: repositorium operum Latinorum apud universitatem Turicensem[34] is a textual repository of Latin texts. This ongoing meta-repository contains links to Latin texts in TEI from a wide range of sources and projects, including the Patrologia Latina as well as the public domain volumes of the CSEL, the Corpus Scriptorum Ecclesiasticorum Latinorum, with free and accessible XML files of this extensive collection of Latin fathers.[35]

There are many noteworthy projects specific to linguistic analyses of the Bible. The Codex Sinaiticus project is a digital project to conserve, digitize, transcribe, and disseminate the *Codex Sinaiticus*, a manuscript of the Bible from the middle of the 4th century with the earliest complete copy of the Greek New Testament.[36] The Codex itself is of utmost importance not just to biblical studies but also to scholars of the history of the book. This exciting digital project, a partner project of the four institutions that have fragments of this Bible,[37] has united the entire Codex and made it available in digitized form. The careful imaging of this critical manuscript gives unprecedented access to its content, and it is all freely accessible. It is a model of collaborative scholarship through digital humanities.

---

33 Perseus Catalog, "Perseus Catalog," *Perseus Digital Library, Tufts University and the University of Leipzig*, http://catalog.perseus.org/.
34 *Corpus Corporum. Repositorum operum Latinorum apud universitatem Turicensem*, http://www.mlat.uzh.ch/MLS/xanfang.php?corpus=2&lang=0.
35 OpenGreekAndLatin, "Corpus Scriptorum Ecclesiasticorum Latinorum," *Csel-Dev*, n.d., http://opengreekandlatin.github.io/csel-dev/.
36 "Codex Sinaiticus," *Codex Sinaiticus–Home*, https://www.codexsinaiticus.org/en/.
37 Namely, the British Library, the Library of the University of Leipzig, the National Library of Russia in St. Petersburg, and the Holy Library of the God-Trodden Mount Sinai (St. Catherine's). "History of Codex Sinaiticus," *Codex Sinaiticus*, http://www.codexsinaiticus.org/en/codex/history.aspx.

Another unique digital resource for the study of the New Testament is the digital scholarly edition of the Greek New Testament text of Nestle–Aland.[38] This edition contains the text of the Greek New Testament with an apparatus created from 2 to 26 manuscripts that the editors checked against the Nestle–Aland edition.

In Coptic studies, we turn to the Coptic Scriptorium, edited by Caroline Schroeder and Amir Zeldes. The Coptic Scriptorium (*Sahidic Corpus Research: Internet Platform for Interdisciplinary multilayer Method*] is a "platform for interdisciplinary and computational research in texts of the Coptic language."[39] The Coptic Scriptorium contains tools, texts, and resources for Coptic studies, all available for free through open access. There are several modules of the Coptic Scriptorium. The Corpus contains Coptic texts for reading, analysis, and complex searches, and the texts contained in the Coptic Scriptorium have stable URNs (Uniform Resource Numbers). The Scriptorium includes different displays of the Coptic texts as well as tools for word analyses. The open-access format and the project's use of linked open data is exemplary.

Syriaca.org is a research portal for Syriac studies with several modules:[40] a Gazetteer or geographical reference work of all places relevant to Syriac studies,[41] a Biographical Dictionary with a multi-volume guide to persons (including saints and authors) related to Syriac culture and history,[42] a reference guide to Syriac works (New Handbook to Syriac Literature),[43] and a digital prosopography of Syriac Events and Relationships (SPEAR).[44] All core entities have their own URIs so that database editors can link them to other digital resources. Minting URIs results in a more robust research tool. The editors of Syriaca.org built

---

[38] "New Testament Transcripts Prototype," *Scholarly Digital Editions*, http://nttranscripts.uni-muenster.de/.
[39] Caroline T. Schroeder and Amir Zeldes, *Coptic Scriptorium: Digital Research in Coptic Language and Literature*, 2013–2017, http://copticscriptorium.org/.
[40] *Syriaca.org: The Syriac Reference Portal*, http://www.syriaca.org/.
[41] Thomas A. Carlson and David A. Michelson, eds., "The Syriac Gazetteer," *Syriaca.org: The Syriac Reference Portal*, 2014, http://www.syriaca.org/geo/index.html.
[42] David A. Michelson, ed., "Syriac Biographical Dictionary", *Syriaca.org: The Syriac Reference Portal*, http://syriaca.org/persons/index.html. For Syriac saints, see Jeanne-Nicole Mellon Saint-Laurent and David A. Michelson, eds., "Qadishe: A Digital Catalogue of Saints in the Syriac Tradition," *Syriaca.org: The Syriac Reference Portal*, 2016, http://syriaca.org/q/index.html. For Syriac authors, see Nathan P. Gibson and David A. Michelson, eds., "A Guide to Syriac Authors," *Syriaca.org: The Syriac Reference Portal*, 2016, http://syriaca.org/authors/index.html.
[43] Nathan P. Gibson, David A. Michelson, and Jeanne-Nicole Mellon Saint-Laurent, eds., "The New Handbook of Syriac Literature," *Syriaca.org: The Syriac Reference Portal*, https://syriaca.org/nhsl/index.html.
[44] Michelson, "Syriac Biographical Dictionary".

their project upon the best practices in digital humanities and collaboration. The database is freely accessible, open access, and community built. Also, Syriaca.org has partnered in the sharing of data and code with several other digital projects connected to Syriac studies. The Digital Syriac Corpus is a curated digital repository of TEI-encoded texts written in classical Syriac.[45] Users can download individual texts to produce critical editions and research.

It is worth noting here resources available for the transmission of texts from one ancient language to another. The digital humanities are exceptionally well suited for these types of projects. Computerization can help with translation as well as the serialization of word forms. An exemplary project of this type is the Arab and Latin Glossary, based out of the Institute of Philosophy at the Julius-Maximilians-Universität Würzburg, under the direction of Dag Nikolaus Hasse.[46] This project is a digital dictionary of vocabulary used in Arabic–Latin translations of the Middle Ages. The dictionary is easy to use, and one need not even know Arabic to benefit from it. A user simply clicks on a word (Arabic letters transliterated into the Latin alphabet). The dictionary then directs him or her to the Arabic word itself, a definition, and lists of quotations in Latin and Arabic in which the word is used, from authors like Avicenna and Alkindi. What is particularly noteworthy about this database is its relatively modest interface, despite the depth and substantive nature of the resource itself. The project brings awareness of the influence of the Arabic language and culture Latin-speaking countries.

A similar project that works with the transmission of texts from one language to another is the Database of Greek Loan Words in Coptic, hosted at the Egyptological Institute of Leipzig University and funded by the Deutsche Forschungsgemeinschaft.[47] The extraordinarily large corpus of texts in Coptic includes texts both written in Coptic and translated into Coptic. As explained by the editors of the database, Coptic borrowed extensively from the Greek language: "it is no exaggeration to say that the Greek–Egyptian contact is the most broadly attested case of language contact in antiquity."[48] Thus, to handle

---

[45] James E. Walters, *Digital Syriac Corpus*, https://syriaccorpus.org/index.html.
[46] Dag Nikolaus Hasse, ed., "Welcome to the Online Arabic and Latin Glossary," *Arabic and Latin Glossary*, Institute of Philosophy of the Julius-Maximilians-Universität Würzburg, http://www.arabic-latin-glossary.philosophie.uni-wuerzburg.de/.
[47] Stephen Emmel, "Coptic Literature in Byzantine and Early Islamic Egypt," in *Egypt in the Byzantine World: 300–700*, ed. Roger S. Bagnall (New York: Cambridge University Press, 2007): 83–102.
[48] Tonio Sebastian Richter, ed., "Database and Dictionary of Greek Loanwords in Coptic," *DDGLC – Home*, http://research.uni-leipzig.de/ddglc/.

all this linguistic data, this project aims "to produce a systematic, comprehensive and detailed lexicographical compilation and description of Greek loanwords as attested in the entire Coptic corpus throughout all dialects and genres of text."[49] This project records any instance of any borrowing from another language into Coptic. Attestations of words are displayed, and then one sees an English translation of the word as well as grammatical notes. This data is then aggregated according to linguistic "type" in lemmata and sub-lemmata and shows textual and manuscript sources as well as regional dialects. At the time of the writing of this article, in January of 2019, this database was still under construction.

Finally, we turn our attention to the Digital Corpus for Greco–Arabic Studies, a collaborative project between classicists at Harvard and Tufts Universities.[50] This corpus contains an open-access collection of Greek and Arabic philosophical works. While this project does not treat Christian texts directly or exclusively, it is significant as far as the history of the transmission of classical texts into the medieval world. This project took printed editions of Greek–Arabic texts and had them digitized, and then they were tagged in XML. The digital corpus includes a list of texts and authors that can be categorized by language, subject, and text type. Also, a user can search for individual Arabic or Greek phrases within the corpus or within an author or text. The Digital Corpus for Graeco–Arabic Studies is an outstanding research instrument that grants greater access to this corpus of literature and attestations of textual translations and transmission.

5 Christian manuscripts and textual objects

The second part of this article addresses digital projects focused on Christian textual objects. Here we describe some outstanding and exemplary digital scholarship on early Christian and medieval manuscripts, papyri, and epigraphy.

One can find an impressive collection of digitized manuscripts and codices at the website of the British Library.[51] This collection contains almost nine hundred Greek manuscripts, including many early Christian and Byzantine ones, as

---

49 Richter, "Database and Dictionary."
50 Gregory Crane, Mark Schiefsky, and Uwe Vagelpohl, eds., "A Digital Corpus for Graeco–Arabic Studies," *Texts | Digital Corpus for Graeco–Arabic Studies: The Andrew Mellon Foundation*, Harvard University, and Tufts University, 2020, https://www.graeco-arabic-studies.org/texts.html.
51 For a link to Greek manuscripts of the British Library's collection, see here: "Greek Manuscripts," *British Library Website*, 2 February 2015, https://www.bl.uk/collection-guides/greek-manuscripts.

well as papyri. Biblical scholars, as well as historians of Christianity, find many resources in the site of the British Library, including "two of the three oldest Greek Bibles, the remains of some 227 manuscripts of the Greek New Testament, and around 50 Greek codices dating from the first millennium."[52] Scholars have not only digitized much of the Greek manuscript collection but have also provided scholarship to introduce students and researchers to the treasures of the collection. Kathleen Maxwell describes the collection's Greek illuminated Gospels, Gospel manuscripts, and other manuscripts with Gospel readings from the lectionary – their place in the Orthodox liturgy, their importance for art historians and scholars of liturgy, and the system of pre-modern biblical concordances or canon tables contained in these Gospels. All this scholarship is beautifully displayed and available to users of the database, with elegant images of these treasures.[53] Other articles of note include the fascinating study by Dr. Peter Toth exploring the British Library's collection of multilingual manuscripts from Byzantium.[54] Finally, the collection of the British Library is essential for scholars of the Greek Old Testament, the Septuagint.[55]

Another essential database for manuscripts is Pinakes, a database of Greek manuscripts produced by the Greek section of the Institute for Research and History of Texts.[56] Pinakes is named after the first catalogue of Greek writers of the library of Alexandria that Callimachus of Cyrene compiled.[57] It is a database of Greek manuscripts that scholars created through the examination of printed manuscript catalogues from a large number of libraries. When Pinakes was put online in 2008, it contained information of 13,000 works from 40,000 manuscripts preserved from 1,300 libraries worldwide. The information in the database is intentionally concise, with authors and works contained in the manuscripts along with some historical data.

A similar effort to digitize and encode bibliographic information on Syriac manuscripts is E-ktobe, a database of Syriac manuscripts.[58] Scholars have col-

---

52 "Greek Manuscripts," *British Library Website*.
53 Kathleen Maxwell, "Illuminated Byzantine Gospels," *British Library Website*, 6 July 2016, https://www.bl.uk/greek-manuscripts/articles/illuminated-byzantine-gospels.
54 Peter Toth, "Multilingualism in Greek Manuscripts," *British Library Website*, 11 July 2016, https://www.bl.uk/greek-manuscripts/articles/multilingualism-in-greek-manuscripts.
55 Peter Toth, "Manuscripts of the Greek Old Testament," *British Library Website*, 11 July 2016, https://www.bl.uk/greek-manuscripts/articles/manuscripts-of-the-greek-old-testament.
56 *Pinakes | Πίνακες: Textes et manuscrits grecs*, Institut de recherche et d'histoire des textes, 2016, http://pinakes.irht.cnrs.fr/.
57 "Pinakes | Πίνακες – Présentation," *Pinakes | Πίνακες: Textes et manuscrits grecs*, Institut de recherche et d'histoire des textes, 2016, http://pinakes.irht.cnrs.fr/presentation.html.
58 *E-Ktobe: Manuscrits Syriaques*, http://syriac.msscatalog.org/.

lected information on texts, physical characteristics, colophons, and notes of Syriac manuscripts. The team of Syriacists constructing this database, led by Drs. André Binggeli and Muriel Debié, has garnered information from some of the world's most important manuscript collections, including those from the libraries of Paris and Charfet, as well as Syriac hagiographical collections from the Vatican, London, and Damascus.

The Hill Museum and Manuscript Library (HMML) at St. John's University in Collegeville, Minnesota, is performing some of the world's most valuable digital work on Christian manuscripts. HMML has nearly 100,000 manuscripts in its Western European collection.[59] HMML's collection of manuscripts is also noteworthy for its collection of manuscripts from Malta, with collections representative of the written culture of Malta and the sovereign military order of Saint John of Jerusalem.[60] HMML has an extensive collection of images of manuscripts from the Arabic, Armenian, Coptic, Ge'ez (Ethiopic), Church Slavonic, and Syriac traditions:[61] "Partnerships with some 70 libraries have now created a unique resource for the study of Eastern Christianity in its historic cradle and in areas of its early expansion: Egypt, India, Iraq, Jerusalem, Lebanon, Syria, and Turkey."

Many of these manuscripts are now available for study through vHMML, a database with a Reading Room. vHMML provides access to thousands of items in the catalogue of HMML. Access to vHMML is free, but users must be registered. Scholars can search for manuscripts by country of origin, keyword, language, and date. The catalogue gives the country and city of the manuscript's origin, the shelf-mark of the manuscript, number of pages, special features, language, size, and title of the work it contains. Many of the manuscripts remain in situ, but through vHMML scholars have access to their contents. This work of protecting cultural heritage and providing access to the contents of the manuscripts themselves exemplifies the strides that digital humanities make both for scholars and cultural traditions threatened by war and political instability.

Syriaca.org is also using linked open data to create a union catalogue of Syriac manuscripts and TEI XML standards for its cataloguing. Each manuscript contains its own unique URI so that databases at other libraries can access the information contained in the record. At present, Syriaca.org has completed

---

59 "Western European Manuscripts," *Hill Museum and Manuscript Library*, St. John's University, 2018, https://hmml.org/collections/western-european/.
60 "Malta Study Center," *Hill Museum & Manuscript Library*, St. John's University, 2018, https://hmml.org/collections/malta/.
61 "Eastern Christian Manuscripts," *Hill Museum and Manuscript Library*, 2018, https://hmml.org/collections/eastern-christian/.

the encoding of the catalogue of William Wright: A Digital Catalogue of Syriac Manuscripts of the British Library.[62] The model for this linked open union catalogue was that of Fihrist, also done in TEI XML, which aims to become a union catalogue for all manuscripts in the Arabic script.[63]

Another relevant database for the study of Christian manuscripts in Italy is the MANUS database.[64] MANUS is a digital database with "catalogue descriptions and digital images of manuscripts, private papers and archives held by Italian public, private and ecclesiastical libraries."[65] MANUS is primarily concerned with the cataloguing of Latin manuscripts dating from the medieval period. Users can search the names of scribes, illustrators, and owners of these manuscripts. This aggregated data displays interesting historical information. For instance, one learns that both manuscripts contained the works of Dante Alighieri[66] as well as manuscripts owned by his family. The descriptions of the manuscripts are robust, with data on content, dates, condition, history, possessors, copyists, and scribes.

The meta-database Trismegistos gives information about inscribed texts on objects: inscriptions, manuscripts on parchment, or papyrus. Each text has its own unique and stable ID to which one can link (a Trismegistos number: www.trismegistos.org/text/1234). The database has an outstanding section on languages and scripts.[67] This list elucidates the sheer breadth of languages spoken by ancient and medieval Christians, and it also charts the full range of materials and objects onto which they inscribed their texts. Thanks to Trismegistos, the scholar or student can research data on objects with inscriptions in the following languages: Caucasian Albanian (records from the Caucasian Albanian palimpsests of the New Testament and Gospel Lectionaries found in St. Catherine's Monastery on Mt. Sinai),[68] the Southern Semitic languages of the South

---

62 See https://archive.org/details/catalogueofsyria03brituoft.
63 "Fihrist," *Fihrist – Home*, Fihrist, 2018, www.fihrist.org.uk/home.
64 *Manus Online*, Istituto Centrale per il Catalogo Unico, 19 December 2017, https://manus.iccu.sbn.it/.
65 "Census of Manuscripts Held by Italian Libraries," *Manus Online*, Istituto Centrale per il Catalogo Unico, https://manus.iccu.sbn.it//index.php?lang=en.
66 Gennaro Ferrante, ed., "Census and Analysis of the Earliest Dante Iconography (14th–15th Centuries)," *Illuminated Dante Project*, Compagnia San Paolo, http://www.dante.unina.it/public/frontend.
67 "Languages and Scripts of the Ancient World (under Construction)," *Trismegistos*, http://www.trismegistos.org/about_languages.php.
68 "The Caucasian Albanian Manuscripts of Mt. Sinai 1 p. 25–38 & III.2–21 (Gippert, Jost / Schulze, Wolfgang / Aleksidze, Zaza / Mahé, J.-P.) + The Caucasian Albanian Manuscripts of

Arabian peninsula (with linked data from DASI or the Digital Archive for the Study of Pre-Islamic Arabian Inscriptions),[69] Arabic (linked to the Arabic Papyrology Database, with records of Arabic documents written on Arabic parchment, papyrus, or paper),[70] and Aramaic texts from Egypt, Armenian, and Brittonic. Trismegistos has records for over 17,000 Coptic Texts, Ethiopic texts from Axum, inscriptions in Georgian (linked to the Epigraphic Corpus of Georgia),[71] Greek manuscripts and papyri up to the year 800 (over 98,000 records), and Hebrew inscriptions from Egypt. Trismegistos links to the Inscriptions of Israel/Palestine project, directed by Michael Satlow, which contains approximately 15,000 published inscriptions from Israel/Palestine from 500 BC to 614 CE. It offers images and contextualization of these inscriptions, as well as some translations. An example of a Christian inscription from a church complex in Bethlehem (dating between 300 and 700 CE), for instance, contains a prayer for the priest, pilgrims, and benefactors of their sacred site.[72] Trismegistos has over 200,000 texts in Latin up to the year 800 CE, from manuscripts to papyri and over 800 Syriac texts in its database. As of January 2020, however, parts of Trismegistos are available to paid subscribers only.[73]

Papyri.info is a research portal for papyrological studies. The Papyrological Navigator provides a way to search and browse contents from several databases with papyrological information: Advanced Papyrological Information System, the Duke Databank of Documentary Papyri, Heidelberger Gesamtverzeichnis der grieschischen Papyrusurkunden Ägyptens, and Bibliographie Papyrologique.[74] A user can search through the papyri documented in all these databases, retrieve results, and search for content in ancient languages or modern translations. All papyri have been assigned a unique identifier or URI by the Trismegis-

---

Mt. Sinai 2 V.1–119 (Gippert, Jost / Schulze, Wolfgang / Aleksidze, Zaza / Mahé, J.-P.)," *Trismegistos*, 15 June 2020, http://www.trismegistos.org/text/220519.
69 Alessandra Avanzini, ed., "DASI," *DASI: Digital Archive for the Study of Pre-Islamic Arabian Inscriptions – Home*, Università degli studi di Pisa, 2013, http://dasi.cnr.it/.
70 Andreas Kaplony, ed., "The Arabic Papyrology Database," *APD – The Arabic Papyrology Database*, http://www.apd.gwi.uni-muenchen.de:8080/apd/project.jsp.
71 Tamar Kalkhitashvili and Eka Kvirkvelia, "Epigraphic Corpus of Georgia," *Epigraphic Corpus of Georgia*, the Institute of Linguistic Research, Ilia State University, https://www.eagle-network.eu/wp-content/gallery/digital-poster-exhibition-rome/img_epigraphic-corpus-of-georgia.jpg.
72 Michael Satlow, ed., "Inscriptions of Israel/Palestine," *Brown Library Website*, Goldhirsh–Yellin Foundation and Brown University, https://library.brown.edu/iip/viewinscr/abur0001/.
73 "What Changes on 1 January 2020?" *Trismegistos*, last updated 22 June 2020, https://www.trismegistos.org/keeptrismegistosalive_whatchanges.php.
74 *Papyri.info*, The Duke Collaboratory for Classics Computing & the Institute for the Study of the Ancient World, http://papyri.info/.

tos portal described above.⁷⁵ The records give the name or title of the papyrus, the places of publication, provenance, material, and date, and links to images when they exist.

This remarkable resource makes a large body of material available to scholars, and some of its components are free to use. To give an example of how one might navigate its contents, a user looking for hagiographical data can run a search for the term "saint." He or she would then find a Christian liturgical calendar in a papyrus from the 7th century CE, with the feast days of Christian saints like Saints Menas and Saint Jeremiah, along with an image of the document. The records have URIs in Trismegistos⁷⁶ and papyri.info.⁷⁷ Images are also included and linked where possible.⁷⁸

6 Use and pedagogy

The study of ancient languages like Latin, Greek, Syriac, Coptic, Ethiopic, Armenian, Georgian, and Arabic gives scholars access to the texts and inscribed objects of the ancient Church. In this article, I have enumerated the scope and contents of some digital projects that scholars of the early and medieval Church should know, use, and help to improve. These resources introduce users to a vast body of texts and collections of objects and manuscripts in many different languages. It should be clear that there is still much work to be done in mining these databases for the treasures that they contain.

The *Instrumenta Studiorum* or tools of the trade for scholars of early Christianity have changed dramatically in the past 20 years. Indeed, the computational turn has arrived as researchers and students are increasingly dependent on

---

75 Mark Depauw, ed., "Trismegistos," *Trismegistos*, http://www.trismegistos.org/. See also Mark Depauw and Tom Gheldof, "Trismegistos: An Interdisciplinary Platform for Ancient World Texts and Related Information," Paper presented at the 17th International Conference on Theory and Practice of Digital Libraries, Valletta, Malta, 22–26 September 2013, in *Theory and Practice of Digital Libraries – TPDL 2013 Selected Workshops*, ed. Łukasz Bolikowski et al., Communications in Computer and Information Science 415 (Cham: Springer, 2014): 40–52.
76 "P. Gen. 4 170 (Gaffino Moeri, Sarah / Poget, Noemi)," *Trismegistos*, http://www.trismegistos.org/text/129793.
77 "P.gen.4.170 = HGV P.Gen. 4 170 = Trismegistos 129793," *Papyri.info*, http://papyri.info/ddbdp/p.gen;4;170.
78 Paul Schubert, *Geneva Papyrus 496. Papyrus De La Bibliothèque De Genève*, Bibliothèque de Genève, http://www.ville-ge.ch/musinfo/imageZoom/?iip=bgeiip/papyrus/pgen496-ri.ptif.

computers and digital technology to do their research.⁷⁹ Students and scholars must still learn ancient languages to read and translate texts and to study the distinct nature of texts found in inscriptions, manuscripts, or papyri. Yet now, digital projects, particularly those constructed according to linked and open data structures, help us to organize and connect texts and objects of the ancient Christian world to the places, regions, and traditions that made them. If one wishes to perform a diachronic study of the Christian traditions from a specific location, for instance, she now has many portals through which to begin her research. A scholar can learn about the persons, stories, treatises, events, and objects that comprised an area's Christian patrimony, from Georgia, to Mesopotamia, to Constantinople, to Rome, and as far as the Emerald Isle. She can internalize and practice the languages of these regions. We should no longer, therefore, classify ourselves as scholars of "text," "manuscript," or "object." The scholarly tools of the digital humanities help scholars of early Christianity to incorporate all these subspecialties into our research and pedagogy. I have only included projects here that users can access for free (no subscription, no paywall). For the sake of clarity, I have also repeated projects mentioned in the body of the article.

7 Select digital projects for scholars of early Christianity

1. Arabic and Latin Glossary, https://algloss.de.dariah.eu/
2. Ancient Greek Tutorials, http://atticgreek.org/
3. Beth Mardutho: The Syriac Institute, http://www.bethmardutho.org
4. Bibliographia Iuris Synodalis Antiqui, https://www.ktf.uni-bonn.de/Einrichtungen/institut-fur-kirchengeschichte/alte-kirchengeschichte-und-patrologie/bisa-deutsch/
5. Bibliographical Information Base in Patristics (BIBP), http://www4.bibl.ulaval.ca/bd/bibp/english.html – online database of patristic literature
6. BiblIndex, http://www.biblindex.mom.fr/ – an index of Biblical references found in Christian literature
7. Bibliographies for Theology, http://moses.creighton.edu/JRS/toc/bibliographies.html

---

79 David M. Berry, "The Computational Turn: Thinking about the Digital Humanities," *Culture Machine* 12 (2011): 1–22, http://sro.sussex.ac.uk/id/eprint/49813/.

8. Clavis Patrum Copticorum, http://www.cmcl.it/~cmcl/chiam_clavis.html – an index of authors and works in the Coptic language
9. Codex Sinaiticus Project, https://www.codexsinaiticus.org/en/
10. Comprehensive Bibliography of Syriac Christianity, http://www.csc.org.il/db/db.aspx?db=SB
11. Coptic Scriptorium, https://copticscriptorium.org/ – tools, texts, and resources for Coptic studies
12. Corpus Corporum: repositorium operum Latinorum apud universitatem Turicensem, http://www.mlat.uzh.ch/MLS/xanfang.php?corpus=2&lang=0
13. Database of Greek Loan Words in Coptic, http://research.uni-leipzig.de/ddglc/
14. Digital Archive for the Study of Pre-Islamic Arabian Inscriptions, http://dasi.cnr.it/
15. Digital Corpus for Greco–Arabic Studies, https://www.graeco-arabic-studies.org/texts.html.
16. De Imperatoribus Romanis: An Online Encyclopedia of Roman Rulers and Their Families, http://www.roman-emperors.org/ – encyclopedia on Roman emperors through the Byzantine period
17. Digital Syriac Corpus, https://syriaccorpus.org/index.html – curated digital repository of TEI-encoded texts written in classical Syriac
18. E-ktobe, http://syriac.msscatalog.org/ – a database of Syriac manuscripts
19. Fourth Century Christianity, https://www.fourthcentury.com/ – tools and texts for the study of 4th-century Christianity
20. Greek New Testament, http://nttranscripts.uni-muenster.de/
21. Hill Museum and Manuscript Library (HMML), https://hmml.org/
22. Inscriptions of Israel/Palestine, https://library.brown.edu/iip/index/
23. Internet History Sourcebook Projects, https://sourcebooks.fordham.edu/index.asp
24. Latinitium, https://www.latinitium.com/learn-latin-links/ – a hub for studying Latin
25. Logeion, http://www.perseus.tufts.edu/hopper/collection?collection=Perseus%3Acollection%3AGreco-Roman
26. MANUS Database of Manuscripts, https://manus.iccu.sbn.it/
27. Manuscripts and Resources of the British Library, https://www.bl.uk/collection-guides/greek-manuscripts
28. The Latin Lexicon – Numen, https://latinlexicon.org/
29. National Archives of the United Kingdom, http://www.nationalarchives.gov.uk/latin/
30. Papyri.info, http://papyri.info/
31. Patrologia Latina, http://patristica.net/latina/

32. Perseids Project, https://www.perseids.org/ – supports access to scholarship in classics for students and members of the public at all levels of competence; included the Perseids Platform (production of a data-driven edition of ancient documents), digital editions, and library tools.
33. Perseus Digital Library of Greek and Latin Texts, https://www.perseus.tufts.edu/hopper/
34. Pinakes: Greek Manuscript Catalogue, http://pinakes.irht.cnrs.fr/presentation.html
35. SEDRA: Syriac Electronic Data Research Archive, https://sedra.bethmardutho.org/ – linguistic and literary database of the Syriac language and literature
36. Surayt–Aramaic Online Project, http://www.surayt.com/
37. Sources littéraires: Auteurs chrétiens, http://bcs.fltr.ucl.ac.be/SLChr.html
38. Syriaca.org, http://syriaca.org/ – a research portal for the study of Syriac Christianity.
39. Trismegistos: Interdisciplinary Portal of the Ancient World, https://www.trismegistos.org/index.php

8 Bibliography

Almas, Bridget. "Perseids: Experimenting with Infrastructure for Creating and Sharing Research Data in the Digital Humanities." *Data Science Journal* 16 (2017). http://dx.doi.org/10.5334/dsj-2017–019.

Avanzini, Alessandra, ed. "DASI." *DASI: Digital Archive for the Study of Pre-Islamic Arabian Inscriptions – Home*. Università degli studi di Pisa, 2013. http://dasi.cnr.it/.

Banerjee, Shubrodeep. "XML: Basics." *GeeksforGeeks*, 6 November 2017. https://www.geeksforgeeks.org/xml-basics/.

Freie Universität Berlin et al. "Start Learning Surayt." *Surayt-Aramaic Online*, 2017. http://www.surayt.com.

Berners-Lee, Tim. "Linked Data." *Linked Data – Design Issues*, 2006. https://www.w3.org/DesignIssues/LinkedData.html.

Berry, David M. "The Computational Turn: Thinking about the Digital Humanities." *Culture Machine* 12 (2011): 1–22. http://sro.sussex.ac.uk/id/eprint/49813/.

Beth Mardutho. *The Syriac Institute*, 2018. http://www.bethmardutho.org.

Bibliotheca Augustana. https://www.hs-augsburg.de/~harsch/augustana.html.

Buckingham, Timothy, "Teach the Teachers Summer 2017", *Perseids* (blog), 17.03.17, http://sites.tufts.edu/perseids/2017/03/17/teach-the-teachers-summer-2017/.

Carlson, Thomas A., and David A. Michelson, eds. "The Syriac Gazetteer." *Syriaca.org: The Syriac Reference Portal*, 2014. http://www.syriaca.org/geo/index.html.

"The Caucasian Albanian Manuscripts of Mt. Sinai 1 p. 25–38 & III.2–21 (Gippert, Jost / Schulze, Wolfgang / Aleksidze, Zaza / Mahé, J.-P.) + The Caucasian Albanian

Manuscripts of Mt. Sinai 2 V.1–119 (Gippert, Jost / Schulze, Wolfgang / Aleksidze, Zaza / Mahé, J.-P.)." *Trismegistos*, 15 June 2020. http://www.trismegistos.org/text/220519.
"Census of Manuscripts Held by Italian Libraries." *Manus Online*. Istituto Centrale per il Catalogo Unico. https://manus.iccu.sbn.it//index.php?lang=en.
"Codex Sinaiticus." *Codex Sinaiticus – Home*. https://www.codexsinaiticus.org/en/.
Crane, Gregory. "Why We Need User Profiles and a New Perseus." *Perseus Digital Library Updates* (blog), 17 August 2017. https://sites.tufts.edu/perseusupdates/2017/08/18/why-we-need-user-profiles-and-a-new-perseus/.
Crane, Gregory, ed. "Perseus Collection Greek and Roman Materials." *Greek and Roman Materials: Perseus Digital Library*, n.d. http://www.perseus.tufts.edu/hopper/collection?collection=Perseus%3Acollection%3AGreco-Roman.
Crane, Gregory, and Anna Krohn, eds. "Breaking the Language Barrier." *Perseids*, Tufts University, and the Perseus Digital Library, n.d. https://sites.tufts.edu/perseids/breaking-the-language-barrier/.
Crane, Gregory, Mark Schiefsky, and Uwe Vagelpohl, eds. "A Digital Corpus for Graeco–Arabic Studies." *Texts | Digital Corpus for Graeco–Arabic Studies: The Andrew Mellon Foundation*, Harvard University, and Tufts University, 2020. https://www.graeco-arabic-studies.org/texts.html.
Depauw, Mark, ed. "Trismegistos." *Trismegistos*. http://www.trismegistos.org/.
Depauw, Mark, and Tom Gheldof. "Trismegistos: An Interdisciplinary Platform for Ancient World Texts and Related Information." Paper presented at the *17th International Conference on Theory and Practice of Digital Libraries*, Valletta, Malta, 22–26 September 2013. In *Theory and Practice of Digital Libraries – TPDL 2013 Selected Workshops*, edited by Łukasz Bolikowski, Vittore Casarosa, Paula Goodale, Nikos Houssos, Paolo Manghi, and Jochen Schirrwagen, 40–52. Communications in Computer and Information Science 415. Cham: Springer, 2014.
Dik, Helma. *About ΛΟΓΕΙΟΝ*. http://logeion.uchicago.edu/about.html.
"Eastern Christian Manuscripts." *Hill Museum and Manuscript Library*, 2018. https://hmml.org/collections/eastern-christian/.
E-Ktobe: Manuscrits Syriaques. http://syriac.msscatalog.org/.
Emmel, Stephen. "Coptic Literature in Byzantine and Early Islamic Egypt." In *Egypt in the Byzantine World: 300–700*, edited by Roger S. Bagnall, 83–102. New York: Cambridge University Press, 2007.
Ferrante, Gennaro, ed. "Census and Analysis of the Earliest Dante Iconography (14th–15th Centuries)." *Illuminated Dante Project*. Compagnia San Paolo. http://www.dante.unina.it/public/frontend.
"Fihrist." *Fihrist – Home*. Fihrist, 2018. www.fihrist.org.uk/home.
Gazarov, Petr. "What Is an API? In English, Please." *freeCodeCamp.org*, 26 March 2020. https://www.freecodecamp.org/news/what-is-an-api-in-english-please-b880a3214a82/.
Gibson, Nathan P. "Challenges of Polyvalent Infrastructures: The Case of Syriac Studies and Syriaca.org." Lecture presented at the *Global Philology Open Conference*, Leipzig, Germany, 22 February 2017.
Gibson, Nathan P., and David A. Michelson, eds. "A Guide to Syriac Authors." *Syriaca.org: The Syriac Reference Portal*, 2016. http://syriaca.org/authors/index.html.

Gibson, Nathan P., David A. Michelson, and Jeanne-Nicole Mellon Saint-Laurent, eds. "The New Handbook of Syriac Literature." *Syriaca.org: The Syriac Reference Portal*. http://wwwb.library.vanderbilt.edu/nhsl/index.html.
"Greek Manuscripts." *British Library Website*, 2 February 2015. https://www.bl.uk/collection-guides/greek-manuscripts.
Hasse, Dag Nikolaus, ed. "Welcome to the Online Arabic and Latin Glossary." https://hmml.org/collections/malta/. http://www.arabic-latin-glossary.philosophie.uni-wuerzburg.de/.
"History of Codex Sinaiticus." *Codex Sinaiticus*. http://www.codexsinaiticus.org/en/codex/history.aspx.
Kalkhitashvili, Tamar, and Eka Kvirkvelia. "Epigraphic Corpus of Georgia." *Epigraphic Corpus of Georgia. The Institute of Linguistic Research*, Ilia State University. https://www.eagle-network.eu/wp-content/gallery/digital-poster-exhibition-rome/img_epigraphic-corpus-of-georgia.jpg.
Kaplony, Andreas, ed. "The Arabic Papyrology Database." *APD – The Arabic Papyrology Database*. http://www.apd.gwi.uni-muenchen.de:8080/apd/project.jsp.
"Languages and Scripts of the Ancient World (under Construction)." *Trismegistos*. http://www.trismegistos.org/about_languages.php.
"Learn Latin: Resources. Subsidia Latine Discentibus." *Latinitium*. https://www.latinitium.com/learn-latin-links/.
"Malta Study Center." *Hill Museum & Manuscript Library*. St. John's University, 2018. https://hmml.org/collections/malta/.
Manus Online. Istituto Centrale per il Catalogo Unico, 19 December 2017. https://manus.iccu.sbn.it/.
Mastronarde, Donald. "Ancient Greek Tutorials @ AtticGreek.org." *AtticGreek.org*. University of California Press, 2013. http://atticgreek.org/.
Maxwell, Kathleen. "Illuminated Byzantine Gospels." *British Library Website*, 6 July 2016. https://www.bl.uk/greek-manuscripts/articles/illuminated-byzantine-gospels.
Michelson, David A., ed. "Syriac Biographical Dictionary". *Syriaca.org: The Syriac Reference Portal*. http://syriaca.org/persons/index.html.
Miller, Eric. "An Introduction to the Resource Description Framework." *Association for Information Science & Technology*. John Wiley & Sons, 31 January 2005. https://asistdl.onlinelibrary.wiley.com/doi/pdf/10.1002/bult.105.
The National Archives. "Latin 1086–1733: An Advanced Practical Online Tutorial." *Beginners' Latin. The National Archives*, 31 March 2007. http://www.nationalarchives.gov.uk/latin/.
The National Archives. "Latin 1086–1733: An Advanced Practical Online Tutorial." *Advanced Latin. The National Archives*, 31 March 2007. http://www.nationalarchives.gov.uk/latin/.
"New Testament Transcripts Prototype." *Scholarly Digital Editions*. http://nttranscripts.uni-muenster.de/.
Oaktree Software. "Accordance Bible Software." *Accordance Bible*. https://www.accordancebible.com/.
Ontotext. "What Are Linked Data and Linked Open Data?" https://ontotext.com/knowledgehub/fundamentals/linked-data-linked-open-data/.
OpenGreekAndLatin. "Corpus Scriptorum Ecclesiasticorum Latinorum." *CSEL-Dev*, n.d. http://opengreekandlatin.github.io/csel-dev/.

"P. Gen. 4 170 (Gaffino Moeri, Sarah / Poget, Noemi)." *Trismegistos*. http://www.trismegistos.org/text/129793.

"P.gen.4.170 = HGV P.Gen. 4 170 = Trismegistos 129793." *Papyri.info*. http://papyri.info/ddbdp/p.gen;4;170.

Papyri.info. *The Duke Collaboratory for Classics Computing & the Institute for the Study of the Ancient World*. http://papyri.info/.

"Patrologia Latina." *Mlat.uzh.ch. Corpus Corporum*. 23 January 2019. http://www.mlat.uzh.ch/MLS/xanfang.php?corpus=2&lang=0.

Perseus Catalog. "Perseus Catalog." *The Perseus Digital Library*. Tufts University and the University of Leipzig. http://catalog.perseus.org/.

"Pinakes | Πίνακες – Présentation." Pinakes | Πίνακες: Textes et manuscrits grecs. Institut de recherche et d'histoire des textes, 2016. http://pinakes.irht.cnrs.fr/presentation.html.

Pinakes | Πίνακες: Textes et manuscrits grecs. Institut de recherche et d'histoire des textes, 2016. http://pinakes.irht.cnrs.fr/.

Richter, Tonio Sebastian, ed. "Database and Dictionary of Greek Loanwords in Coptic." *DDGLC – Home*. http://research.uni-leipzig.de/ddglc/.

Saint-Laurent, Jeanne-Nicole Mellon, and David A. Michelson, eds. "Qadishe: A Digital Catalogue of Saints in the Syriac Tradition." *Syriaca.org: The Syriac Reference Portal*, 2016. http://syriaca.org/q/index.html.

Satlow, Michael, ed. "Inscriptions of Israel/Palestine." *Goldhirsh–Yellin Foundation and Brown University*. http://library.brown.edu/cds/projects/iip/viewinscr/abur0001/.

Schroeder, Caroline T., and Amir Zeldes. *Coptic Scriptorium: Digital Research in Coptic Language and Literature*, 2013–2017. http://copticscriptorium.org.

Schubert, Paul. *Geneva Papyrus 496. Papyrus De La Bibliothèque De Genève*. Bibliothèque de Genève. http://www.ville-ge.ch/musinfo/imageZoom/?iip=bgeiip/papyrus/pgen496-ri.ptif.

"Sedra." *Beth Mardutho: the Syriac Institute*, 2018. https://sedra.bethmardutho.org.

Shockey, Nick. "Open Access Week." *International Open Access Week*. http://www.openaccessweek.org/page/about.

Syriaca.org: The Syriac Reference Portal. http://www.syriaca.org/.

TEI Text Encoding Initiative. https://tei-c.org/.

TLG. "The History of the TLG." *Thesaurus Linguae Graecae: A Digital Library of Greek Literature*. http://stephanus.tlg.uci.edu/history.php.

TLG. "Home." Thesaurus Linguae Graecae: A Digital Library of Greek Literature. http://stephanus.tlg.uci.edu/.

A Third Way Technologies. Glossa: A Latin Dictionary. https://orbilius.org/glossa/.

Tombeur, Paul, ed. Library of Latin Texts – Series A; Database for the Western Latin Tradition, Users' Guide 2017. *Brepols Publishers*, 2017. http://www.brepols.net/Pages/BrowseBySeries.aspx?TreeSeries=LLT-O.

Toth, Peter. "Manuscripts of the Greek Old Testament." *British Library Website*, 11 July 2016. https://www.bl.uk/greek-manuscripts/articles/manuscripts-of-the-greek-old-testament.

Toth, Peter. "Multilingualism in Greek Manuscripts." *British Library Website*, 11 July 2016. https://www.bl.uk/greek-manuscripts/articles/multilingualism-in-greek-manuscripts.

Upadhyay, Anu. "Difference Between Programming, Scripting, and Markup Languages." *GeeksforGeeks*, 6 January 2020. https://www.geeksforgeeks.org/difference-between-programming-scripting-and-markup-languages/.

Walters, James E. *Digital Syriac Corpus*. https://syriaccorpus.org/index.html.
"Western European Manuscripts." *Hill Museum and Manuscript Library*. St. John's University, 2018. https://hmml.org/collections/western-european/.
"What Is SPARQL – Semantic Search Query Language." *Ontotext*. https://www.ontotext.com/knowledgehub/fundamentals/what-is-sparql/.
Woodell, Keith Alexander. *Numen: The Latin Lexicon*. http://latinlexicon.org/index.php.

Mathias Coeckelbergs

Between statistics and hermeneutics: the interplay between digital and traditional methods in Hebrew linguistics as evidenced from the study of *hapax legomena*

1 Introduction

This chapter seeks to reflect on the identity of digital humanities from a linguistic point of view. Contemporary discussions on digital humanities and its future revolve around the problem of how to incorporate new methods, statistical and algorithmic, into research fields historically built up without such intention.[1] Often this creates divisions between researchers as to the importance attached to these new methods. This shift is also noticeable within the field of linguistics, wherever more emphasis is placed on the study of countable entities, such as syntactic constituents, often decreasing space for interpretative research, which is more difficult to study from a statistical or algorithmic point of view.[2]

This development within linguistics can be approached from a variety of fields and subjects. We choose a particular subject, the treatment of hapax legomena. The term derives from ancient Greek, ἅπαξ λεγόμενον, which literally means "read only once." This definition signals that we are dealing with a clearly defined set of words given a concrete corpus, but this could not be farther from the truth. As we will see throughout this chapter, different accounts have provided strongly varying accounts of hapax legomena, using both computational and non-computational elements to justify their validity, each with particular goals in mind. Discussing the issues regarding hapax legomena will bring several aspects of reconciling computational and non-computational approaches to the forefront, due to the indebtedness of research on this topic to both approaches.

---

[1] Paolo Gerbaudo, "From Data Analytics to Data Hermeneutics: Online Political Discussions, Digital Methods and the Continuing Relevance of Interpretive Approaches," *Digital Culture & Society* 2 (2018): 95–112.
[2] Jan Hajič, "Linguistics Meets Exact Sciences," in *A Companion to Digital Humanities*, ed. Susan Schreibman, Ray Siemens, and John Unsworth (Oxford: Blackwell, 2004): 79–87.

https://doi.org/10.1515/9783110574043-007

After this introduction, the second section will provide an overview of the historical attention for the phenomenon of hapax legomena. This in turn will allow us in a third section to more systematically present issues regarding its historical development, and to discuss their application in fields related to linguistics. After these two sections, we will have a thorough understanding of the phenomenon, allowing the fourth section to place the discussion more closely within the framework of digital humanities.

2 *Status quaestionis* of biblical Hebrew hapax legomena

The Greek expression ἅπαξ λεγόμενον was first attested by 3rd century grammarians from Alexandria, who used the term to indicate that a word occurs in one specific instance within the entire corpus of classical Greek literature.[3] Although the definition of the expression seems clear, the underlying paragraphs will point out that it has been given different meanings by several authors. Moreover, as Martinazolli has pointed out, several related Greek expressions were competing – ἅπαξ εἴρηται, ἐχρήσατο, εἰρημένον, μόνον, ἐνταῦθα – much to the same extent as during the Middle Ages, as we will describe below.[4] Nevertheless, we had to wait until the 20th century for Hebrew scholars to take up the term to refer to rare words in the Hebrew Bible,[5] and to underline the importance of the chosen corpus for the definition of hapax legomena. In this section, we will discuss how rare words have been discussed throughout time, making a distinction between medieval and modern studies.

2.1 Hapax legomena in the Middle Ages

The first attestation of interest in word frequency in general and hapax legomena in particular for the Hebrew Bible can be found in the Masoretic text. This is the edition of the Hebrew Bible accompanied by the Masora, a series of critical notes indicating what the Masoretes, Jewish scribe–scholars interested in the preserva-

---

3 Folco Martinazzoli, *Hapax Legomena* (Rome: Gismondi, 1953), 83–84.
4 Martinazzoli, *Hapax Legomena*, 83–84.
5 Elke Verbeke, "Hebrew Hapax Legomena and Their Greek Rendering in LXX Job" (PhD diss., Leuven, 2011), 8.

tion of the Bible, found important about the text.⁶ Word frequency plays an important role here, with unique words being indicated by the siglum ל. This sign is short for איתי לא or ליתא, meaning "there is no." Hence, they did not use the word hapax legomena, and used their denotation for unique words in a specific manner. The main interest of the Masoretes was the preservation of the Hebrew Bible,⁷ which is why they put a heavy emphasis on orthography. Nevertheless, other numeric attestations are indicated as well, such as the unique attestation of a particular word or phrase at the beginning of the line. This particular Masoretic interest in this high level of uniqueness is very different from other approaches, which bring in other factors, most notably its meaning.⁸ For this reason, we will not refer back to the Masoretic system in this article.

Most of the other works in the Middle Ages do not show a particular interest in word frequency, but they nevertheless treat the words considered by others as hapax, without naming it as such. We find several lists among different scholars, each with their own reasons for fabricating the lists, but never from a systematic interest in the phenomenon of hapax legomenon.

The first explicit interest in word frequency can be found in the works of the 9th–10th century rabbi Sa'adia Gaon.⁹ In his work *Kitab al-Sab'in lafza al-mufrada*, he does not primarily deal with word frequency, but uses arguments using hapax legomena. Following the general scholarly consensus, the work is written as a polemic against the Karaites, religious scholars believing that only the Hebrew Bible has authority regarding Jewish law.¹⁰ As counter-argument, Sa'adia argued that Mishna and Talmud are necessary to explain the meaning of rare words found in the Hebrew Bible. During his argumentation, he does not provide a systematic overview of what he considers to be rare words, nor does he present a definition of such words. He solely presents a list of words for which he considers Mishna and Talmud necessary to explain. Hence, his discussion of rare words serves only his argumentation and lacks a general interest in linguistics or the statistical occurrences of words.

---

6 Emanuel Tov, *The Text-Critical Use of the Septuagint in Biblical Research* (Indiana: Eisenbrauns, 2015), 72.
7 Aron Dotan, "Homonymous Hapax Doublets in the Masora," *Textus* 14 (1988): 131–45.
8 Page Kelley, Daniel Stephen Mynatt, and Timothy Crawford, *The Masorah of Biblia Hebraica Stuttgartensia. Introduction and Annotated Glossary* (Grand Rapids, MI: Eerdmans, 1998), 9.
9 Michael Friedländer, "Life and Works of Saadia," *The Jewish Quarterly Review* 5 (1893): 177–99.
10 Chaim Cohen, *Biblical Hapax Legomena in the Light of Akkadian and Ugaritic* (Cambridge: Scholars Press, 1978), 9; Max Schloessinger, "Hapax legomena in Rabbinic literature," *Jewish Encyclopedia* 6 (New York: Funk and Wagnalls, 1904), 229.

Among other medieval Jewish scholars, we do find a specific interest in rare words as such. However, they do not use the word "hapax legomena" to refer to them, but rather use a variety of phrases, among which אם אב או לו/לה אין is the most frequently attested, with variation in אב/אם being replaced by רע/ריע, עמית, חבר,בן, אחות, אח, דומה, משפחה. These forms literally mean "for it (the word) is no father/mother," whereas the variant forms replace father/mother with sister/brother/equal/friend/family[11]. Their terminology makes clear that they do not necessarily focus on the uniqueness of the word, in that it would only occur once, but rather that it has to be a word for which no related word can be found. These medieval scholars, of which Abraham ibn Ezra and Rashi are the most well known, have a clear definition of relatedness, namely that to be related means to share the same consonantal root.[12] The main constituent of Hebrew words is a (tri)-consonantal root, which expresses the general semantics. By adding morphemes, consonants, and/or vowels, the root gets a specific instantiation as a word. An example can clarify this. The root RKB signifies "riding," specifically in the context of "horseback riding." This root can be conjugated as a regular verb, giving for example RAKAB "he drove," RAKABTI "I drove," ROKEB "driver," but other, related words are also derived from this, such as MERKABA "chariot." The usage of this root makes their semantic relation clear. This root system is flexible, and semantic shifts are visible diachronically. For example, the root RKB has given rise to the modern Hebrew term RAKEBET "train." Returning to the medieval stance on rare words, an unrelated word is a word containing a root not attested elsewhere. It is clear that this category contains words for which the determination of its precise meaning can be difficult, because only context can help. In summary, we can state that medieval Jewish scholarship is mainly interested in the etymology of words.

2.2 Hapax legomena in modern research

In the modern period – which for our purposes starts in the 19th century, when a purely linguistic interest in textual studies arises – we can sporadically find a more systematic treatment of rare words. Not surprisingly, then, it is this period that characterizes questions as to the exact definition of a hapax legomenon. This question results in quite elaborate discussions; this is the subject of the

---

11 Leo Prijs, *Jüdische Tradition in der Septuaginta. Die Grammatikalische Terminologie des Abraham Ibn Esra* (Hildesheim: Georg Olms, 1987), 24.
12 Frederick Greenspahn, *The Meaning of "ein lo domeh" and Similar Phrases in Medieval Biblical Exegesis* (Cambridge: Cambridge University Press, 1979), 61.

third section, which gives a systematic overview of problems encountered in defining unique words. In this subsection, we will continue to discuss the revolving goals of this shift.

Under influence of the historical–critical method – which defined briefly aims at the development of methods to investigate the process underlying the final text of the Bible – other possibilities of explaining or using hapax legomena came to the front. Under the auspices of this method, it becomes possible to nuance several long-held opinions, for example David's authorship of many Psalms; or that the book of Isaiah is written by the prophet with the same name, and therefore written in entirely in the same century.

Most of the work published in the 19th and 20th century regarding hapax legomena deals with specific passages for exegesis. When stumbling upon a word that occurs only once, it is indicated as such, but usually not followed by further information. Many researchers treat the word as if it is essentially hapax, and not in need of further clarification. It is often mentioned as difficult to translate, although it is a myth that hapax legomena in general would be difficult to translate.[13] Hence, most researchers do not pay further attention to this word group.[14] However, emendation is the most common reason given in such cases for explaining why the word is difficult to fit into the context. More systematizing works, such as the ones by Casanowicz or Greenspahn, clearly indicate that, although it is possible some texts are corrupted,[15] the explanation of emendation should only be given if no other possibility exists, and if emendation in the particular context is likely. Both of these authors can be considered the most important voices of modern scholarship on hapax legomena. Casanowicz is most famous for introducing the conceptual difference between, on the one hand, "either absolutely new coinages of roots, or [words that] can not be derived in their formation or in their specific meaning from other occurring stems" and, on the other hand, words that "while appearing once only as a form, can easily

---

[13] Frederick Greenspahn, *Hapax Legomena in Biblical Hebrew: A Study of the Phenomenon and Its Treatment since Antiquity with Special Reference to Verbal Forms* (Eugene, OR: Wipf & Stock, 2016), 13.

[14] An important reason can be found in John Huehnergard, "Review of F.E. Greenspahn, Hapax Legomena in Biblical Hebrew (Chico, CA, 1984)," *Bulletin of the American Schools of Oriental Research* 264 (1986): 88–90, who explains that this word group does not constitute a true class of words. The group is solely defined by its statistical properties, not by a more syntactically motivated category such as nouns, or semantically, for example words referring to a given field of reference. This reason would then explain why most researchers referring to hapax legomena do so for practical exegetical purposes, running into unique words which need explanation. These instances indicate the need for systematic study of the phenomenon.

[15] Bruno Kirschner, *Hapax legomena, Jüdisches Lexikon* (Berlin: Jüdischer Verlag, 1931), 1429.

be connected with other existing words."¹⁶ These words have since become known as respectively absolute and non-absolute hapax legomena.

This distinction uses the notion of relatedness from medieval Jewish scholars to classify hapax legomena in two categories, whether they have a related root elsewhere in the Bible or not. Although this is an important distinction that will be taken up by following scholars, he does not delve deeper into related problems, such as how to discern whether homonyms have related roots or merely similar surface forms. Greenspahn's work does go into these issues and expands the work of Casanowicz with statistical information and derivations. We will come back to these issues in the third section.

2.3 Conclusion

At the end of this second section, we can conclude that hapax legomena have been discussed for centuries, but that any systematic account of this word group is fairly recent and still exceptional within the field of exegesis. A careful analysis makes clear that the search for useful definition is by no means easy and requires several decisions before a quantitative assessment can be embarked upon. It is precisely these decisions that we will discuss at length in the next section, leaving behind the current historical overview to focus on the specific issues for a scientific study of hapax legomena.

3 A systematic overview of issues

In this section, we want to enrich the historical overview we have put forward by investigating which issues are related to the study of hapax legomena. Our goal is to emphasize, to begin with, the difficulty and influence of decisions on the quantitative analysis and its subsequent interpretation. This will be the subject of the first subsection, which will discuss methodological problems arising in the definition and scope of hapax legomena, within the context of both textual studies in general, and Hebrew studies in particular. The subsequent subsections will then focus on the extent to which we can use the quantitative analyses in a variety of domains. We will study its influence on translation, lexical variation, poetry, and the study of cognates.

---

16 Immanuel Casanowicz, "Hapax legomena. Biblical data," *Jewish Encyclopedia* 6 (New York: Funk and Wagnalls, 1904): 226–28.

3.1 Methodological issues

The methodological issues we set out to study here are limited to the field of linguistics and textual studies. We limit our scope to exclude inquiries from other fields, of which psychology and philology are the most important. A particular brand of psychological research might be of interest here, namely the investigation of word uses and vocabulary to classify persons.[17] It is established that people have a very broad passive knowledge of words, of which they only use a fraction actively. From this perspective, texts can be classified according to origin in place, time, and, in part, the identity of the writer. However, this is only an ideal case and strongly abstracts the concrete textual situation, which is more chaotic. For example, authors, and ancient ones more prominently than modern, have a tendency to (partly) copy texts or authors with high authority, so as to bring honor to the original writer. This principle, known by the Latin phrase *imitatio et aemulatio*, is prevalent among the writers of the ancient world and is evidenced by the large amount of texts ascribed in anachronism, for example for certain Psalms to David or the Pentateuch to Moses.

It is important to notice from the start that it can be argued as to whether or not the class of hapax legomena constitutes a separate category of words. Of course, they can be considered as such from a statistical point of view, but a case could be made that their uniqueness in a given corpus is the sole characteristic they have in common. Some of these words may be inherently rare, but a short investigation into the hapax legomena of novels or newspaper articles indicates that common words can also be found to be unique accidentally. On the other hand, if a writer invents new terms, but uses them at least twice, they are no longer considered hapax, even though they are inherently rare words for any linguistic community or subdivision of texts. In other words, we could state that no word can be said to be essentially hapax – as they can be said to be essentially a verb, feminine, or possessive – but the category can provide an interesting insight into the vocabulary of the given corpus, relevant, for example, to the study of translation.

Looking at the feature of word frequency from a strictly statistical point of view, an interesting distribution can be discovered. Named after the American linguist George Kingsley Zipf, although he only popularized the notion and did not invent it,[18] Zipf's law states that the frequency of a given word is inver-

---

[17] Helen Slocomb Eaton, *Semantic Frequency List for English, French, German and Spanish* (Chicago: Chicago University Press, 1940), 7.
[18] David Powers, "Applications and Explanations of Zipf's Law," *Association for Computational Linguistics* (1998): 151–60.

sely proportional to its rank in the frequency table. In other words, this means that the second most frequent word occurs half as many times as the most frequent one, the third one third, and so forth. As can be seen in the table, for any corpus this means that a select number of words occurs extremely often (words such as interjections, articles, prepositions), while some words in the middle are most relevant to determining the topics dealt with in the text. The final part of the graph contains a long tail of words that occur only once or a few times. In accordance with the prediction of Zipf, any corpus will have between 40% and 60% of its entire vocabulary occurring only once. This Zipfian distribution lies at the basis of the statistical treatment of language, with several application in areas such as stylometry and topic modeling.

Throughout the modern history of exegesis, researchers have often stumbled upon the fact that a word is unique for the corpus, but do not go further in discussing patterns within the set of these hapaxes. For example, Zakovitch deals with hapax legomena in his commentary of the Song of Songs but does not provide a clear definition of what he considers hapax, apart from the fact that the word has to occur once in the book and not somewhere else in the Bible.[19] This means that a word can appear several times in Song of Songs, but as long as it does not occur elsewhere, it is considered hapax. This raises the question of the influence of the chosen corpus on the identification of the hapax legomena. Wagner makes an important distinction in his study of hapax legomena in the Septuagint between *Autorbezogen* and *Textkorpusbezogen*, indicating that one can limit the range of hapaxes by considering all works by a certain author, or a given canon of text.[20] Although the study of hapax legomena brings these general concerns, studying them within the context of Hebrew also necessitates an investigation into the effects of the language on the unique words.

The problem of homonymy, to which we have above, is more stringent for Hebrew than it is for English, due to the higher number of ambiguous words. In our historical overview, we saw that medieval Jewish scholars put an emphasis on etymology and considered a word rare not on the basis of the frequency it is attested, but on whether the same root is attested elsewhere. This idea has to be nuanced further, because words sharing the same root do not necessarily lie in the same semantic field. For example, the word LKM is far from the meaning of MLKMH, or DBR is far from MDBR. Although it can be said that the word for desert shares a root with that of speech, because the desert is considered a place

---

[19] Yair Zakovitch, *Das Hohelied. Herders Theologischer Kommentar zum Alten Testament* (Freiburg: Herder, 2004), 64.
[20] Christian Wagner *Die Septuaginta-Hapaxlegomena im Buch Jesus Sirach* (Berlin: De Gruyter, 2012), 75–7.

where important words are spoken from God, it is clear that the desert is not intrinsically linked to speech. Hence, it becomes a problem to derive the lexeme from a surface form that may show the same root but does not necessarily pertain to the same lexeme. This is the reason Greenspahn excludes homonyms, which he calls homographs, because the underlying lexeme cannot be guaranteed without discussion.[21]

A related problem to the determination of homonyms is the habits in spelling and vocalization. An important question is whether a different spelling of a word constitutes a new word. In general, researchers agree that variation in the use of *matres lectionis* is a mere surface feature, leaving the word itself untouched. From this point of view, it is only the Masoretes who are interested in the unique spelling forms. However, we also find cases where similar sounding letters, such as *ayin* and *alef*, or *tav* and *tet*, are mixed up, producing a hapax legomenon. Here the discussion becomes more nuanced, because this seems to constitute a new root. Some examples are clear corruptions of the text due to scribal errors or genuine changes in the writing style that do not, however, influence the meaning of the root. For the variety in vocalization, we can state that this is a problem for Masoretic studies, since it was the Masoretes who provided the original consonantal text with vocalization. Since the text was meant to be read out loud, it is possible that the small variations we find, leading technically to a hapax legomenon, were put in place for prosodic reasons. Exploring this question in depth is beyond the scope of this article, but these issues do question further evidence for the behavior of triconsonantal roots, to be able to address to what extent variation between roots is occurring.

A final point of interest on the word-level is the distinction between absolute and non-absolute hapax legomena. As we indicated in our historical overview, this terminology derives from Casanowicz,[22] who uses the medieval interest in unique roots to make a classification among all words occurring only once, according to whether they have a connection to other, more frequently attested words through their root, or not. All these problems contribute to the fact that one cannot simply search a database for words occurring once, without knowing how the database has encoded all of the above-mentioned intricacies.

---

21 Greenspahn, *Hapax legomena*, 23–4.
22 Casanowicz, "Hapax legomena," 226–8.

3.2 Hapax legomena and translation

As we have discussed already, it is difficult if not impossible to systematically categorize the nature of hapax legomena, let alone be able to predict them in literature. An important marker of this variation can be found in translations.

Do older translations bear witness to preserving a meaning that in more modern translations is lost? Are some words untranslatable, or do they refer to realities that are no longer familiar to us? Do translations consider faithfulness to the original text to be of utmost importance, or do they prioritize a fluid and contemporaneous text in the target language? To what extent can a translator be said to be creative? These are examples of important questions regarding translation that can be addressed by considering the use of hapax legomena.

A large part of translation studies of the Hebrew Bible focus on the Septuagint, because it is the oldest non-Semitic translation of the Bible. From the hapax legomena point of view, this is interesting because its vocabulary is completely different. As evidenced by Lemmelijn,[23] a clear difference between quantitative and qualitative approaches to translation studies can be discerned. Quantitative arguments are mainly brought forward by Barr and Tov, whereas the qualitative approach is dominated by Finnish scholars, of whom Soisalon-Soininen, Aejmelaeus, and Sollamo are the most prevalent. The quantitative branch sets out to use statistical methods to discuss the literalness of the text against the freedom and influence of the translator. Whether the proposed methods are suitable and sufficient to discuss this issue depends on the point of view. The qualitative branch of research criticizes this approach for reducing the discussion of translation merely to the most common cases, since these are able to be discussed from a statistical standpoint. Emanuel Tov would nuance this view by pointing out that one has to start from a statistical quantification of the text in order to prevent researchers from following their intuition rather than the data.[24] This is when exegesis is in danger of becoming eisegesis, projecting theoretical frameworks onto the text instead of letting them be challenged by the text. Nevertheless, the Finnish school, which can be characterized as focusing on the qualitative assets of the text, does not deny the usefulness of statistics, but claims that the essence of translation can be found in those places where the translation di-

---

[23] Bénédicte Lemmelijn, "Two Methodological Trails in Recent Studies on the Translation Technique of the Septuagint," in *Helsinki Perspectives on the Translation Technique of the Septuagint*, ed. Raija Sollamo and Seppo Sipilä (Helsinki: The Finnish Exegetical Society in Helsinki, 2001): 43–63.
[24] Tov, *Text-Critical Use of the Septuagint*, 25.

verges from what is expected.²⁵ But, of course, what is expected is determined by a statistical approach to the textual material. In this regard, it has to be underlined that the branches are not defending mutually exclusive standpoints, but rather that researchers tend to focus on different aspects that contribute to an overall evaluation of the translation process. Several methodologies to bring both approaches together have been proposed, one of the most well known being the focus on content-related criteria, promulgated by the Leuven center for Septuagint Studies.²⁶ Their proposition is to evaluate translation for specific semantic fields, or other content-related criteria such as the collection of all toponyms, declaring hapax legomena as one of multiple features for assessing translation quality. This means that they do not select features to be examined based on syntax or grammar, but rather on a specific semantic field, which then in turn can be investigated in both languages.

3.3 Lexical richness and hapax legomena

A further context in which hapax legomena are discussed, beyond translation, is the lexical richness of a collection of texts. As we have pointed out before, following Zipf's law we can infer that about half of the vocabulary of any corpus consists of hapax legomena. It is important to notice that this law holds for any kind of text, whether it is literature, a code of law, poetry, or the scriptural representation of a speech. This means that we cannot directly make conclusions on the lexical richness of a text based solely on hapax legomena as such. If one were to write a text trying to drastically diminish the use of one's vocabulary, this would not reduce the percentage of hapax legomena – unless the same sentence is written over and over again – but would result in hapax legomena that have a relatively high frequency score in other corpora of the same language. The law of Zipf is inevitable and impossible to avoid.

However, as Greenspahn's research points out, it is possible to study lexical richness of a language in general, to put the number of hapax legomena into perspective.²⁷ One would be tempted to state that the more hapax legomena are found in a text, the more lexically rich it tends to be, which in turn could be in-

---

25 Ilmari Soisalon-Soininen, Anneli Aejmelaeus, and Raija Sollamo, *Studien zur Septuaginta-Syntax* (Helsinki: Suomalainen Tiedeakatemia, 1987).
26 Hans Ausloos and Bénédicte Lemmelijn, "Content-Related Criteria in Characterising the LXX Translation Technique," in *Die Septuaginta: Texte, Theologien, Einflüsse*, ed. Wolfgang Kraus, Martin Karrer, and Martin Meiser (Tübingen: Mohr Siebeck, 2010), 368.
27 Greenspahn, *Hapax legomena*, 36–41.

dicative of a rich vocabulary, such as we typically associate with poetic language. This bears on whether the hapax legomena in question have a tendency to be rare in other corpora, making this an essential feature. In other words, the important question is how to determine whether certain hapax legomena are merely accidentally attested. "If the choice of hapax legomena is purely random, resulting solely from the nature of word-frequency distribution, then they should not be found concentrated in any identifiable part(s) of the Bible."[28] In other words, if hapax legomena are accidental, and therefore occur without the conscious intent of the writer, this could be traced statistically via a probabilistic distribution, and no specific concentrations of higher numbers of hapax legomena should be found.[29] He uses data from the entire Bible to determine a baseline for the number of hapaxes one can expect on average. In relation to this number, he uses chi-square tests on biblical texts to determine their respective place on the graph. The use of biblical texts rather than books is intentional; using results from historical–critical research, he separates multiple biblical books along the lines of broadly accepted coherent units according to their dating and content. So, for example, the book of Isaiah is divided into its three constituents, the book of Psalms in five, and the book of Job according to the speakers of the five monologues.

Greenspahn's mapping of biblical texts is taken up here because it is the first thorough examination of hapax legomena from a modern standpoint. His results are in line with the accepted view of poetic and prose texts, where the former are found above the baseline and the latter below. The graph is particularly useful because it seems to reflect an intuition about the nature of these biblical texts into numerical data, which can then in turn be further explored. As Greenspahn himself indicates, the interpretative value of these data may not be overestimated. It correctly separates poetry from prose but does not take the nature of vocabulary into consideration. So, for example, although the vocabulary of Samuel and Kings, on the one hand, and that of Chronicles, Ezra, and Nehemiah, on the other hand, is quite distinct, they are mapped closely together on this graph.

3.4 Hapax legomena and poetry

The poetic nature of a text cannot solely be approached from the point of view of lexical richness or frequency of attestation. As discussed above, the Semitic sys-

---

[28] Ibid., 36.
[29] Ibid.

tem of roots leaves space to construct neologisms, sharing the same root but constituting a novel word, such as the modern word for train. This fact evidences that the Hebrew word system provides ample space for flexibility and even creativity. Just as the root RKB has diachronically shifted from a specific meaning of horseback riding to riding in general, including cars and trains, so too can a poet invent new words to suit his expressive needs. As pointed out above, further research into the behavior of roots can determine the likelihood of such explanations.

Furthermore, there is a tendency within Hebrew poetry fort certain structures to have a high likelihood of attracting hapax legomena. An important characteristic of Hebrew poetry is its heavy reliance on parallelism. This is a poetic device where two cola (grammatically correct but not logically complete phrases) that make up a verse contain a similar structure.[30] Three varieties of parallelism exist, namely synthetic, antithetic, and synonymous. Synthetic parallelism presents two ideas, which, although disparate, express a certain affinity, whereas antithetic parallelism presents two different sides of the same idea. Synonymous parallelism, on the other hand, expresses the same idea in different words, and is most important for hapax legomena. In this case, both cola in essence present the same information, albeit in different phrasing. Research into the nature of these verses has pointed out that in the large amount of verses, its second part consists of words lower on the frequency scale than the first colon. In other words, the second colon gives a rarer representation of the content contained in the first. This technique forces the poet to be creative and show his richness of vocabulary.

Returning to the work of Greenspahn cited in the previous subsection, we notice that, beyond the distinction between poetry and prose, he also claims to be able to discern different styles of literature based on the deviation of the distribution of hapax legomena.[31] He does indicate that this data is insufficient to determine authorship, in that it only shows the different identities of texts. It clearly is not the case that any difference in the statistical distribution of hapax legomena has to be interpreted meaningfully. This can be seen when other divisions of texts in a random fashion are carried out.

This insight places an important limit on the interpretative radius of statistical results. The value of comparing the distribution of hapax legomena for an individual text within the entire biblical collection is valuable to a certain extent but cannot be interpreted deterministically. Not every distinction we find is

---

30 Robert Lowth, *De sacra poesi hebræorum prælectiones. Lecture 6* (Montana: Kessinger, 2004).
31 Greenspahn, *Hapax legomena*, 42–3.

meaningful, and we also need to take into account the preprocessing steps been undertaken before the quantitative evaluation. Concerning the distinction between prose and poetry, the hapax distribution seems to be a salient feature but is still in need of further comparison with others. In essence, poetry is captured not only by the lexical richness or diversity of a text, but also in other features such as sentence length, variation in inflection, and the like. This in turn leads to other research questions, embarking upon the influence of different features on the poetry/prose distinction. An example would be to question whether the lexical variety of poetry is paralleled by variety in attested roots.

3.5 Hapax legomena and cognates

In our historical overview, we discussed the focus on etymology of the medieval Jewish scholars. A point of contention among those scholars, however, was the relation between etymology and context. In the interpretation of Yellin, Sa'adia gave more importance to context than to etymology.[32] The rationale behind this opinion is that whatever the etymology of a word may be, in the end it is the company the word keeps that determines its meaning. After all, we know that semantic shifts occur throughout history, which means that etymology by itself can at most indicate a historical link of significance, rather than predict the semantic value of a word. Of course, this argument from context is difficult within the context of rare words that have no root in common with other words, since context is the only constituent to determine its meaning. If we take the subsection of hapax legomena for which this is the case, about four hundred words – the exact numbering depending on a number of choices, which we discussed above – we have words for which one specific context is all we have to determine its meaning. Nevertheless, this does not seem to form a particular problem for almost all of these words.

The interest in etymology for rare forms seems to be divided in two sections, which both find related words in other Semitic languages. The difference lies in the fact of whether this related word is itself rare or not. In most cases, it seems to be the case that rare roots are equally infrequent in other corpora. Some researchers have investigated links with Ugaritic in this regard,[33] but comparisons remain indecisive in most cases, due to the theory-leadenness of these examples. On the other hand, some cases report explanations of the same root being much

---

32 David Yellin, תולדות התפתחות הדקדוק העברי (Jerusalem: Qohelet, 1945), 33, 39.
33 Cohen, *Biblical Hapax Legomena*.

more abundant in other corpora. The problem with a simple identification of the hapax legomenon with the meaning of the cognate is that this etymology is only useful when it is applied appropriately. The difficulty, of course, lies in the definition of appropriateness, which we will not go into further here.

This problem ties in with the question of the scope within which we consider words to be hapax. In essence, we could imagine the entire corpus of Semitic languages to be one corpus, in which we consider basic semantic roots, some of which are language specific and a series of false friends, which undergo semantic shifts interlinguistically and intralinguistically. Considering the corpus of the Bible as such, we may not forget that the text has been through layers of redaction, which probably has also interpreted some hapax legomena as corruptions, which then were corrected afterwards to make them more understandable.

4 From hermeneutics to statistics and back

As we have seen throughout this chapter, analyses of hapax legomena can be characterized as a series of back-and-forth movements between quantitative arguments based on the counting of patterns and the consideration of individual rare words and their significance. The study of categories among hapax legomena indicates important limits to the statistical enterprise, which can only be part of a broader picture in which we hermeneutically interact with the text in order to gain ever more insight into its nature, provenance, and, ultimately, meaning. For example, the occurrence of a significant portion of words of different origin, as in Job and Ezekiel, for instance, poses the question as to the extent of influence from outside the Hebrew community. However, this seems to be a question where we gain only minor insight from the study of rare words, since they merely provide an explanandum about the reason for this foreign provenance. In other words, the study of hapax legomena indicates limits of what we can know where statistical approaches will not provide further insight.

An important distinction we have made throughout this chapter is between word and root, most notably in the section on translation and poetry. The literature on Hebrew rare words is divided as to whether to consider words that occur only once as the center of their attention, or whether one should focus on the root and its (un)relatedness to other words. Modern studies of language evolution put high emphasis on the semantic change of words throughout time, but the evolution of root meanings has remained understudied. Work done by medieval Jewish scholars has put an emphasis on the significance of the root system and the aberrations to which it can be witness.

This distinction between the focus on roots rather than words indicates the possibility of Indo-European bias against the stance of Semites towards words. We have a tendency to regard the word as the smallest basis for meaning – or more specifically morphemes, but its meaning is rather minute, not that it can be taken up in an ontology – whereas it is more logical from a Semitic point of view to think in roots rather than words. The question of comparison of both systems, the root-based focus on relatedness, and the word-based focus on number of occurrences, which are both statistical in nature, places question marks as to the evolution of roots themselves. If words are not seen as places of meaning in themselves, but rather as constituents in which the more basic entity of root is instantiated, we can see that words are related to roots in the same way as sentences relate to words. This is an example of the hermeneutical approach requiring further statistical evidence.

In machine learning research, the science of designing algorithms that mimic learning behavior, an important question lies in finding salient features and engineering them to achieve meaningful results in tasks such as text summarization and information retrieval. The correspondence between features, of which hapax legomena can be one, also gives us a more thorough understanding of the essence of literary features, such as the essence of poetry. In the future, we will be able to answer questions pertaining to this characteristic identity of Hebrew poetry, such as whether the lexical variation is more important than structural differences such as word order variation or high frequency of attested roots. This is an important example of how statistical evidence will allow us to gain insight in (future) hermeneutical questions.

Guiding ourselves by the systematic accounts of hapax legomena in recent scholarship, we have indicated how a movement between interpretation and quantitative assessment is not only necessary for any meaningful results but is also useful to consider fields related to lexical semantics, such as the study of translation methods, lexical variation, the identification of poetry, and the study of cognates in related languages. The outset was not only to show the meaningfulness of hapax legomena in these fields, but also to illustrate that the interpretative decisions that had to be made prior to our quantitative analyses were once again put into question by the results of these analyses. From this point, we made the case that computational analyses should be taken up as part of the hermeneutical circle to increase our insight into the text. Hapax legomena should not be considered as a deterministic category, which we need to carefully define, but rather as a group of words that can serve as a marker of several traits of the text and author, and as a computational feature.

5 Bibliography

Ausloos, Hans, and Bénédicte Lemmelijn. "Content-Related Criteria in Characterising the LXX Translation Technique." In *Die Septuaginta: Texte, theologien, einflüsse*, edited by Wolfgang Kraus, Martin Karrer, and Martin Meiser. Tübingen: Mohr Siebeck, 2010.

Casanowicz, Immanuel. "Hapax Legomena. Biblical data." *Jewish Encyclopedia* 6. New York: Funk and Wagnalls, 1904.

Cohen, Chaim. *Biblical Hapax Legomena in the Light of Akkadian and Ugaritic*. Cambridge: Scholars Press, 1978.

Dotan, Aron. "Homonymous Hapax Doublets in the Masora." *Textus* 14 (1988): 131–45.

Eaton, Helen Slocomb. *Semantic Frequency List for English, French, German and Spanish*. Chicago: Chicago University Press, 1940.

Friedländer, Michael. "Life and Works of Saadia." *The Jewish Quarterly Review* 5 (1893): 177–99.

Gerbaudo, Paolo. "From Data Analytics to Data Hermeneutics: Online Political Discussions, Digital Methods and the Continuing Relevance of Interpretive Approaches." *Digital Culture & Society* 2 (2018), 95–112.

Greenspahn, Frederick. *Hapax Legomena in Biblical Hebrew: A Study of the Phenomenon and Its Treatment since Antiquity with Special Reference to Verbal Forms*. Eugene, OR: Wipf & Stock, 2016.

Greenspahn, Frederick. *The Meaning of "ein lo domeh" and Similar Phrases in Medieval Biblical Exegesis*. Cambridge: Cambridge University Press, 1979.

Hajič, Jan. "Linguistics Meets Exact Sciences." In *A Companion to Digital Humanities*, edited by Susan Schreibman, Ray Siemens, and John Unsworth, 79–87. Oxford: Blackwell, 2004.

Huehnergard, John. "Review of F.E. Greenspahn, Hapax Legomena in Biblical Hebrew (Chico, CA, 1984)." *Bulletin of the American Schools of Oriental Research* 264 (1986): 88–90.

Kelley, Page, Daniel Stephen Mynatt, and Timothy Crawford, *The Masorah of Biblia Hebraica Stuttgartensia. Introduction and Annotated Glossary*. Grand Rapids, MI: Eerdmans, 1998.

Kirschner, Bruno. *Hapax Legomena, Jüdisches Lexikon* Berlin: Jüdischer Verlag, 1931.

Lemmelijn, Bénédicte. "Two Methodological Trails in Recent Studies on the Translation Technique of the Septuagint." In *Helsinki Perspectives on the Translation Technique of the Septuagint*, edited by Raija Sollamo and Seppo Sipilä, 43–63. Helsinki: The Finnish Exegetical Society in Helsinki, 2001.

Lowth, Robert. *De Sacra Poesi Hebræorum Prælectiones. Lecture 6*. Montana: Kessinger, 2004.

Martinazzoli, Folco. *Hapax Legomena*. Rome: Gismondi, 1953.

Powers, David. "Applications and Explanations of Zipf's Law." *Association for Computational Linguistics* (1998): 151–60.

Prijs, Leo. *Jüdische Tradition in der Septuaginta. Die Grammatikalische Terminologie des Abraham Ibn Esra* Hildesheim: Georg Olms, 1987.

Schloessinger, Max. "Hapax Legomena in Rabbinic Literature." *Jewish Encyclopedia* 6. New York: Funk and Wagnalls, 1904.

Soisalon-Soininen, Ilmari, Anneli Aejmelaeus, and Raija Sollamo. *Studien zur Septuaginta-Syntax*. Helsinki: Suomalainen Tiedeakatemia, 1987.

Tov, Emanuel. *The Text-Critical Use of the Septuagint in Biblical Research*. Indiana: Eisenbrauns, 2015.
Verbeke, Elke. "Hebrew Hapax Legomena and Their Greek Rendering in LXX Job." PhD diss., University of Leuven, 2011.
Wagner, Christian. *Die Septuaginta-Hapaxlegomena im Buch Jesus Sirach*. Berlin: De Gruyter, 2012.
Yellin, David. תולדות התפתחות הדקדוק העברי. Jerusalem: Qohelet, 1945.
Zakovitch, Yair. *Das Hohelied. Herders Theologischer Kommentar zum Alten Testament*. Freiburg: Herder, 2004.

Matthew Munson
Lexicography, the Louw–Nida Lexicon, and computational co-occurrence analysis

1 Introduction

This study considers the ways in which computational methods for the automatic extraction of semantic data can improve our understanding of the lexical semantics of a word when their results are compared to the Louw–Nida New Testament Lexicon,[1] which organizes all the words in the New Testament according to semantic domains. I will begin with a brief description of the computational methods used and the linguistic theory behind them. I will then follow this with a brief literature review, which will consider the place of the Louw–Nida Lexicon in the context of lexicography in general and New Testament lexicography in particular. Then I will consider two different use cases where the distributional methods can deepen the lexical understanding gained from Louw–Nida by introducing data reflecting how these two words were actually used by the New Testament writers.

The first use case will deal with the word σάρξ, a word normally translated as "flesh" but which actually has an extremely complex meaning[2] that Louw–Nida, in conjunction with these distributional methods, will be able to describe much more fully. The second use case will consider the word δαιμόνιον, which Louw–Nida says belongs in only one semantic sub-domain, "Supernatural Beings." My methods, while not disputing this placement, will demonstrate that the New Testament writers showed a different focus on demons[3] than this domain would suggest.

Note: This article is a revision of a portion of my dissertation: Matthew Munson, *Biblical Semantics: Applying Digital Methods for Semantic Information Extraction to Current Problems in New Testament Studies*, Theologische Studien (Aachen: Shaker Verlag, 2017), 47–67. It has been reproduced here by permission of the publisher.

1 Johannes P. Louw and Eugene A. Nida, *Greek–English Lexicon of the New Testament: Based on Semantic Domains*, 2nd ed. (New York: United Bible Societies, 1989).
2 According to Louw–Nida, it is part of ten different semantic domains.
3 Note that I will use the English words "demon" and "demons" throughout this paper to refer to the type of being for which the New Testament writers would have used the Greek word δαιμόνιον. I do not intend with this substitution to project the modern understanding of "demons"

2 Theory: distributional semantics and word context

The method I am using to extract semantic information from the biblical corpora is based on the work of the linguist Zellig Harris. In his 1954 article "Distributional Structure,"[4] he asserted that words demonstrate their meanings in texts by means of the words that occur around them. His hypothesis has come to be called the distributional hypothesis based on the name that he gave the contexts in which words tend to occur, i.e. their "distributions." The most developed expression of this hypothesis came in a series of lectures he did in 1986 in which he stated, "The most precise way of determining a word's meaning is by investigating the meanings of the words that occur along with that word."[5] Harris' theory has wide-ranging applications, and is the basis for the field of statistical semantics, i.e. the "statistical study of meanings of words and their frequency and order of recurrence."[6] According to the Association for Computational Linguistics Wiki page, statistical semantics is used, among other things, for "measuring the similarity in word meanings," "measuring the similarity in word relations," "measuring the cohesiveness of text," "discovering the different senses of words," "distinguishing the different senses of words," and "subcognitive aspects of words."[7]

Coming back to Harris' statement that the meaning of a word is determined by the meanings of the words around it, this statement makes perfect sense if we think about how native speakers of a language deal with words they have never encountered. For instance, if a speaker of English saw the following sentence, "They built a frack to their god," that speaker would have a good idea of the meaning of frack even if they had never encountered it before. A frack is something that one builds to a god and thus would be classified as being similar to a temple or an altar, which could be substituted for frack in this sentence without it becoming nonsensical. And if the reader were to see frack in a text several

---

back into the New Testament. That is, in fact, the whole purpose of this paper: to show that our modern view of "demons" was not necessarily shared by the NT writers.

4 Zellig Harris, "Distributional Structure," *Word* 10, no. 23 (1954): 146–62.
5 Zellig Harris, How Words Carry Meaning, Columbia University, 1986, http://zelligharris.org/BL3.2.Words.html.
6 E. Delavenay, *An Introduction to Machine Translation* (New York: Thames and Hudson, 1960).
7 Association for Computational Linguistics, "Statistical Semantics," Wiki of the Association for Computational Linguistics, last modified 25 May 2010, https://aclweb.org/aclwiki/Statistical_Semantics.

more times, each occurrence would enrich the meaning of frack. For instance, if the next sentence were, "They poured the blood of their sacrifice on the frack," the reader would know that its meaning is probably closer to altar than to temple because it belongs to those things upon which things are poured after a sacrifice.[8]

In this vein, Harris observes that "a person's store of meanings grows and changes through the years while his language remains fairly intact."[9] From a distributional standpoint, this means that as we encounter known words in new contexts, i.e. new distributions, our understanding of the meanings of those words changes slightly to fit the newly encountered context. And while the import of this is obvious in language learning, i.e. the more one encounters a language, the better one knows the language, it is also the basic assumption of the computational method put forth here. That is, if we set a computer up to encounter and learn from enough word contexts, the computer will be able to start building a distributional, semantic profile of the word, which will, at least to some extent, represent the meaning of that word. And the more contexts the computer encounters, the better this profile, and thus the semantic representation, will be. The extent to which these methods produce a representation of a word's meaning is the subject of investigation in this article.

And, finally, one last citation from Harris adds the last bit of theoretical information needed for this study: "If we consider words or morphemes A and B to be more different in meaning than A and C, then we will often find that the distributions of A and B are more different than the distributions of A and C. In other words, difference of meaning correlates with difference of distribution."[10] This means that one can compare the distributional profiles of two different words to measure the similarity in meaning of the two words. It is upon this statement that the method used in this study rests. That is, by first building distributional profiles of the words in a corpus, which are based on their co-occurrence patterns (i.e. their distributions), and then comparing the profiles of words within and between corpora, we will achieve a better understanding of how similar and how different words are. For instance, if the profiles of θεός (God) and κύριος (lord) in the Septuagint are similar, then we should expect the meanings of these two words to be similar. On the other hand, if the profile of θεός in the Septuagint is significantly different from that of θεός in the New Testament, then

---

8 Eugene A. Nida, *Componential Analysis of Meaning* (The Hague: Mouton, 1975).
9 Harris, "Distributional Structure," 151.
10 Harris, "Distributional Structure," 156.

this is an indication that the meaning of θεός has shifted between the Septuagint and the New Testament.

The theory behind the computational method should now be clear. Instead of a precise description of the algorithms used to produce the data for this study, I will briefly and generally describe how the method works. This can be most succinctly done by referring to the previous work on this subject in two studies by John Bullinaria and Joseph Levy, one in 2007[11] and one in 2012.[12] Bullinaria and Levy, in both of these studies, used the method described here of counting word co-occurrences, measuring the significance of these co-occurrence counts, and then determining the similarity of the resulting distributional vectors to complete three rather difficult tasks that have a direct bearing on what I am doing in this study. The first of these tasks was the synonym test of the standardized Test of English as a Foreign Language (TOEFL). This test gives a single word and a list of four synonym possibilities. The test-taker must then select the correct synonym from the 4 possibilities. In their 2007 study, Bullinaria and Levy were able to score 85% correct on this test,[13] while the addition of singular value decomposition (SVD) in the 2012 study allowed them to score nearly 100% on this test.[14] The second task was similar to the first, one they named "Distance Comparison."[15] In this task, they chose 200 pairs of "semantically related words (e.g. "king" and "queen," "concept" and "thought,"…)," introduced 10 other random words to each of these pairs, and then computed "the percentage of the control words that are further from the target than its related word."[16] So if their methods determined that "king" and "queen" were the closest two words in that group of 12 words, the score would be 100% for that cluster. In their 2007 study, they scored approximately 98% on this test[17] and in 2012 nearly 100%.[18] The third test they call "Semantic Categorization."[19] In this test, they took "ten words from each of 53 semantic categories (e.g. cities, flowers, insects, vegetables, dances)"

---

[11] John A. Bullinaria and Joseph P. Levy, "Extracting Semantic Representations from Word Co-Occurrence Statistics: A Computational Study," University of Birmingham, 2007, https://www.cs.bham.ac.uk/~jxb/PUBS/BRM.pdf.
[12] John A. Bullinaria and Joseph P. Levy, "Extracting Semantic Representations from Word Co-Occurrence Statistics: Stop-Lists, Stemming and SVD," University of Birmingham, 2012, http://www.cs.bham.ac.uk/~jxb/PUBS/BRM2.pdf.
[13] Bullinaria and Levy, "Extracting Semantic Representations," 13.
[14] Bullinaria and Levy, "Stop-Lists, Stemming and SVD," 14.
[15] Ibid., 4.
[16] Ibid., 4.
[17] Bullinaria and Levy, "Extracting Semantic Representations," 13.
[18] Bullinaria and Levy, "Stop-Lists, Stemming and SVD," 14.
[19] Ibid., 4–5.

and then calculated how often their methods put each of these words closer to its own category than any of the other 52 categories.[20] In 2007 they scored about 80% on this test and in 2012 about 90%.

These are all very impressive scores, with Bullinaria and Levy asserting that their methods "provide new state-of-the-art performance"[21] on the TOEFL synonym test. And if one looks at the list of performances on the TOEFL test at the Association for Computational Linguistics Wiki page, one sees that theirs is the highest published performance on this test.[22] These two studies demonstrate the ability of the methods used in this study to extract usable semantic information from large corpora. Further, studies by Landauer and Dumais[23] and Turney et al.[24] have also demonstrated the usefulness of this basic methodology. And this is also the basic method described by Jurafsky and Martin in their textbook *Speech and Language Processing*.[25] So, we can see that distributional semantics offers a promising way into the computational comparison of corpora on the basis of word meaning.

In preparation for this study, I ran parameterization tests using these methods and comparing their results to the semantic domains described in the Louw–Nida lexicon. I chose the best parameters by simply choosing the ones where the results were closest to those of Louw–Nida.[26] For the lemmatized text of the New Testament, the best performance was achieved using a fairly small 12-word, weighted context window.[27] This means that I only counted the co-occurrents for a single target word if they occurred within 12 words to the left and 12 words to the right of that target word. And the weighted context window means that words that occur closer to the target word were weighted more heavily in the calculations than words that occurred farther from the target word. The

---

20 Ibid., 4–5.
21 Ibid., 1.
22 Association for Computational Linguistics (ACL), "TOEFL Synonym Questions (State of the Art)," Wiki of ACL, https://aclweb.org/aclwiki/TOEFL_Synonym_Questions_(State_of_the_art).
23 Thomas K. Landauer and Susan T. Dumais, "A Solution to Plato's Problem: The Latent Semantic Analysis Theory of Acquisition, Induction, and Representation of Knowledge," *Psychological Review* 104, no. 2 (1997): 211–40, https://doi.org/10.1037/0033–295X.104.2.211.
24 Peter D. Turney et al., "Combining Independent Modules to Solve Multiple-Choice Synonym and Analogy Problems," *CoRR* cs.CL/0309035 (2003), http://arxiv.org/abs/cs.CL/0309035.
25 Daniel Jurafsky and James H. Martin, *Speech and Language Processing: An Introduction to Natural Language Processing, Computational Linguistics, and Speech Recognition*, 2nd ed., Prentice Hall Series in Artificial Intelligence (Upper Saddle River, NJ: Pearson Education, 2009), 693–701.
26 Munson, *Biblical Semantics*, 22–46.
27 Munson, *Biblical Semantics*, 46.

significance of these raw co-occurrence counts was measured using the log-likelihood hypothesis-testing algorithm.[28] This mathematically complex algorithm essentially measures how likely the number of times that two words co-occur is due to chance. A high log-likelihood score suggests that the occurrence of one word makes the occurrence in the same context of a second word more likely and thus suggests a semantic relationship between the two words. The similarity of the log-likelihood scores for any two words was then measured by the cosine similarity algorithm,[29] which determines the similarity of two ordered lists of values by comparing the matching values of each list with each other. Two lists of log-likelihood values that show similar values for the same words will be counted as being similar to each other.

3 The Louw–Nida lexicon and semantic domains

The Louw–Nida Greek–English Lexicon of the New Testament Based on Semantic Domains, in its introduction, claims to be "a unique type of dictionary primarily because it is based on the concept of semantic domains, and secondly because of the manner in which the domains are organized and the data presented."[30] Nida and Louw also assert that their lexicon is based on "a completely new approach to lexicography."[31] Any brief look at the lexicon will reveal the most obvious difference: the lexicon is organized not alphabetically but, instead, by semantic similarity, i.e. words with similar meanings occur together in the lexicon. This obvious difference, however, is simply the outward appearance of the "new approach" cited above.

Of most interest to this study is that the focus on semantic domains changed significantly how the semantic data for the individual words was analyzed. The words were considered from the beginning as belonging to a network of semantic features that consist of shared features, distinctive features, and supplementary features. Shared features "are those elements of the meaning of lexical items which are held in common by a set of lexical items. The distinctive features are those which separate meanings one from another, and supplementary features

---

[28] Ted Dunning, "Accurate Methods for the Statistics of Surprise and Coincidence," *Computational Linguistics* 19 (1993): 61–74.
[29] For a description of the cosine similarity algorithm, see Munson, *Biblical Semantics*, 20.
[30] Louw and Nida, *Greek–English Lexicon*, vi.
[31] Eugene A. Nida, Johannes P. Louw, and Rondal B. Smith, "Semantic Domains and Componential Analysis of Meaning," in *Current Issues in Linguistic Theory*, ed. Roger William Cole (Bloomington, IN: Indiana University Press, 1977), 139.

are those which may be relevant in certain contexts or may play primarily a connotative or associative role."[32] So instead of reconstructing the meaning of each word in isolation from others, all words were considered in relation to all other words. This means that the definitions that are given for each lexical item always depend on its relationship to other lexical items, especially in its own semantic sub-domain.[33] This leads to what Louw and Nida call "the primary value of a lexicon based upon semantic domains ... that it forces the reader to recognize some of the subtle distinctions which exist between lexical items whose meanings are closely related and which in certain contexts overlap."[34] An example of how this type of analysis can be useful to the user of the lexicon is within domain 19, "Physical Impact." As Louw and Nida explain,

> κολαφίζω, ῥαβδίζω, and μαστίζω and μαστιγόω all share the features of physical impact involving hitting or striking. They differ, however, in certain distinctive features in that κολαφίζω designates striking or beating with the fist, ῥαβδίζω designates beating or striking with a stick or rod, and μαστίζω and μαστιγόω designate beating with a whip. The terms μαστίζω and μαστιγόω also differ from κολαφίζω and ῥαβδίζω in that they normally refer to officially sanctioned punishment.[35]

At this point, it is interesting to point out that while the most widely used New Testament lexicon, the BDAG,[36] differentiates these items in terms of the object used for impact (fist, rod, or whip), it almost completely ignores the second aspect of official sanctioning. This important aspect, however, becomes clear when one focuses on (all of) the distinctive aspects of each lexical item. And the reader's ability to recognize these aspects is enhanced since the lexicon places the most similar lexical items, like the four mentioned above, together along with the advice to read also "those entries which immediately precede and follow [the item in question], [so that] can one fully appreciate the referential range of any meaning... . This will provide a good deal of insight as to the way in which different meanings relate to one another."[37] As mentioned above, these shared, distinctive, and supplementary aspects are made clear precisely because this is the analytical scheme used in the preparation of this lexicon.

---

[32] Louw and Nida, *Greek–English Lexicon*, vi.
[33] Ibid., ix.
[34] Ibid., x.
[35] Ibid., vi.
[36] Frederick W. Danker, Walter Bauer, and William Arndt, *A Greek–English Lexicon of the New Testament and Other Early Christian Literature*, 3rd ed. (Chicago: University of Chicago Press, 2000).
[37] Louw and Nida, *Greek–English Lexicon*, 11.

In the end, as will become clear below, the distributional methods I use in this study measure the relationship between the shared and distinctive elements of each lexical item, with the supplementary elements being considered shared if they are common to several items and distinctive if not. A higher cosine similarity score suggests a greater proportion of shared elements while a lower score suggests the opposite. Another aspect that will become clear below is that we are measuring less what Louw calls the lexical meaning of a word, i.e. the meaning that a word "contributes in and of itself" but, instead, the "contextual meaning," i.e. the meaning "involving the circumstances of and the objects referred to in a specific context in terms of its usage in such a context along with other words or phrases contributing to the context."[38] Louw also states that it was the purpose of the Louw–Nida lexicon to focus only on lexical meaning.[39] However, the Semantic Dictionary of Biblical Hebrew, a lexicon similar in concept to Louw–Nida that is in preparation under the guidance of Reinier de Blois,[40] separates the lexical from the contextual meanings of the lexical items, analyzing them both separately. Finally, the utility of extracting primarily the contextual as opposed to the lexical meaning will also become evident below, as we compare the contextual meanings of lexical items in order to determine their relationships as it is communicated by the context of the corpus under investigation: the New Testament in this study.

4 Comparison to Louw–Nida

After this brief literature review, the next step is to examine the results to see what they can tell us about our methods, the text of the NT, the sub-domains of the Louw–Nida lexicon, and our own views of NT semantics. For this discussion, I start by considering all the words as they relate to their various sub-domains to discover places where words do not seem to fit as well as we would expect them to. The data shows two typical cases in which a word's cosine similarity score with the other words in its sub-domain differs significantly (around one standard deviation) from the average similarity score for every word in its sub-domain(s). The first is in the case of words with high polysemy, i.e. with a large number of senses. This is an expected result since not all senses

---

38 Johannes P. Louw, "How Do Words Mean – If They Do?" *Filología Neotestamentaria* 4 (1991): 131.
39 Ibid., 137.
40 United Bible Societies, "A Semantic Dictionary of Biblical Hebrew," https://semanticdictionary.org/.

of a word will be equally represented in any corpus. So the senses of a word that are used less frequently in a corpus will result in a smaller cosine similarity score for that word in the sub-domain that contains that sense. For instance, the word ἀκούω appears in seven different semantic sub-domains (24.52–70 B Hear; 31.50–57 G Accept As True; 32.1–10 A Understand; 32.42–61 E Lack of Capacity for Understanding; 33.189–217 O Inform, Announce; 36.12–30 C Obey, Disobey; 56.12–19 D Judicial Hearing, Inquiry). The sub-domain in which the other words are the most similar to ἀκούω is 24.52–70 B Hear, which should not surprise us since most would consider the primary meaning of ἀκούω to be "to hear." The other sub-domains are in the order listed above, with the sub-domains of 36.12–30 (Obey, Disobey) and 56.12–19 (Judicial Hearing, Inquiry) showing the least average similarity. To demonstrate such cases, I will investigate the word σάρξ, normally understood to mean "flesh." I have chosen this word because this definition is actually one of the weakest of its senses in the New Testament. So this is an excellent case, as I will demonstrate below, of the semantics of a word outside of the New Testament, and especially in later Christian literature, actually covering up the semantics of the word as used by the New Testament writers. The second category of words that do not fit into their sub-domain is words where the semantic sub-domain has been chosen correctly but where the word's usage in our corpus shows that it actually has importance in a different semantic sphere. I will use the word δαιμόνιον, "demon," to investigate this phenomenon. I have chosen δαιμόνιον because it actually has the poorest fit with its single semantic domain of any single-domain word that occurs at least 50 times, making it a perfect candidate for investigation.

4.1 ΣΑΡΞ

Let us begin by considering the word σάρξ, "flesh." According to Louw–Nida, σάρξ belongs to ten different semantic sub-domains. This analysis will help to solve the problem of disentangling "the constellations of closely related meanings of single lexical units" described by Nida, Louw, and Smith in their 1977 article introducing the lexical methodology of the Louw–Nida lexicon.[41] As we will see below, our methods not only allow a more complete picture of the relation of these constellated meanings, but my analysis of these meanings in relation to the varying lexical sub-domains[42] will also allow us to describe the use of σάρξ in

---

41 Nida, Louw, and Smith, "Semantic Domains," 153.
42 Ibid., 153.

the New Testament much better than any translation gloss could. The 10 Louw–Nida sub-domains are listed in Table 1 along with the Louw–Nida gloss(es) of σάρξ into English in that sub-domain, the average similarity of σάρξ with the other words in that sub-domain (Ave CS), and the average standard score for this average cosine similarity score (Ave z-score). A few introductory comments will serve as a general orientation to the data in this table. First, the average cosine similarity score of every word in the New Testament with every other word is 0.0494. Notice that all of the similarity scores are well above this average, with the lowest of 0.0598 being 0.2792 standard deviations above this average. That means that even the weakest sense of σάρξ ("physical nature") coheres more closely within its semantic sub-domain than the average word would. Second, notice that its second weakest sense in the New Testament is actually what would normally be considered its basic meaning, "flesh" as a part of the body.[43]

Table 1: Louw–Nida Sub-domains for σάρξ.

Semantic sub-domain	Gloss(es)	Ave CS	Ave z-score
26 Psychological Faculties	f human nature	0.1236	1.9860
25.12–32 B Desire Strongly	sexual desire	0.1047	1.4782
9.1–23 A Human Beings	c people	0.1041	1.4641
23.88–128 G Live Die	h life	0.0943	1.2004
88.271–282 J Sexual Misbehavior	homosexual intercourse	0.0825	0.8845
10.1–13 A Groups and Members of Groups of Persons Regarded as Related by Blood but without Special Reference to Successive Generations	e nation	0.0812	0.8511
22.15–20 B Experience Trouble Hardship	trouble	0.0801	0.8221
8.1–8 A Body	b body	0.0771	0.7416

---

[43] For an interesting discussion on the dangers of always translating σάρξ as flesh, see Nida, Louw, and Smith, "Semantic Domains," 140–1.

Table 1: Louw–Nida Sub-domains for σάρξ. *(Continued)*

Semantic sub-domain	Gloss(es)	Ave CS	Ave z-score
8.9–69 B Parts of the Body	a flesh	0.0625	0.3523
58.1–13 A Nature Character	g physical nature	0.0598	0.2792

So, now, what does this information tell us about σάρξ in the NT? First, it tells us that σάρξ in what would be considered its more metaphorical meanings of "human nature," "sexual desire," "people," and "life," are more strongly present in the NT than its less metaphorical senses of "flesh" and "physical nature." At this point we need to take a closer look inside the actual sub-domains in order to see exactly why σάρξ is drawn so closely to those sub-domains. This should give us a more complete picture of the constellation of meaning for σάρξ in the NT rather than relying on a single misleading gloss like "flesh." For this exercise, it is important to remember that σάρξ is not drawn to the sub-domain as such but, instead, to the other words in that sub-domain. Thus, we must look at the cosine similarity score of σάρξ with each of the other words in each sub-domain in order to determine why each sub-domain has its specific strength of attraction to σάρξ. I will start with the sub-domain "26 Psychological Faculties." Table 2 shows the other words in this sub-domain in the order of descending cosine similarity scores with σάρξ. The gloss for each word is its primary meaning from Louw–Nida as opposed its specific gloss in the sub-domain of "Psychological Faculties." I have chosen this more general gloss since it should, in theory, better represent a word's range of meaning than the specific gloss for one of its sub-domains. While this is not always the case, as it is not with σάρξ, it should be less misleading than the more specific meanings of words in certain sub-domains.

Table 2: Σάρξ similarity with semantic sub-domain "psychological faculties."

Word	Gloss	CS w/ σάρξ	Word	Gloss	CS w/ σάρξ
φρόνημα	thoughtful planning	0.5664	σύμψυχος	Harmonious	0.0904
πνεῦμα	(Holy) spirit	0.4616	ἄνθρωπος	human being	0.0853
σαρκικός	human	0.1504	ψυχή	inner self	0.0775
νοῦς	mind	0.1462	νεφρός	Desires	0.0737

Table 2: Σάρξ similarity with semantic sub-domain "psychological faculties." *(Continued)*

Word	Gloss	CS w/ σάρξ	Word	Gloss	CS w/ σάρξ
διάνοια	mind	0.1361	ἔσω	Inside	0.0677
σάρκινος	of people	0.1349	κοιλία	Belly	0.0672
φρονέω	to have an attitude	0.1198	νόημα	Mind	0.0635
καρδία	inner self	0.1157	φρήν	thoughtful planning	0.0561
πνευματικός	from the spirit	0.1122	ἔσωθεν	from inside	0.0531
φρόνησις	thoughtful planning	0.1053	πνευματικῶς	from the spirit	0.0495
κρυπτός	secret	0.0992	ἰσόψυχος	similarly minded	0.0406
συνείδησις	be aware of	0.0965	ὁρμή	Will	0.0310
σπλαγχνίζομαι	feel compassion for	0.0922			

If we consider just the first half of this list, since these are the words that draw σάρξ most strongly into this sub-domain, we see four major themes in these 13 words. The one with the most representatives (7 of the 13) gathers around the words for "mind" and represents thought and feeling: φρόνημα and φρόνησις (both "thoughtful planning"), νοῦς and διάνοια (both "mind"), φρονέω ("to have an attitude"), σπλαγχνίζομαι ("feel compassion for"), and συνείδησις ("to be aware of"). So one major aspect of σάρξ that draws it to this sub-domain is that of "thought and feeling." The other three themes are each represented by two words apiece: καρδία and κρυπτός representing the inner and hidden as opposed to outward things, πνεῦμα and πνευματικός representing the spirit, and σαρκικός and σάρκινος representing the human side. Thus, we can say that σάρξ is psychological inasmuch as it represents the thinking, inner human faculty that is somehow related to the spirit (more on this below).

Table 3: σάρξ with semantic sub-domain "human beings"

Word	Gloss	CS w/ σάρξ	Word	Gloss	CS w/ σάρξ
αἷμα	blood	0.2160	γλῶσσα	Tongue	0.0896
ὄνομα	name	0.1573	ἄνθρωπος	human being	0.0853
γῆ	earth	0.1519	ἀνθρώπινος	Human	0.0845

Table 3: σάρξ with semantic sub-domain "human beings" *(Continued)*

Word	Gloss	CS w/ σάρξ	Word	Gloss	CS w/ σάρξ
σῶμα	body	0.1422	σκεῦος	Object	0.0822
σάρκινος	of people	0.1349	κοινωνέω	to share	0.0795
χείρ	hand	0.1145	ψυχή	inner self	0.0775
τέλειος	perfect (moral)	0.1014	οἰκουμένη	Earth	0.0748
πρόσωπον	face	0.0994	κόσμος	Universe	0.0593
ἐπίγειος	on the earth	0.0969	γόνυ	Knee	0.0571
υἱός	son (own)	0.0913	ἀνήρ	Man	0.0480

Now, let us look at the sub-domain "9.1–23 A Human Beings." Table 3 presents the words in this sub-domain ordered by their strength of relationship to σάρξ. Again, let us consider the first half of this table. In these ten words, we see two primary categories and then two words that do not easily fit with the others: τέλειος ("perfect [moral]") and υἱός. The largest category are those words that refer either directly or metonymically to the human being: αἷμα ("blood"), ὄνομα ("name"), σῶμα ("body"), σάρκινος ("of people"), χείρ ("hand, finger"), and πρόσωπον ("face"). Not surprisingly, then, σάρξ has a strong, probably metonymic relationship to the category "human being." The second category, represented by two words, deals with physical creation: γῆ ("earth") and ἐπίγειος ("on the earth"). One could posit several reasons for this strong relationship to the physical universe. Perhaps it is because the human being is represented as the pinnacle of creation, which would tie in τέλειος ("perfect [moral]"), the last word in the top 10. Or perhaps it is because the human being was formed from the material of the earth in the second creation story. It is, however, unclear why this relationship is so strong besides the fact that σάρξ, σάρκινος, γῆ, and ἐπίγειος all appear to represent the physical nature of creation/the human being. So σάρξ is drawn closely to this sub-domain because of its relationship to the physical side of the human being.

Table 4: σάρξ with semantic sub-domain "nature, character"

Word	Gloss	CS w/ σάρξ	Word	Gloss	CS w/ σάρξ
σπέρμα	seed	0.1305	πλάσσω	to make	0.0381
ὑπόστασις	substance	0.1138	μόρφωσις	embodiment	0.0377
φύσις	nature	0.0837	φυσικός	natural	0.0376

Table 4: σάρξ with semantic sub-domain "nature, character" *(Continued)*

Word	Gloss	CS w/ σάρξ	Word	Gloss	CS w/ σάρξ
σύμμορφος	similar in form	0.0810	πλάσμα	what is formed	0.0358
μορφή	nature	0.0577	μορφόω	to form	0.0351
συμμορφίζομαι	have same likeness	0.0509	φυσικῶς	by nature	0.0283
σχῆμα	form	0.0472			

The next sub-domain we will investigate is "58.1–13 A Nature, Character." The format of Table 4 follows that of those above. This sub-domain is, unsurprisingly, full of words that refer to the nature or the form of something. That leads us to believe that σάρξ also refers to the nature and the form of a thing. One word that sticks out among these words referring to form and nature is the word σπέρμα ("seed"). And the fact that it is so closely related to σάρξ (first on the list) suggests that σάρξ also has something to do with the origin of the human being, just as σπέρμα does. And, finally, the strong relationship of σάρξ to "form" (σύμμορφος, μορφή, συμμορφίζομαι, and σχῆμα) in this category supports our assertion from the analysis of the previous sub-domain that σάρξ refers also to the physical nature of the thing, that which is also represented by the thing's form.

Table 5: σάρξ with semantic sub-domain "desire strongly"

Word	Gloss	CS w/ σάρξ	Word	Gloss	CS w/ σάρξ
ἐπιθυμία	deep desire	0.4431	πλεονεξία	Greed	0.0651
θέλημα	desire	0.2223	διψάω	to be thirsty	0.0592
ἐπιθυμέω	to desire greatly	0.2019	αἰσχροκερδῶς	shamefully greedy	0.0565
πλησμονή	gratification	0.1812	ὀρέγομαι	to strive to attain	0.0517
πάθημα	suffering	0.1337	ὁμοιοπαθής	same kinds of desires	0.0489
ἐπιπόθησις	deep desire	0.0888	ἅρπαξ	Vicious	0.0488
ἡδονή	pleasure	0.0872	ἐπιποθία	deep desire	0.0478
θυμός	fury	0.0842	ἁρπαγή	Plunder	0.0427
πάθος	passion	0.0805	καταστρηνιάω	to have lust	0.0422

Table 5: σάρξ with semantic sub-domain "desire strongly" *(Continued)*

Word	Gloss	CS w/ σάρξ	Word	Gloss	CS w/ σάρξ
ἐπιποθέω	to deeply desire	0.0804	ἐπιθυμητής	one who greatly desires	0.0402
ζηλόω	to set one's heart on	0.0786	αἰσχροκερδής	shamefully greedy	0.0361
πεινάω	to be hungry	0.0716	πλεονέκτης	greedy person	0.0325
πυρόομαι	to be on fire	0.0673	ἐκκαίομαι	to burn out	0.0181
κοιλία	belly	0.0672	ὄρεξις	Desire	0.0171

The final category that we will consider in this brief analysis of σάρξ is "25.12–32 B Desire Strongly." All the words in Table 5, of course, have to do with strong desire and the close relationship of σάρξ with this sub-domain demonstrates that σάρξ also has to do with desire. The primary reason for considering this list, however, is to see how many clearly negative words appear here: πλησμονή ("gratification"), πάθημα ("suffering"), ἡδονή ("pleasure"), θυμός ("fury"), πεινάω ("to be hungry") and πυρόομαι ("to be on fire") show up just on the first half of the list. This list should make it clear that "strong desire" is considered primarily as a negative thing in the New Testament and that the close relationship of σάρξ with this sub-domain certainly casts it in a negative light.

Having considered the order of the sub-domains to which σάρξ belongs and its relationship with the words in the top four sub-domains in that ranking, we can say that the evidence strongly suggests that σάρξ in the New Testament has moved away from its original sense of "flesh" and towards a more metaphorical meaning, something like "the physical, thinking, desiring part of human nature." It is also worth noting, however, that, while it does have the negative sense of "sexual desire" and it is related to many negative words in the sub-domain "25.12–32 B Desire Strongly," the negative connotations of σάρξ are not the primary ones in the New Testament. But it is also clear that the way has been paved for the negative aspects of σάρξ to become stronger, if for no other reason than that its primary meaning of "human nature" can be easily set against "divine nature" and, thus, given a negative cast. We see this happening already in the New Testament, primarily in Paul, and nowhere more clearly than in Galatians 5, where, for example, he writes ἡ γὰρ σὰρξ ἐπιθυμεῖ κατὰ τοῦ πνεύματος, τὸ δὲ πνεῦμα κατὰ τῆς σαρκός (Galatians 5:17, NRSV: "For what the flesh desires is opposed to the Spirit, and what the Spirit desires is opposed to the flesh"). And while statements like this are the exception in the New Testament, even for Paul, they plant σάρξ as "human nature" firmly against the divine nature, in the citation above represented by πνεῦμα, paving the way for more extreme representations of σάρξ in later Christianity.[44]

4.2 ΔAIMONION

The next word I will consider, δαιμόνιον ("demon"), shows the opposite pattern to what we saw above with σάρξ: it is a word that falls into only one semantic sub-domain, "12.1–42 A Supernatural Beings," into which it fits rather poorly. The average domain similarity score of δαιμόνιον in this sub-domain is only 0.0727, which, with an average standard score of only 0.6241, is the lowest for any word that occurs over 50 times and falls into only a single semantic sub-domain.[45] In our modern world, a demon is considered an other-worldly creature, some sort of spirit sent to possess a person or cause general trouble. For this reason, the Louw–Nida categorization as a supernatural being makes sense. So the question I will investigate in this section is why it fits so poorly in the semantic domain to which it would seem to us to fit most naturally. Since placement in the sub-domain for "Supernatural Beings" is primarily a statement about the nature and origin of demons, I will begin my investigation below by looking at the other semantic domains that would seem to deal with the nature and origin of objects and beings, i.e. domains 2 (Natural Substances), 3 (Plants), 4 (Animals), 9 (People), and 12 (Supernatural Beings and Powers). I take this as the first step in order to investigate if the New Testament writers may have categorized demons as some other sort of being as opposed to a heavenly one. Having looked at these five upper level semantic domains, I will drill down into sub-domains in each of these domains to determine if δαιμόνιον fits with any of them better than it does with "Supernatural Beings." If it does, then I will consider the individual words in the sub-domains in which it fits better and see if I can discover what type of being the writers of the New Testament thought demons were. If it does not fit better in any other sub-domain, then I will spend the last part of this section considering why it does not.

---

44 See, for instance, Teresa M. Shaw, *The Burden of the Flesh: Fasting and Sexuality in Early Christianity* (Minneapolis: Fortress Press, 1998).

45 Note that λοιπός has a lower score in its single domain (63.21–22 E Remnant), but each of the other words in its domain (ἐπίλοιπος, κατάλοιπος, λεῖμμα, ὑπόλειμμα) occurs only once, so the amount of data on which the score for λοιπός depends is too small to make any decisions from it. The word εἴτε also has a lower score with its single domain (89.65–70 J Condition), but as a conjunction, it carries more syntactic than semantic value and thus I did not choose it.

Table 6: Similarity of other "creature" domains with δαιμόνιον.

Domain	Ave CS	Ave σ
2 Natural Substances	0.0374	−0.3182
3 Plants	0.0347	−0.3924
4 Animals	0.0471	−0.0591
9 People	0.0570	0.2031
12 Supernatural Beings and Powers	0.0716	0.5958

Listed in Table 6 are the five top-level domains I listed above. The results of this table show that, despite the fairly low similarity with the "Supernatural Beings" sub-domain, δαιμόνιον is still drawn most closely to this upper level domain. This first, very general piece of evidence suggests that, like us, the New Testament writers would have considered demons also to be supernatural creatures. In order to flesh out this evidence, Table 7 shows more detail in terms of how δαιμόνιον relates to the individual sub-domains within these five top level domains. Notice that I have added one sub-domain that is outside of these five, i.e. "23.142–184 I Sickness, Disease, Weakness." I added this on the hunch that the New Testament authors may have seen demons more as a disease that needs to be cured instead of a creature.[46] Notice, first, that almost all of these sub-domains have a negative average standard score, which means that they fall below the mean similarity of all words in the New Testament with each other. I have highlighted the sub-domains that have positive scores in gray to set them apart. But even among these, there is not a single sub-domain that scores better than the "Supernatural Beings" sub-domain.

Table 7: Similarity of δαιμόνιον with "creature" sub-domains.

Sub-domain	CS Score with δαιμόνιον	Standard Score
2.1 A Elements	0.0430	−0.1705
2.2 B Air	0.0547	0.1429
2.3–6 C Fire	0.0411	−0.2211

---

[46] I admit that this view is perhaps a more modern one in which we would consider as a psychological illness what in the New Testament is classified as demon possession and its results. The results of this hunch that we see below, however, are quite interesting.

Table 7: Similarity of δαιμόνιον with "creature" sub-domains. *(Continued)*

Sub-domain	CS Score with δαιμόνιον	Standard Score
2.7–13 D Water	0.0398	−0.2549
2.14–28 E Earth, Mud, Sand, Rock	0.0429	−0.1723
2.29–48 F Precious and Semiprecious Stones and Substances	0.0185	−0.8243
2.49–62 G Metal	0.0545	0.1397
3.1 A Plants [General Meaning]	0.0229	−0.7069
3.2–12 B Trees	0.0301	−0.5125
3.13–32 C Plants That Are Not Trees	0.0399	−0.2525
3.33–46 D Fruit Parts of Plants	0.0288	−0.5484
3.47–59 E Non-Fruit Parts of Plants	0.0311	−0.4865
3.60–67 F Wood and Wood Products	0.0578	0.2265
4.1–37 A Animals	0.0515	0.0595
4.38–46 B Birds	0.0408	−0.2267
4.47–50 C Insects	0.0224	−0.7202
4.51–57 D Reptiles and Other "Creeping Things"	0.0536	0.1155
4.58–61 E Fishes and Other Sea Creatures	0.0246	−0.6615
9.1–23 A Human Beings	0.0699	0.5495
9.24–33 B Males	0.0466	−0.0714
9.34–40 C Females	0.0414	−0.2110
9.41–45 D Children	0.0472	−0.0558
9.46–48 E Persons For Whom There Is Affectionate Concern	0.0703	0.5614
12.1–42 Supernatural Beings	0.0727	0.6241
12.43–50 Supernatural Powers	0.0695	0.5393
23.142–184 I Sickness, Disease, Weakness	0.0709	0.5776

Since this evidence strongly suggests that Louw–Nida was correct in classifying the nature of demons as supernatural, I need to look at the evidence more carefully to determine why the CS score of δαιμόνιον in "Supernatural Beings" is so low. My next step, then, will be to consider all of the individual words in all of these sub-domains to see if any patterns emerge as to the type of being (or "Natural Substance" or "Sickness, Disease, Weakness") that the authors of the New Testament might have imagined δαιμόνιον to be.

Table 8: Top 10 most similar "creature" sub-domain words with δαιμόνιον.

Word	CS Score with δαιμόνιον	Standard Score
ἄρχων (supernatural power)	0.4529	10.7832
δαιμονίζομαι (be demon possessed)	0.2426	5.1638
νόσος (sickness)	0.2357	4.9794
ἄρρωστος (ill)	0.2228	4.6347
κάρφος (splinter, speck)	0.2097	4.2846
ἀκάθαρτος (unclean spirit)	0.1936	3.8544
ὄνομα (name)	0.1904	3.7689
μαλακία (sickness)	0.1809	3.5151
λεπρός (leper)	0.1792	3.4696
βάτραχος (frog)	0.1757	3.3761

Table 8 shows the top ten most similar words to δαιμόνιον from among the 26 semantic sub-domains listed in Table 7.[47] On this list, two of the ten words come from the "Supernatural Beings" sub-domain (δαιμονίζομαι and ἀκάθαρτος). These words either name demons themselves or the results of their activity. The top word that is not on this list, δαίμων, reinforces this pattern. We have to go down to number 19 on the list of most similar words to find the next word from the "Supernatural Beings" sub-domain with θεός (CS: 0.1236, Standard Score: 1.9839). That strongly suggests that most of the strength of the relationship between δαιμόνιον and this semantic sub-domain comes from the other words that are directly related to demons and demonic activity rather than their supernatural nature. But if we include the one word on this list from the "Supernatural

---

[47] See Table C in the Appendices of my dissertation for the full list of words in these domains with their similarity to δαιμόνιον: Munson, *Biblical Semantics*, 145–47.

Powers" sub-domain, ἄρχων, then perhaps we do get some insight into the nature of demons as the New Testament writers saw them. But it is not as simple as saying that instead of "Supernatural Beings" they were seen as "Supernatural Powers." The similarity score between δαιμόνιον and ἄρχων is an extreme exception within the "Supernatural Powers" sub-domain, with the next most similar word, δόξα coming in with a standard score of only 1.217. There are five other words in the "Supernatural Beings" domain that are more similar: θεός (Z-Score: 1.9839), εἴδωλον (1.8958), πονηρός (1.7755), υἱός (1.4762), and πειράζω (1.2384). This means that, even more so than in the "Supernatural Beings" sub-domain, its similarity with the "Supernatural Powers" sub-domain comes from a single aspect of the semantics of δαιμόνιον: its relationship to ἄρχων. Besides these three supernatural words, we also see four of the 10 words from the "Sickness" sub-domain (νόσος, ἄρρωστος, μαλακία, and λεπρός). And besides these four, there are three more words from this sub-domain in the top 20 on our list of most similar words from these sub-domains: κακῶς, συσπαράσσω, and πονηρός. The evidence that I will present below will provide even stronger evidence that the New Testament writers saw demons and demon-possession as a kind of disease.

Before coming to that discussion, however, the last three words in this list, κάρφος, ὄνομα, and βάτραχος, will require a deeper analysis since they do not obviously fit into any of obvious semantic pattern. ὄνομα occurs 229 times in the New Testament, but the explanation as to why it is so similar to δαιμόνιον is surprisingly simple: they co-occur quite significantly together. They both land as the number 16 co-occurrent on the other's list, according to Log-Likelihood, and, thus, share many similar co-occurrents simply by the fact that the words that occur in all of these passages co-occur with both words. In fact, in five different passages (Matthew 7:22, Mark 9:38, Mark 16:17, Luke 9:49, and Luke 10:17) demons are said to be cast out in the name (τῷ ὀνόματί) of Jesus. So the name of Jesus relates very closely to demon exorcism.[48] The word κάρφος appears only 6 times in the New Testament: Matthew 7:3, 7:4, 7:5, Luke 6:41, and 6:42 (2x). These are all in the context of Jesus instructing his listeners to look first to their own sins by telling them to "first take the log out of your own eye, and then you will see clearly to take the speck [κάρφος] out of your neighbor's eye" (Matthew 7:5 = Luke 6:42). But this saying is in neither Gospel related in any way to demon possession or even heavenly beings at all. Why, then, should this word be so closely related to δαιμόνιον? We need look only briefly at the top three co-

---

[48] This relationship of demons to miraculous deeds done by or in the name of Jesus will be strengthened below.

occurrents for each word, as represented by their log-likelihood score, between these two words (shown in Figure 4) to discover the answer to the question. There we see that the top co-occurrent for δαιμόνιον and the third for κάρφος are the same: ἐκβάλλω. ἐκβάλλω is the word used to describe the exorcism of demons and, in the stories about specks and logs in Matthew and Luke, the word is used three times in each story to describe removing either the speck or the log from the eye. So δαιμόνιον and κάρφος are not similar because they somehow share the same nature but, instead, because in the New Testament they both fall into the category of ἐκβαλλόμενοι, i.e. "things that are removed/expelled."

Figure 4: Top 3 co-occurrents with δαιμόνιον and κάρφος.

Δαιμόνιον		κάρφος	
ἐκβάλλω	182.6842	ὀφθαλμός	72.1339
δαιμόνιον	110.1079	δοκός	70.8468
Βεελζεβούλ	88.1081	ἐκβάλλω	31.1088

The example of βάτραχος is more straightforward. This word appears only once, in Revelation 16:13, and the word δαιμονίων appears only four words away, at the beginning of 16:14. Not only this, but another word that co-occurs significantly with δαιμονίων, ἀκάθαρτος, occurs only two words before βάτραχος in 16:13. This is a similarity that actually focuses on the nature of demons as evil spiritual beings since, as the only occurrence of βάτραχος in the New Testament, "frogs" are very closely related to πνεύματα ἀκάθαρτα (16:13), which would seem to be the category under which demons would also fall (see e.g. Mark 1:23–45). As a final step in this investigation I will consider the case of the words from the "Sickness" sub-domain, νόσος, ἄρρωστος, μαλακία, and λεπρός. Figure 5 shows the top 10 most similar words for each of these. While there is a lot of data in this figure, most of it falls within just a few categories. The first of these categories, highlighted in light gray, represents words that serve as descriptions of a malady: κωφός, μαλακία, δαιμονίζομαι, ἄρρωστος, σεληνιάζομαι, βάσανος, μάστιξ, νόσος, βλάπτω, ἐνοχλέω, λέπρα, and χωλός. These descriptions concentrate under the 4 sickness words, with λεπρός having three, ἄρρωστος and μαλακία four, and νόσος five while there is only one in the top 10 with δαιμόνιον. The second group, in medium gray, describe the action of curing someone or the results of this action: ἐκβάλλω, θεραπεύω, ἐπιτίθημι, ἰάομαι, καθαρίζω, διαβλέπω, and εὐθέως. These words are fairly evenly distributed among the individual lists with νόσος having one, ἄρρωστος, λεπρός and μαλακία two, and δαιμόνιον three. The words in dark gray are descriptions of the surrounding in which the healing act takes place: ἔξω, πολύς, ὄχλος, ὑποχωρέω, and παράλιος. This group of words shows no representatives with λεπρός, one representative with μαλακία and δαιμόνιον, two with ἄρρωστος, and three with νόσος. And, finally, the words in black are the two words that tie all of these words together: θανάσιμον and δωρεάν. θανάσιμον occurs only in Mark 16:18 and δωρεάν, while occurring nine times throughout the New Testament, occurs twice in a similar context in Matthew 10:8. In both of these passages, Jesus is commissioning his apostles to go out and perform wondrous deeds. The former mentions casting out demons in 16:17 and healing the sick in 16:18 while the latter also mentions curing the sick and casting out demons. It is with these two words that we finally find the key to how to interpret demons and sickness together: both of them represent miracles that Jesus, and his disciples, perform. And, as we saw in my brief analysis of the relationship of ὄνομα and δαιμόνιον, these miraculous deeds were performed ἐν τῷ ὀνόματί σου.

Figure 5: Top 10 most similar words to δαιμόνιον, νόσος, ἄρρωστος, μαλακία, and λεπρός.

δαιμόνιον	νόσος	ἄρρωστος	μαλακία	λεπρός
βεελζεβούλ	Μαλακία	θανάσιμον	νόσος	Καθαρίζω
ἐκβάλλω	Δαιμονίζομαι	νόσος	θεραπεύω	Λέπρα
ἄρχων	Θεραπεύω	βλάπτω	κηρύσσω	ἀλάβαστρος
ἔξω	ἄρρωστος	πολύς	ποικίλος	Κωφός
κωφός	Σεληνιάζομαι	ὄχλος	παράλιος	Θέλω
διαβλέπω	βάσανος	θεραπεύω	ἄρρωστος	Χωλός
συροφοινίκισσα	πολύς	μαλακία	πᾶς	Καταχέω
θανάσιμον	ὄχλος	ἐπιτίθημι	βάσανος	εὐθέως
ἔννυχα	Μάστιξ	κἄν	ἐνοχλέω	Δωρεάν
θεραπεύω	ὑποχωρέω	δαιμονίζομαι	ἰάομαι	ἀλάβαστρον

This, I think, is finally the key to understanding why δαιμόνιον fits so poorly into its proper semantic sub-domain of "Supernatural Beings." The reason is that, for the New Testament authors, it does not matter where demons come from, what other beings they are related to, or how they were created. Instead, what is important is that demons act throughout the Gospels, along with illness, as one major motivation for miracle stories. This demonstrates something that we should have already expected: when one relies on distributional semantics the text and the context determines the meaning of a word. If our text would have been an excursus on the nature of demons, then I expect that δαιμόνιον would have been more similar to other "Supernatural Beings" words. As it is, this is not a description of the text of the New Testament and so it returns very little information of this sort (though see βάτραχος). And distributional semantics does not read this outside knowledge about demons back into the text. In terms of lexical and contextual meaning mentioned above, what our investigation shows is that distributional methods return information about the contextual meaning of words, which is exactly what we should expect given their reliance on distributional data to represent meaning. We, as readers, can bring our own knowledge of a word's lexical meaning to bear as we see fit, but we should always be careful not to let it overwhelm what the text itself tells us.[49]

5 Bibliography

Association for Computational Linguistics. "Statistical Semantics." Wiki of the Association for Computational Linguistics, 2010. https://aclweb.org/aclwiki/Statistical_Semantics.

Association for Computational Linguistics. "TOEFL Synonym Questions (State of the Art)." Wiki of the Association for Computational Linguistics. https://aclweb.org/aclwiki/TOEFL_Synonym_Questions_(State_of_the_art).

Bullinaria, John A., and Joseph P. Levy. "Extracting Semantic Representations from Word Co-Occurrence Statistics: A Computational Study." University of Birmingham, 2007. https://www.cs.bham.ac.uk/~jxb/PUBS/BRM.pdf.

Bullinaria, John A., and Joseph P. Levy. "Extracting Semantic Representations from Word Co-Occurrence Statistics: Stop-Lists, Stemming and SVD." University of Birmingham, 2012. http://www.cs.bham.ac.uk/~jxb/PUBS/BRM2.pdf.

Danker, Frederick W., Walter Bauer, and William Arndt. *A Greek–English Lexicon of the New Testament and Other Early Christian Literature*. 3rd ed. Chicago: University of Chicago Press, 2000.

Delavenay, E. *An Introduction to Machine Translation*. New York: Thames and Hudson, 1960.

Dunning, Ted. "Accurate Methods for the Statistics of Surprise and Coincidence." *Computational Linguistics* 19 (1993): 61–74.

Harris, Zellig. "Distributional Structure." *Word* 10, no. 23 (1954): 146–62.

Harris, Zellig. How Words Carry Meaning. Columbia University, 1986. http://zelligharris.org/BL3.2.Words.html.

Jurafsky, Daniel, and James H. Martin. *Speech and Language Processing: An Introduction to Natural Language Processing, Computational Linguistics, and Speech Recognition*. 2nd ed. Prentice Hall Series in Artificial Intelligence. Upper Saddle River, NJ: Pearson Education, 2009.

Landauer, Thomas K., and Susan T. Dumais. "A Solution to Plato's Problem: The Latent Semantic Analysis Theory of Acquisition, Induction, and Representation of Knowledge."

---

[49] Again, a reference to the discussion of the danger of translating σάρξ as "flesh" is germane here: Nida, Louw, and Smith, "Semantic Domains," 140–41.

Psychological Review 104, no. 2 (1997): 211–40. https://doi.org/10.1037/0033-295X.104.2.211.

Louw, Johannes P. "How Do Words Mean – If They Do?" *Filología Neotestamentaria* 4 (1991): 125–42.

Louw, Johannes P., and Eugene A. Nida. *Greek–English Lexicon of the New Testament: Based on Semantic Domains*. 2nd ed. New York: United Bible Societies, 1989.

Munson, Matthew. *Biblical Semantics: Applying Digital Methods for Semantic Information Extraction to Current Problems in New Testament Studies*. Theologische Studien. Aachen: Shaker Verlag, 2017.

Nida, Eugene A. *Componential Analysis of Meaning*. The Hague: Mouton, 1975.

Nida, Eugene A., Johannes P. Louw, and Rondal B. Smith. "Semantic Domains and Componential Analysis of Meaning." In *Current Issues in Linguistic Theory*, edited by Roger William Cole, 139–67. Bloomington, IN: Indiana University Press, 1977.

Shaw, Teresa M. *The Burden of the Flesh: Fasting and Sexuality in Early Christianity*. Minneapolis: Fortress Press, 1998.

Turney, Peter D., Michael L. Littman, Jeffrey Bigham, and Victor Shnayder. "Combining Independent Modules to Solve Multiple-Choice Synonym and Analogy Problems." *CoRR* cs.CL/0309035 (2003). http://arxiv.org/abs/cs.CL/0309035.

United Bible Societies. "A Semantic Dictionary of Biblical Hebrew." https://semanticdictionary.org/.

ём # Part III: **Digital Christian history**

Delfi I. Nieto-Isabel and Carlos López-Arenillas
From inquisition to inquiry: inquisitorial records as a source for social network analysis

In October 1248, Pope Innocent IV decided that the part of the ecclesiastical province of Narbonne that politically depended on the King of Aragon would also depend on the inquisitors of that kingdom.[1] He therefore instructed the archbishop of Narbonne to commission a text describing the inquisitorial procedure as it was conducted in the region of Languedoc in order to send it to Aragonese officials. The result of these efforts was the collection of materials known as the *Ordo processus Narbonensis*.[2] Now lost, the *Ordo processus Narbonensis* is the first known official document to address the whole procedure of an inquisition and include a list of questions.[3] Even though this text is a mere outline in comparison to the most sophisticated inquisitors' manuals of the late 13th and early 14th century, it already betrayed the inquisitorial concern about the connections of individuals with suspected heretics.

The aim of this chapter is to show that the relational nature of inquisitorial records makes them an ideal source for the application of the formal methods of social network analysis to the study of personal connections within religious movements, but also that understanding the sociological features and constraints of the inquisitorial procedure is essential for this approach to succeed. Our purpose is to showcase the theoretical considerations behind this specific part of what has become the digital humanist's toolkit, in particular, for the study of Christian realities. Thus, our focus is not a detailed exploration of digital methodologies but a conceptual discussion of formal issues without which the whole digital approach to these sources would be rendered useless.

---

[1] Yves Dossat, "Le plus ancient manuel de l'inquisition méridionale: le Processus inquisitions (1248–1249)," *Bulletin philologique et historique (jusq'à 1715)* (1952): 33–7; Yves Dossat, *Les crises de l'Inquisition Toulousaine au XIIIe siècle (1233–1273)* (Bordeaux: Imprimerie Bière, 1959), 167–8.
[2] The Dominican François Balme discovered the only extant copy of the *Ordo processus Narbonensis* in Manuscript 53 of the Biblioteca Universitaria de Madrid around 1880. Sadly, this library was dismembered by Royal Order of 6 May 1897 into nine autonomous institutions, and its holdings were transferred to nine different venues, some of which merged over time. At present, the manuscript's whereabouts remain unknown.
[3] Adolphe Tardif, "Document pour l'histoire du *processus per inquisitionem* et de l'*inquisitio heretice pravitatis*," *Nouvelle Revue du droit français et étranger* 7 (1883): 669–78.

The current conception of social network analysis was born around the 1970s as an inherently interdisciplinary field that emerged from the unlikely association of sociology, anthropology, and mathematics. Although social networks were indirectly present in the idea of social group developed by Durkheim and Tönnie in the 1890s,[4] it was during the 1930s that this theoretical construct saw its first major developments.[5] Jacob L. Moreno, considered one of the founders of social network analysis, was a pioneer of sociometry, the quantitative study of social relationships, into which he incorporated the mathematical graph theory. A psychiatrist and psychosociologist, he published some of the first sociograms, that is, depictions of social networks, which he used to analyse preferences within small groups.[6]

In the 1970s, the mathematical innovations of the so-called Harvard Revolution represented a major breakthrough for the ever-growing number of scholars devoted to the study of social networks. Harrison White, a theoretical physicist and sociologist who was very much concerned about the lack of scientificity of the analysis of social structures, influenced many scholars, among them his student Mark Granovetter, whose renowned article "The Strength of Weak Ties" fostered the application of network analysis to a variety of case studies and popularized the methodology.[7] Finally, in the 1990s, the most recent addition to social network analysis was the contribution of physicists to network studies and the application of their models to social phenomena. Although harshly criticized by sociologists for their apparent disregard for (or lack of knowledge of) previous research, the works of Watts and Strogatz, and Albert and Barabási have undeniably opened up new perspectives and de facto created the new field of sociophysics.[8]

Social science studies based on historical data showed that the methods of social network analysis can be successfully applied to specific sets of historical

---

4 Émile Durkheim, *De la division du travail social: étude sur l'organisation des sociétés supérieures* (Paris: Félix Alcan, 1893); Ferdinand Tönnies, *Gemeinschaft und Gesellschaft* (Leipzig: Fues' Verlag, 1887).
5 For an overview of the development of social network analysis from the 1930s to the present, see John P. Scott, *Social Network Analysis* (Los Angeles: SAGE, 2013), 11–39.
6 Jacob L. Moreno, *Who Shall Survive: A New Approach to the Problem of Human Interrelations* (Washington D.C.: Nervous and Mental Disease Publishing Co., 1934).
7 Mark S. Granovetter, "The Strength of Weak Ties," *American Journal of Sociology* 78, no. 6 (1973): 1360–80.
8 See Scott, *Social Network Analysis*, 38. For the seminal papers of social physics, see Duncan J. Watts and Steven H. Strogatz, "Collective Dynamics of 'Small-World' Networks," *Nature* 393, no. 6684 (1998): 440–42; Réka Albert and Albert-László Barabási, "Statistical Mechanics of Complex Networks," *Reviews of Modern Physics* 74 (2002): 48–97.

data,[9] and this merge of network theory and historical methods is what characterizes the young and burgeoning field of Historical Network Analysis. Moreover, the inclusion of social network analysis as part of the methodological background of digital humanists has allowed innovative approaches to the study of correspondences, social movements, kinship, relations of power, and economic history.[10]

In general, the dearth of data characteristic of many medieval contexts hinders the systematic collection and recording of information, but the fact is that the specific case of inquisitorial sources offers a distinct vantage point that so far has mostly been explored theoretically.[11] The inquisitorial procedure and the textual sources it generated stemmed from a relational worldview. As will be discussed below, inquisitors only saw individuals to the extent that they were connected to each other, which was in fact the basis for the whole inquisitorial system. Thus, despite the inaccuracies and obstacles inherent to this kind of sources, they allow for a strong structural approach. Such an approach, which potentially involves thousands of historical actors and relations, would not be possible, or would be much more complicated, without the use of digital tools.

The present chapter proposes some theoretical reflections based on the analysis of the inquisitorial registers copied in Manuscripts 21 to 37 of the Doat Collection (Bibliotèque nationale de France), the *Book of Sentences* of the Dominican inquisitor Bernard Gui (1308–1323, Add. MS 4697 British Library), and the records of the inquisitions held by Jacques Fournier (1318–1325, MS Lat. 4030 Biblioteca Apostolica Vaticana). The first step of this analysis consisted in breaking down the sources into information units, a process that is both quantitative and qualitative. Given the initial estimate of the number of actors involved in the

---

9 Peter S. Bearman, *Relations into Rhetorics: Local Elite Social Structure in Norfolk, England, 1540–1640* (New Brunswick: Rutgers University Press, 1993); Roger V. Gould, *Insurgent Identities: Class, Community, and Protest in Paris from 1848 to the Commune* (Chicago: University of Chicago, 1995); John F. Padgett and Christopher K. Ansell, "Robust Action and the Rise of the Medici, 1400–1434," *American Journal of Sociology* 98 (1993): 1259–1319; Charles Tilly, *Popular Contention in Great Britain, 1758–1843* (Cambridge, MA: Harvard University Press, 1995).
10 Andreas Gestrich and Martin Stark, eds., *Debtors, Creditors, and Their Networks: Social Dimensions of Monetary Dependence from the Seventeenth to the Twentieth Century* (London: German Historical Institute London, 2015); Margaret Mullett, *Theophylacht of Ochrid: Reading the Letters of a Byzantine Archbishop* (Aldershot: Variorum, 1997); Isabelle Rosé, "Reconstitution, représentation graphique et analyse des réseaux de pouvoir au haut Moyen Âge: Approche des pratiques sociales de l'aristocratie à partir de l'exemple d'Odon de Cluny († 942)," *Redes. Revista hispana para el análisis de redes sociales* 21 (2011): 199–272.
11 Paul Ormerod and Andrew P. Roach, "The Medieval Inquisition: Scale-Free Networks and the Suppression of Heresy," *Physica A* 339 (2004): 645–52.

case studies considered – around 2,000 – digital humanities proved as the only valid framework for such an analysis. A data model was designed to deal with information, the management of unstructured data, and its transformation into a structured format ready for analysis. This model enabled the collection of data enriched with relational, geographical, and temporal attributes, but also allowed for a modelization of uncertainty, that is, the codification of ambiguity and vagueness in names, dates, places and the other categories of the model.[12] Information units were in turn handled and rearranged to help test hypotheses, and digital resources assisted with the exploration and visualization of data in space and time. These included a MySQL database, statistical analysis software, and UCINET 6.620, a general package focused on the analysis of sociometric data.[13]

We have simultaneously worked on two different fronts: reconstructing the process of information gathering and reconstructing the sample. The former involves using additional sources, such as inquisitorial manuals, while, in turn, reconstructing the sample entails considering the special circumstances under which the depositions took place. This double reconstruction process, together with the data model that builds on it, has allowed us to address structural questions such as the community performance of dissident groups, the identification of network topologies and common patterns, and the reassessment of the participation of women, which we have addressed elsewhere.[14]

Our purpose is not to liken inquisitors to sociologists but to compare the methods of inquisitorial inquiry to current sociological techniques in order to better understand the dissident networks that were the subject of their persecution. To that end, it is imperative to establish the criteria of inquisitors as to what defined "heretics," for these will determine the kind of individuals that were likely to be considered as part of said networks, and the social structures that we can expect to extract from these sources. In the following pages we will first introduce the features and limitations of inquisitorial sources and then

---

12 On the need for a modelization of uncertainty in theoretical digital humanities, see Michael Piotrowski, "Accepting and Modeling Uncertainty," *Zeitschrift für digitale Geisteswissenschaften*, Sonderband 4 (2019), http://dx.doi.org/10.17175/sb004_006a.

13 Stephen P. Borgatti, Martin G. Everett, and Linton C. Freeman, eds., "UCINET," in *Encyclopedia of Social Network Analysis and Mining*, ed. Reda Alhajj and Jon Rokne (New York: Springer, 2014): 2261–67.

14 Delfi I. Nieto-Isabel, "Communities of Dissent: Social Network Analysis of Religious Dissident Groups in Languedoc in the Thirteenth and Fourteenth Centuries" (PhD diss., University of Barcelona, 2018).

will turn to the analysis of the inquisition as a sociological inquiry and the study of its sampling techniques.

1 The lights and shadows of inquisitorial records

The vicissitudes of time have drastically reduced the vast inquisition archives of Carcassonne and Toulouse. Most records of 13th-century inquisitions have only survived in 17th-century copies, and a handful were preserved by chance in the bindings of later volumes.[15] The fortune of 14th–century inquisitorial records was better, although the extant sources are but a very small part of what they originally were.[16] Therefore, it is crucial to bear in mind that any research on inquisitorial sources builds on partial evidence, not only because of their uneven preservation over time and the limitations inherent to them, but also because it stands to reason that inquisitors were not that efficient and that many of the people involved in dissident groups were able to remain undetected.

The wealth of data compiled in inquisitorial records and their confessional character convey a twofold purpose. On the one hand, inquisitorial registers and other types of inquisitorial texts acted as a sort of collective textual memory for inquisitors, reflecting a common discourse on heresy and establishing a classification of the different categories of transgression.[17] On the other hand, recording events and the people involved in them had a distinct coercive goal.[18] Individuals whose names were associated with the crime of heresy were forever placed under suspicion, for the inquisitorial register granted a certain degree of timelessness to their implication. For instance, on 30 November 1243, the widow Bernarda Targueira confessed that 30 years before she had been a vested heretic for three years and a half;[19] and in February 1324, Peire Astruc testified about his

---

[15] Dossat, *Les crises de l'Inquisition*, 29–55; James B. Given, *Inquisition and Medieval Society: Power, Discipline, and Resistance in Languedoc* (Ithaca: Cornell University Press, 1997), 26–28.
[16] See the well-referenced reflection on this subject in Mark Gregory Pegg, *The Corruption of Angels: The Great Inquisition of 1245–1246* (Princeton: Princeton University Press, 2001).
[17] John H. Arnold, *Inquisition and Power: Catharism and the Confessing Subject in Medieval Languedoc* (University Park, PA: Pennsylvania State University Press, 2001), 37–47.
[18] The provincial council held in Béziers in 1232 set forth the idea of using the record of past transgressions as a means to monitor the spiritual performance of a community; see Giovanni Domenico Mansi, ed., *Sacrorum conciliorum nova et amplissima collection*, vol. 23 (Venice: Antonio Zatta, 1779), col. 271.
[19] MS Doat 22, fol. 2r: "testis iurata dixit quod fuit haeretica induta per tres annos et dimidium, et sunt triginta anni."

contact with two *good men*, which had also taken place 30 years earlier.[20] The register was meant to deter from further involvement, given that a previous recorded abjuration and sentence would put the accused in the difficult position of being condemned as a relapser and handed over to the secular arm. Furthermore, a conviction for heresy also affected the descendants of the accused, who often found themselves dispossessed.[21] Registers were instruments of repression in their own right, for they put in writing the creation of the new social group of convicted heretics. Thus, whereas other inquisitorial and ecclesiastic materials allow us to reconstruct beliefs as well as to study Church history and the persecution of dissident religious movements, inquisitorial records enable a shift of focus towards the target of such persecution, the members of those movements.

The particularities of inquisitorial records raise the need for a few generic methodological remarks regarding their use as historical sources.[22] First, it is necessary to bear in mind that testimonies underwent several successive alterations before ending up as written evidence.[23] Deponents, inquisitors, notaries, and scribes selected what they said or wrote down according to their own criteria and constraints, exercising their sometimes quite restricted agency; but adding to it, the inquisitorial procedure inherently contained a fundamental mechanism of alteration, that is, depositions were built on a delayed "dialogue" that was simultaneously maintained in two different languages.[24] Questions were posed and answered in the vernacular, and the essential parts of the answers were translated into Latin while mostly changing the first person into the third.

---

[20] MS Doat 27, fols. 33v–34r: "viginti octo anni vel triginta potuerunt esse vel circa tempore confessionis factae per eum de infrascriptis, duo homines de Albia quos nominat venerunt ad operatorium suum."

[21] See MS Doat 21, fols. 52r–58r for the papal constitutions issued by Pope Alexander IV (d. 1261) banning convicted heretics from holding public offices until the second generation.

[22] Medieval inquisitorial registers present a paradigmatic case where a great potential for research is hindered by a high density of uncertainty. The formal characterization and systematization of the different degrees of uncertainty inherent to these sources as well as their operationalization into machine-readable information is the subject of a paper currently in progress.

[23] Caterina Bruschi, *The Wandering Heretics of Languedoc*, Cambridge Studies in Medieval Life and Thought Fourth Series (New York: Cambridge University Press, 2009), 14–26; Caterina Bruschi, "'Magna diligentia est habenda per inquisitorem': Precautions before Reading Doat 21–26," in *Texts and the Repression of Medieval Heresy*, ed. Caterina Bruschi and Peter Biller, York Studies in Medieval Theology 4 (York: York Medieval Press, 2003): 81–110.

[24] We are foregoing here the debate on the accuracy of the word "dialogue" to describe the interaction between inquisitors and deponents; on this matter, see Arnold, *Inquisition and Power*, 8–13, and Carlo Ginzburg, "The Inquisitor as Anthropologist," in *Clues, Myths, and the Historical Method*, ed. Carlo Ginzburg, trans. J. and A. Tedeschi (Baltimore: Johns Hopkins University Press, 1989), 158.

These summarized versions of the depositions were then orally translated back into the vernacular and read out loud to the deponents so that they could verify them, and finally the verified deposition was again rendered in Latin and became public instrument. Even in the best-case scenario, this process resulted in a record that was biased both in form and substance.

The differences in form were not only due to the formulaic nature of the questions and, consequently, the answers, but also to the recording itself, for scribes and notaries shared the legal background, language, and vocabulary of inquisitors. Thus, it is only in the brief passages kept in the original language that we can be fairly certain about the deponents' own words.[25] As for the alterations in content undergone by the original testimonies, the record was neither literal nor comprehensive: not all questions were recorded, and neither were the complete answers. The Dominican inquisitor Bernard Gui in his *Practica inquisitionis heretice pravitatis* – completed between 1323 and 1324 – advised his fellow inquisitors not to record all the questions and answers, but only those relevant to the truth they were seeking.[26] Moreover, in the context of inquisitorial questioning, deponents did not give their testimony freely but were forced to do so under stressful circumstances, for their own fate often depended on it. Fear played a major role in the construction of their discourse, most likely leading them to hide as much of the truth as they could or to play down their involvement. But many of these deponents were prepared to stay true to their faith whatever the cost; after all, the fear of the stake weighed little against risking the eternal condemnation of their souls.[27]

To conclude this brief overview of inquisitorial sources, it must be noted that the copies of inquisitorial records in the volumes of the Collection Doat add very specific problems to the aforementioned set of difficulties. First, given that these are 17th-century copies of mostly 13th- and 14th-century originals, the mistakes of Doat copyists need to be considered along with the classic problem of scribal errors.[28] Secondly, Doat volumes are compilations and excerpts of previous re-

---

25 Annie Cazenave, "De la parole au texte: les termes de Langue d'Oc dans les actes latins," *Bulletin philologique et historique* (1979): 77–98.
26 Guillaume Mollat, ed., *Manuel de l'inquisiteur Bernard Gui*, vol. 1 (Paris: Les Belles Lettres, 1964), 32.
27 Bruschi, *Wandering Heretics*, 142–89; Mary Douglas, *Risk Acceptability According to the Social Sciences*, Social Research Perspectives 11 (New York: Russell Sage Foundation, 1986); David L. Scruton, "The Anthropology of an Emotion," in *Sociophobics: The Anthropology of Fear*, ed. David L. Scruton (Boulder, CO: Westview Press, 1986): 7–49.
28 Peter Biller, Caterina Bruschi, and Shelagh Sneddon, eds., *Inquisitors and Heretics in Thirteenth-Century Languedoc: Edition and Translation of Toulouse Inquisition Depositions, 1273–1282*, Studies in the History of Christian Traditions 147 (Leiden: Brill, 2011), 117–20.

cords, which further altered the contents and the overall appearance of the original inquisitions, for the selection and the arrangement that followed were made according to the purposes and constraints of the Doat mission.[29] Finally, from the standpoint of historical network analysis, the main problem is the fact that this selection had little to do with the actual circumstances surrounding the original dissident groups and the inquisitions that involved them. However, this does not make the results of their analysis less valid, it only hides information that could be useful for a better reconstruction of dissident networks.

2 Inquisition: a very particular type of sociological inquiry

In the eyes of inquisitors, individuals were only persons of interest inasmuch as they were related to other persons of interest, that is, only to the extent that they belonged to a specific group. The succinct *Ordo processus Narbonnensis* focused on the connections with suspected heretics, as if inquisitors acted already knowing who those "heretics" were,[30] and then turned to their neighbors, acquaintances and, in general, the whole population of the area, in order to assess and truncate the expansion of heretical tenets.

Inquisitors shaped the discourse of the deponents, which severely limits the capability of historians to piece together any kind of individuality. Therefore, it is legitimate to ponder whether the interference of inquisitors obtrudes the validity of the relational structure we can extract from inquisitorial records. In our view, far from being a veil that needs to be torn down, inquisitorial questions formed a pattern, and it is both the text that escapes such pattern and the pattern itself that constitute invaluable sources of information. Furthermore, said patterns evolved over time, and whereas early records showed a more factual interest, later sources evince a shift in focus to a more elaborate account that also provides information about motivation, personal decisions and opinions.[31]

The main focus of medieval inquisitors was not the sociological dimension of heretical movements, but rather the identification of the men and women who either held and endorsed certain beliefs, or had been in contact with "proven" heretics. Thus, their questions about the things said, shared, and exchanged

---

29 Ibid., 20–26.
30 Lucy Sackville, *Heresy and Heretics in the Thirteenth Century: The Textual Representations* (Suffolk: Boydell & Brewer, 2011), 142.
31 Arnold, *Inquisition and Power*, 98–99.

by certain individuals produced a wealth of relational information that can be used to analyze the social networks extracted from their records. It is in this sense that we can regard an *inquisitio* as a sociological inquiry into dissident movements. Moreover, as we will discuss in the following section, inquisitors used a sampling method that closely resembled snowball sampling.

The usual course of action when the suspicion of heresy aroused in a specific area was conducting an inquest. During a *predicatio generalis*, delivered before the local clergy and an assembly of other people, inquisitors publicly announced the purpose of the *inquisitio* and read out loud the letters of commission from the Pope and the provincial prior. A period of grace was established during which all who came forward were granted a relative leniency,[32] and, at the same time, a general summons was issued for all men older than 14 and all women older than 12 to appear before the inquisitors and answer their questions.

As noted in the previous section, the interrogation that followed had a strong formulaic character. The specific words with which deponents answered were not as important as the way in which their replies fitted into the inquisitorial narrative. Inquisitorial questions provided the basic script for the confessions that were to be extracted from deponents. The relation between inquisitors and deponents was thus openly asymmetrical and hierarchical, for the punitive and normative nature of the inquisitorial procedure corresponds to an exercise of power.[33] The fact that this power relation was in plain sight, placing inquisitors and deponents in well-established hermeneutical frameworks, limits the information available to both inquisitors and historians, but facilitates the task of identifying eventual biases.

The core of the inquisition was conducted in secrecy, thus, the accused did not know the name of their accusers nor the specific charges brought against them; people whose testimony was usually not accepted in secular trials were accepted as inquisitorial witnesses, suspects were forced to confess under oath at the risk of being declared impenitent heretics otherwise, and the sentences of inquisitorial tribunals were unappealable. Moreover, inquisitors were the first to resort to long-term imprisonment as a coercive strategy meant to extract confessions from reluctant deponents.[34] Self-incriminating statements were not only essential for true repentance, but also turned suspects into a source of information about other members of their network.

---

32 Mansi, *Sacrorum conciliorum*, vol. 23, cols. 690–703.
33 Arnold, *Inquisition and Power*, 90–93.
34 James B. Given, "The Inquisitors of Languedoc and the Medieval Technology of Power," *American Historical Review* 94, no. 2 (1989): 336–59; Given, *Inquisition and Medieval Society*.

The *Ordo processus Narbonensis* was the first official document to address the whole procedure of an inquisition and to include a list of questions, which, as befits mid-13th century inquisitions, were focused on the deponents' actions and not on their beliefs.[35] Inquisitorial treatises on heresy also placed under suspicion all those who visited heretics when captured, brought them victuals, lamented their capture or death, excused them or claimed that they had been unjustly condemned, and those who kept their bones as relics. The resulting degrees of involvement would still be functioning in the early 14th century, although by then the concept of heresy involved a wider variety of cases than it did a century before. This situation translated into a need for more varied formulas to properly interrogate the suspected members of each group and ascribe them to the most suitable category of transgression. Thus, the evolution of inquisitorial question lists was the result of both a diversification of evidence between the mid-13th and the early 14th century and the consolidation of the inquisitorial practice and discourse that made the prosecution of spiritual dissent more efficient.

Inquisitors were interested in knowing who had been in contact with heretics in order to gauge and ultimately end the spread of heresy. But they also wanted details on individual involvement so that they could impose the proper penance and obtain relational information about other people with a similar degree of implication. Thanks to the relational nature of the documents left by such a line of questioning, the acquaintanceship network of suspected heretics can be reconstructed through the application of the methods of social network analysis. Furthermore, it is also possible to extract other networks based on specific types of relations from the same set of actors, which, according to our data model, has allowed us to separately analyze, among others, the distribution of victuals and money, commensality, and assistance and teaching practices. In addition, through the use of UCINET we have jointly analyzed these multiplex relations. This has furthered our understanding of the structure of these communities and has helped us to level down the bias of inquisitorial sampling methods towards the overrepresentation of some actors, which will be discussed below.

From a social constructionist perspective, the inquisitorial procedure was a process of social construction of heretical identities, which is rather different from the invention of heretical structures that some authors have proposed.[36] Im-

---

35 Tardif, "Document pour l'histoire," 672.
36 Antonio Sennis, ed., *Cathars in Question* (Suffolk: Boydell & Brewer, 2016); Robert I. Moore, *The War on Heresy. Faith and Power in Medieval Europe* (London: Profile Books, 2012); Pegg, *The Corruption of Angels*.

posing yellow crosses on convicted heretics was a punishment, but also an attempt on the part of the inquisitors to break social ties and operationalize a sort of constructed otherness. However, the so-called heretics undertook their own social construction. Against the "constructed typification"[37] devised by inquisitors, dissidents put forward an "existential typification," that is, a social construction of the environment in which they were immersed. This clash of social constructions becomes clear in the use of language.[38] Thus, in contrast to the inquisitors' term "heretic," the respondents used the terms "just" or "righteous," in contrast to "burned heretics," "martyrs," in contrast to "errors," "beliefs," and in contrast to "acts against the Christian faith," they claimed to "lead a good life." On the one hand, these construction processes show that heretics opposed the inquisitorial narrative with their own alternative construction and were therefore endowed with agency. On the other, the interaction of these two conflicting typifications brought about a new discourse that evolved from their process of co-evolution. Thus, the punitive action of inquisitorial tribunals engaged with the social construction of some of these groups, legitimating it and, in some cases, even prompting their "desire" to become willing martyrs as the ultimate community-binding act.

The characteristics of the *inquisitio* highlight a reality that all sociological inquiries share: the resulting networks are likely to reflect the interaction between interviewer and interviewee. Therefore, it is not so much that the dissident networks extracted from inquisitorial records are "contaminated" by inquisitors and their narrative but that they are built upon inquisitors, deponents, and their specific way of interacting. Understanding their interaction is thus vital to gauge the representativeness of said networks.

3 Sampling the network: actors and relations

The different groups marked as "heretical" in 13th- and 14th-century Languedoc were formed by individuals and structures that were fully embedded into the social landscape of the period long before inquisitorial action was launched against them. Once the inquisitorial prosecution began, common gestures more rooted in tradition, courtesy, and charitable practices than in doctrinal displays ran the risk of being perceived as heretical when their recipients were la-

---

37 John C. McKinney, "Typification, Typologies, and Sociological Theory," *Social Forces* 48, no. 1 (1969): 1–12.
38 Peter L. Berger and Thomas Luckmann, *The Social Construction of Reality: A Treatise in the Sociology of Knowledge* (London: Penguin Books, 1991).

belled as heretics.[39] Therefore, all those who had contact with people suspected of doctrinal deviance were in turn likely to be "infected" and became suspects themselves. However, inquisitors were only able to build a case thanks to the information relayed by said suspects. In other words, what we could call the sampling methods of inquisitors were based on referrals made among people who participated or had knowledge of heretical activities, which broadly fits the definition of snowball sampling.[40] Snowball sampling is a method used in sociological research that is particularly suited for collecting information from and about hidden populations – namely groups of people that cannot be easily accessed[41] – and suspected heretics certainly responded to this description. Although inquisitors obviously acted as prosecutors and not as researchers, comparing the methods they used with those designed by social scientists to approach the problem of concealed groups can help assess the representativeness of the sample, and point out eventual misrepresentations.

Snowball sampling depends on the subjective choices of the respondents, to the point that the information is entirely supplied by them; thus, in a way, the inquirer surrenders the sampling itself to the subjects of the study.[42] This was also the case for inquisitors, although the specific features of inquisitorial inquiries and sources somewhat minimized the effects of subjective responses. Deponents could still lie about their connections – not so much making up false relations as keeping some of their actual connections hidden – but they were certainly not immune to the coercive power of the inquisitorial machinery and probably ended up saying much more than they originally intended to. Additionally, inquisitors were well aware of the possibility of untruthful or incomplete and vague statements, as can be seen in Gui's *Practica inquisitionis*, where Gui acknowledges the painstaking efforts the inquisitors must make to unveil the truth.[43] Registers are especially informative regarding the active use of strategies to catch deponents in a lie, such as repeated questionings, contrasting the depositions of different suspects, and asking them about the discrepancies over and

---

39 Julien Théry, "L'hérésie des bons hommes. Comment nommer la dissidence réligieuse non vaudois ni béguine en Languedoc (XIIe–début du XIVe siècle)?" *Heresis* 36/37 (2002): 75–117.
40 Patrick Biernacki and Dan Waldorf, "Snowball Sampling: Problems and Techniques of Chain Referral Sampling," *Sociological Methods & Research* 10, no. 2 (1981): 141–63.
41 Chaim Noy, "Sampling Knowledge: The Hermeneutics of Snowball Sampling in Qualitative Research," *International Journal of Social Research Methodology* 11 (2008): 327–44.
42 Ibid.
43 Mollat, *Manuel de l'inquisiteur*, vol. 1, 6.

over without explaining why.⁴⁴ The thoroughness of inquisitorial questionings is precisely one of the factors that, from a modern perspective, might have improved the representativeness of the sample. The fact that the records on the same actors often span many years, the inquisitors' power to summon any individual that might be considered of interest, and their cross-referencing of information between depositions allowed for longer referral chains, which in turn strengthen the aforementioned representativeness according to current standards.⁴⁵

Inquisitors unintentionally relinquished a considerable amount of control over the sampling to the deponents, but they had full authority over the way in which relations between deponents were evaluated. According to our analysis, inquisitors generally gauged the strength of the connections between actors depending on the existence of a specific set of relations such as sharing meals, almsgiving, and conversing, among others. They used a similar method regarding beliefs, asking for how long a belief had been maintained, who was its source, and with whom it had been shared, on which basis they determined the respondent's involvement. Therefore, prior to the implementation of network analyses, it is necessary to develop a data model that is capable of accommodating all this relational information along with its directionality. Our data model is thus based on the relations that inquisitors deemed relevant in regard to the spread of heresy, but since these were based on the common modes of socialization of that specific social context, they can be used to naturally characterize the group.

According to Ormerod and Roach,⁴⁶ by the 1320s the century long experience of the *officium inquisitoris* had helped inquisitors understand how heretical communities worked; thus, eliminating the most important individuals in a group – or rather the most connected people – seemed a reasonable repressing response. Despite agreeing with these authors on the fact that the accumulated expertise of inquisitors played a role in the evolution of their performance, in our opinion, this specific practice of trying to remove the most connected actors was not so much motivated by a newly acquired knowledge about the inner workings of these communities, but on lingering prejudices related to the view of spiritual

---

44 Irene Bueno, *Defining Heresy: Inquisition, Theology, and Papal Policy in the Time of Jacques Fournier*, Studies in Medieval and Reformation Traditions 192 (Leiden: Brill, 2015); Danielle Laurendeau, "Le village et l'inquisiteur. Faire parler et savoir taire au tribunal d'Inquisition de Pamiers (1320–1325)," *Histoire & Sociétés Rurales* 34, no. 2 (2010): 13–52.
45 Lisa G. Johnston and Keith Sabin, "Sampling hard-to-reach populations with respondent driven sampling," *Methodological Innovations Online* 5, no. 2 (2010): 38–48.
46 Ormerod and Roach, "The Medieval Inquisition."

dissenters as groups of gullible people who let themselves get carried away under the influence of a heresiarch. In this regard, snowball sampling presents another problem that is particularly relevant for the representativeness of the social networks extracted from inquisitorial records. The samples obtained by using this technique are biased towards the inclusion of these most connected individuals,[47] in other words, their importance is overplayed to the detriment of more isolated members of the network. Since inquisitors were mostly interested in learning about people who engaged in heretical practices and beliefs within what we could call the relational space, the men and women who adhered to such principles more privately went all but undetected. In addition, inquisitors tended to use some individuals as markers of heresy and asked for them during the inquiry, thus artificially increasing the number of times they were mentioned by others, which leads to an overemphasis of their role in the network.[48] In this sense, the referral chains prompted by inquisitors seem in some cases not so much a method to increase the sample size and improve their knowledge about a specific dissident movement, but a mechanism to assess the implication of some deponents and build a stronger case against others whose acquaintance was considered as an aggravating circumstance.

The most immediate result of inquisitorial sampling techniques is the snowball effect experienced by some of the members of the network. The inquisitorial procedure, as any modern snowball sampling, was a dynamic process, and as it developed, and also as different inquisitions took place, some individuals started attracting the attention of the inquisitors, thus becoming new markers of heresy in their eyes. This resulted in an enhanced visibility of these individuals, which is liable to affect even the most qualitative approach to the sources, for some names were explicitly included in the interrogation and the number of mentions they received increased accordingly. Consequently, the sooner that being acquainted with them became an incriminating factor, the larger the number of connections we can expect for each of these actors, traditionally seen as "leaders" of the movement. Furthermore, different symbolical and behavioral traits that were not initially considered in the question lists emerged, and with them new means to identify heretics and to start new referral chains. However, the presence of gaps in the information available is undeniable. After all, unlike social scientists, who can device their sampling techniques according to their social group of choice, historians working with inquisitorial sources are not merely

---

47 Rowland Atkinson and John Flint, "Accessing Hidden and Hard-to-Reach Populations: Snowball Research Strategies," *Social Research Update* 33 (Summer 2001), http://sru.soc.surrey.ac.uk/SRU33.html.
48 See, in particular, Nieto-Isabel, "Communities of Dissent," 254–63, and 330–46.

looking into a hidden population, but into the extant and oftentimes scarce traces of the incomplete sample produced by the inquisitions.

4 Conclusions

The objective of conducting a formal network analysis on inquisitorial sources is not to show that social relationships were important, but to shed light on the way in which very specific spiritual networks worked. This needs first and foremost an understanding of the framework that was developed for their persecution and of the sources it generated. Fraught with uncertainty as they are, these sources nonetheless provide a volume of relational information whose structural analysis requires both the use of digital tools and tailor-made formal models, the actual core of digital humanities.[49]

This paper addresses two key aspects that have a direct impact on the validity of the results of any quantitative analysis of historical data: the representativeness of the sources on which it is based, and the way information is gathered and processed. As for the first, inquisitorial registers were carefully produced and kept with the intention of recording events and to serve as future reference, but other mechanisms have also intervened in the survival of the extant sources, such as personal initiatives and interests, selective deposit, and even chance. The whole process is quite random, that is, no obscure purposes underlie the preservation of some specific inquisitorial records and not others, which, in turn, grants a certain initial degree of representativeness to the records that have actually survived. Thus, the only purposes that need concern researchers are those of the producers of these documents, namely, uprooting heresy, keeping records that would facilitate this task, and keeping track of the individuals involved in heretical activities.

Regarding the way the information was generated, the endeavor of stopping the spread of heretical errors and bringing the heretics back into the fold was conceived by inquisitors as a problem based on social interactions whose solution depended on exposing those relationships and classifying them. These conceptions of heresy, together with the low social visibility, allegedly deviant behavior, and unwillingness to cooperate of the target populations, led to a kind of inquiry that shares the characteristics of what we now call "snowball sampling." There was a certain lack of uniformity among inquisitions, for inquisitors were allowed much flexibility in the way they conducted the procedure, but

---

[49] Piotrowski, "Accepting and Modeling Uncertainty," 6.

there is also evidence of an effort to unify criteria and improve question lists in order to adapt them to the different characteristics of each heretical group.[50]

Finally, looking into inquisitorial techniques from a perspective that takes into account current knowledge on the workings of snowball sampling has proven instrumental to understanding the networks that can be extracted from inquisitorial sources. The techniques used by inquisitors to glean information from suspects introduced a bias in the number of connections that could be expected for each individual – and therefore in their relative centrality – that does not only affect network analysis but, more generally, qualitative approaches based on the relative visibility of certain individuals in the record. It is by acknowledging this trait of the inquisitorial procedure that we have been able to grasp the extent to which the resulting networks are socially representative of medieval dissident religious cultures.

5 Bibliography

Albert, Réka, and Albert-László Barabási. "Statistical Mechanics of Complex Networks." *Reviews of Modern Physics* 74 (2002): 48–97.

Arnold, John H. *Inquisition and Power: Catharism and the Confessing Subject in Medieval Languedoc.* University Park, PA: Pennsylvania State University Press, 2001.

Atkinson, Rowland, and John Flint. "Accessing Hidden and Hard-to-Reach Populations: Snowball Research Strategies." *Social Research Update* 33 (Summer 2001). http://sru.soc.surrey.ac.uk/SRU33.html.

Bearman, Peter S. *Relations into Rhetorics: Local Elite Social Structure in Norfolk, England, 1540–1640.* New Brunswick: Rutgers University Press, 1993.

Berger, Peter L., and Thomas Luckmann. *The Social Construction of Reality: A Treatise in the Sociology of Knowledge.* London: Penguin Books, 1991.

Biernacki, Patrick, and Dan Waldorf. "Snowball Sampling: Problems and Techniques of Chain Referral Sampling." *Sociological Methods & Research* 10, no. 2 (1981): 141–63.

Biller, Peter, Caterina Bruschi, and Shelagh Sneddon, eds. *Inquisitors and Heretics in Thirteenth-Century Languedoc: Edition and Translation of Toulouse Inquisition Depositions, 1273–1282.* Studies in the History of Christian Traditions 147. Leiden: Brill, 2011.

Borgatti, Stephen P., Martin G. Everett, and Linton C. Freeman, eds. "UCINET." In *Encyclopedia of Social Network Analysis and Mining*, edited by Reda Alhajj and Jon Rokne, 2261–67. New York: Springer, 2014.

Bruschi, Caterina. "'Magna diligentia est habenda per inquisitorem': Precautions before Reading Doat 21–26." In *Texts and the Repression of Medieval Heresy*, edited by Caterina Bruschi and Peter Biller, 81–110. York Studies in Medieval Theology 4. York: York Medieval Press, 2003.

---

50 Sackville, *Heresy and Heretics*, 135–53.

Bruschi, Caterina. *The Wandering Heretics of Languedoc*. Cambridge Studies in Medieval Life and Thought Fourth Series. New York: Cambridge University Press, 2009.
Bueno, Irene. *Defining Heresy: Inquisition, Theology, and Papal Policy in the Time of Jacques Fournier*. Studies in Medieval and Reformation Traditions 192. Leiden: Brill, 2015.
Cazenave, Annie. "De la parole au texte: les termes de Langue d'Oc dans les actes latins." *Bulletin philologique et historique* (1979): 77–98.
Durkheim, Émile. *De la division du travail social: étude sur l'organisation des sociétés supérieures*. Paris: Félix Alcan, 1893.
Dondaine, Antoine. "Le manuel de l'inquisiteur (1230–1330)." *Archivum Fratrum Praedicatorum* 17 (1947): 97–101.
Dossat, Yves. "Le plus ancient manuel de l'inquisition méridionale: le Processus inquisitions (1248–1249)." *Bulletin philologique et historique (jusq'à 1715)* (1952): 33–37.
Dossat, Yves. *Les crises de l'Inquisition Toulousaine au XIIIe siècle (1233–1273)*. Bordeaux: Imprimerie Bière, 1959.
Douglas, Mary. *Risk Acceptability According to the Social Sciences*. Social Research Perspectives 11. New York: Russell Sage Foundation, 1986.
Feld, Scott L., and William C. Carter. "Detecting measurement bias in respondent reports of personal networks." *Social Networks* 24, no. 4 (2002): 365–383.
Gestrich, Andreas, and Martin Stark, eds. *Debtors, Creditors, and Their Networks: Social Dimensions of Monetary Dependence from the Seventeenth to the Twentieth Century*. London: German Historical Institute London, 2015.
Ginzburg, Carlo. "The Inquisitor as Anthropologist." In *Clues, Myths, and the Historical Method*, edited by Carlo Ginzburg, translated by J. and A. Tedeschi, 141–48. Baltimore: Johns Hopkins University Press, 1989.
Given, James B. "The Inquisitors of Languedoc and the Medieval Technology of Power." *American Historical Review* 94, no. 2 (1989): 336–59.
Given, James B. *Inquisition and Medieval Society: Power, Discipline, and Resistance in Languedoc*. Ithaca: Cornell University Press, 1997.
Gould, Roger V. *Insurgent Identities: Class, Community, and Protest in Paris from 1848 to the Commune*. Chicago: University of Chicago, 1995.
Granovetter, Mark S. "The Strength of Weak Ties." *American Journal of Sociology* 78, no. 6 (1973): 1360–80.
Johnston, Lisa G., and Keith Sabin. "Sampling Hard-to-Reach Populations with Respondent Driven Sampling." *Methodological Innovations Online* 5, no. 2 (2010): 38–48.
Laurendeau, Danielle. "Le village et l'inquisiteur. Faire parler et savoir taire au tribunal d'Inquisition de Pamiers (1320–1325)." *Histoire & Sociétés Rurales* 34, no. 2 (2010): 13–52.
Mansi, Giovanni Domenico, ed. *Sacrorum conciliorum nova et amplissima collectio*. Vol. 23. Venice: Antonio Zatta, 1779.
McKinney, John C. "Typification, Typologies, and Sociological Theory." *Social Forces* 48, no. 1 (1969): 1–12.
Mollat, Guillaume, ed. *Manuel de l'inquisiteur Bernard Gui*. Paris: Les Belles Lettres, 1964.
Moore, Robert I. *The War on Heresy. Faith and Power in Medieval Europe*. London: Profile Books, 2012.
Moreno, Jacob L., *Who Shall Survive: A New Approach to the Problem of Human Interrelations*. Washington D.C.: Nervous and Mental Disease Publishing Co., 1934

Mullett, Margaret. *Theophylacht of Ochrid: Reading the Letters of a Byzantine Archbishop.* Aldershot: Variorum, 1997.

Nieto-Isabel, Delfi I. "Communities of Dissent: Social Network Analysis of Religious Dissident Groups in Languedoc in the Thirteenth and Fourteenth Centuries." PhD diss., University of Barcelona, 2018.

Noy, Chaim. "Sampling Knowledge: The Hermeneutics of Snowball Sampling in Qualitative Research." *International Journal of Social Research Methodology* 11 (2008): 327–44.

Ormerod, Paul, and Andrew P. Roach. "The Medieval Inquisition: Scale-Free Networks and the Suppression of Heresy." *Physica A* 339 (2004): 645–52.

Padgett, John F., and Christopher K. Ansell. "Robust Action and the Rise of the Medici, 1400–1434." *American Journal of Sociology* 98 (1993): 1259–1319.

Pegg, Mark Gregory. *The Corruption of Angels: The Great Inquisition of 1245–1246.* Princeton: Princeton University Press, 2001.

Piotrowski, Michael. "Accepting and Modeling Uncertainty." *Zeitschrift für digitale Geisteswissenschaften.* Sonderband 4 (2019). http://dx.doi.org/10.17175/sb004_006a.

Rosé, Isabelle. "Reconstitution, représentation graphique et analyse des réseaux de pouvoir au haut Moyen Âge: Approche des pratiques sociales de l'aristocratie à partir de l'exemple d'Odon de Cluny († 942)." *Redes. Revista hispana para el análisis de redes sociales* 21 (2011): 199–272.

Sackville, Lucy. *Heresy and Heretics in the Thirteenth Century: The Textual Representations.* Suffolk: Boydell & Brewer, 2011.

Scott, John P. *Social Network Analysis.* Los Angeles: SAGE, 2013.

Scruton, David L. "The Anthropology of an Emotion." In *Sociophobics: The Anthropology of Fear,* edited by David L. Scruton, 7–49. Boulder, CO: Westview Press, 1986.

Sennis, Antonio, ed. *Cathars in Question.* Suffolk: Boydell & Brewer, 2016.

Tardif, Adolphe. "Document pour l'histoire du *processus per inquisitionem* et de l'*inquisitio heretice pravitatis*." *Nouvelle Revue du droit français et étranger* 7 (1883): 669–78.

Théry, Julien. "L'hérésie des bons hommes. Comment nommer la dissidence religieuse non vaudois ni béguine en Languedoc (XIIe–début du XIVe siècle)?" *Heresis* 36/37 (2002): 75–117.

Tilly, Charles. *Popular Contention in Great Britain, 1758–1843.* Cambridge, MA: Harvard University Press, 1995.

Tönnies, Ferdinand, *Gemeinschaft und Gesellschaft.* Leipzig: Fues' Verlag, 1887.

Waters, Jaime. "Snowball Sampling: A Cautionary Tale Involving a Study of Older Drug Users." *International Journal of Social Research Methodology* 18 (2015): 367–80.

Watts, Duncan J., and Steven H. Strogatz. "Collective Dynamics of 'Small-World' Networks." *Nature* 393, no. 6684 (1998): 440–42.

Katherine Faull
Visualizing religious networks, movements, and communities: building Moravian Lives

1 Introduction

This chapter investigates the intersection of the digital, the autobiographical and the theological in the age of the internet and discusses how the implementation of social network analysis and the methods of the digital humanities might aid in an examination of Moravian religious networks and their claims to constitute the "invisible church." The large memoir corpus referred to in this chapter comes primarily from the archives of the Moravian Church in Bethlehem, PA, USA, which holds the records of the activities of the Moravians in the American Northern Province (Pennsylvania, New York, New Jersey) from 1740 to the present day. The chapter will discuss first the history behind the composition of the Moravian memoir, then the creation of a digital platform that incorporates the metadata and also digitized images of a subset of these memoirs, then the methodology employed in visualizing networks contained within that corpus, and then finally discuss what those visualized networks reveal in terms of new knowledge about the interactions between authors of the Moravian memoirs. Visualizing networks might lead us to understand what Nikolaus von Zinzendorf, the founder of the Moravian Church understood to be the reconstitution of "the invisible church."

Within the context of the Protestant Reformation and subsequent Pietist thought, the term "invisible church" has been understood as a deliberate rejection of the earthly edifices of the Roman Catholic Church.[1] According to early Pietists, the invisible church emphasizes the individual believer's personal relationship with Christ without the intermediary of the earthly church. Further, within the Protestant movements of Pietism in the German-speaking states (primarily Frankfurt am Main, Halle and Leipzig in Sachsen-Anhalt) of the 17th and 18th centuries, this concept became instantiated in the conventicles or "ecclesio-

---

[1] Douglas H. Shantz, "The Origin of Pietist Notions of New Birth and the New Man: Alchemy and Alchemists in Gottfried Arnold and Johann Henrich Reitz," in *The Pietist Impulse in Christianity*, ed. Christian T. Collins Winn et al., with forewords by James H. Barnes III and Peter C. Erb (James Clarke & Co Ltd, Cambridge, 2011): 29–41.

https://doi.org/10.1515/9783110574043-010

lae in ecclesia"[2] in which, as Peter Vogt has recently argued, a community of believers supports each other's faith in "a dynamic of reciprocity."[3]

The practices of meeting in private houses, forming groups for prayer and Bible study, and the application of faith to everyday life that constituted some of the distinguishing features of German Pietism were also complemented by the relation to other believers of one's life and conversion. Indeed, the beginnings of Pietism in Frankfurt am Main have been argued to be simultaneous with an "autobiographical turn"[4] by which the reciprocal relation of the lives of all "brothers and sisters" became a constitutive act in the creation of a true church of all believers.[5] To support their lives of faith, Pietist leaders read the lives of those women and men who had inspired the formation of "der neue Mensch" or the "new human being."[6] In turn, the composition of the life story of the "new human beings" modelled paradigmatic lives of faith for others.

The advent of Web 2.0, with its promise of universal access to both data/information and instant authorship, has offered a radical change in both the delivery of content and in the creation and maintenance of spirituality.[7] Like the technological invention of the printing press at the time of the Protestant Reformation, the advent of the digital has the potential to change radically the concept and practice of religion, as we have indeed seen in the recent pandemic and its concomitant social/physical distancing mandates. To this end, scholars of the sociology of religion have begun to explore both the practices and possibilities for religion and theology that inhere in the digital and included in these investigations are questions about how the digital can both constitute and support religiosity.[8]

However, this chapter is not about how the digital realm supports religiosity today, but rather about how the field of digital humanities can be combined with studies in the history of religion to see how, almost 300 years ago, a perhaps par-

---

2 Douglas Shantz, *An Introduction to German Pietism: Protestant Renewal at the Dawn of Modern Europe* (Baltimore: Johns Hopkins University Press, 2013), 115.
3 Peter Vogt, "Spiritual Autobiography and Ecclesiology," in *Moravian Memoirs: Pillars of an Invisible Church*, ed. Christer Ahlberger and Per von Wachtenfeld (Artos, 2017), 35.
4 Shantz, *Introduction to German Pietism*, 7.
5 Vogt, "Spiritual Autobiography and Ecclesiology," 39.
6 Lucinda Martin, "Female Reformers as the Gatekeepers of Pietism: The Example of Johanna Eleonora Merlau and William Penn," *Monatshefte* 95, no. 1 (2003), 35.
7 Boris Groys, "Invisibility of the Digital: Religion, Ritual, Immortality," *RES: Anthropology and Aesthetics* 55/56 (2009), 336.
8 Pauline Cheong et al., eds., *Digital Religion, Social Media and Culture: Perspectives, Practices, and Futures* (New York: Peter Lang, 2012); Heidi A. Campbell, ed., *Digital Religion: Understanding Religious Practice in New Media Worlds* (Oxford: Routledge, 2013).

allel concept of networks, media and reciprocal authorship and readership supported lives of faith in a Protestant group and might have constituted the invisible church. To aid this investigation, I draw on the international DH project "Moravian Lives."[9] The theoretical underpinnings of this project are questions rooted in recent work on the genre of autobiography, the history of Pietism, gender studies, and digital humanities, especially in the emerging field of historical network research.[10] The question I will address in this chapter is how the application of the methods of social network analysis can help to visualize the connections between a subset of members of the Moravian Church in the 18th century, and how the tools of digital humanities (most notably working with the open source software, Gephi) can reveal new knowledge about those networks. Specifically, does the visualization of these social networks allow a more accurate understanding of the role of gender, family, and ethnicity within these early Pietist networks?

2 Who are the Moravians?

The Moravian Church, known in Germany as the *Brüdergemeine, Brüder-Unität,* and *Herrnhuter,* traditionally places its pre-Reformation origins in the present-day Czech Republic and was "renewed" in the early 18th century by Count Nikolaus Ludwig von Zinzendorf (1700–1760) when groups of peasants, artisans, and craftsmen, mostly Protestant, flocked to the nobleman's estates in Berthelsdorf, Saxony, seeking a different kind of spiritual life. In the mid-18th century, as the congregations grew, these men and women from all social classes found the freedom to practice their religion in intentional communities designed to foster individual spirituality and communal faith in settlements like Herrnhut in Saxony, Herrnhaag in Wetteravia and Bethlehem in Pennsylvania.[11] Fired by the enthusi-

---

9 Moravian Lives, University of Gothenburg and Bucknell University, http://moravianlives.org/.
10 Whereas network theory has long been in the critical toolbox of sociological research, only recently has it been applied as an analytical practice to the field of historical research. See, for example, the publication of a new journal, *Journal of Historical Network Research,* from the University of Luxembourg in 2017, in which the editors argue that such a publication will "help advance the epistemological and theoretical understanding of social network analysis in the historical sciences and promote empirical research on historical social interactions." (Düring Rollinger and Stark Gramsch-Stehfest, "Editors' Introduction," *Journal of Historical Network Research* 1 (2017), v.
11 J. Taylor Hamilton and Kenneth G. Hamilton, *History of the Moravian Church: The Renewed Unitas Fratrum, 1722–1957* (Bethlehem, PA: Interprovincial Board of Christian Education, Moravian Church in America, 1983).

asm of the Great Awakening among the textile workers of the West Riding in Yorkshire and the miners of Kingswood in north Bristol, similar Moravian congregations were established in Great Britain.[12] Furthermore, mission congregations were set up in the Caribbean, Greenland, South Africa, and North America. One of the consequences of this worldwide Moravian mission was that men and women, from the 18th century to today, could be called to serve the church on the other side of the world.

Since the mid-18th-century, members of the Moravian Church (known in Germany as the Brüdergemeine or Unitas Fratrum) have written or dictated an account of their life to read at their funeral. These memoirs total now over 65,000 and are housed primarily in archives in Herrnhut, Germany and Bethlehem, Pennsylvania in the US, but there also exist smaller collections of documents in many of the Moravian settlements across the world. Less than 10% of the earliest manuscript material composed in the century between 1750–1850 has been published, and thus most memoirs remain inaccessible to researchers in the myriad fields to which they represent a potentially vital resource.

The origins of the practice of writing or dictating one's memoir within the Moravian church have been much discussed, researched, and debated (see bibliography). Traditionally, the origin of the practice of dictating or writing a Moravian memoir before each brother or sister died has been attributed to a speech by Zinzendorf on 22 June 1747 at the Moravian congregation in Herrnhaag, Wetteravia.[13] In that speech, Zinzendorf expressed his regret that nothing material remained of the departed except their "earthly vessel" and decided that from now on the memoir of the departed person should be read at the *Singstunde* (service of song) on the day he or she was buried in order that the congregation and the individual could wish each other one final adieu. Most recently, Stephanie Böß has argued that the accretion of memoirs constituted for Zinzendorf the history of the Moravian Church, a history written not from the top down but from the bottom up, consisting of the lives of all its members, whether women or men, African or German, noblewoman or indentured servant or slave.[14]

The practice of composing a spiritual autobiography is not peculiar to the Moravian Church. Having been raised within Pietist circles, Zinzendorf knew the tradition of writing a spiritual memoir that had been revived by August Her-

---

[12] Colin Podmore, *The Moravian Church of England 1728–1760* (Oxford: Oxford University Press, 1998) 88–96.
[13] Jüngerhausdiarium, 22 June 1747, UA Herrnhut, R.03.A 08. 245.
[14] Stephanie Böß, *Gottesacker-Geschichten: Eine Ethnographie zur Herrnhuter Erinnerungskultur am Beispiel von Neudietendorfer Lebensläufen* (Münster: Waxmann, 2016), 65.

mann Francke (1663–1727) in whose hands the genre followed a definite pattern of relating an individual's trials of atonement, followed by a sudden awakening or conversion experience. However, the Moravian memoir is unique as a theological and literary genre in that both the reason for writing the narrative and the point in the author's life at which this was done distinguish these texts both from contemporary German Pietist versions and from North American Quaker journals and Puritan spiritual narratives. Moravian memoirs do not necessarily contain a single pattern of spiritual conversion that is to be followed; rather they frequently depict the truth, whether good or bad, about the individual's life. Moravian memoirs sometimes include dreams and visions, that can act as indications of either a troubled soul or imminent grace. For some, these are moments of possible revelation.

Whereas both Methodist and Puritan narratives were required of the applicant for admission into the community, the Moravian memoir can span an individual's entire lifetime as it meshes with and illumines the life of the Moravian community. Almost all the memoirs describe both inner and outer lives: the personal relationship with Christ, feelings at first communion, the atmosphere in the early, almost experimental, community, parents' reactions (not always positive) to their child's decision to join the Moravian Brethren.

In addition to the reading of others' memoirs, the Moravians were trained in the act of self-relation. Integral to the spiritual and discursive development of each Moravian was the practice of the monthly Speakings that were held before communion to ascertain the health of the subject in body, mind and soul.[15] The Speakings were one of the most important, and yet until recently critically neglected, events in the lives of 18th-century Moravians. In addition to the letters, memoirs, reports and diaries, the Speakings constituted an important form of communication within the Moravian communities and are a crucial factor in the process of shaping conceptions of self, identity, and Christ's presence in the world. The regular acts of introspection and the subsequent discussion of the most private and intimate of personal concerns (marital relations, desires, fantasies and faith) developed in individuals a high degree of awareness and fluency of the self that could then be manifested in the relation of the memoir.[16]

Over the last 25 years, the genre of the Moravian "Lebenslauf" or memoir has become the focus of increased academic interest in many different scholarly fields. This interest has been fueled by the more general recognition of autobiog-

---

15 Katherine M. Faull, *Speaking to Body and Soul: Instructions for the Moravian Choir Helpers, 1785–1786*, Pietist, Moravian, and Anabaptist Studies (University Park, PA: Pennsylvania State University Press, 2017).
16 Faull, *Speaking to Body and Soul*, xvii–xx.

raphy as a genre worthy of scrutiny, and by the increased accessibility of the main repository of the manuscript sources in the Unity Archives in Herrnhut, Germany and the Moravian Archives in Bethlehem, PA. Concurrent with this, changes in conceptual models in social and religious history, and gender/race theory see such "ego-documents" as valuable primary sources for a perspective from the social classes that do not usually have a voice in the writing of histories, such as women and men of the artisan classes and non-Europeans. The attached bibliography of recent publications in English and German reveals a healthy, vibrant, and multi-dimensional set of inquiries.

One of the constant foci of critical attention within this genre is the question of the freedom allowed to each individual to express authentic and unique reflections on the lived experience. Whereas some critics have argued that the very institutional edict to write a self-narration necessarily limits that act in terms of form, formulation, and individuality, others have argued that the Pietistic environment in which these self-relations were created, encouraged, at least in the 18th century, a balance between the demands of the community and the self. As Peter Vogt has so aptly stated, the Moravian memoir constitutes "a dynamic of reciprocity between individual witness and community identity."[17] Within the theory of autobiography, such reciprocity in the narration of the self has also been discussed by Paul Eakin, who argues that without a story there is no self, and, in the age of the digital, this self is "not only reported but performed, certainly by any of us as we tell or write stories of our lives, and perhaps to a surprising degree by the rest of us as we listen to them or read them."[18]

For millennia in the West, autobiography has served the purpose of providing a public model of the exemplary life. Whether in the form of saints' *vitae*, the chronicles of kings and queens, the political autobiography, or conversion narratives like that of St. Augustine, autobiographies have been disseminated and retold to serve the purpose of shaping others' lives. Straddling the precarious bridge between the private and public, or, in Jan Assmann's terms, between communicative and cultural memory, autobiography allows the writing subject to examine his or her own past, to (re)shape that history, and to interrogate the reasons for action and examine personal conscience.[19] For the reader, the genre

---

[17] Vogt, "Spiritual Autobiography and Ecclesiology," 37.
[18] Paul John Eakin, "Autobiography as Cosmogram," *Storyworlds: A Journal of Narrative Studies* 6, no. 1 (2014), 24.
[19] Jan Assmann, *Das kulturelle Gedächtnis: Schrift, Erinnerung und politische Identität in frühen Hochkulturen* (München: Beck, 2007), 55–6.

provides an opportunity to view these processes within another human subject, to witness the relation of authentic (or inauthentic) experience and emotion.

The classic definition of the genre, according to Philippe Lejeune, posits that autobiography is "a retrospective prose narrative produced by a real person concerning his own existence, focusing on his individual life, in particular on the development of his personality."[20] The narrative voice is "autodiégétique"; it points simultaneously to both the narrator and the protagonist, the author's position as the narrator and the narrator's position as the protagonist. According to Lejeune, one of the strongest forces that draws the reader to the autobiographical genre is this "autobiographical contract": that is, the reader knows that there is a contract between the author, the narrator, and the "I that is speaking" and that they are co-equal. This utterance of the "I" is a performative act: namely, the "I" comes into existence when it is uttered. More recently, Eakin has connected this concept of autobiography as a performative act to the neuro-biological investigations of human consciousness in which the connection between mind and consciousness is one that inheres in the very act of the narration.[21] This idea of the self as one that is created in the act of telling one's story is deeply evocative of Zinzendorf's own concept of the role of the individual life in the creation and sustaining of the "invisible church."

The required record of Moravians' both outer and inner journey was first read at the individual's funeral lovefeast, a simple service of songs and thanks. Then copies of these memoirs were sent to the central archive in Herrnhut from where they could also be disseminated to Moravian congregations around the world, where they were read by and to other Moravians to serve as a means of edification. The memoirs of leaders and role models (male and female, nobility or artisan, European or not) were first reproduced by hand and then in print, and circulated in the *Gemeinnachrichten* (Congregational Accounts).[22] Because of the worldwide reach of the Moravian church, Moravian archives preserve some of the earliest "ego documents" produced by 18th-century Africans and Native Americans. Archiving these documents has fulfilled a twofold purpose: storing and ordering them in the institutional archival memory of the Church and

---

[20] Philippe Lejeune, "The Autobiographical Contract," in *French Literary Theory Today: A Reader*, ed. Tzvetan Todorov (Cambridge: Cambridge University Press, 1982), 193.
[21] Eakin, "Autobiography as Cosmogram," 24.
[22] Gisela Mettele, *Weltbürgertum oder Gottesreich? Die Herrnhuter Brüdergemeine als globale Gemeinschaft 1760–1857* (Göttingen: Vandenhoeck & Ruprecht, 2009), 208–11.

also, for those who access this archival memory, as a locus of presence and interactivity in the lived memory of the Church.[23]

As noted above, the relation of the lives of exemplary believers, as Vogt argues, helped to create "a tangible impression of the invisible church community."[24] In an examination of several centuries' worth of memoirs from the Herrnhut archives, Christine Lost describes the communicative structure of Moravian experience and finds that, like the genre of autobiography outlined above, the Moravian memoir is both inwardly and outwardly directed; that is, it serves as a means of self-examination for the writing "I," as well as participating in the construction of a communal identity.[25] This dialectic of individual/community reflects very much Zinzendorf's own understanding of the function of the memoir.[26] The relation of one's life within this community serves as an act of witness and testimony to the invisible host of those who had gone before and who were still to come.

In her examination of the memoirs from the Moravian congregation of Neudietendorf, Stephanie Böß discusses the various means implemented in the community to bring its members into fellowship with their peers.[27] Multiple opportunities existed to record and hear autobiographical reflections in letters, memoirs, and diaries. According to both Lost and Böß, these oral and written forms of communication came together with the gender-specific structures of the community, through the choir system, to underscore the Moravian notion that the human being is not divided into realms of mind/body/spirit, but rather constitutes an interrelated, holistic entity.[28] Within the context of scholarship on the Moravian memoir, this notion of an instantiation of selfhood stands in a powerful relationship with the formation of what the founder of the Moravian Church, Nikolaus von Zinzendorf, called a universal, invisible "*Gemeine*" or congregation.[29]

Many of the manuscript memoirs are also prefaced by biographical information such as birthplace and date, original religious affiliation, and choir membership that are supplied by either the choir helper, the minister, or family member

---

[23] Ekaterina Haskins, "Between Archive and Participation: Public Memory in a Digital Age," *Rhetoric Society Quarterly* 37, no. 4 (2007), 401.
[24] Vogt, "Spiritual Autobiography and Ecclesiology," 39.
[25] Christine Lost, *Das Leben als Lehrtext: Lebensläufe aus der Herrnhuter Brüdergemeine* (Herrnhut: Herrnhuter Verlag, 2007), 26–33.
[26] Jüngerhausdiarium, 22 June 1747.
[27] Böß, *Gottesacker-Geschichten*, 68–70.
[28] Lost, *Das Leben als Lehrtext*, 55–64; Böß, *Gottesacker-Geschichten*, 119.
[29] Vogt, "Spiritual Autobiography and Ecclesiology," 53.

at the time of death. The memoir is then completed with details of the final moments of the person's life supplied by the choir helper. From this version, a report of the individual's life and death was composed which might appear in the congregation diary, the official diary of the local Moravian congregation that recorded all comings and goings, religious services, births, deaths, and marriages. A third version could also be drawn up, based on the original version, that was included in the *Gemeinnachrichten*, the handwritten "newsletter" that was circulated to all the Moravian communities around the globe.[30] These three versions can also differ significantly from each other, with the most public version, circulated in the *Gemeinnachrichten*, omitting overtly personal detail and any particulars that might contradict the accepted picture of the community. In addition, the writing style is improved, spelling is standardized, and very occasionally the whole story is completely rewritten.

The Moravian Church's emphasis on the relation of one's life story also accompanies its movement into the colonial settler spaces of North America and the North Atlantic. Removed from the states regulated by the Reformed or Lutheran orthodoxies, the relation of the personal memoir fulfilled the desire for fellowship and community in these contested geospatial contexts. In Pennsylvania, for example, many of the authors of memoirs faced challenges to their faith from the encounter with non-European and non-Christian peoples. In a recent article on the writing of the memoir, Thomas McCullough argues that the memoir's self-relation served not only to provide the Choir Helpers of the congregation with an account of each individual's life to be read at his or her funeral (as many have assumed the purpose to be), but rather the *Lebenslauf* also functioned, very pragmatically, as a kind of census mechanism to account for the church membership. Especially in North America, where the members were not living in closely controlled town congregations (*Ortsgemeinen*), such a census was an important means with which to construct a database of church membership.

> Hehl's memorandum [. . .] ultimately provided three purposes for the collection of personal information from church members. First, he intended to create a master catalog of all Moravians living in Pennsylvania. Second, the information would serve as personalia to be shared with the congregations, if and when such a member had been "called home." This confirms the well-established and -studied tradition of memorialization through autobiographical accounts.[31]

---

30 Mettele, *Weltbürgertum oder Gottesreich*, 199.
31 T. J. McCullough, "The Most Memorable Circumstances: Instructions for the Collection of Personal Data from Church Members, circa 1752," *Journal of Moravian History* 15, no. 2 (2015), 166.

Whatever the driving reason for composition of a memoir, the expectation that an account of the self's relationship to Christ was to be a constitutive part of everyone's religious experience, whether from the nobility, the artisan class, or an indentured servant or enslaved African reveals how Moravian life-writing was a deeply embedded practice of the church. Through the composition of a memoir, Moravians since the 18th century have been presented with multiple opportunities to reflect on their lives as aesthetic and verbal constructs. How does having these opportunities change their concept of themselves as members of an invisible church?

3 Looking through the digital lens

The extraordinarily large number (over 60,000) of memoirs in the worldwide archives of the Moravian church presents both opportunities and challenges for researchers who wish to draw on this large corpus, who wish to access the archival memory for the purposes of lived memory. Like other DH projects that focus on autobiographical writings, such as those found in the Francke Foundations in Halle[32] and at the Rylands Library in Manchester,[33] Moravian Lives faces multiple issues from digitization of manuscript sources, to transcription of materials in multiple languages, to the development of protocols in the creation of a gazetteer and personography. One of the initial and potentially overwhelming questions is, how can we read so many documents, not just in terms of their numbers but also because the vast majority of them are in German Script (an archaic manuscript hand) or printed in *Fraktur?* What patterns can we identify that might reveal differences in style, voice, lexicon? How can this access to such a wide-ranging corpus be a radical force in changing perceptions of the 18th century and also of the nature of the writing self?

Lack of access to these documents has severely curtailed the ability of researchers to conduct comparative analyses between time periods, place of composition, ethnicity, or gender. With access to such a large corpus of ego-documents (and their metadata) from around the world that span social class, race, and gender over the last 270 years, then scholars in many fields could ask and attempt to answer major research questions. From within the field of re-

---

[32] "Digital Collections," Franckesche Stiftungen, https://digital.francke-halle.de/mod2/nav/index/all.
[33] "Digitisation Services," University of Manchester Library, https://www.library.manchester.ac.uk/search-resources/manchester-digital-collections/digitisation-services/projects/rapture-and-reason/.

ligious history and autobiography, a number of questions still remain: for example, is there a distinctively woman's voice that can be heard in the memoirs that is not subordinated to a male voice?[34] Is there an identifiable linguistic pattern of secularization in the 19th century?[35] How do individuals conceive of their own death and the death of others through time?[36] What kinds of lives did women live within the Moravian Church and how did they change? Future questions might include, how does the exploration of this corpus challenge commonly hold assumptions about mobility and emigration? How does mobility affect language change?

The development of tools in the field of digital humanities affords researchers a way of not only approaching these questions but also of thinking in new ways about how to conceptualize notions of self, narrative, and language. Some digitized corpora have already been constructed by archives, such as the Moravian Archives, Bethlehem, PA, and also by individual scholars working on questions in the fields of demographics, religious community, missions, and memoirs in Moravian history. The development of digital tools in text analysis, such as Voyant, Antconc, or Lexos, permits the investigation of large corpora in search of topic models, keywords, lexical "keyness" in comparison to non-Moravian corpora. Looking for meaningful patterns in the exercise of "distant reading" (the use of computational methods to analyze literary texts) transforms digital tools into integral parts of the process of understanding the study of Christianity.

Extracting semantically tagged entities such as the names of people and places, from marked-up texts enables both network visualization and geospatial analysis. This, in turn, allows the researcher to visualize and analyze the networks of groups of people, drawing on the methods of historical social network analysis. For example, a network visualization of the people that are mentioned in the women's memoirs brings to light the centrality of certain "nodes" or agents to a network, reveals the link between groupings that might consist of only one person, or if more finely tuned to account for "attributes" such as gender, marital status, or even language group, a network visualization can demonstrate the role that these attributes play in the formation of groups, small worlds, and networks.

---

34 Katherine M. Faull, ed. and trans., *Moravian Women's Memoirs: Their Related Lives, 1750–1820* (Syracuse, NY: Syracuse University Press, 1997).
35 Beverly Prior Smaby, *The Transformation of Moravian Bethlehem: From Communal Mission to Family Economy* (Philadelphia: University of Pennsylvania Press, 1988).
36 Böß, *Gottesacker-Geschichten*, 115.

In many ways reenacting the archival drive of the Moravians in the 18th century, that is their desire to keep a record of the activities and lives of the members of the church for the purpose of creating "a history from below," the methods of DH permit analyses of both the metadata and the text of large amounts of information that allows the other function of memoir to be fulfilled, the function of lived memory in which the archived materials of the past may become present and interact with others.[37] The Moravian Lives project, initiated in 2014, and based at Bucknell University in the US and Gothenburg University in Sweden, is aimed at precisely this. The project realizes the potential of DH approaches to opening up the memoir corpus, namely through the construction of a searchable database of the memoir metadata of all the holdings in the main archives of the Moravian Church in Bethlehem, PA and Herrnhut, Germany, and also linking the metadata visualizations with the facsimile and transcribed memoirs and their extracted named entities.

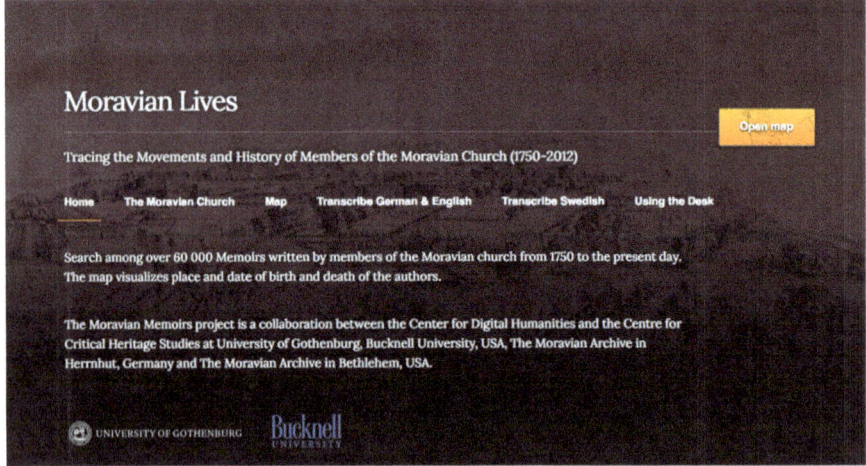

Figure 1: Home page of "Moravian Lives" http://moravianlives.org (Bucknell University, USA).

The first step in this process can be found at moravianlives.org, where a map interface provides a responsive search query engine (via php protocol) to a MySQL database of the metadata from the Herrnhut and Bethlehem archival repositories. The database can be filtered to answer a researcher's questions about: a) the centers of Moravian activity through the last 250 years; b) the movements of men and women at various times throughout the "Moravian world"; and c)

---

37 Haskins, "Between Archive and Participation," 401.

genealogies through the metadata linked to the visualization. Even the metadata search engine and map visualization alone provides insights into the way in which specific Moravian centers were connected to each other. For example, just using the birth and death locations and dates, the movements of Moravians from Herrnhut to the rest of the world in the 18th century can be quickly visualized.

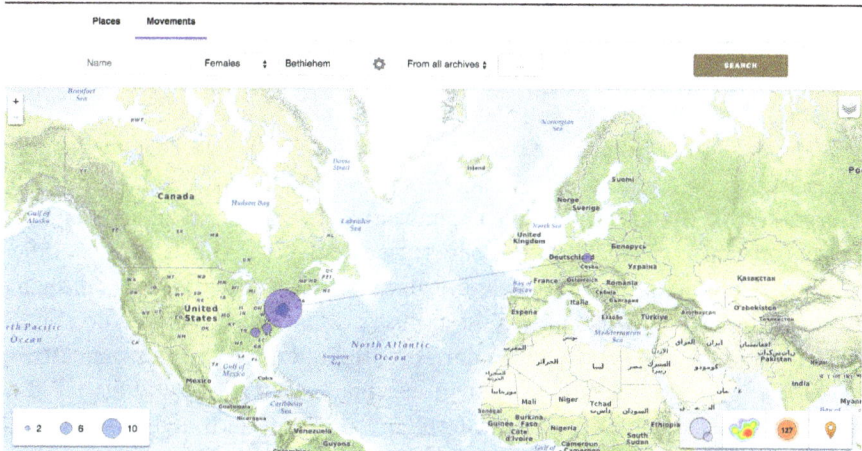

Figure 2: Visualization of the movement of 124 Moravian women from Bethlehem to other parts of the world, 1700–1800 (using Bethlehem as a birthplace) (http://moravianlives.org/map).

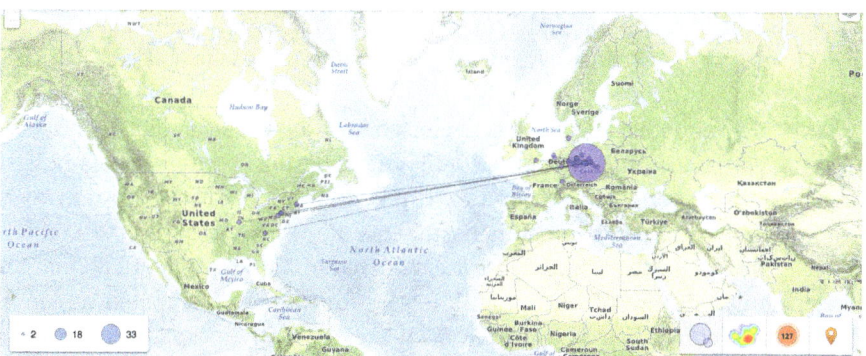

Figure 3: Visualization of movement of 360 Moravian women from Herrnhut to other parts of the world, 1700–1800 (using Herrnhut as birthplace) (http://moravianlives.org/map).

Two observations can be made immediately from these geospatial visualizations. First, there is far more movement by women born in Herrnhut, Germany to the rest of the world in the 18th century; and second, Moravian women born in Bethlehem in the 18th century tend to die in the United States.

If we examine this distant geospatial visualization of the metadata more closely through access to the transcribed memoirs of the women, we might then also be able to drill down further to reveal patterns of behavior and narration. To this end, the next phase of this project has consisted in the digitization of the earliest sections of the Bethlehem Archives' memoir collection (MemBeth), resulting in 260 documents and the custom build of a responsive and stable transcription desk where digital image and transcription page are linked together side by side (http://moravian.bucknell.edu/transcribe/). The custom-designed transcription desk encourages researchers to employ their paleographical skills in transcribing German and English manuscripts. The transcription desk currently runs on a customized WordPress site. The custom plugin consists of a modified version of the Scripto, CKEditor, and jQuery Panzoon while the custom theme controls the styling. This enables the transcription desk to be portable and allows it to run on any system with a current installation of WordPress and MediaWiki. The transcriptions and user login information are stored and managed in the MediaWiki database while the front-end user interface and metadata are managed through WordPress. The customized configurations in CKEditor allow us the flexibility to add and manipulate different TEI and other markup tags to our needs. Metadata such as author, date, gender, archive, and location are added as custom WordPress taxonomies or categories that are stored in the WordPress database and allow for fast and easy category linking, sorting and filtering. Our modified version of Scripto allows us to load images from any external server and then seamlessly integrate them into the image and editing interface.

In order for both scholarly and interested lay transcribers to adhere to scholarly standards, the project team has built guidelines for the transcribers in best practices for drafting transcriptions and preparing them for peer review. As a team of undergraduate and graduate students are working on the transcription process, the transcribed documents are rendered in XML-compliant TEI, and researchers can download files in XML format for further parsing and research.

In the last six months, we have been able to mark up approximately 100 documents in XML-compliant TEI and also extract entities. Once tagged, the people and places entities within each document can be extracted and visualized. Multiple documents form a representative corpus and within that corpus geospatial and network visualizations can be created that reveal new networks, relationships, and movements. Such visualizations provide insight into the constitu-

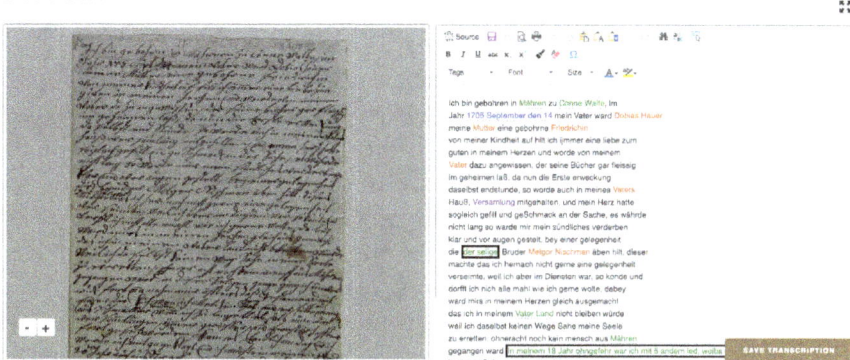

Figure 4: The transcription desk. Memoir of Rosina Neubert (http://moravian.bucknell.edu/scripto/?scripto_action=transcribe&scripto_doc_id=10286&scripto_doc_page_id=26390).

tion of the Moravian network and its worldwide diaspora by exploring social relationships among the authors through their memoirs. With such a potentially large corpus, scholars can analyze Moravian ego-documents in multiple ways: from the tracking of social change over the last 250 years, to the analysis of immigration history, to the creation of a vast corpus for linguistic analysis, and the investigation of race and gender history.

3.1 Visualizing networks

In discussions of church history, the role of missions and networks is one that has only come into critical focus in the last two decades. Andrew Porter, arguing against the prevalent tone in the field that had dismissed mission history as "excessively dull" and prone to "missionary hagiography,"[38] makes a plea instead for the recognition of the deeply political role these frequently decentralized, self-financing, self-governing and self-propagating indigenous churches played in settler cultures.[39] Communications between missions, relationships between White missionaries and indigenous people, kinship systems within indigenous

---

[38] Andrew Porter, "Church History, History of Christianity, Religious History: Some Reflections on British Missionary Enterprise Since the Late Eighteenth Century," *Church History* 71, no. 3 (2002), 558.
[39] Porter, "Church History," 561.

cultures, and invisible affinities between women played an enormous role in the spread of Christianity in the mission field.[40] Additionally, communications about language, customs, polities, religious beliefs of the peoples to be evangelized were all vital to the longevity of a mission.[41]

For example, contrary to the dominant historical accounts that elide the agency of women from the mission field in the Moravian church of the 18th and 19th centuries, visualized networks reveal the fact that Moravian women were crucial to the development of Christian communities in the mission field in their work with Native American women, in their negotiations with Colonial authorities, and in their leadership of the mission movement overall. Although some recent already cited historical scholarship has pointed to archival evidence that shows the centrality of women's activities to an understanding of the Colonial North American frontier, visualizing the networks of the married women's activities in the Moravian mission field among the Lenape (Delaware), Mahican, and Wampanoag nations compellingly reveals the crucial role women in the Moravian church played in its history.

Focusing on the ego-documents that are available in the digital memoir database of 11 Moravian women who were active in the missions in New York state and Pennsylvania in the mid-18th century, we can trace such communication networks through the extraction of named entities. Extracting named entities from the memoirs of Susanna Partsch (1722–1795), Martha Powell 1704–1774), Anna Mack (1720–1772), Johanette Schmick (1721–1795), Jannetje Mack (1722–1749), Marianne Rösler (1719–1804), Margarethe Jungmann (1721–1793), Martha Büninger (1723–1812), Maria Agnes Roth (1735–1805), Catharina Schmidt (n.d.), Sister Hagen (n.d.) we are able to construct a network diagram which visualizes the strength of relationship between these women by extracting the number of times the names of each woman appears in the memoirs and can then be represented through the "weight" of the links (Figure 5).

---

[40] See the more recent work of, among others, James Merrell, "The Other 'Susquehannah Traders': Women and Exchange on the Pennsylvania Frontier," in *Cultures and Identities in Colonial British America*, ed. Robert Olwell and Alan Tully (Baltimore: Johns Hopkins University Press, 2015): 197–222; Jane T. Merritt, "Cultural Encounters along a Gender Frontier: Mahican, Delaware, and German Women in Eighteenth-Century Pennsylvania," *Pennsylvania History: a Journal of Mid-Atlantic Studies* 67, no. 4 (2000): 502–31; Katherine M. Faull, "Women, Migration and Moravian Mission: Negotiating Pennsylvania's Colonial Landscapes," in *Babel of the Atlantic: Language and Cultural Politics in Colonial Pennsylvania*, ed. Bethany Wiggin (University Park, PA: Pennsylvania State University Press, 2019): 101–28.
[41] Porter, "Church History," 577.

Using the same method we can also represent the varying number of relationships (degree) each woman has with another woman in the network. So, looking at Figure 5 we can see that Johanette Schmick has a degree of 8, Janette Mack has a degree of 7, and are thus at the center of the network; whereas Martha Powell, with a degree of 3 appears at the periphery as does Marie Roth (with degree of 1). A network diagram partitioned for modularity (Figure 6) (in which the network is divided into modules or clusters based on the strength of ties between groups of individuals) reveals the small world community between Sisters Powell, Mack. Hagen, and Schmidt who all worked together in the Moravian mission of Shamokin, Pennsylvania in the 1740s and 50s.

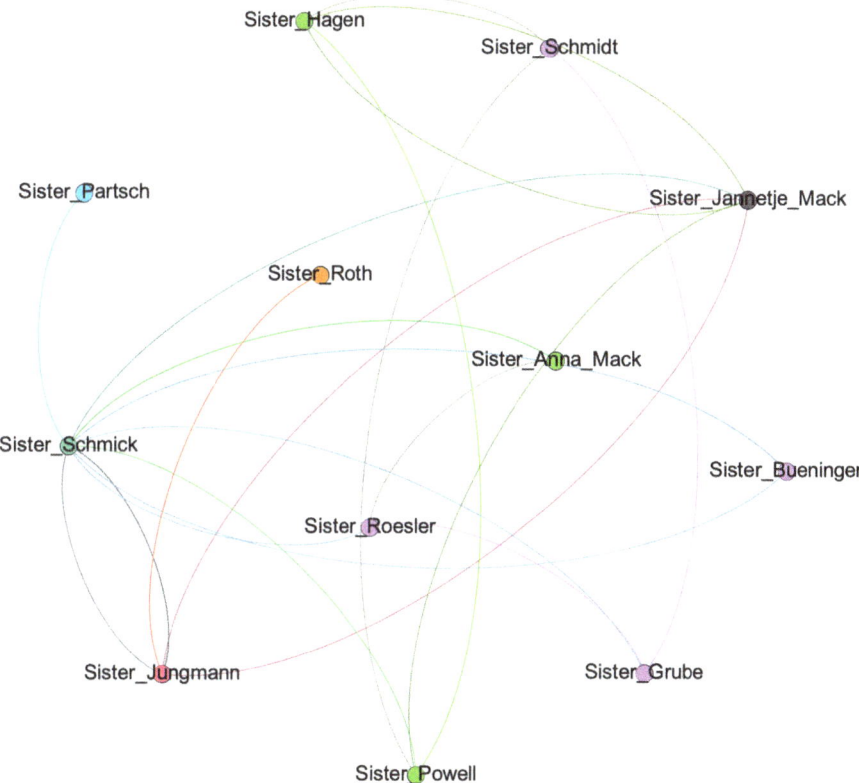

Figure 5: Visualization of network between Married Sisters who were Moravian missionaries in Pennsylvania in the 1740s–1770s partitioned for degree (# of connections).

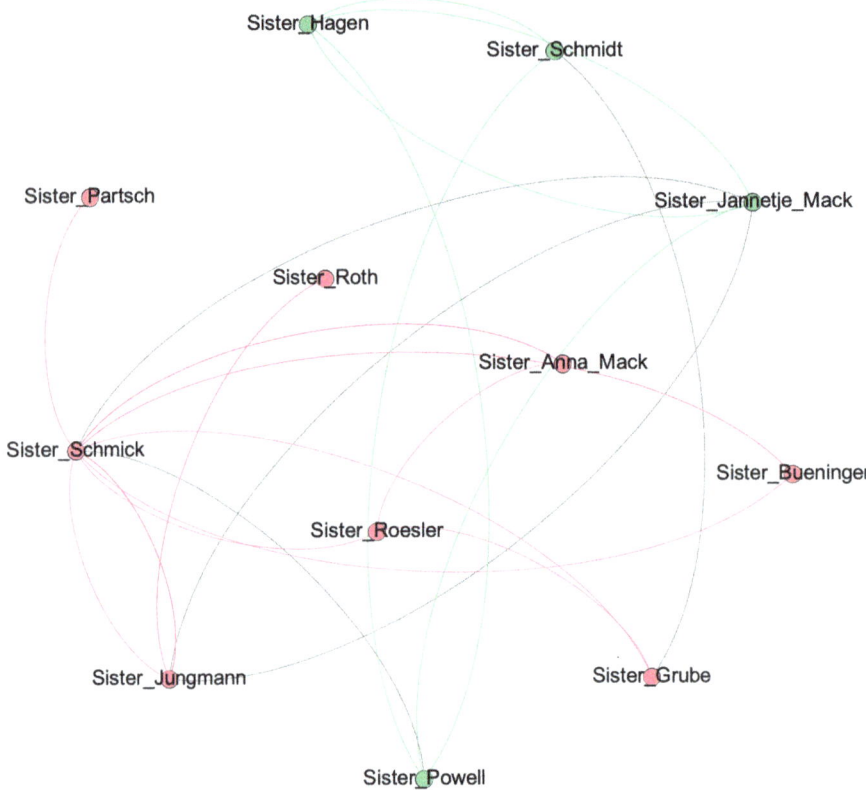

Figure 6: Network diagram partitioned for modularity, revealing the small world community between Sisters Powell, Mack, Hagen, and Schmidt who all worked together in the Moravian mission of Shamokin. The strongest relationship based on shared place and time of work is between Jennetje Mack and Martha Powell. However, all women are connected to each other through their work in the Moravian missions in the mid-Atlantic (rendered in Gephi by Faull 2017).

As seen in Figures 5 and 6, network analyses demonstrate that these 11 Moravian women in the 18th-century mid-Atlantic region formed their own strong networks in the mission field, exchanging knowledge between themselves and also to and from the Lenape and Mohican women with whom they came into contact in the mission towns.[42]

In a religious community that, for almost two hundred years, separated genders into "choirs," groups that were organized by gender, age and marital status,

---

[42] Faull, "Women, Migration and Moravian Mission," 106.

we can now delve further into the question of what the social networks of the individual Moravians looked like and examine women's networks.

Taking the albeit small digital corpus of women's memoirs that was first published in the volume *Moravian Women's Memoirs: Their Related Lives (1750–1820)*, the connections between the people that appear in the memoirs can be visualized and entered as nodes and edges in Gephi, creating a network graph (Figure 7).

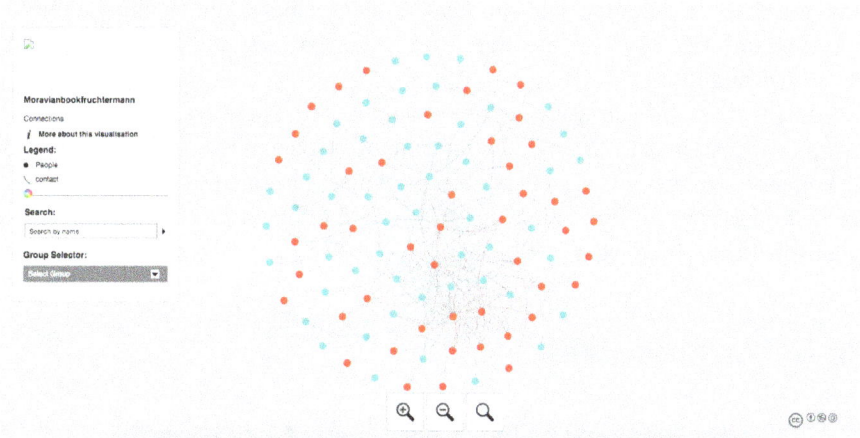

Figure 7: Network visualization of all the "persName" tags in Faull, *Moravian Women's Memoirs*, 1997. Available at http://katiefaull.net/network-memoirbook/index.html.

Exploring this graph reveals several interesting things. First, it is clear that the majority of Moravian women whose memoirs are in the corpus were connected to an extended network of both men and women. For example, Anna Boehler, one of the married sisters, has connections with 13 people: 12 Moravians and one non-Moravian; 4 women and 9 men. Sarah Hussey, a widowed sister, originally from Paris, is part of quite a tight cluster of 9 people (all Moravian) that is almost equally divided between men (4) and women (5). Unsurprisingly, single sisters' networks are the smallest, with the most intimate clustering being around the "Heiland," that is Jesus Christ.

This particular network visualization also reveals the interconnectedness of those whose names are mentioned in the memoirs but who are not actually authors of the memoirs in the corpus. Over the time span of the corpus (1750–1800), Count Zinzendorf has 16 named connections in the network, evenly divided between men and women. Anna Nitschmann has 19 connections, 8 women and 11 men. Augustus Spangenberg has 13 connections, 5 men and 8 women;

Martha Spangenberg has 8 connections, 3 women and 5 men. Again, despite the traditional scholarly claims that there was strict gender segregation among the Moravians, it is interesting to note that all four leaders of the church had more connections in this network with people of the opposite sex than with their own sex. There are obvious reasons for this among the leaders of the church, as they come into contact with and are mentioned by everyone, regardless of gender. Those sisters who were not in the church leadership did not have as much contact with members of the opposite sex: however, this did not mean that the sisters did not mention brothers in their memoirs. For example, the widowed Sister Marie Worbass, mentions three Moravian men and one Moravian sister in her memoir.

In this way we can see how the communicative network of the Moravian world was instantiated through the memoirs of Moravian women. And, contrary to common perceptions of Pietistic women as living isolated lives with little contact with men and/or non-Moravians the resultant network reveals how rich and connected their lives were.

4 Networked lives

To return to the question that was posed at the outset of this chapter: how might the act of visualizing digitally this large corpus of religious memoirs be understood as what Nikolaus von Zinzendorf, the founder of the Moravian Church understood to be the reconstitution of the invisible church?

Much of the previous discussion has focused on the extraction of positivistic historical data in the form of names, dates, and places, which is then manipulated and visualized to provide insights into the lives of Moravians in the past. But how does the medium of the digital affect the conceptualization of selfhood, both historically in terms of accessing "archival memory" and also phenomenologically in terms of participating in "lived memory"?

Recently, scientific research has revealed that St. Augustine's notion of memory, outlined in Book X of the Confessions as a great "store house of memory" repository archive, is indeed partially accurate.[43] An additional concept to that of archival memory adheres to the "connectionist" paradigm by which is understood that the past is not only stored but is recreated and reconstructed every

---

[43] Lilianne Manning, Daniel Cassel, Jean-Christophe Cassel, "St. Augustine's Reflections on Memory and Time and the Current Concept of Subjective Time in Mental Time Travel," *Behavioral Sciences* (Basel) 25, no. 3 (April 2013): 232–43.

time it is invoked by the present subject in a new associative context: "Every memory ... is a new memory because it is shaped (or reconsolidated) by changes that have happened to our brain since the memory last occurred to us."[44]

If we apply van Dijk's insights into the working of memory and autobiography to the reading of thousands of digitally transcribed memoirs, we need to ask how the experience of reading a digitized material manuscript of a Moravian man or woman's life substantively changes the re-presentation of that life. Will the existence of the digital archive of memoirs bring these memoirs back into a lived present? If the original Zinzendorfian tradition of writing a memoir was conceived theologically, does the digital medium transform and make immediate that particular instantiation of the word and kingdom of God?

Moravian Lives, as a digital platform, provides insight into the records of Moravian lives contained within the archived memoirs, leading to interpretive and analytical texts that can illuminate the rich and varied ways in which personal history becomes universal history. The project already allows access to a large database of the metadata attached to the "ego-documents" from a socially and ethnically diverse group of men and women. Investigation of such a large collection of mainly first-person narratives from the mid-18th century to the present allows researchers in many historical fields access to the "big data" of the memoir collections in the two major archives in Europe and North America. It provides a flexible and growing platform that will enable the collection to be added to from other smaller Moravian archives (such as those in Sweden, the United Kingdom, South Africa, Australia, and other locations in the Moravian diaspora and mission field), thus subverting the tendency of making public only those memoirs of the social and spiritual elites (ministers and male elders and European missionaries). The digital archive also makes available the recorded lives of artisans, women, enslaved peoples, and indigenous peoples. In addition, applying a new phenomenological reading to the function of the archive could have enormous implications for theology. In this new digital way, Moravian memoirs might achieve their truly Zinzendorfian purpose: to create a living history of the church that consists of the lived history of all its members.

---

44 José Van Dijk, *Mediated Memories in the Digital Age* (Stanford: Stanford University Press, 2007), 18.

5 Primary Sources

Unity Archives, Herrnhut, Germany
Jüngerhausdiarium, 22 June 1747, UA Herrnhut, R.03.A 08. 245

Memoirs
Anna Mack (1720–1772) R.22.147.23

Moravian Archives, Bethlehem, PA Memoirs
Martha Büninger (1723–1812) MemBeth 0545
Martha Powell (1704–1774) MemBeth 0224
Margarethe Jungmann (1721–1793) MemBeth 0356
Susanne Louise Partsch (1722–1795) MemBeth 0377
Maria Agnes Roth (1735–1805) MemBeth 0475
Johanette Schmick (1721–1795)
Jannetje Mack (1722–1749)
Marianne Rösler (1719–1804)
Catharina Schmidt (n.d.),
Anna Hagen (n.d.)

6 Bibliography

Assmann, Jan. *Das kulturelle Gedächtnis: Schrift, Erinnerung und politische Identität in frühen Hochkulturen.* Beck: München, 2007.
Augustine. *Confessions*, trans. Henry Chadwick. Oxford: Oxford University Press, 1998.
Böß, Stephanie. *Gottesacker-Geschichten: Eine Ethnographie zur Herrnhuter Erinnerungskultur am Beispiel von Neudietendorfer Lebensläufen.* Münster: Waxmann, 2016.
Campbell, Heidi A., ed. *Digital Religion: Understanding Religious Practice in New Media Worlds.* Lomdon/New York: Routledge, 2013.
Cassel, Jean-Christophe, Daniel Cassel, and Lilianne Manning. "From Augustine of Hippo's Memory Systems to Our Modern Taxonomy in Cognitive Psychology and Neuroscience of Memory: A 16-Century Map of Intuition before Light of Evidence." *Behavioral Sciences* 3 (2013): 21–41.
Cheong, Pauline, Peter Fischer-Nielsen, Stefan Gelfgren, and Charles Ess, eds. *Digital Religion, Social Media and Culture: Perspectives, Practices, and Futures.* New York: Peter Lang, 2012.
Eakin, Paul John. "Autobiography as Cosmogram." *Storyworlds: A Journal of Narrative Studies* 6, no. 1 (2014): 21–43.
Faull, Katherine M., ed. and trans. *Moravian Women's Memoirs: Their Related Lives, 1750–1820.* Syracuse, NY: Syracuse University Press, 1997.
Faull, Katherine M. *Speaking to Body and Soul: Instructions for the Moravian Choir Helpers, 1785–1786.* Pietist, Moravian, and Anabaptist Studies. University Park, PA: Pennsylvania State University Press, 2017.

Faull, Katherine M. "Writing a Moravian Memoir: The Intersection of History and Autobiography." In *Life Writing and Lebenslauf: Pillars of an Invisible Church*, edited by Christer Ahlberger and Per van Wachtenfeld, 9–34. Artos Publishers, 2018.

Faull, Katherine M. "Women, Migration and Moravian Mission: Negotiating Pennsylvania's Colonial Landscapes." In *Babel of the Atlantic: Language and Cultural Politics in Colonial Pennsylvania*, edited by Bethany Wiggin, 101–30. University Park, PA: Pennsylvania State University Press, 2019.

Groys, Boris. "Invisibility of the Digital: Religion, Ritual, Immortality." *RES: Anthropology and Aesthetics* 55/56 (2009): 336–40.

Hamilton, J. Taylor, and Kenneth G. Hamilton. *History of the Moravian Church: The Renewed Unitas Fratrum, 1722–1957*. Bethlehem, PA: Interprovincial Board of Christian Education, Moravian Church in America, 1983.

Haskins, Ekaterina. "Between Archive and Participation: Public Memory in a Digital Age." *Rhetoric Society Quarterly* 37, no. 4 (2007): 401–22.

Lejeune, Philippe. "The Autobiographical Contract." In *French Literary Theory Today: A Reader*, edited by Tzvetan Todorov, 192–222. Cambridge: Cambridge University Press, 1982.

Lost, Christine. *Das Leben als Lehrtext: Lebensläufe aus der Herrnhuter Brüdergemeine*. Herrnhut: Herrnhuter Verlag, 2007.

Manning, Lilianne, Daniel Cassel, Jean-Christophe Cassel, "St. Augustine's Reflections on Memory and Time and the Current Concept of Subjective Time in Mental Time Travel." *Behavioral Sciences* (Basel) 25, no. 3 (April 2013): 232–43.

Martin, Lucinda. "Female Reformers as the Gatekeepers of Pietism: The Example of Johanna Eleonora Merlau and William Penn." *Monatshefte* 95, no. 1 (2003): 33–58.

McCullough, T. J. "The Most Memorable Circumstances: Instructions for the Collection of Personal Data from Church Members, circa 1752." *Journal of Moravian History* 15, no. 2 (2015): 158–75.

Mettele, Gisela. *Weltbürgertum oder Gottesreich? Die Herrnhuter Brüdergemeine als globale Gemeinschaft 1760–1857*. Göttingen: Vandenhoeck & Ruprecht, 2009.

Merrell, James. "The Other 'Susquehannah Traders': Women and Exchange on the Pennsylvania Frontier." In *Cultures and Identities in Colonial British America*, edited by Robert Olwell and Alan Tully, 197–222. Baltimore: Johns Hopkins University Press, 2015.

Merritt, Jane T. "Cultural Encounters along a Gender Frontier: Mahican, Delaware, and German Women in Eighteenth-Century Pennsylvania." *Pennsylvania History: A Journal of Mid-Atlantic Studies* 67, no. 4 (2000): 502–31.

Podmore, Colin. *The Moravian Church of England 1728–1760*.Oxford: Oxford University Press, 1998.

Porter, Andrew. "Church History, History of Christianity, Religious History: Some Reflections on British Missionary Enterprise Since the Late Eighteenth Century," *Church History* 71, no. 3 (2002): 555–84.

Rollinger, Düring, and Stark Gramsch-Stehfest. "Editors' Introduction." *Journal of Historical Network Research* 1 (2017): v.

Shantz, Douglas H. "The Origin of Pietist Notions of New Birth and the New Man: Alchemy and Alchemists in Gottfried Arnold and Johann Henrich Reitz." In *The Pietist Impulse in Christianity*, edited by Christian T. Collins Winn, Christopher Gehrz, G. William Carlson, and Eric Holst, with forewords by James H. Barnes III and Peter C. Erb, 29–41. Cambridge: James Clarke & Co Ltd, 2011.

Shantz, Douglas. *An Introduction to German Pietism: Protestant Renewal at the Dawn of Modern Europe.* Baltimore: Johns Hopkins University Press, 2013.

Schutt, Amy. *Peoples of the River Valleys: The Odyssey of the Delaware Indians.* Philadelphia: University of Pennsylvania Press, 2007.

Smaby, Beverly Prior. *The Transformation of Moravian Bethlehem: From Communal Mission to Family Economy.* Philadelphia: University of Pennsylvania Press, 1988.

Van Gent, Jacqueline. "The Lives of Others: Moravian Religious Converts' Writings and the Politics of Colonial Autobiographies." In *Selbstzeugnis und Person: Transkulturelle Perspektiven,* edited by Claudia Ulbrich, Hans Medick, and Angelika Schaser, 87–100. Köln: Böhlau, 2012.

Vogt, Peter. "Spiritual Autobiography and Ecclesiology." In *Moravian Memoirs: Pillars of an Invisible Church,* edited by Christer Ahlberger and Per von Wachtenfeld, 35–56. Artos, 2017.

Van Dijk, José. *Mediated Memories in the Digital Age.* Stanford: Stanford University Press, 2007.

Wheeler, Rachel. *To Live upon Hope: Mohicans and Missionaries in the Eighteenth-Century Northeast.* Ithaca: Cornell University Press, 2008.

John N. Wall
The theology of relational practice: digital modeling and the historical study of Christianity

Digital modeling technology is transforming our study of post-Reformation Christianity because it enables us to recreate the experience of reformed public worship in the spaces in which it was originally conducted. In our Virtual Paul's Cross Project (vpcp.chass.ncsu.edu), for example, we have made it possible for users to hear John Donne's Paul's Cross sermon for November 5, 1622 as an event that unfolds in real time from within a digital model of Paul's Churchyard, outside St. Paul's Cathedral in London.[1] This sermon, preached by Donne at the request of King James on the day set aside to commemorate James' escape from the Gunpowder Plot of 1605, defends James for his actions earlier in 1622 to control the preaching of Calvinist opponents of his efforts to secure an alliance with the Spanish.

On the Project's website,[2] one can explore questions about the audibility of the unamplified voice – and thus Donne's ability to communicate with such a large crowd of people in a large outdoor space – by listening to Donne's sermon from eight different positions within Paul's Churchyard as well as in the company of four different sizes of crowd. One can also explore the workings of early modern worship, as we come to understand how this event was organized and

---

[1] Prof. David Hill, my colleague at NC State University, and I were the co-Principal Investigators of the Virtual Paul's Cross Project, which was funded by a grant from the National Endowment for the Humanities. The Virtual Paul's Cross Project recreates one of many sermons preached at Paul's Cross, the Preaching Station located in the northeast section of Paul's Churchyard, outside the cathedral. Standing inside Paul's Cross, a preacher delivered a public sermon almost every Sunday from 10 AM until noon from the early 16th century until the 1630s, to crowds of as many as 5,000 or 6,000 people. The choice of preacher was made by the Bishop of London or, after the Reformation, the reigning monarch. This was the site at which the political and theological controversies of the English Reformation were argued and the religious policies of the Tudor and Stuart monarchs were defended. The outdoor site was chosen because the only alternative, the Choir of the cathedral, seated fewer than 150 people. For more on the Paul's Cross sermon, see Mary Morrissey, *Politics and the Paul's Cross Sermons, 1558–1642* (Oxford: Oxford University Press, 2011); and Torrance Kirby and Paul Stanwood, eds., *Paul's Cross and the Culture of Persuasion in England, 1520–1640* (Toronto: Brill, 2013).

[2] The Virtual Paul's Cross website has attracted over 150,000 visitors since going live in 2013. It received the John Donne Society's Award for Distinguished Digital Publication in 2013 and the Award for Best DH Data Visualization from DH Awards in 2014.

https://doi.org/10.1515/9783110574043-011

staged. One can also examine the effect on the experience of hearing this sermon of random ambient noise, including the sounds of horses, birds, and dogs, as well as the regular and recurring sound of the cathedral's clock tolling the hours.

The Virtual Paul's Cross Project's companion, the Virtual St. Paul's Cathedral Project,[3] will soon enable us to experience worship and preaching inside the cathedral, recreating use of the Book of Common Prayer on two full liturgical days, including all worship services, sermons preached in the cathedral, and music for choir and organ composed by the cathedral's musicians. Both these projects help us reorient our thinking about post-Reformation religious history because they remind us of the importance of public worship in the formation of Christian faith and the centrality of oral communication in a country where everyone was by law a member of the Church of England and congregations contained a complex mix of literacies and a significant proportion of the population were non-readers. These two projects also help set the agenda for digital modeling still to come of various styles and arrangements of parish worship.

Our websites function, therefore, as examples of what Christophe Schuwey calls "interfaces," practices that serve as "ways to renew our relationship" to the objects of our study.[4] Taking this approach to the study of post-Reformation Christianity enables us to explore more fully the performative, interactive, and relational dimensions of the English Reformation. We can consider afresh how post-Reformation religious identities developed in England through use of the Book of Common Prayer to form and sustain religious communities and to guide the reading and hearing of the Bible. We can also reformulate our understanding of broadly held theological positions, now based on our consideration of liturgical worship as consisting of contextual, community-based events. These events – performances enabled through words, through objects like water and bread and wine, and through interactive participation by clergy and laity – grounded the religious life of the country in a network of interpersonal relationships that served as the movement's theological and practical point of departure,

---

[3] Prof. Hill and I have been joined as co-Principal Investigators for the Virtual St Paul's Cathedral Project by Prof. Yun Jing, then also at NC State University, but now on the faculty at Penn State University. This project, also funded by a grant from the National Endowment for the Humanities, seeks to recreate the look and sound of the cathedral on Easter Sunday 1624, during which we will experience a full day of worship with choir and organ performing music composed by the cathedral's musicians and sermons by Bishop Lancelot Andrewes in the morning and Dean John Donne in the afternoon.

[4] See his *Interfaces: l'apport des humanités numériques à la littérature* (Neuchâtel, Switzerland: Editions Livreo-Alphil, 2019), esp. 125–6.

in addition to, or even rather than, the independent and private spaces of theological reflection.

1 The reconstruction of liturgical practice

The Virtual Paul's Cross Project and the Virtual St Paul's Cathedral Project use visual modeling technology to integrate the surviving physical traces of pre-Fire St Paul's Cathedral and its surrounding churchyard (including measurements of the foundations still in the ground) with the historic visual record of the cathedral and its surroundings into a highly accurate visual model of the Cathedral and its churchyard.[5] The Paul's Cross model depicts the northeast corner of Paul's churchyard, including the choir and north transept of the Cathedral, the Paul's Cross Preaching Station, and the buildings surrounding the churchyard, chiefly mixed-use houses with retail book shops on the ground floor and living accommodations above. The model also includes the buildings along the streets that run alongside the northeast corner of the Churchyard, specifically Paternoster Row to the north and The Old Change Street to the east, as well as their intersection at the west end of Cheapside. The Cathedral Project model completes the model of the cathedral itself, both inside and out, and adds the buildings that surrounded the Cathedral to the northwest along Paternoster Row, to the west along Ave Maria Lane, and to the south along Carter Lane.

The depiction of buildings in our visual models are based on visual images in paintings, drawings, and engravings from the late 16th and early 17th centuries, most notably the drawings and engravings of St Paul's Cathedral done in the mid-1650s by the Dutch artist Wenseslaus Hollar for William Dugdale's *History of St Paul's Cathedral* (1658). The size, location, and physical dimensions of these buildings are based on surveys conducted of these buildings in the middle of the 17th century and on archaeological excavations from the 19th and 20th cen-

---

5 The basic software packages used for visual modeling were SketchUp 3D Modeling Software for the basic models and Photoshop for renderings that added details of time, weather, and the effects of aging on the buildings. While other visual modeling projects, such as *Rome Reborn* (https://romereborn.org/) also integrate historic and archaeological data to create their models, they almost always avoid the inclusion of signs of time's passage. As a result, the whole model looks like the buildings are of equal age, and are all brand new, with the paint still wet. Although our basic models share this look, we have gone to great lengths in individual views of the models to include this important element. So, the buildings are dirty, the sky is usually overcast, and the older construction looks more worn than the newer ones.

turies.⁶ The representation of structures in our models ranges from the highly accurate (especially the cathedral, for which we have Hollar's work, Christopher Wren's measurements, and archaeologists' findings) to the generically accurate (when we have the measurements of the foundations, numbers of stories, and design of roofs from the contemporary surveys but not details of the specific appearance) to the approximate (when we have some but not all of the dimensions of a structure, such as for the Paul's Cross preaching station, for which we have the dimensions of the foundations from archaeologists and the look of the structure from contemporary depictions but not the exact height).

Our visual models provide the basis for acoustic models that enable us to recreate the experience of hearing the sounds of early modern worship and preaching, recorded in our time but now heard as though they had been made in the spaces in which they were originally performed.⁷ The acoustic models are simplified versions of our visual models, containing the basic geometrical forms of the structures and spaces in the visual models, together with information about the reflective, dispersive, or absorptive characteristics of the materials out of which the original structures were made. Acoustic modeling programs map the behavior of sound in these spaces, enabling us to hear the sounds of worship services as though we were hearing them in the spaces we have modeled.

To recreate the services we wish to hear, we have followed the rubrics of the Book of Common Prayer of 1604, the edition in use at the cathedral while Donne was Dean, from 1621 until his death in 1631. We have recreated two full days of worship in the cathedral – Easter Day in 1624 (a festival day) and the Tuesday after the First Sunday in Advent in 1625 (a ferial, or ordinary day on the Calendar of the Church Year). The Easter Sunday services include Morning Prayer, the Great Litany, and Holy Communion (including Bishop Launcelot Andrewes' sermon for that day), as well as Evensong (followed by Dean Donne's sermon for that day). Music for this festival occasion includes pieces by the most distinguished musicians of the day; music for the Advent service includes pieces composed by Adrian Batten, a musician at St Paul's hired by Dean Donne in 1625.

---

6 For more on the post-Great Fire surveys, see Peter Blayney, *The Bookshops in Paul's Cross Churchyard, Occasional Papers of the Bibliographical Society* 5 (London: The Bibliographical Society, 1990). For work by archaeologists surveying the foundations of St Paul's and other structures in Paul's Churchyard, see John Schofield, *St Paul's Cathedral Before Wren* (Swindon: English Heritage, 2011).
7 The software packages used for acoustic modeling were CATT Acoustic and iPack Simpa, an open-source software package developed specifically for the Cathedral Project.

To use the acoustic modeling software effectively, we start with recordings made to include only the sounds made by speakers, singers, and musicians while minimizing any reverberation or echo from the walls of the studio in which the recordings were made.[8] To approximate the sounds of early modern worship, we use scripts using original early modern London English pronunciation prepared by the linguist David Crystal (Crystal himself performs Andrewes' sermon).[9] For the sound of St Paul's organ in the early 17th century, we used the Hauptwerk electronic recreation of an early modern organ, the instrument of the Holy Trinity church in Smecno, in the Czech Republic, built around 1587.

Combining our acoustic models with our visual models, we can experience early modern worship services in their full scale and duration within spaces that approximate the sits of their original performances. Within the Paul's Cross model, we can hear Donne's sermon along with the ambient noises of horses, dogs, and birds, as well as the sound of the cathedral's clock marking the passage of the hours and quarter-hours. We can join a range of different sizes of crowd as they gather to experience a historically faithful interpretation of Donne's preaching style, performed by the actor Ben Crystal and based on contemporary descriptions of Donne's capacity to engage his congregations imaginatively and emotionally and to delight them with his wit. Within the Cathedral model, we can experience the full extent of the liturgical day, notice how the rites of Easter Sunday frame the Bishop's sermon in the morning and the Dean's sermon in the afternoon, and how the Prayer Book rites weave extensive scripture readings into a framework of fixed and variable prayers and sacramental activities. We can also get a sense of how the noise made by crowds gathered in Paul's Walk – the cathedral's nave – might have interrupted the daily and weekly round of worship services taking place in the Choir.[10]

---

8 The best studio for such recordings is an anechoic (or "non-echo-producing") chamber, a studio lined over the walls, ceiling, and floor with highly absorbent foam, and with a steel net for the performer to stand on. We used the anechoic chamber at the University of Salford, in Manchester, England, for our recordings for Paul's Cross. For the Cathedral Project, we used a semi-anechoic recording studio in Cambridge, England and employed highly directional microphones (one for each performer) to produce the kinds of anechoic recordings we required.

9 Other performers on the recordings include the professional actors Ben Crystal (who performed Donne's role for both projects), William Sutton, and Colin Hurley, and the Choir of Jesus College, Cambridge, under the direction of Choirmaster Richard Pinel, who also played the organ for our recordings.

10 We have chosen to model St Paul's Cathedral in part because of its importance to the career of John Donne, who was ordained to the diaconate and priesthood on 23 January 1615 in the Chapel of the Bishop of London, attached physically to the northwest side of St Paul's nave. Donne was also Dean of St Paul's from 1621 until his death in 1631. But we also chose it because,

2 Worship and belief in post-Reformation England

The Virtual Paul's Cross and Cathedral Projects help us understand more fully the daily and weekly worship experiences of early modern Londoners. While some clergy objected to the Prayer Book's use of set prayers and specified times and forms for public worship, English law nonetheless required citizens to attend worship in their local parish churches, to have their new-born children baptized in this churches within a few days of birth, and to have the major events of their lives, from marriage to burial, organized and informed by use of the texts of the Book of Common Prayer.[11] Hence, we must recognize that for the vast majority of English folk in the post-Reformation period what they believed about their faith was what they experienced in worship and were told about the meaning of their experience by the Prayer Book in explanation of the Church's public acts of worship. In spite of some historians' claim that the theology of the reformed Church of England was essentially Calvinist,[12] what mattered to folks who took part in its public ceremonies was that those ceremonies were meaningful and effective, providing reassurance of their value and standing before God.

In contrast to the bleak pessimism of Archbishop Whitgift's Lambeth Articles,[13] for example, the rites of the Prayer Book created for ordinary parishioners, in the words of David Bagchi, "a daily and weekly framework of comfort and assurance."[14] Those whose children were baptized by a priest using the Baptismal

---

as a cathedral, having no formal congregation of its own, its basic reason for existence was to carry out the full round of worship services called for by the Book of Common Prayer.

11 Historians inflate the extent of Puritan dissent in post-Elizabethan settlement of religion arguments about use of the Prayer Book. See Judith Maltby, *Prayer Book and People in Elizabethan and Early Stuart England* (Cambridge: Cambridge University Press, 1998) for a balanced review of this topic.

12 Hence convinced that one's status before God depended on God's eternal decree regarding someone rather than on any temporal event in which that person might participate; for how the history of the post-Reformation Church of England looks from within this perspective, see Alec Ryrie, *Being Protestant in Reformation Britain* (Oxford: OUP, 2013) and "The Reformation in Anglicanism," in *The Oxford Handbook of Anglican Studies*, ed. Mark Chapman, Sathianathan Clarke, and Martyn Percy (Oxford: OUP, 2015): 34–45.

13 The Lambeth Articles, never officially adopted by the Church hierarchy, embody Calvinist beliefs about human depravity and human dependence for hope on the eternal will of a remote and abstract God. See "Lambeth Articles," Wikipedia, last modified 22 September 2019, https://en.wikipedia.org/wiki/Lambeth_Articles for the full text.

14 David Bagchi, "'The Scripture Moveth Us in Sundry Places': Framing Biblical Emotions in the Book of Common Prayer and the Homilies," in *The Renaissance of Emotion: Understanding Affect*

rite of the Book of Common Prayer had assurance that they had been "embraced" by God "with the arms of his mercy," and had been given "the blessing of eternal life." Those who "have duly received these holy mysteries "at Holy Communion could be assured that they were "very members incorporate in the mystical body of thy Son...and heirs through hope of thy everlasting kingdom."[15] Those who had received the Last Rites of the Church could believe that they approached their deaths forgiven for their offences, absolved "from al [their] synnes," and abiding "in sure and certain hope of resurrection to eternall lyfe." As far as the vast majority of English folk were concerned, therefore, "as they prayed, so did they believe," and the Book of Common Prayer provided the script for their prayers.[16]

When we recognize the importance of the lived experience of corporate worship in the post-Reformation Church of England,[17] we must reimagine the concept of "text" when we consider the writings that the faithful in early modern England found to embody their beliefs, whether they be the Creeds, or official statements of dogma, or the writings of notable theologians, whether Augustine, or Aquinas, or Luther, or Calvin.

While Christianity is one of the world's "religions of the book,"[18] we are reminded that, as Paul wrote to the Church at Corinth, "The letter killeth, but the Spirit giveth life." [19] In a world where communication of religious subjects was primarily oral, primarily about speaking and hearing, we are reminded that

---

in Shakespeare and His Contemporaries, ed. Richard Meek and Erin Sullivan (Manchester: Manchester University Press, 2015), 54.
15 All quotations in this essay from the Book of Common Prayer are, for the purposes of convenience, from the edition of 1559, ed. John Booty (Folger Library, 1976). Donne at St Paul's would have used the edition of 1604, essentially a reprint of the 1559 edition except for updating in various prayers and other texts to reflect changes brought by the accession to the throne of James I).
16 A loose translation of the traditional Latin affirmation *lex orandi, lex credendi*.
17 The style of parish worship – although not the rites performed – would have been different in parish churches, where few had organs or choirs that survived the iconoclasm of the early Reformation period. So, the services would have been spoken rather than sung (although the Psalms would have been sung in at least some places), there would have been fewer celebrations of Holy Communion, and clergy would have worn cassocks and surplices rather than the copes they wore at the cathedral. We hope, given time and support, to create visual and acoustic models of one or more parish churches so we can explore more fully these differences.
18 For interesting discussions of this term, see Matthew Dimmock and Andrew Hadfield, *The Religions of the Book: Christian Perceptions, 1400–1660* (Houndmills: Palgrave Macmillan, 2008).
19 2 Corinthians 3:6. All biblical citations in this essay will be from the Authorized (King James) Version of 1611.

the core texts of Christian faith – the Gospels – are not formulations of belief so much as they are stories about events and relationships; Jesus' early followers did not join him because they were persuaded by a logical argument but because they met someone who invited them to follow him. Even the Creeds are narratives at heart; while the Nicene Creed does devote several of its 32 lines to defining the relationships among the persons of the Trinity in philosophical language, it is, mostly, a series of narratives about the actions of these persons, as well as their interactions, and their relationships with us, relationships that give us identity and locate us in time as we recite them.

When scholars address the topic of sermons in their studies of early modern literature, however, they typically treat early modern sermons as theological essays, not as traces of public events. Whatever the topic of their study, whether it is the sermon's theological content, its rhetorical structure, the style of composition, or the use of scripture, or of classical or contemporary allusions, they base their discussions on, and support their arguments with, quotes from the texts, whether they survive in manuscript or printed form. Scholars write about early modern sermons, therefore, as though the text of the sermon that comes down to us, either in manuscript or printed form, is the sermon, is the goal and culmination of the process that lies behind the production of that text.[20] In these approaches, sermons-as-text can be read in extract, in prooftext, backwards or forwards, with sections viewed as important read repeatedly, more closely than other sections, highlighted for our attention while other sections recede from view.

Christianity's focus on texts, while understandable given the transitory character of lived experience, has a way of foregrounding some aspects of the Christian tradition, or of our understanding what is meant by the term "Christian," and disregarding others. Definitions of Christianity that focus chiefly on texts privilege the cognitive meaning-making of the faithful, thus isolating the work of the study, of the scholar or theologian alone in the process of thinking and writing. In so doing, we lose sight of what is of course at the heart of what it means to be Christian from the earliest days – the gathering of the Church's members, continuing "steadfastly in the apostles' doctrine and fellowship, and in breaking of bread, and in prayers."[21]

---

[20] For examples, see Winfried Schleiner, *The Imagery of John Donne's Sermons* (Providence, RI: Brown University Press, 1970), Deborah Shuger, *Habits of Thought in the English Renaissance: Religion, Politics, and the Dominant Culture* (Berkeley: University of California Press, 1990); P. M. Oliver, *Donne's Religious Writing: A Discourse of Feigned Devotion* (Longman, 1997); and Jeffrey Johnson, *The Theology of John Donne*, Studies in Renaissance Literature (D. S. Brewer, 1999).
[21] Acts 2:42 (Authorized Version).

Hence, through approaching early modern sermons from the perspective of their oral performances, we can more fully appreciate the significance of Cranmer's emphasis on the Book of Common Prayer as a unifying force in the development of a national religious identity. We can explore how through use of the Prayer Book, the Bible was received into the public worship of English folk through the public performance of lectionary readings, through public preaching from biblical texts, and public performance of biblically derived Prayer Book liturgies. We can also explore more fully how, through the performance of relational events, English folk were formed as post-Reformation Christians and developed their understanding of the Reformed faith through their corporate practice, leaving theological controversies to occupy the spare time and extra energies of the learned and the privileged.

This is especially true for the Church of England, where the early modern reformers placed the public gathering of the faithful at the center of their Reformation. In the Preface to the first Book of Common Prayer (1549), Archbishop Cranmer stresses the importance of uniform public worship, noting that

> heretofore, there hath been great diversitie in saying and synging in churches within this realme: some folowyng Salsbury use, some Herford use, some the use of Bangor, some of Yorke, and some of Lincolne: Now from hencefurth, all the whole realme shall have but one use.[22]

Cranmer's vision is of a nation united in prayer through "use" of common forms of worship and texts for prayer. To enable this uniformity of worship, the Church of England in the reign of Edward VI, produced a series of monumental publications stretching from the Great Bible (1539),[23] through the first Book of Homilies (1547) and the first Books of Common Prayer (1549, 1552), investing enormous resources in enabling English folk to have "one use."[24]

Every parish and collegiate church and every cathedral across the land was required by the Injunctions of Edward VI and Elizabeth I to purchase this set of

---

22 From the Preface to the Book of Common Prayer (1549), here: http://justus.anglican.org/resources/bcp/1549/front_matter_1549.htm#Preface.
23 The Great Bible was deliberately printed as "the largest volume in English" because it was a Bible to be used for public, not private, reading; to be "set up in some convenient place within the said church that ye have care of, whereas your parishioners may most commodiously resort to the same and read it" in the public space of the church.
24 For discussions of these official books, and of the program they embody, see John Booty, ed., *The Godly Kingdom of Tudor England: Great Books of the English Reformation* (Wilton, CT: Morehouse-Barlow, 1981).

books.[25] The point of all this printed paper was to enable all English folk to engage in the public worship of God in the language "understanded of the people,"[26] a publicly enacted intersection of oral reading – in English – of the Bible, of prayers and public acts of confession, intercession, and thanksgiving and observation of the sacraments of Baptism and Holy Communion. Public reading of the Bible was systematically structured by the Daily Office lectionary and the assigned readings for services of Holy Communion. By following the Lectionary, clergy made sure that the Book of Psalms was read over in the context of public worship once a month, the Old Testament once a year, and the New Testament three times a year. The Bible provided the essential readings; the Prayer Book provided texts for the worship services; the Books of Homilies provided sermons for use when the local parish priest did not qualify for a license to preach his own sermons.

As a result of the general implementation of Cranmer's plan for the transformation of corporate religious life in England, as Eamon Duffy puts it, "Cranmer's somberly magnificent prose, read week by week, entered and possessed their minds, and became the fabric of their prayer, the utterance of their most solemn and their most vulnerable moments."[27] Or, as William Harrison put it in his contemporary account of Tudor social life, "the minister saith his service commonly in the body of the church, with his face toward the people" so "the ignorant doo not onelie learne diuerse of the psalmes and vsuall praiers by heart, but also such as can read, doo praie togither with [the priest]: so that the whole congregation at one instant powere out their petitions vnto the liuing God."[28]

Harrison's reference to the "ignorant" (meaning illiterate) reminds us that, while literacy was high among the male elite, a majority of those who gathered for worship in early modern England typically could not read. We must conclude, therefore, that for everyone to some degree and for a majority in fact, the knowledge and experience of Christianity in the early modern period was acquired chiefly through hearing, most especially through hearing other people recite

---

25 The canonically prescribed list also included, over time, an English translation of Erasmus' *Paraphrases upon the New Testament* (1548) and a second *Book of Homilies* (1571).
26 From Article XXIV of the *Thirty-Nine Articles of Religion* (1571): https://www.churchofengland.org/prayer-and-worship/worship-texts-and-resources/book-common-prayer/articles-religion.
27 In Eamon Duffy, *The Stripping of the Altars: Traditional Religion in England, c. 1400–c. 1580*, 2nd ed. (New Haven, CT: Yale University Press, 2005), 593. See also Maltby, *Prayer Book and People*, for an informed discussion of the limits on implementation of the English liturgical reformation and on lay response to dissenting clergy.
28 William Harrison, *The Description of England*, 2nd ed. (1587; rpt. Dover, 1968), 36.

the creeds, responses, and prayers found in the Book of Common Prayer. As the English prayed, so did they believe, or at least the vast majority of them did so. In this context, the world of texts, and the theological controversies that were enabled and driven by that world of texts, seem remote from the actual experience of the Christian faith, as experienced within and learned from, the worship life of the reformed Church of England, carried out day by day, week by week, season by season, and year by year.

To understand the theological beliefs of early modern English Christians, therefore, we need to attend to this lived experience of the practice of the Christian faith. Sermons-as-delivered were events, occurring through time, in the context of specific occasions and in specific places, organized by and situated within use of the Book of Common Prayer. Sermons-as-delivered were not one-sided activities, but interactive performances, collaborations of preacher and congregation.[29] Sermons-as-delivered were not so much about their theological content but, as rhetorical events, put their theological content into use as part of the preacher's engagement with his congregation. As rhetorical events, they were intended by their preachers to persuade their specific congregations to deepen their sense of community, to promote their sense of corporate identity, and to provide meaning and purpose to their lives.[30]

3 Some things we have learned about worship and preaching in their public setting

With our experience of the Virtual Paul's Cross Project, and our development of the Virtual St Paul's Cathedral Project, we have begun to take the sermon–in-performance as the proper subject of our study, with the surviving text of the sermon now viewed as a trace of the performed sermon. The sermon-in-performance, as delivered, is reframed as an interactive event led by a particular individual in a specific architectural space over the course of a specified period of time, in the presence of a specific gathering of listeners, in the context of a specific set of his-

---

29 John Donne tells us that preachers at Paul's Cross could expect their congregations to respond vocally to their sermons, on occasion to converse among themselves so actively after the preacher made a point that they delay his moving on to his next point by as much as "one quarter of an hour." John Donne, *Sermons*, ed. G. R. Potter and E. M. Simpson, vol. 10 (Berkeley, 1953–62), 132–3.
30 On sermons-as-heard, see Arnold Hunt, *The Art of Hearing: English Preachers and their Audiences, 1590–1640* (Cambridge: Cambridge University Press, 2010).

toric and cultural circumstances. In light of that recognition, we will now review some of the ways that approaching Donne's sermon for Gunpowder Day within a digital environment has changed our understanding of the act of preaching, as well as what aspect of the preaching process we are clearer about, and what parts of Donne's sermon for Gunpowder Day, November 5th, 1622, we are now drawn to value.[31]

3.1 Audibility

Based on our experience with the Paul's Cross acoustic model, we have concluded that Donne's sermon was probably audible anywhere one stood or sat in Paul's Churchyard on a Sunday morning in November,[32] and that his audibility was enhanced because he delivered his sermons at Paul's Cross in a slow and deliberate fashion. Doing so enabled him to take advantage of the amplification of his voice level due to the reverberation of sound in that space but also to avoid losing his hearers' comprehension due to the muddling of his words that would have resulted from the reverberation if he had spoken faster.[33]

3.2 Ambient noise: the bells

We have also come to believe that the kinds and levels of ambient noise present in Paul's Churchyard would not have impeded Donne's audibility, with one exception. Thanks to Tiffany Stern's recent research, we know that part of the soundscape of early modern London was the sound of the bell at St Paul's, activated by a clock mechanism, that rang on the quarter-hours and hours of each passing day.[34] English cathedrals in the 16th-century are known to have mechanical clocks that recorded time by striking bells; one of these survives at Salisbury

---

[31] For a fuller discussion of the relationship between King and pulpit at Paul's Cross, see Morrissey, *Politics and the Paul's Cross Sermons*.
[32] So long as the crowd remained relatively quiet and attentive.
[33] For a detailed discussion of the audibility of human speech in Paul's Churchyard, see Ben Markham, "Acoustics at Paul's Cross," on the Paul's Cross website at https://vpcp.chass.ncsu.edu/hear/.
[34] Tiffany Stern, "'Observe the Sawcinesse of the Jackes': Clock Jacks and the Complexity of Time in Early Modern England," Paper presented at Convention of the Modern Language Association, Seattle, Washington, 5–8 January 2012.

Cathedral.[35] The clock at Salisbury had no face; the ringing of a bell was its sole means of communicating the time. The sounding of this clock/bell was not discretionary. It could not be stopped and started again without disrupting its accuracy as a timepiece.

Stern's research into the ringing of church bells in early modern London has taught us that St. Paul's Cathedral had such a clock and that the clock at St. Paul's Cathedral rang on the quarter hour as well as on the hour, marking the passage of time in 15-minute increments. We have incorporated into the acoustic model the sound of a struck bell ringing on the hour and the quarter hour. This addition to the soundscape of the acoustic model has raised, however, the question of how the preacher dealt with the bells. He either talked over them (or tried to) or paused when they rang. The bells must have been loud enough to be heard over a good bit of London; that would have been part of the cathedral's role as center of city life, as focus of the community's attention, as marker, and organizer, of the passage of time in human affairs.

Thus we believe that the sound of church bells ringing out the 11 o'clock hour at the cathedral and at the many churches surrounding St Paul's Cathedral in the City of London would have rendered his words inaudible for a minute or more if he had insisted on trying to speak while the bells were ringing. It seems unlikely, therefore, that the preacher could have talked over them. So, presumably, he would have had to pause in his delivery until the sound of these bells died away, before continuing with his sermon. The pause at 15 minutes past the hour would have been fairly brief, but it would have gotten longer with each passing quarter hour. The pause on the hour, at 11:00 a.m., would have been of a significant length, about a minute.

The length of the pause required to prevent the sound of his voice, hence the content of his sermon, from being obscured by the sound of the bell, means that Donne had options about how to deal with this inevitable but also predictable interruption. The sound of the bell would have been an interruption, coming at some otherwise random moment in the unfolding of the sermon. It would have been a pause to be dealt with in some fashion, otherwise Donne's congregation's attention could wander, perhaps causing them to lose track of where the preacher was in the unfolding of his argument when the interruption began.

In an attempt to explore this question further, we have modeled the delivery of Donne's sermon on the assumption that Donne was able to anticipate the tolling of the cathedral's clock bell; as a result, he could incorporate a pause for the

---

35 "Salisbury Cathedral Clock," Wikipedia, last updated 10 May 2020, https://en.wikipedia.org/wiki/Salisbury_cathedral_clock.

clock's bell to strike the time into the oratorical structure of his sermon's delivery.[36] Instead of simply ignoring this pause and resuming his delivery of content when the interruption was over where he left off when the interruption began, our model of Donne preaching assumes he could shape the organization of his sermon to reach a point of closure, then be silent while the bell tolls, then begin again on a new topic, refocusing the congregation's attention, calling them back to the task at hand, and perhaps reminding them what was being said at the beginning of the tolling.

Hence, in our model, the predictable, and hence anticipatable, interruption by the bell every 15 minutes is regarded by our hypothetical Donne not just as an annoyance to be accommodated but, with planning, an opportunity to complete a thought, then treat the bell as an underlining of that point, then treat the pause created by the bell as a chance to catch his breath, perhaps take a sip of the wine we are told preachers kept in the pulpit at Paul's Cross, and then begin the next section of his sermon afresh.

3.3 Ambient noise: the crowd

Also, in our model, Donne's preaching is but one part of a collaborative experience, an experience that results from the encounter of occasion, preacher, and audience, a negotiated experience through which tradition, expectation, intention, and response merge into a one- or two-hours traffic upon the pulpit. We assume that Donne preached for an audience well-experienced in sermon-going, with a high regard for the quality of performance, for the techniques of delivery, the techniques of text-handling, of division and application.[37] Therefore, in our

---

[36] We are not sure how Donne would have been able to anticipate the ringing of the bell; the hourglass next to him in the pulpit would not have been able to do so, since, as Stern points out, hourglasses varied from day to day in their accuracy in marking the passage of time in response to changes in humidity. One possibility is that the ringing of another clock bell in the vicinity of St Paul's took place just before St Paul's bell began to ring, providing a guide to the timing of his delivery. I have learned through correspondence with Paul Glennie, Senior Lecturer in Geography at the University of Bristol and author, with Nigel Thrift, of *Shaping the Day: A History of Timekeeping in England and Wales 1300–1800* (Oxford: Oxford University Press, 2009), that there were at least 11 churches with clock bells in audible distance of St Paul's Cathedral in 1622. These clocks were not synchronized with each other, so that some of them must have rung early, giving Donne a signal that the clock at St Paul's was about to strike.

[37] For a helpful discussion of the relationship between preachers and their congregations in post-Reformation England, see especially Arnold Hunt's chapter "Preaching and the people," in his *The Art of Hearing*, pp. 229–91.

model, we have tried to build into the experience of Donne's sermon the response of the audience gathered to hear him. As the sound of Ben Crystal's voice rises and falls with the ebb and flow of Donne's text, so, too, does the sound of the congregation rise and fall in response.[38] The effect is sometimes not as pronounced or as clear as we might have hoped,[39] but we believe the result does help us identify passages in the sermon important for what they tell us about Donne's sermon as a sermon-in-performance rather than as a theological essay.

To approach this topic, we must remember the social and political context for this sermon, recognizing that Donne's central goal in his sermon for Gunpowder Day was to build support for James I's ongoing negotiations for the Spanish Match, a plan to join the royal families of England and Spain through the marriage of James' son Charles to Maria Anna, a daughter of the king of Spain. The possibility of such a match between the royal families of protestant England and Catholic Spain caused unrest among many of James' subjects, especially among clergy and laity already convinced that the English Reformation had not distinguished the Church of England sufficiently from its medieval predecessor. Negotiations for the Spanish Match ignited fears that the reformed church in England might be under threat, that, in an extreme case, the Church of England might once more become Catholic, once more under papal authority.

James had sought to quell opposition to his plans in the summer of 1622 by issuing his *Directions concerning Preachers*, orders restricting the subjects of their sermons preached "in any popular auditory" to noncontroversial subjects, rather than "presume to preach the deep points of predestination, election, reprobation or of the universality, efficacy, resistibility or irresistibility of God's grace." They were also ordered not to "presume from henceforth in any auditory within this kingdom to declare, limit, or bound out, by way of positive doctrine, in any lecture or sermon, the power, prerogative, jurisdiction, authority, or duty of sovereign princes, or otherwise meddle with these matters of state."[40]

Donne, at James' request, had preached a sermon defending the *Directions for Preachers* at Paul's Cross on September 15, 1622. In this sermon, Donne, in addition to affirming the benefit of James' imposition of limits on preaching, re-

---

[38] Listen to the whole sermon with audience response here: https://vpcp.chass.ncsu.edu/listen-from-the-cross-yard/. Explore the acoustic model here: https://vpcp.chass.ncsu.edu/listen/.
[39] As one of the colleagues said, we could have done much more if we had the support of a feature-length movie's sound effects budget.
[40] James I, "Directions concerning Preachers," in *Documents Illustrative of English Church History*, ed. Henry Gee and William John Hardy (New York: Macmillan, 1896): 516–8, last updated March 2001, https://history.hanover.edu/texts/ENGref/er90.html.

minds his auditors that the subject here is really one of royal authority, that subjects are called upon to obey their monarchs, and that obedience includes trust in their wisdom, and hence that subjects should trust James' stated reasons for issuing the *Directions* rather than connect them to the negotiations for the Spanish Match. Now, with the summer turning into autumn and public unrest continuing, Gunpowder Day in 1622 offered the crown yet another opportunity to reassure the populace about the King's religious allegiances and also to reassert the royal prerogative in religious as well as political affairs. After all, James was the person whom Catholic plotters intended to kill, above all others, in the original Gunpowder Plot of 1605.

So James called on Donne to provide a second public effort to shore up support for him. In this sermon, Donne insists that good subjects owe their trust and obedience to the monarch regardless of whether he is a good king like King Josiah or a bad king like King Zedekiah, simply because he is king. The fault of Catholics is precisely in their disobedience, in their refusal to "have this man to reign over us" (Luke 19:14). Nevertheless, Donne is also quick to defend James as a Josiah, a "good king," echoing the rhetoric of the reign of Edward VI when Edward in his efforts to transform the Church of England from a Latin to an English church was leading a reformation like the one Josiah led.

4 The rhetoric of congregational engagement

Our experience with the Virtual Paul's Cross Project, however, leads us away from a narrow concern with the cognitive content and logical construction of Donne's argument in this sermon in the direction of considering those moments in the sermon through which Donne seeks to establish a strong connection between himself as priest and preacher and his congregation, to develop a community of orientation, a common perspective on the subject of the sermon, and on the individuals who figure in it. Donne undertakes this effort from the sermon's very beginning, from its opening prayer, in which Donne creates an image of a nation gathered in many different places, yet as one people, to remember and to give thanks, and to praise God for James' deliverance from the Gunpowder Plot.[41]

---

[41] The discussion that follows takes its quotes from Jeanne Shami's transcription of the manuscript of Donne's Gunpowder Day Sermon, published in her *John Donne's 1622 Gunpowder Plot Sermon: A Parallel-Text Edition* (Pittsburg: Duquesne, 1996). We now know that this text of Donne's sermon is at best a trace of what Donne actually said, but it is the best we can do.

In this our Day, and in these houres, We praise thee, O God, we knowledge thee, to bee the Lord; All our Earth doth worship thee; The holy Church throughout all this Land, doth knowledge thee, with commemorations of that great mercy, now in these houres. Now, in these houres, it is thus commemorated in the Kings House, where the Head and Members praise thee; Thus, in that place, where it should have been perpetrated, where the Reverend judges of the Land doe now praise thee; Thus in the Universities, where the tender youth of this Land, is brought up to praise thee, is a detestation of their Doctrines, that plotted this; Thus it is commemorated in many severall Societies, in many severall Parishes, and thus, here, in the shadow of this Mother Church, in this great Congregation of thy Children, where, all, of all sorts, from the Lieutenant of thy Lieutenant, to the meanest sonne of thy sonne, in this Assembly, come with hearts, and lippes, full of thanksgiving.

In the model, the congregation grows silent as Donne begins this prayer. Donne's use here of repetitive language – the almost incantatory "In these houres," and the linking of places and peoples by "Thus in" and "praise thee" – and the progress he makes by naming places where people gather, unite time and place and people into a common gathering with a common purpose. The volume of congregational response grows as Donne leads us from "the King's house" to the place where the bomb was supposed to be detonated, to the "Universities," to the "severall Societies," to the "Parishes," finally winding up "here...in this great Congregation," where people of every level of the social hierarchy, "from the Lieutenant of thy Lieutenant" to "the meanest son of thy sonne" all gathering to "praise thee." This sense of movement towards a metaphoric unity is then fulfilled by a real unity of voice in "the shadow of this Mother Church," as Donne leads the congregation in an energetic recitation of the Lord's Prayer.[42]

Donne's vision here of community and commonality amid diversities of place, rank, and relationships is fortified almost immediately by the definition of an "Other," a community of difference. After taking a moment to announce and read his text for the day, as the congregation quietens down to listen, Donne immediately evokes "the Councell of Trent,"[43] thus Catholicism, and on the subject of special interest to Protestants, the text of the Bible, specifically the authorship of the Hebrew Bible text called Lamentations. Donne's congregation begins to respond audibly once more when Donne builds on the fact that the Council of Trent, when giving a list of the canonical books of the Bible, leaves

---

42 My understanding of events here involves trusting that Donne and his congregation that day followed what must have been a customary pattern of following an opening prayer by the preacher with a communal recitation of the Lord's Prayer. This is a practice spelled out in the Canons of the Church of England; one would assume that it would be implemented at the most important church in the most important city in England.
43 Shami, 45.

out the Book of Lamentations. Donne says that while he does not doubt they intended to include Lamentations in their canon, nevertheless, by including two books under the same writer's name, they raise the possibility that they should have clumped the first five books of the Bible together under "one name of Moses: and so they might haue comprehended and inuolud, the Apocalypse and some Epistles in the name of John, and haue left out the booke it selfe in the number."

Not only are Catholics, in Donne's view, inadequate or silly in their handling of the Bible, they really cannot agree among themselves on this subject, since "one of their owne Iesuits, though some…make this of Lamentations but an Appendix to the booke of Jeremie, determins for all that Canon, that it is a distinct booke."[44] The congregation responds anew when Donne points out that in the face of Catholics' inadequate skills in Biblical scholarship and disagreement among themselves about the status of the Lamentations, Donne goes on, we who know better know that "It is Jeremies; and a distinct booke"; further, since "it concerns the Iews, and vs too," Donne has reached a point at which he can launch into the heart of his argument.

This opening section of the sermon constitutes a joke, perhaps not a knee-slapper of a joke, but a joke nonetheless. But it also performs a move to divide the world into two parts; those who like us know their Bibles, and those who don't. Moreover, this division also makes it clear which side is the side any reasonable person would like to be on, so, in case there are any people in the crowd who are equivocating about which side they are on, they are likely to join in the moment's positive energy and align themselves with the good, loyal English monarchists in the audience.

From this opening, Donne again draws on the power of repetition to build community, to evoke adoption by members of his congregation of the view that they are one people, under one king, all subjects of one God. In the second 15-minute section of the sermon, Donne starts with the idea that all creation starts from "an Idæa in God; there was a Model, a platforme, an exemplar, of euery thing, which God producd, and created in tyme." Of Monarchy," Donne claims, "of Kingdome, God, who is but one, is the Idæa; God himselfe, in his vnity, is the Model, he is the Type of Monarchy."[45]

While the murmuring in the crowd indicates the congregation is listening attentively, Donne expands on this concept, building on repetition of "one," of the

---

44 Ibid., 47.
45 Ibid., 63, 64.

concept of the One, so that "love of one Soueraine" is the connection between God's creation of "one world" and God's promise of a better world to come:

> He made but one world; [...] He made this one world, but one Eye, the Sun; the Moone is not another Ey, but a glasse vpon which the Sun reflects. He made this one world but one Ear, the Church: he tells not vs that he hears in a left ear, by Saints, but by his right ear, the Church, he does. One God, one faith, one Baptisme, and these leade vs to the loue of one Soueraigne, of Monarchy, of Kingdome. In that name he hath convayd to vs the state of grace, and the state of Glorie too; and promisd both, in enioyninge that prayer, adueniat regnum; Thy kingdome of grace here, thy kingdome of Glorie hereafter.[46]

Donne repeatedly during this sermon can be heard using the power of language to evoke energy, to elicit approving response. Towards the end of his first hour, Donne reconstructs for his congregation the events of that first Gunpowder Day. Drawing once more on the power of repetition, here of letters as well as words, Donne paints a strongly evocative account of what happened that day.

> What they did historically we know: They made that House which is the hyue of this kingdome, from whence all her Hony comes, that House, where Justice herselfe is conceyud, in their preparing of good laws, and inanimated and quickned and borne by the Royall assent there giuen, they made that whole house, one Murdring peece: and hauing put in theyr powder, they chargd that peece with Peers, with people, with Princes, with the King, and ment to discharg it vpward at the face of heauen, to shoote God at the face of God, Him, of whome God had sayd, *Dij estis*, you are gods, at the face of that God who had said so: as though they would haue reprochd the God of heauen, and not haue been beholden to him for such a king, but shoote him vp to him and bid him take his king againe, for *Nolumus hunc regnare*, we will not haue this king to reigne ouer vs.[47]

In our recreation, Donne's voice here starts matter-of-factly with the appeal to common knowledge, for "What they did historically we know," then rises in energy and volume and urgency before falling back into a skeptical and ironic and contemptuous tone at that final line. Surely, one concludes, no one in Donne's audience would want to be part of that selfish, arrogant group of conspirators. On the website, the congregation's agitation builds as Donne's repetition of "h's" and "p's," his stringing together of short phrases, combine with the visual impact of his imagining the meeting hall of the government as itself a cannon, a "Murdring peece," to achieve the captivating image of the Gunpowder conspirators seeking to "shoot God at the face of God." The congregation's response suggests that Donne is creating a compelling experience, one that ends with the con-

---

46 Ibid., 65.
47 Ibid., 95, 97.

clusion that the conspirators' actions were in fact a very personal expression of their contempt for social order and their personal pique as having "this king to reigne ouer us."

Donne's joke at the beginning of this sermon about Catholics' inadequacy as readers and interpreters of the Bible is not the only point in the sermon that Donne draws on his skills as a teller of jokes and master of the witty aside to engage and sustain his congregation's attention. In the third segment of the sermon, scheduled for delivery between 10:30 and 11:00 AM, Donne is arguing for the idea that James' subjects who do not support him are in fact injuring themselves. To explore this topic, Donne conjures up the possibility of one's having an affair with Anne of Denmark, James' wife: "Euery where the king is *Sponsus regni*," says Donne, "the husband of the kingdome; and to make loue to the kings wife, and vndervalew him, must needs make any king iealous."[48]

Yet this witty aside, perhaps planted to recover the attention of anyone in the crowd whose thoughts have begun to wander, opens the way for a broader discussion of the relationship between king and country. Here, in a dramatic shift in tone, Donne focuses his audience's attention by arguing that king and country are one, so that the well-being of the one depends on the well-being of the other:

> The king is *Anima regni*, the Soule of the kingdome; and to prouide for the health of the body, by the detriment of the Soule, is yll phisick. The king is *Caput regn*i, the head of the kingdome, and to cure a member, by cutting off the head, is yll Surgery. Man and wife, Soule and body, Head and Members, God hath ioynd, and those whome God hath ioynd let no man seuer: *Salus regni asylum proditorum*, to pretend to vphold the kingdome, and to ouer throw the king hath euer been the tentation before, and the excuse after in the greatest treasons.[49]

Again, in the second hour of the sermon, Donne seeks to close the distance between his audience and King James by imagining himself able to ask the King in person a theological question in person:

> If I had the honor to ask this question in his royall presence, I know he would be the first Man, that would say no; No; your Souls are not myne, so. And as he is a most perfit text man in the booke of God (and by the way I should not easily fear his beeing a papist that is a good text man) I know he would cite Daniel, though our God do not deliver vs, yet know, O king that we will not worshipp thy Gods; I know he would cite Saint Peter, we ought to obey God rather then men; And he would cite Christ himselfe, fear not them (for the soule) that cannot hurt the soule. He claimes not your Souls so.[50]

---

48 Ibid., 87.
49 Ibid., 87, 89.
50 Ibid., 139.

In the midst of his confident testimony about James' ability to cite scripture – and the appropriate scripture, at least in Donne's opinion – Donne is able to slip in a reassuring comment for those in his congregation who doubt James' Protestantism, who fear James is really a Catholic who might try to undo the English Reformation. As James "is a most perfit text man in the booke of God (and by the way I should not easily fear his beeing a papist that is a good text man) I know he would cite Daniel." As we have known since the beginning of this sermon, at least in Donne's construction, Catholics are confused and divided about their understanding of the Bible; James, according to Donne, demonstrates he is not a "papist" both because he is "a text man," a man who knows his Bible, and because what he knows about his Bible is true, or at least recognizable as true by his Protestant subjects.

Each section of Donne's sermon thus displays rhetorical tools to further Donne's goal of creating a community of support for James. In a later passage, for example, we get more information about how to identify that "Other," that party to which, Donne hopes, he is dissuading us from joining. To an appreciative congregation, Donne describes that person who would question James' skill in ruling or his judgment in his policies:

> That Man must haue a large Comprehension that shall aduenture to say, of any king He is an yll king. He must know his office well and his actions well, and the actions of other princes too, who haue correspondence with him, before he can say so. When Christ says let your Communication be yea yea, and nay, nay, for whatsoeuer is more then these, when it comes to swearinge, that commeth of evill, Saint Augustine does not vnderstand it of the evyll disposition of the Man that swears, but of them who will not beleeue him without swearinge.[51]

Donne argues that while James sometimes acts in a way that "departs from the exact rule of his duty," it is not because he objects to "truth and clearness," but because he is carrying out a plan to "countermyne vndermyners," for "With craftie neighbours a prince will be craftie, and perchance false with the false." So his behavior is perfectly understandable, and no one should mention it again.

Thus, in Donne's plan for this sermon, everything leads back to where it began, with his congregation, gathered in Paul's Churchyard on this crisp November day. To them, Donne says, as a conclusion, in the words with which he leaves them, let us preserve our King by "preserving God amongst vs in the true and sincere profession of his religion":

> Looke thou seriously to thine owne dores, to thyne owne family, and keepe all right there. Cities are built of families, and so are Churches too; Euery man keepe his own family, and

---

51 Ibid., 109.

then euery pastor shall keepe his flock; and so the Church shalbe free from Scisme, and the state from sedition, and our Josiah preserud, prophetically, for euer, as he was historically, this day.[52]

To demonstrate their capacity for continued alertness and their gratitude for what he has said to them, the congregation responds with a resounding "Amen" as the cathedral clock tolls the 12 strokes of noonday and the crowd begins to disperse, energetically discussing Donne's sermon (or perhaps their plans for lunch) among themselves.

5 Conclusion

Hence, for Donne on 5 November 1622, it is ultimately the event itself that is theologically significant. Donne's sermon-in-performance on this day promotes loyalty to the King by informing and encouraging his congregation to recognize the significance of this day and of this event, the gathering of God's people, in memory of their history, and, especially, in their understanding of their place in God's salvation history now and in anticipation of the future to which it leads, precisely because of the nature of this people, and their Church, and the role of their King. Hence, the Church of England, as a state church, as a church in which everyone who was English was a member, with the King as its Governor, living together in harmony and in hope of a future to which this corporate activity will take them, is the blessed assembly of God's people.

The Virtual Paul's Cross and the Virtual Cathedral Projects thus help us recognize that Donne's preaching was not the univocal delivery of a lecture to a passive, quiet, cognitively attentive audience but an interactive performance delivered on a specific occasion for a specific congregation, in a format that was shaped by performer's and hearers' expectations about the event, and by their interactive participation in the event. Most important, digital modeling has brought us to consider questions and explore issues about the religious culture of the past that have previously not occurred to us. In doing so, we have reached the point described by Willard McCarty, concerning the Virtual Paul's Cross Project. This project, writes McCarty, take "the observer to the limits of what is securely known, then offers a standpoint from which securely to infer more."

> Does knowledge result? If not quite that, then what gives – knowledge or what we mean by "knowledge"? And by the nature of the medium, the observer, having done that, can then

---

52 Ibid., 185.

return to the sermon (which is, at this point, what exactly?) to look and listen again, then incorporate what has been inferred into the simulation model. And so it goes, "where no one has gone before." I am tempted to say, if this does not make you nervous and excited all at once, then either you or I are at fault.[53]

"Along this trajectory," McCarty continues, "lies the creative scholarship in digital humanities that we must have for the discipline to become strong." All of us involved in the Virtual St Paul's Cathedral and Virtual Paul's Cross Projects are honored to be so recognized by McCarty and look forward to continuing our leadership in work that is helping us explore more fully the preaching and worship of early modern England as events intelligible only in the context of the time, place, and occasion of their performance.

6 Primary Sources

Book of Common Prayer
Book of Common Prayer (1559), edited by John Booty. Folger Library, 1976.

Bible
The Holy Bible (1611), edited by David Norton. London: Penguin, 2006.

John Donne
Donne, John. *John Donne's 1622 Gunpowder Plot Sermon: A Parallel-Text Edition*, edited by Jeanne Shami. Pittsburgh: Duquesne, 1996.
Donne, John. *Sermons*, edited by G. R. Potter and E. M. Simpson. 112 vols. Berkeley: University of California Press, 1953–62.

Lambeth Articles
"Lambeth Articles." Wikipedia. Last modified 22 September 2019. https://en.wikipedia.org/wiki/Lambeth_Articles.

7 Bibliography

Bagchi, David. "'The Scripture Moveth Us in Sundry Places': Framing Biblical Emotions in the Book of Common Prayer and the Homilies." In *The Renaissance of Emotion: Understanding Affect in Shakespeare and His Contemporaries*, edited by Richard Meek and Erin Sullivan, 45–64. Manchester: Manchester University Press, 2015.

---

53 From a lecture by Professor McCarty, shared privately with the author.

Blayney, Peter. *The Bookshops in Paul's Cross Churchyard*. Occasional Papers of the Bibliographical Society 5. London: The Bibliographical Society, 1990.

Booty, John, ed. *The Godly Kingdom of Tudor England: Great Books of the English Reformation*. Wilton, CT: Morehouse-Barlow, 1981.

Dimmock, Matthew, and Andrew Hadfield, *The Religions of the Book: Christian Perceptions, 1400–1660*. Houndmills: Palgrave Macmillan, 2008.

Duffy, Eamon. *The Stripping of the Altars: Traditional Religion in England, c. 1400–c. 1580*. 2nd ed. New Have, CT: Yale University Press, 2005.

Glennie, Paul, and Nigel Thrift. *Shaping the Day: A History of Timekeeping in England and Wales 1300–1800*. Oxford: Oxford University Press, 2009.

Hunt, Arnold. *The Art of Hearing: English Preachers and their Audiences, 1590–1640*. Cambridge: Cambridge University Press, 2010.

Johnson, Jeffrey. *The Theology of John Donne*. Studies in Renaissance Literature. D. S. Brewer, 1999.

Kirby, Torrance, and Paul Stanwood, eds. *Paul's Cross and the Culture of Persuasion in England, 1520–1640*. Toronto: Brill, 2013.

Maltby, Judith. *Prayer Book and People in Elizabethan and Early Stuart England*. Cambridge: Cambridge University Press, 1998.

Markham, Ben. "Acoustics at Paul's Cross." Virtual Paul's Cross Project. https://vpcp.chass.ncsu.edu/hear/.

Morrissey, Mary. *Politics and the Paul's Cross Sermons, 1558–1642*. Oxford: Oxford University Press, 2011.

Oliver, P. M. *Donne's Religious Writing: A Discourse of Feigned Devotion*. Longman, 1997.

Ryrie, Alec. *Being Protestant in Reformation Britain*. Oxford: Oxford University Press, 2013.

Ryrie, Alec. "The Reformation in Anglicanism." In *The Oxford Handbook of Anglican Studies*, edited by Mark Chapman, Sathianathan Clarke, and Martyn Percy, 34–45. Oxford: Oxford University Press, 2015.

Schleiner, Winfried. *The Imagery of John Donne's Sermons*. Providence, RI: Brown University Press, 1970.

Schofield, John. *St Paul's Cathedral Before Wren*. Swindon: English Heritage, 2011.

Schuwey, Christophe. *Interfaces: l'apport des humanités numériques à la littérature*. Neuchâtel, Switzerland: Editions Livreo-Alphil, 2019.

Shuger, Deborah. *Habits of Thought in the English Renaissance: Religion, Politics, and the Dominant Culture*. Berkeley: University of California Press, 1990.

Stern, Tiffany. "'Observe the Sawcinesse of the Jackes': Clock Jacks and the Complexity of Time in Early Modern England." Paper presented at Convention of the Modern Language Association, Seattle, Washington, 5–8 January 2012.

Louis Chevalier
Liturgical history in a digital world: principles and future developments

Liturgical history examines the expression, evolution, and theological significance of liturgy in Christian societies at different times. The digital humanities continue to play an increasingly significant role in this particular discipline as scholars look to apply various digital technologies to it. As a result, digital tools and techniques have created new research challenges, which, in turn, have led to a profound transformation in working methods. This is partly due to an increase in scholarly research and collaboration, which has been facilitated by increased access to an ever-greater number of sources. In raising new questions, computer-based technologies have helped incorporate liturgical history within a wider "digital culture" by providing it with networks of exchange, publication, and data analysis. Continuing to rise to the digital challenge is therefore of critical importance for liturgical history.

This article will examine the consequences of this digital revolution for liturgical history by looking first and foremost at the methodological and philosophical approach to research. It will then turn to look at the digital impact upon this social and historical science, before finally proposing some areas for future study.

1 A paradigm shift in a digital context

The term liturgy refers to the actions and words that underpin the public and collective rites performed by both clergymen and believers in order to worship God, and to ask for divine gifts and forgiveness.[1] The liturgy (including mass and canonical hours) is best studied in its many forms, including chants, prayers, mass readings, rites and gestures, vestments and objects (vases, sacred vessels, etc.), as well as in the interpretation of religious space (churches or any place where

---

Note: I would like to express deep gratitude to Aileen Jang, Marion Gilles, and Richard Allen for their help in writing this chapter in English.

[1] e.g. Aimé-Georges Martimort, ed., *The Church at Prayer: An Introduction to the Liturgy*, trans. Matthew J. O'Connell, 4 vols. (Collegeville, MN: Liturgical Press, 1987).

processions take place) and the interpretation of time through a cyclical liturgical calendar of feasts (Christmas and Easter, interspersed with saints' days).[2]

Using different sources, liturgical history simultaneously observes and interprets past rituals and their evolution. Liturgical history was and remains, according to Ernst Kantorowicz, "one of history's most important auxiliaries,"[3] particularly when it is studied within a political and social framework. Indeed, those prayers offered by clergymen for the coming of God's Kingdom embody, through their form and scriptural content, the matrix of their very thinking and existence.

The sources that allow historians access to ancient liturgies are primarily textual in nature. These include prayer books such as sacramentaries, ordinals, missals, lectionaries, Psalters and graduals, which contain the liturgy, psalms, scriptural lessons, hymns, sermons, calendars, etc., and which are necessary for performing the liturgy and are required during mass or Divine Offices.[4] However, they also include texts that show how liturgical change was enacted either at the level of individual churches (for example, the statutes of cathedral or monastic chapters) or for the Church in general (canons of a council, etc.). Besides such texts, scholars have also examined buildings dedicated to the liturgy, as well as theological tracts on the meaning of liturgy and iconography, and objects of worship.

The historical study of liturgy is based on a dual approach. On the one hand, a diachronic approach focuses on the ways Christian liturgy has evolved from its beginnings. It thus studies its roots, which are generally found in cultural models outside the Christian world, in particular within the Jewish faith.[5] It also examines the development of the different branches of Christian liturgy in the East and West,[6] which gave birth to the liturgies of the various modern denomina-

---

2 e.g. Jacques Dubois and Jean-Loup Lemaitre, *Sources et méthodes de l'hagiographie médiévale* (Paris: Cerf, 1993).
3 Ernst Kantorowicz, *Laudes Regiae: A Study in Liturgical Acclamations and Medieval Ruler Worship* (Berkeley: University of California Press, 1946), IX.
4 e.g. Cyrille Vogel, *Medieval Liturgy: An Introduction to the Sources* (Washington: The Pastoral Press, 1986).
5 e.g. Paul Bradshaw, *The Search for the Origins of Christian Worship: Sources and Methods for the Study of the Early Liturgy* (New York: Oxford University Press, 1992).
6 Historical studies of Eastern liturgy mainly take Syrian liturgies into account (i.e. the liturgies of Mesopotamia and Persia; Chaldean liturgies; Jerusalem and Antioch) as well as Armenian, Egyptian (Coptic liturgy), Ethiopian (Abyssinian liturgy), and Byzantine liturgies. Historical studies of Western liturgy mainly take Gallican liturgies (i.e. the liturgy used in Gaul between the 5th and 9th centuries) into account, as well as Ambrosian, Mozarabic (i.e. the liturgy used in Spain until the 12th century), Celtic (gradually replaced by an Anglo-Roman rite in the 12th century, after the Synod of Cashel in 1172), and Roman liturgies.

tions.[7] The structure or integration of the liturgy in the lives of individuals varies greatly depending on the geographical area or chronological period in question.

The other approach is synchronic, and focuses on liturgical exchange between different rites. Using this approach, historians look to identify those liturgical elements (chants, prayers, etc.) of one liturgical family that have been borrowed from another.[8] The comparison of different liturgies, in which digital tools play a significant role, is essential for establishing links between different usages and for identifying various influences. The question of liturgical exchange is thus one posed at both local and national level (with regards to local liturgies, this means those rites observed in a particular diocese or abbey, or by a particular religious order, such as the Benedictines and the Roman liturgy). By making such comparisons, scholars are able to identify the existence of different liturgical traditions that follow the same liturgical structure, but which present differences in those rites used for the same celebration.

Digital resources made their first appearance in the study of liturgical history through chant databases[9] and digital libraries, such as *E-Codices*[10] and *BVMM*,[11] which continue to make available to historians an ever-increasing of number of digitized manuscripts conserved in the libraries of Switzerland and France. The creation of these basic databases resulted in the development of more sophisticated tools, such as *Antiphonale Synopticum* and *Comparatio*, which are dedicated to data analysis. It is important to ask, however, whether the introduction of digital technology to liturgical history has changed the study of its sources and its working methods, and whether this in turn has altered our understanding of its history. In a digital context, we can point to two major developments in the historical study of liturgy: first, the ease with which every liturgical element can be studied simultaneously (through the examination of the complete chant repertoire of a religious house, or the study of various liturgical elements: texts, music, etc.); and second, a larger, more precise concentration and classification of data (such as our understanding of liturgical chants, for example),

---

7 e.g. Anton Baumstark, *Comparative liturgy* (London: Mowbray, 1958).
8 On the Cistercian, Cluniac, and Chartreuse liturgies, see: Paul Tirot, *Un* Ordo Missae *monastique: Cluny, Cîteaux, La Chartreuse* (Rome: Edizioni Liturgiche, 1981).
9 e.g. Andrew Hughes, *Late Medieval Liturgical Offices: Tools for Electronic Research: Texts* (Toronto: Pontifical Institute of Medieval Studies, 1994).
10 Christoph **Flüeler,** *Bibliothèque virtuelle des manuscrits en Suisse, e-codices*, University of Freiburg, https://www.e-codices.unifr.ch/fr.
11 François Bougard, Bibliothèque virtuelle des manuscrits médiévaux, IRHT-CNRS, https://bvmm.irht.cnrs.fr/.

and the diffusion of this data through digital research tools (for example, text-editing programs that include specialized textual analysis tools).

It is possible to list a wide range of digital tools used today for the study of medieval and modern liturgies.

Databases:
Cantus Index: University of Waterloo & al.
Cantus Database: D. Lacoste, University of Waterloo, Canada.
Cantus Planus in Polonia: B. Izbicki, Poland.
Fontes Cantus Bohemiae: J. Koláček, Czech Republic.
Global Chant Database: J. Koláček, Czech Republic.
Gregorien.info: I. Behrendt, G. Messiaen, B. Schmid, Belgium.
Hungarian Chant Database: Z. Czágany, Hungary.
Musica Hispanica: C. J. Gutiérrez, Universidad Complutense de Madrid, Spain.
Musikalische Quellen des Mittelalters in der Österreichischen ationalbibliothek: R. Klugseder, Österreichische Akademie der Wissenschaften, Austria.
Portuguese Early Music Database: M. P. Ferreira, Portugal.
Slovakian Early Music Database: E. Veselovská, Slovakia.

Digital catalogues and libraries of liturgical manuscripts, which may include musical notation:
Census-catalogue of Notated Mediaeval Manuscripts: C. Meyer, France.
Digital Image Archive of Medieval Music: E. E. Leach, University of Oxford, England.
Manuscrits notés en neumes en Occident: C. Massip, École Pratique des Hautes Etudes, France.
Medieval Music Manuscripts Online: D. Gatté, France.

Analysis tools:
Antiphonale Synopticum and *Graduale Synopticum:* H. Buchinger, Universität Regensburg, Germany.
Calendoscope: D. Muzerelle, Institut de Recherche et d'Histoire des Textes – CNRS, France.
Cantus Planus: D. Hiley, Universität Regensburg, Germany, and R. Klugseder, Österreichische Akademie der Wissenschaften, Austria.
Cantus Ultimus: I. Fujinaga, McGill University, Canada.
Comparatio: C. Maître, IRHT – CNRS, France.

Digital editions:
Cantus Network: F. Praßl, R. Klugseder, University of Graz, Austria.
Cursus: J. Cummings, England.

The first question to consider, therefore, is how liturgy can be studied in all its dimensions with the help of such resources. It should be noted that liturgical history is a specific historical discipline within the digital humanities, which has developed as a result of liturgy's numerous modes of expression and the complexity of liturgical texts. There are various digital projects that allow scholars to study these various elements: *DIAMM*, which was developed at the University of Oxford, contains digital images of medieval and early modern (14th–16th c.) European chant manuscripts;[12] *Calendoscope*, which was created by the IRHT (Institut de Recherche et d'Histoire des Textes) in France,[13] focuses on the identification of liturgical calendars.[14] Elsewhere, the website *geesebook.asu.edu* allows users (in particular students) to compare digital images of a 14th-century gradual, to access its Latin text along with an English translation, and to listen to audio files containing 23 chants of the Mass performed by the *Schola Hungarica*.[15]

Moreover, liturgical texts are complex, being formed of various aggregated elements, such as rubrics, mentions of chants or prayer formulas, as well as information relating to the solemnity of the celebration (a manuscript may contain various markers concerning solemnity, which differentiate the feasts according to their importance by indicating the number of lessons at Matins and the number of candles to be lit in the choir, as well as by specifying what vestments are to be worn: alb, cope, etc.). In order to characterize the liturgy of a particular place, scholars must therefore take into account all these liturgical aspects. As a result, their research methods and tools must be designed to deal with these realities. In a digital edition of sources, therefore, the encoding of liturgical texts should allow for each part to be separated into groups of words whose liturgical nature has been clearly defined, thereby allowing users to search by pre-set terms, such as the title of a chant or the designation of a feast.

---

[12] Elizabeth Eva Leach, Digital Image Archive of Medieval Music, University of Oxford, https://www.diamm.ac.uk/.
[13] The IRHT studies medieval manuscripts written in Hebrew, Greek, Latin, Copte, Arabic and Syriac languages; ancient inscriptions; and the humanist book, in the disciplines of paleography, codicology and the history of libraries and heraldry, diplomacy, illuminated manuscript, papyrology, liturgy, and lexicography.
[14] Denis Muzerelle, Calendoscope, IRHT–CNRS, http://calendoscope.irht.cnrs.fr/.
[15] Volker Schier and Corine Schleif, Opening the Geese Book, http://geesebook.asu.edu/.

The second question that arises concerns the bringing together, the classification and the circulation of existing liturgical knowledge. This includes such things as catalogues of manuscripts and liturgical elements,[16] which consist of registers of prayers or chants classified by type (antiphons, hymns, etc.). Each register provides precise information on the origin of each liturgical element, which is crucial for their identification and study. Besides allowing for such things to be easily downloaded, digital technology has resulted in the creation of new registers based on original models. The development of databases has thus allowed for significant progress to be made in the development of these registries.

A good example of this is the collaborative text database, *Cantus Database*, developed at the University of Waterloo (Canada).[17] This provides an inventory of medieval liturgical chants classified by genre, which allows users to find information relating to a specific piece, religious establishment or celebration. It also offers access to digital copies of manuscript sources. For each piece, technical notes indicate the manuscript source, its liturgical context (by taking account of its creation and edition; for example, saints' feasts, masses, office of Hours, etc.), and the liturgical genre, while also providing musical notes and concordance tools. Each work is also assigned an identifier, based on the work of R.J. Hesbert, who published an important registry of antiphons, hymns, responds, and invitatories used in the medieval liturgy, each of which he assigned a unique reference number. For example, the antiphon *A bimatu et infra* bears the number 1187 both in Hesbert's work and in *Cantus Index*.[18] This type of database is thus important in allowing scholars to identify a specific piece and to study its dissemination throughout the abbeys and cathedrals of Europe. The connection between new and pre-existing databases, including publications and analysis tools, goes hand-in-hand with the improvement of this system.

By way of example, let us look at a case study from the *Cantus Database*. It should first be noted that this database allows users to use various methods and to solve diverse problems. A piece of chant, whether it is a verse, an antiphon, etc., must be identified not only with its text, but also with its melody. Indeed, in ancient liturgy, as in its contemporary equivalent, one can find the same text, extracted from the Bible or taken from a prayer celebrating the origins of the

---

16 For example, hymns: Guido Maria Dreves and Clemens Blume, *Analecta Hymnica medii aevi* (Leipzig: R. Reisland, 1886–1920); antiphons: René-Jean Hesbert, *Corpus antiphonalium officii*, 6 vols. and indices (Rome: Herder, 1963–1979); tropes: Gunilla Björkvall, Gunilla Iversen, and Ritva Jonsson, *Corpus Troporum*, 11 vols. (Stockholm: Almqvist & Wiksell, 1975–2009).
17 Debra Lacoste, *Cantus Database*, University of Waterloo, http://cantus.uwaterloo.ca .
18 René-Jean Hesbert, *Corpus antiphonalium officii*, vol. 3 (Rome: Herder, 1968), 21.

Church or a saint, used in liturgies throughout the Christian world. But the same text might have been set to music by various different composers at different times in accordance with the practices of the time. Thus, in an ideal work of comparison, one should be able to confirm that the same chant was used in the liturgy of two different places, and that the text and the music was identical in both. It is only as a result of this that we can speak with certainty of liturgical similarity or of "liturgical filiation."

Let us examine, therefore, an Alleluia verse (during the Mass, an Alleluia verse is inserted between two Alleluias, before the Gospel is proclaimed), namely *Laetatus sum in his quae* (ThK 113),[19] which in the *Cantus Database* bears the reference number g00498a. The note attached to this verse identifies the manuscript in which it is found (Porrentruy, Bibliothèque cantonale du Jura, MS. 18, fol. 14, namely a 12th-century Premonstratensian gradual), its liturgical context (Mass of the 2nd Sunday of Advent), and its melody, with a correspondence between the words and the musical notation. Thanks to this note concerning the chant's text and melody, such as it appears in the Premonstratensian manuscript, it is possible to identify this chant with certainty. For musicologists, the musical interpretation of this chant is facilitated by an accurate transposition of the musical notation. The *Cantus Database* is not only open access, but its contributors are based around the world and come from different academic disciplines. It is regularly updated and, thanks to the use of different media, allows for liturgy to be studied in both its textual and musical form via the *Cantus* Melody Search tool and the *Cantus* Melody Comparison tool, thereby allowing users to conduct multi-dimensional analysis and to disseminate liturgical knowledge. From this point of view, the *Cantus Database* is characterized by collaboration and interdisciplinarity, in particular in the way that it brings together researchers interested in liturgical history with musicologists and computer scientists.

Digital technology is thus helping to revolutionize the historical study of religious chants throughout the various Christian traditions. The study of a community's repertoire is central to the characterization of its liturgical regimen:

> Worship followed a daily, weekly, and yearly pattern of psalmody and reading from Scripture, but it was also used to observe and commemorate each feast in the Christian calendar. On most feast days, special texts and chants, either purpose-written or drawn from appropriate pre-existing material, displaced the ordinary liturgy of the day.[20]

---

19 Karl-Heinz Schlager, *Alleluja-Melodien I: bis 1100* (Kassel: Barenreiter, 1968), 280.
20 Matthew Cheung Salisbury, *Medieval Latin Liturgy in English Translation* (Kalamazoo, MI: Medieval Institute Publications, 2017), 6.

It is also important to study a community's repertoire in order to characterize its liturgical devotions. Besides chants, and their textual variants and lyrical content, prayer texts are also very important from a theological perspective, since they allow scholars to contextualize a community's spirituality at a precise moment in its history. For example, in writing on the subject of the medieval feast of the Conception of the Virgin, Marie-Bénédicte Dary has noted how those communities that adopted the preface *Cuius virginis matris conceptionis sollempnia* (Mont Saint-Michel, Winchester, etc.) believed in the immaculate conception of the Virgin Mary at the same time as figures such as Bernard of Clairvaux were arguing against such doctrine.[21] Liturgical exegesis, that is to say, the theological reasons underpinning the choice of particular office readings and the mass of a feast, might also express theological and spiritual convictions.

Finally, it is important to be able to reconstruct, both scientifically and digitally, every chant in its original form, because each major liturgical family (Coptic, Roman, etc.) has its own form of chant, which is distinguished from other liturgies by its musical notation, its language and its technical performance (with regards to its tone and rhythm). Databases such as *Cantus Database* exist in order to address such issues. Various national databases are currently being built to accompany the historical study of religious chant and to provide access to written liturgical heritage. Thanks to international collaboration, many of these databases (the *Slovakian Early Music Database*,[22] the *Hungarian Chant Database*,[23] etc.) can now be consulted via the *Cantus Index* portal.[24]

These databases are often built in the same way. They bring together digital images and references to liturgical sources, which allow users to perform searches across a source's location, its date of creation, the type of liturgical book, and the title of each piece. By bringing them together in a single digital space, these databases also allow for comparisons to be made between liturgical sources dispersed between a wide range of (inter)national institutions. Consequently, this approach helps re-establish historical links between local liturgies, which would otherwise not have been made if these liturgies had remained separated. Such databases also allow for searches to be performed either from the text or the melody of a liturgical chant, thereby allowing for each liturgical piece to

---

[21] Marie-Bénédicte Dary, "Aux origines de la 'Fête aux Normands': La liturgie de la fête de la Conception de la Vierge Marie en France (XIIe–XIIIe siècles)," in *Marie et la "Fête aux Normands": Dévotion, images, poésie*, ed. Françoise Thelamon (Mont-Saint-Aignan: Presses universitaires de Rouen et du Havre, 2011), 89.
[22] Eva Veselovská, Slovak Early Music Database, 2012–2020, http://cantus.sk.
[23] Gábor Kiss, Hungarian Chant Database, 2020, http://hun-chant.eu.
[24] Cantus Index, University of Waterloo et al., 2012–2018, http://cantusindex.org.

be identified with precision. Sacred music databases also help researchers identify its characteristics and the areas in which chants were disseminated. The breaking down of barriers between various disciplines allows researchers to consider liturgy in a wider sense and in relation to its various forms of expression. This phenomenon itself brings about the development of digital technologies.

2 A digital answer to new problems

The digital world both generates new problems and simultaneously creates tools to help solve these problems. Given this new paradigm, it is important to revisit here the primary methods of liturgical history. Various methodological questions will thus be examined, within which perspectives of digital development are situated.

As was noted above, comparative study is essential to liturgical history for studying the origins and influences of liturgical usages, that is to say "the patterns of text, movement, music and ceremonial associated with a particular venue or region."[25] This work allows, on the one hand, for liturgical books belonging to the same religious house or diocese, but dating from different periods, to be studied, and for light to be shed on the evolution of the liturgy in these places. On the other hand, scholars can look for similarities between liturgical books of different places, and can group these books into liturgical families within which they can identify links between different liturgical usages. In this regard, foundational work has been carried out by the school of *Vergleichendeliturgiewissenschaft* (comparative liturgy) and by its founder, Anton Baumstark.[26] In particular, Baumstark has tried to establish links between the major Western and Eastern liturgical families.

The first limit of the comparative method is the number of available liturgical sources used to reconstruct ancient liturgy and its genealogy. Throughout the centuries, numerous sources have been lost and dispersed, with the result that not every comparison is reliable, given the absence of key witnesses. The creation of large digital registers of manuscripts and liturgical works (such as the

---

25 Matthew Cheung Salisbury, "Rethinking the Uses of Sarum and York: A Historiographical Essay," in *Understanding Medieval Liturgy: Essays in Interpretation*, ed. Helen Gittos and Sarah Hamilton (London: Routledge, 2017), 103.
26 With regards to comparative liturgy, see: Robert Francis Taft and Gabriele Winkler, eds., *Acts of the International Congress Comparative Liturgy Fifty Years After Anton Baumstark (1872–1948), Rome, 25–29 September 1998* (Rome: Pontificio Istituto Orientale, 2001).

*Portuguese Early Music Database,*²⁷ the *Cantus Planus in Polonia,*²⁸ etc.), which include manuscript images, search engines and academic notes, helps partially resolve this problem by making available to researchers a large number of documents. But this problem of sources is resolved through the creation of digital comparison tools specific to liturgy, such as *Comparatio.*²⁹ These tools allow researchers to perform a comparative, synchronic study of works of chant (identified by their text, or by both their text and their music) in dated and localized manuscripts, thereby enabling reliable comparisons to be made between manuscripts and liturgies. These digital tools are able to respond to specific questions and to analyze a large amount of data, since they provide a portal through which users can search a large amount of information stored in various different databases. Such tools have been developed in order to create new links between material information and to reveal unknown historical phenomena relating to liturgical developments.

The *Comparatio* database, developed by the IRHT, brings together and compares the different chants interpreted during the Latin liturgy of the Hours through an edition of these works and their musical variants, which is itself based on a corpus of manuscripts from different geographical regions. *Comparatio* has its own database. Users can use a search tool to bring together sources and to focus on the text of a work, on its liturgical genre (antiphons, responds, etc.), on its liturgical context, or on its musical form. Such tools provide important support to those researchers looking to localize, recover and manipulate information in these databases.³⁰ It is now possible to study ever greater collections of information in order to compare numerous local liturgies, to establish similarities between them, and to reveal the complete structure of the major liturgical traditions and the areas they cover. It is important that researchers, in using such digital resources, use the existing historiography to further the results of their analysis, and thus to explain each established link.

The creation of databases such as *Cantus Database* or *Comparatio,* which are considered to be sophisticated research and analysis tools, provides an initial means by which to study and disseminate information. Another means of diffusion is digital editing. Editing liturgical texts is necessary for restituting sources.

---

27 Manuel Pedro Ferreira, Portuguese Early Music Database, 2010–2020, http://pemdatabase.eu.
28 Bartosz Izbicki, Cantus Planus in Polonia, Cantus Index Group, 2012–2014, http://cantus.ispan.pl/.
29 Claire Maître, Comparatio, IRHT–CNRS and Biblissima, http://comparatio.irht.cnrs.fr.
30 Claire Maître, "Une nouvelle base de données pour la musique et la liturgie médiévales," *Revue Mabillon* 28 (2017): 271–4.

For many years, researchers have been able to make use of the critical editions of numerous liturgical books.[31] These editions provide a standardized text, which is accompanied by the variants found in each related manuscript. They also typically include an introduction that, on the one hand, presents the textual tradition of the work in question, and, on the other, examines the liturgical peculiarities found in the manuscript. Such editions are also accompanied by an index of important liturgical works: prayers, chants, etc. The existence of these editions is of utmost importance.

Thanks to the critical, historical and liturgical apparatus accompanying each edited text, these works allow scholars to examine the liturgical uses of a particular place, even if they are not themselves a specialist of ancient or contemporary liturgy. The introduction of digital technology in the editing of ancient sources makes it possible for researchers to access tools rich in functionality. The need for the liturgical historian to accurately describe both textual and musical data, convey the existence of digital catalogues of chants, and for the interest of creating hypertext links between the edited text and the photographs of manuscripts, should naturally attract editors of liturgical sources to digital editing. However, there presently exists no specialized markup language for the digital editing of these types of sources; such methods still need to be developed and would need to consider the typology of chants or the structure of liturgical calendars. Liturgical historians are currently using recommendations created for the encoding of documents of various natures.

Editing liturgical texts can be done with the help of the TEI ("Text Encoding Initiative") using XML ("Extensible Markup Language"), which is being increasingly used in the critical edition of texts and the creation of databases. Developed over a period of more than 30 years, the TEI was defined by one of its creators, Lou Burnard:

> Its purpose is to provide guidelines for the creation and management in digital form of every type of data created and used by researchers in the Humanities, such as source texts, manuscripts, archival documents, ancient inscriptions, and many others.

And:

---

[31] For example, the publications of: *Alcuin Club Collections; Henry Bradshaw Society; Liturgiewissenschaftliche Quellen und Forschungen; Monumenta Studia Instrumenta Liturgica; Spicilegium Friburgense.*

> The TEI framework provides a useful way of thinking about the nature of text: it constitutes a kind of encyclopedia of generally-agreed textual notions.[32]

According to its guidelines, the TEI should "define a recommended syntax [for the encoding of texts in the same] format," "define a metalanguage for the description of text-encoding schemes," and "describe the new format and representative existing schemes both in that metalanguage and in prose."[33] XML is a mark-up metalanguage. This format defines the structure of a computer text, and promotes the exchange of digital contents through interoperability. The first version of the XML format was released by the World Wide Web Consortium ("W3C") in 2001. XML is universal, flexible, and extensible. The user is responsible for defining tags and attributes, and its format allows users to reuse edited text in other media. Two major projects for editing liturgical texts have been developed using XML–TEI. *Cursus: An Online Resource of Medieval Liturgical Texts*[34], offers the edition of breviaries, antiphonaries, and a diurnal from English abbeys. *Cantus Network: Libri ordinarii of the Salzburg metropolitan province*[35] presents the edition of ordinals of Brixen, Freising, Regensburg, Passau, and Salzburg – and photographs of graduals, missiles and antiphonaries of these dioceses in a digital image viewer with annotations.

What exactly does a digital edition bring to our understanding of liturgical sources in comparison with a traditional printed edition or text analysis? A digital edition should be an authentic research tool: digital resources allow researchers to use several layers of notes, or to conduct a multi-layered reading – for example, of all the liturgical elements found in a text, thus highlighting the liturgical structure linked to a specific liturgical tradition. A digital edition will also allow researchers to develop detailed indexations of a text, thereby resulting in an index of liturgical pieces, the ceremonial vestments worn by the priest, the architectural elements, and the relics used, etc. This detailed encoding divides the text into segments, allowing users to perform precise and specialized queries. A digital edition will present the text of a liturgical work synoptically, thereby allowing liturgical differences between two manuscripts to be identified, and for comparisons to be made. A digital edition might also include an index of

---

32 Lou Burnard, *What Is the Text Encoding Initiative?* (Marseille: Open Edition Press, 2014), 7–13.
33 TEI Vault, *Design Principles for Text Encoding Guidelines*, http://www.tei-c.org/Vault/ED/edp01.htm.
34 James Cummings, Cursus, http://www.cursus.org.uk/.
35 Robert Klugseder and Franz Karl Praßl, Cantus Network, Austrian Academy of Sciences and University of Graz, http://www.cantusnetwork.at.

liturgical pieces, with links to the relevant part of the edited text. Moreover, many liturgical manuscripts include musical notes: neumes, diastematic notation, square notation. The MEI ("Music Encoding Initiative") makes it possible to describe the notations, by giving for example information on the source (sub-element: fileDesc), on the title and the composer (sub-element: workDesc), on the score (sub-element: section), and on audio or video of music interpretations (sub-element: performance) or editor comments (sub-element: front). Close to the TEI, the MEI can be implemented in a file created according to the TEI recommendations.

To illustrate the above, let us take a look at an example of a digital edition of a liturgical text, an XML–TEI edition of a 15th–century ordinal (*liber ordinarius*) from the Mont Saint-Michel abbey (Avranches, Bibliothèque municipale, MS. 216), which is currently being developed by the author of this chapter at the University of Caen Normandy (Centre de Recherches Archéologiques et Historiques Anciennes et Médiévales, in collaboration with the Pôle du Document Numérique). An ordinal is a liturgical book which aims to present to the celebrant a summary of the divine office and the mass for each day of the temporal and sanctoral cycles. It provides the incipit of all chants, prayers and readings, a precise description of all liturgical acts (processions, etc.), and other details concerning the liturgical life of priests and monks: the price and number of candles to be lit in the choir, the liturgical ornaments to be worn by those performing the service, or the list of feasts. An ordinal was connected to the other types of liturgical books, and therefore served as an important witness of the local liturgy. Each diocese and the majority of religious houses and orders had their own ordinal, acting as a book of liturgical legislation.[36] Any edition of an ordinal will therefore take into account numerous and various liturgical aspects. A number of studies dedicated to liturgical ordinals have been published in the past,[37] while Tillmann Lohse's important contribution to the editing of ordinals should not go unrecognized. In one article, Lohse suggests that any edition of an ordinal must take into consideration its "open" aspects by separating those corrections made by the "initial corrector" from those made "subsequently."[38]

Indeed, an ordinal was produced not to be used during the liturgy, but rather to follow the legislation of a particular diocese or abbey. Having been copied,

---

[36] Jean-Baptiste Lebigue, "*Mos orandi*, La législation des usages liturgiques au Moyen Âge (XIIe–XVe s.)," *Revue de l'histoire des religions* 229 (2012): 349–73.

[37] e.g. Edward Foley, "The *Libri Ordinarii*," *Ephemerides liturgicae* 102 (1988): 129–37; Aimé-Georges Martimort, *Les ordines, les ordinaires et les cérémoniaux* (Turnhout: Brepols, 1991).

[38] Tillmann Lohse, "Editer des *libri ordinarii*: réflexions et suggestions autour d'un type particulier de livres liturgiques," *Revue Mabillon* 26 (2015), 164.

each manuscript was regularly corrected to reflect the liturgical changes initiated by the ecclesiastical hierarchy. The editor of an ordinal must therefore take each correction into account, and must reconstruct each stage of the liturgy affected by the corrections made to the manuscript. In a digital edition, this extremely important textual reality can be represented in two ways. First, via notes linked to the edited text (these might provide information on the paleography of the manuscript or on related sources), and then through the creation of a dual note system. Today, it is possible to create a dual system (both paleographical and critical) for the same text stream (that is, the basic version of the main liturgical text), with two independent note systems. This is a technology that needs further development with regards to the digital edition of both liturgical texts and other types of ancient texts.[39]

The normalized text of the ordinal of Mont Saint-Michel was first digitally divided into sections: one for the temporal cycle and one for the sanctoral cycle (element: div, attribute: type, attribute value: "Section I"). Each section was then further divided by the creation of second and third-level sections relating to the different feasts (element: div, attribute: subtype, attribute value: "day") and offices. The liturgical text was divided to create a segment of text within the software corresponding to the name of an office and another segment corresponding to the title of a liturgical piece. Treating a liturgical text in such a way not only allows precise questions to be asked with ease, but also permits users to perform two types of search: first, an analysis of the liturgical unity of a particular feast, which takes into account all the elements of this feast; second, the study of the use of a particular piece throughout the liturgical year.

Each liturgical piece is indexed according to its type (antiphon, epistle, etc.) and its title (element: seg, attribute: subtype, attribute value: "antiphon." Element: title, attribute: ref, attribute value: "ID"). It is thus possible to perform cross-referenced searches of both the title of a piece and the list of liturgical feasts. The index cards of each chant, which are stored in a database of the musical repertoire of the medieval abbey of Mont Saint-Michel, are hyperlinked to the records of the *Cantus Index* database. The formation of the *index rerum* led to the indexing in the text of degrees of solemnity, of the actors of the liturgy (abbot, sacristan, etc.), of the places (altars, chapels, etc.) and of the objects of worship, as bells or censer (element: term, attribute: ref, attribute value: "censer." Attribute: type, attribute value: "indexRerum"). The edited text includes notes (footnotes, etc.), and also brings together different media, namely the edit-

---

39 For more on its application in the digital context, see: Frédéric Duval, "Pour des éditions numériques critiques. L'exemple des textes français," *Médiévales* 73 (2017): 13–30.

ed liturgical text and digital images of the manuscript, which thereby allow for the direct study of manuscript corrections and the use of colored inks (in ancient liturgical books, red and blue inks were used to mark the most important feasts of the calendar, while the color red was also used for the rubrics of a liturgical text). The modifications of the main text are indexed with the precision of the paleographic type and the correction mode (element: add, attribute: hand, attribute value: "hand A: *textualis formata*." Attribute: place, attribute value: "*addidit in margine*").

The development of digital technologies has had a profound impact upon the study of liturgical history. By opening up new horizons, the digital world brings this science closer to the hopes and dreams of its founders by allowing scholars to perform more detailed comparisons and to study liturgy in all its dimensions. Like other disciplines, liturgical history must be pioneering in its approach, enlarging not only its own area of study, but helping to create digital tools for other disciplines. In the development of digital editing technologies, the digital tools constructed by liturgical historians for the editing of texts in XML will have to be sufficiently flexible to handle the particularities of each type of liturgical book, and will also have to be sufficiently sophisticated to allow for the indexing and study of all the different liturgical elements (chants, actions, etc.). Other approaches, such as the improvement of concordance programs, will likewise open up interesting avenues and help reinvigorate the discipline's working methods. By increasing the number of projects dedicated to the digital edition of liturgical texts, researchers will be able to work with an ever-increasing library of normalized, digitized and edited texts, which will in turn help facilitate comparisons between sources. The field of digital object development, developed for research purposes, is also open to the problems of liturgical history.

From another point of view, reflecting on the basic methods of liturgical history and its new challenges, and the development of specifically designed digital research tools, will no doubt lead to the creation of interdisciplinary links with other historical disciplines, such as paleography. The liturgical manuscripts of a single religious house can be shown to have been corrected by different scribes, thus reflecting changes in liturgical practices. Each correction represents a new liturgical layer. The digital analysis of medieval writing and the digital identification of similar hands in numerous manuscripts (using a database of writing samples from the same scriptorium) could allow for each period of change in the liturgy to be reconstructed more precisely. The European project *Himanis* (Historical Manuscript Indexing for user-controlled search, 2018. IRHT – France, in collaboration with the Pattern Recognition and Human Language Technology Research Centre of the Polytechnic University of Valencia, and the

Artificial Intelligence and Cognitive Engineering of the University of Groningen) promises to break new ground in this regard. It aims to make available a large collection of indexed manuscripts of the French royal chancery (14th–15th c.), which will be searchable by keyword, and to develop a digital tool dedicated to the analysis and identification of hands.[40] Other such tools have yet to be designed. As such, liturgical history must take its place in the digital world, which promises a new era for the discipline that will not only build upon the work carried out to date, but will take into account every new problem without being afraid to devise new methods to solve them.

3 Bibliography

Baumstark, Anton. *Comparative Liturgy*. London: Mowbray, 1958.
Björkvall, Gunilla, Gunilla Iversen, and Ritva Jonsson. *Corpus Troporum*. 11 vols. Stockholm: Almqvist & Wiksell, 1975–2009.
Bradshaw, Paul. *The Search for the Origins of Christian Worship: Sources and Methods for the Study of the Early Liturgy*. New York: Oxford University Press, 1992.
Burnard, Lou. *What Is the Text Encoding Initiative?* Marseille: Open Edition Press, 2014.
Dary, Marie-Bénédicte. "Aux origines de la " Fête aux Normands ": La liturgie de la fête de la Conception de la Vierge Marie en France (XIIe–XIIIe siècles)." In *Marie et la " Fête aux Normands ": Dévotion, images, poésie*, edited by Françoise Thelamon, 85–98. Mont-Saint-Aignan: Presses universitaires de Rouen et du Havre, 2011.
Dreves, Guido Maria, and Clemens Blume. *Analecta Hymnica medii aevi*. Leipzig: R. Reisland, 1886–1920.
Dubois, Jacques, and Jean-Loup Lemaitre. *Sources et méthodes de l'hagiographie médiévale*. Paris: Cerf, 1993.
Duval, Frédéric. "Pour des éditions numériques critiques. L'exemple des textes français." *Médiévales* 73 (2017): 13–30.
Foley, Edward. "The *Libri Ordinarii*." *Ephemerides liturgicae* 102 (1988): 129–37.
Hesbert, René-Jean. *Corpus antiphonalium officii*. 6 vols. and indices. Rome: Herder, 1963–1979.
Hughes, Andrew. *Late Medieval Liturgical Offices: Tools for Electronic Research: Texts*. Toronto: Pontifical Institute of Medieval Studies, 1994.
Hughes, Andrew. *Late Medieval Liturgical Offices: Tools for Electronic Research: Sources and Chants*. Toronto: Pontifical Institute of Medieval Studies, 1996.
Kantorowicz, Ernst. *Laudes Regiae: A Study in Liturgical Acclamations and Medieval Ruler Worship*. Berkeley: University of California Press, 1946.
Lebigue, Jean-Baptiste. "*Mos orandi*, La législation des usages liturgiques au Moyen Âge (XIIe–XVe s.)." *Revue de l'histoire des religions* 229 (2012): 349–73.

---

40 Dominique Stutzmann, Himanis, 2018, http://himanis.huma-num.fr/himanis/.

Lohse, Tillmann. "Editer des *libri ordinarii:* réflexions et suggestions autour d'un type particulier de livres liturgiques." *Revue Mabillon* 26 (2015): 155–77.

Maître, Claire. "Une nouvelle base de données pour la musique et la liturgie médiévales." *Revue Mabillon* 28 (2017): 271–4.

Martimort, Aimé-Georges, ed. *The Church at Prayer: An Introduction to the Liturgy*, trans. Matthew J. O'Connell. 4 vols. Collegeville, MN: Liturgical Press, 1987.

Martimort, Aimé-Georges. *Les ordines, les ordinaires et les cérémoniaux.* Turnhout: Brepols, 1991.

Salisbury, Matthew Cheung. *Medieval Latin Liturgy in English Translation.* Kalamazoo, MI: Medieval Institute Publications, 2017.

Salisbury, Matthew Cheung. "Rethinking the Uses of Sarum and York: A Historiographical Essay." In *Understanding Medieval Liturgy: Essays in Interpretation*, edited by Helen Gittos and Sarah Hamilton, 103–23. London: Routledge, 2017.

Schlager, Karl-Heinz. *Alleluja-Melodien I: bis 1100.* Kassel: Barenreiter, 1968.

Taft, Robert Francis, and Gabriele Winkler, eds. *Acts of the International Congress Comparative Liturgy Fifty Years After Anton Baumstark (1872–1948), Rome, 25–29 September 1998.* Rome: Pontificio Istituto Orientale, 2001.

TEI Vault. *Design Principles for Text Encoding Guidelines.* http://www.tei-c.org/Vault/ED/edp01.htm.

Tirot, Paul. *Un* Ordo Missae *monastique: Cluny, Cîteaux, La Chartreuse.* Rome: Edizioni Liturgiche, 1981.

Vogel, Cyrille. *Medieval Liturgy: An Introduction to the Sources.* Washington: The Pastoral Press, 1986.

World Wide Web Consortium. "Extensible Markup Language." W3. https://www.w3.org/XML/.

Part IV: **Theology and pedagogy**

Tim Hutchings and Karen O'Donnell
Digital pedagogy and spiritual formation: training for ministry and games for children

1 Introduction

> Go therefore and make disciples of all nations, baptizing them in the name of the Father and of the Son and of the Holy Spirit and teaching them to obey everything I have commanded you.
>
> Mt. 28. 19–20

The text cited above, known to many Christians today as "the Great Commission,"[1] draws the Gospel of Matthew to a close. Jesus' last words to his followers, in this text, are pedagogical words. His followers are exhorted to "make disciples" by baptizing and teaching new believers. From its foundational texts to the present day, Christianity has been deeply connected with teaching, formation, and education. There is a pedagogical aspect at the heart of Christian faith and ministry. We can see Christian teaching at work in the widest array of contexts and audiences, including the catechizing of new believers, the training of monks, pastors and priests, the hallowed halls of university theology departments and the simple stories told to children in Sunday School.

In the contemporary world, this pedagogical work has grown to include digital tools, resources, and platforms. This chapter will argue that many Christian churches and institutions are already engaging in something that could be considered "digital humanities," even if that term is not always used explicitly. Using two case studies, introduced below, we will look for common interests and concerns between practitioners of Christian digital pedagogy and academic digital humanities, hoping to encourage greater mutual awareness and closer collaborations across these fields in the future.

David Berry has summarized the digital humanities (or DH) as "the complex field of understanding culture through digital technology."[2] This definition implies a central role for pedagogy, looking for new ways to use digital technology

---

[1] Robbie F. Castleman, "The Last Word: The Great Commission: Ecclesiology," *Themelios* 32 (2007/3), 68.
[2] David Berry, "Introduction: Understanding the Digital Humanities," in *Understanding Digital Humanities*, ed. David Berry (Basingstoke: Palgrave Macmillan, 2012), 5.

to help others to attain this understanding. In practice, however, digital humanists have not always paid such close attention to teaching. Stephen Brier argues that digital humanities work has tended to focus on research and academic publication, while "minimizing and often obscuring the larger implications of DH for ... how we prepare the next generation of graduate students for careers inside and outside of the academy."[3] In the introduction to his volume *Digital Humanities Pedagogy*, Brett Hirsch agrees: reflecting on a survey of key DH journals and volumes, he reports "the almost systematic relegation of the word 'teaching' (or its synonyms) to the status of afterthought."[4]

Nonetheless, Hirsch still argues that "pedagogy is at the heart of the digital humanities,"[5] in a way that should challenge wider university systems and assumptions. The digital humanities "embrace a hacker ethos," he claims, in which the pedagogical focus is on "learning *by* doing," leading to a "shift from vertical to horizontal structures of learning."[6] If so, then the gap between teaching and research in the digital humanities might be overcome: "The teaching–research relationship... appears to be more symbiotic in the digital humanities than it is in other fields because our research, like our teaching, is founded on collectivity and collaboration in the pursuit and creation of new knowledge."[7]

Where digital humanists have turned their attention to pedagogy, their focus has tended to be inward, towards the institutional contexts in which undergraduate and postgraduate students are explicitly trained to become digital humanists. In response, Kara Kennedy has called for a "long-belated welcome" for the teaching methods of the digital humanities into mainstream humanities classrooms. Digital humanities, digital pedagogy, and digital literacy all share "a clear overlap," she suggests, "regarding the importance of critically analyzing technology while engaging with it."[8] All students need digital literacy, Kennedy

---

[3] Stephen Brier, "Where's the Pedagogy? The Role of Teaching and Learning in the Digital Humanities," in *Debates in the Digital Humanities*, ed. Matthew Gold (Minneapolis: University of Minnesota Press, 2012), 390.
[4] Brett Hirsch, "‹/Parentheses›: Digital Humanities and the Place of Pedagogy," in *Digital Humanities Pedagogy: Practices, Principles and Politics*, ed. Brett Hirsch (Cambridge: Open Book Publishers, 2012), 5, https://www.openbookpublishers.com/reader/161#page/24/mode/2up.
[5] Ibid., 16.
[6] Ibid., 15.
[7] Ibid., 16.
[8] Kara Kennedy, "A Long Belated Welcome: Accepting Digital Humanities Methods into Non-DH Classrooms," *DHQ* 11, no. 3 (2017), para. 2, http://www.digitalhumanities.org/dhq/vol/11/3/000315/000315.html.

argues, and the digital humanities allow them to gain these skills by engaging with topics they already care about.⁹

In Christian communities, such projects are already well underway.¹⁰ Berry's call to understand culture through technology has been answered by a host of commercial and non-profit projects, and digital teaching methods have been welcomed into colleges, homes and churches worldwide. The Bible and other religious texts have been digitized to increase their accessibility,¹¹ and are now widely discussed and circulated through websites, study apps and social media. New digital tools and techniques have been produced to help organize and analyze those texts in new ways, producing new kinds of understanding and insight. Christian ideas are studied and critiqued across networks of blogs and social media channels, or shared with new audiences through digital texts, videos, animations, and games.

Christians have been using the most recent advances in communications technology to engage in educational and formational activities for centuries. Distance learning courses in theology and Christianity have been available since the early 19th century, with letters and course materials travelling by both stage coach and postal service. This kind of learning capitalized on the earlier technological development of the printing press, which was used to make the Bible, biblical commentaries, polemics, and other literature widely available. Alongside these enthusiastic uses of new media technologies, Christians have engaged in centuries of critical analysis and appraisal, assessing how their new systems of communication might be changing their faith, practice and understanding.

In this chapter, we will begin by considering how Christian theologians have responded to the challenges and opportunities of digital pedagogy. As we shall see, the role of embodiment and physical presence in learning have been key concerns, articulated theologically through the concept of the Incarnation (the doctrine that God became a human being, Jesus). We will then explore how these concerns have been addressed in practice, by analyzing two examples of Christian digital pedagogy aimed at very different audiences in the UK. Previous discussion of Christian digital learning has focused on US seminaries, so these British case studies will expand the conversation to a new international context.

Our first case study is the Common Awards provision for the formation for ministry in the Church of England and partner denominations, overseen by Dur-

---

9 Ibid., para. 10.
10 Heidi Campbell, *When Religion Meets New Media* (Abingdon: Routledge, 2010); Heidi Campbell (ed.), *Digital Religion. Understanding Religious Practice in New Media Worlds*, Routledge, 2013.
11 Tim Hutchings, "Design and the Digital Bible: Persuasive Technology and Religious Reading," *Journal of Contemporary Religion* 32, no. 2 (2017): 205–19.

ham University but located in smaller learning institutions (TEIs, or Theological Education Institutes – not to be confused with the more common DH use of TEI, the Text Encoding Initiative) in England and Scotland. Co-author Karen O'Donnell has worked closely with Common Awards to study and support the use of digital pedagogy in participating institutions. Our second case is *Guardians of Ancora*, a game for 8–11-year-old children developed by the charity Scripture Union England and Wales.[12] Each case report is based on hour-long expert interviews conducted in February 2018. O'Donnell interviewed Professor Mike Higton, who oversees the Common Awards program, and Mike Hull, Director of the Scottish Episcopal Institute in Edinburgh. Co-author Tim Hutchings interviewed Maggie Barfield, Product Developer for *Guardians of Ancora*. In each case study, we will consider the ways in which formational activities attend – or fail to attend – to the questions of embodiedness, incarnationality, and community raised by Christian critics of digital pedagogy. We will then contrast the pedagogical choices made by each of these providers, highlighting two common strategies with many echoes in Christian and DH pedagogical literature: hybrid blending of digital and face-to-face formational activities, and the careful development of a community of learners.

2 Spiritual formation and physical presence

Christian education is interested not just in key topics, skills and understanding, but in spiritual formation. This concept of formation is shaped around ideas of "the nourishment of practices of prayer and study, of community building and of nurture in a denominational tradition."[13] Spiritual formation is usually seen as communal, taking place over a lifetime of being together in Christian community, and the term "incarnational" is frequently used to emphasize the importance of being physically present with others in this formative process. John Gresham notes that "the heart of the divine pedagogy is the personal embodiment of divine revelation in the incarnation,"[14] arguing that the second person of the Trinity became flesh so that humans might learn what God is like, know God, and become more like Christ through his example.

---

[12] Scripture Union, "*Guardians of Ancora* for Churches," 2018. https://content.scriptureunion.org.uk/resource/guardians-ancora-churches.
[13] Ian McIntosh, "Formation in the Margins: The Holy Spirit and Living with Transitions in Part-Residential Theological Education," *Journal of Adult Theological Education* 11, no. 2 (2014), 139.
[14] John Gresham, "The Divine Pedagogy as a Model for Online Education," *Teaching Theology and Religion* 9, no. 1 (2006), 25.

In the incarnational approach to spiritual formation represented by Gresham, the emphasis on Jesus' flesh and his presence with humans becomes the primary way of understanding the Incarnation. The association of Jesus' human flesh with his divine nature in the hypostatic union of the Incarnation serves to redeem human flesh more broadly from its association with materiality as opposed to spiritual matters. Spiritual progress can, therefore, be achieved within the fleshly body. Incarnation is, in this mode of thinking, equated with embodiment and physical presence such that both terms ("incarnation" and "embodiment") come to take on meanings of being present together. In terms of spiritual formation, the invocation of these concepts comes to give physical presence together primacy in the ways in which people are spiritually formed. When training for ministry, for example, it is in the sharing of physical space that people are spiritually formed.

Inspired by this Incarnation-centered model of spiritual formation, a number of Christian teachers have raised questions regarding the nature of digital pedagogy and its compatibility with Christian theology. For example, in her 1999 essay on embodiedness in online learning, Mary Hess notes that she often faces a common critique – that Christian formation is incompatible with distance learning. These critics ask:

> is it even possible, let alone appropriate, to be using digital technologies in the context of theological education? ... they fear that theologically focused learning has something uniquely and integrally relational about it to which we cannot attend in the "disembodied" context of the Internet.[15]

Three years later, theologian and Christian anthropologist David Kelsey articulated the theological concerns regarding digital technology and theological education in a paper exploring the nature of the human. Kelsey argued that the human is complex organic matter that God relates to incarnationally, but also that God creates and sustains. This God affirms, delights, and rejoices in the human. Kelsey links this anthropological perspective to theological education:

> The theological anthropology that undergirds programs of theological schooling should focus on the implications of the view that what we are is not spiritual souls contained in bodies, not ghosts in machines, not even centers of consciousness floating somehow

---

[15] Mary Hess, "Attendance to Embodiedness in Online Theologically Focused Learning," presented at Going the Distance: Theology, Religious Education, and Interactive Distance Education, University of Dayton, Ohio, November 1999, https://web.archive.org/web/20161202041436/http://meh.religioused.org/dayton.pdf, 1.

above brains, but extraordinarily complex organic bodies with an extraordinary range of powers.[16]

For Kelsey, bodies are inherently involved in our efforts to communicate ourselves as persons. Therefore, all teaching and learning, not just theological education, involves the organic, personal bodies of both teachers and learners. If learning abstracts the personal, bodily presence of students from each other and from their teachers then such theological learning is not, in Kelsey's opinion, in keeping with the Christian tradition. He writes:

> Can genuine theological schooling really be accomplished entirely on the Web? Perhaps some aspects of theological schooling can – say, language instruction or the transfer of historical data and chronicles. Are there some aspects of theological schooling that cannot at all be accomplished by using the Web, and if so, what are they? Are virtual space and virtual presence adequate media for communication among personal, organic bodies, or is "virtual" just a euphemism for "bodiless"?[17]

Since Kelsey outlined his concerns regarding the formational and incarnational nature of theological learning and its supposed incompatibility with the digital mode, a variety of research has been undertaken on the topic of Christian formation in digital spaces.[18] Almost all of this research indicates that spiritual formation can and does happen in digital contexts, but that this is heavily dependent on the quality of teaching and learning, course or activity design, and the attitudes of both the learners and the teachers. As Gresham points out, simply

---

[16] David H. Kelsey, "Spiritual Machines, Personal Bodies, and God: Theological Education and Theological Anthropology," *Teaching Theology and Religion* 5, no. 1 (2002), 7.

[17] Kelsey, "Spiritual Machines," 9.

[18] Helen Cepero, "Writing Your Way Home: Spiritual Direction Teaching in an Online Format," *The Covenant Quarterly* 70, no. 1/2 (2012): 60–72; Benjamin K. Forrest and Mark A. Lamport, "Modeling Spiritual Formation from a Distance: Paul's Formation Transactions with the Roman Christians," *Christian Education Journal Series 3* 10, no. 1 (2013): 110–24; Diane Hockridge, "'What's the Problem?' Spiritual Formation in Distance and Online Theological Education," *Journal of Christian Education* 54, no. 1 (2011): 25–38; Stephen D. Lowe and Mary E. Lowe, "Spiritual Formation in Theological Distance Education: An Ecosystems Model," *Christian Education Journal Series 3* 7, no. 1 (2010): 85–102; Mary Lowe, "Spiritual Formation as Whole-Person Development in Online Education," in *Best Practices of Online Education: A Guide for Christian Higher Education*, ed. Mark Maddix, James Estep, and Mary Lowe (Charlotte, NC: IAP, INC., 2012): 55–64; Ron Mercer and Mark Simpson, "What Would Kant Tweet? The Utilization of Online Technology in Courses Involving Formation, Meaning, and Value," *Theological Education* 49, no. 2 (2015): 1–18; Daniel Schrock, "Using Technology in Spiritual Direction," *Vision* (2015): 19–26; Roger White, "Promoting Spiritual Formation in Distance Education," *Christian Education Journal Series 3* 3, no. 2 (2006): 303–15.

being physically present in a classroom with other Christians has never been enough to guarantee that something spiritually formative will take place. Instead, Gresham places the emphasis on the character of the teacher and the life experiences of students as the locus of divine saving action,[19] and suggests that these more fundamental factors can be transferred to online learning.

This body of research has highlighted the specific advantages of the digital setting for learning for spiritual formation. For example, traditional hierarchies between teacher and learner are destabilized in this context. Learning, including learning that is spiritually formative, in the digital setting is at its best when it is collaborative and tutors and students construct knowledge together, an observation shared by Christian educators[20] and digital humanists.[21] For Christian educators, however, digital formation extends the reach of the learning. It is not confined to the four walls of the classroom, but rather is embedded into the daily lives of learners and can provide a context for an interactive learning community that is spiritually formative.[22] This extension of reach, in turn, honors the ecosystems of learners' lives. Christians have always been formed in a variety of settings: the classroom, the Sunday school, the college, church placements, "home" church, mentors, friendships, non-church life. Recognizing these as natural parts of lifelong formation allows the recognition of the online context as simply another part of this rich ecosystem.[23]

This brief summary of two decades of Christian thinking about digital pedagogy has emphasized embodiment, embeddedness, and collaboration. Supporters and critics have debated the effectiveness and appropriateness of distance learning, but they have tended to agree that spiritual formation involves the whole person, working together in a learning community with colleagues and teachers. We now turn to our two empirical case studies, to explore the extent to which this scholarly concern for embedded collaboration is shared by contemporary formational projects.

---

19 Gresham, "Divine Pedagogy."
20 Cepero, "Writing Your Way Home."
21 Hirsch, "‹/Parentheses›."
22 Mercer and Simpson, "What Would Kant Tweet?"
23 Lowe and Lowe, "Spiritual Formation."

3 Digital pedagogy: two case studies

3.1 Common Awards: formation for Christian ministry

In 2011, the Church of England undertook a "radical restructuring"[24] of its training for ministry, in partnership with four smaller denominations: the Methodist, Baptist, Scottish Episcopal, and United Reformed Churches. Seminaries and teaching institutions were encouraged to enroll in a national suite of Common Awards, validated by a single higher education institution, and Durham University was selected to perform this accreditation. At the time of writing, courses registered for the Common Awards program are taught by 17 Theological Education Institutes (TEIs) in England and one in Scotland.

All of these TEIs now ostensibly offer the same degree course, but not all TEIs operate in the same manner. There are three distinct modes of training. The first is the traditional manner of training which requires the student to live in a residential college for the 2 or 3 years of their training. The second manner is that offered by the non-residential colleges: students come to college once or twice a week for intensive lectures, usually in the evening. These are supplemented by residential weekends and week-long spring or summer schools. Most of the students on these courses work part or full-time alongside their studies, although some are retired, and some fit their studies around family life. The third manner of training is the mixed mode. This combines one or two days of lectures per week with extended placements in a local church, focusing on experiential learning alongside the more traditional theological education for ministry.[25]

No Common Awards provision is offered through solely online courses. Whole modules may be taught online, but the whole diploma or degree will not be. At some point in their training, however, almost all Common Awards students are likely to experience digital pedagogy, whether through the use of a virtual learning environment like Moodle or Blackboard, live or asynchronous streaming of lectures, online seminars, or self-directed online learning. Obviously, students who are not full-time residents of a theological college are most likely to experience the bulk of this digital pedagogy given that they are, by their

---

24 Interview with Mike Higton. For an overview of the training ministry in the Church of England, see https://www.churchofengland.org/resources/diocesan-resources/ministry/training-institutions.
25 An outline of all the different teaching approaches currently offered by TEIs can be found at https://www.durham.ac.uk/departments/academic/common-awards/policies-processes/teis/

nature, already more distant from the perceived community of a residential college.

The TEIs around the UK have various different strategies for using digital pedagogy and for addressing the issues of incarnationality, embodiment, and community outlined above. Their responses to these issues tend to fall into two categories: strategies of hybridity, and strategies of intentional community. These strategies are complementary, and individual TEIs are likely to combine both approaches in different ways.

Most online learning provision is offered in a hybrid mode, in which students will, at some point, meet together. This might be for weekly evening classes, or for a study day, weekend, or longer period of time.[26] TEIs marshal a variety of resources to ensure that they are providing opportunity for formative experience to take place within this hybrid system. For example, the TEI All Saints, based in the northwest of England, teaches weekly evening classes on campus but invites a number of students to join the class remotely. Where possible, these remote students are encouraged to meet in small groups to connect to the class. This means that they are still meeting physically with other students, engaging in interaction, and developing community, even if they cannot attend the main lecture setting.

Multiple TEIs run online modules that include a study day near the beginning of the course, where all the students meet together with tutors for teaching. This has the advantage of, again, facilitating the development of community. Often the connections made on this study day are maintained and developed by students throughout the course through the use of social media, such as a closed Facebook group or WhatsApp group, and these media can be used to share updates, prayer requests, and mutual support.

This appeal to hybridity on the part of the TEIs reflects the contemporary nature of engagement with digital technology. While the nomenclature of "online" and "offline" remains, there are very few times where the distinction is clear cut. Digital technology is substantially enmeshed in contemporary life. Co-author Karen O'Donnell interviewed Professor Mike Higton, who oversees Common Awards, and his view of digital connectivity reflects this enmeshment:

> The interesting questions are around what different spaces we have for interaction, what different spaces do we have for reflection and how do they connect to the other parts of our lives. And there are lots of interesting questions to ask about that. But the questions

---

26 Church of England, "Ordination Training on Courses: The Report of the Working Party on the Structure and Finance of Theological Colleges," ACCM Occasional Paper, Second Series, no. 30, 1989.

don't divide up into how do the unreal bits of our lives connect to the real bits, or how do the online bits to the physical bits? Those seem to me to just be mistaken ways of dividing things up. How do these forms of interaction relate to everything else that's going on? How do these spaces for thinking and reflection relate to everything else that's going on? You need to ask that about any kind of formation.

The second key strategy employed by TEIs is one of intentional, deliberately cultivated community. Intentional community is one in which time spent together in community is expected to be spiritually formative.[27] Despite the best intentions of a course designer, neither formation nor community in an online context happens automatically. Formation is more likely to happen in the digital context if it is stated as an explicit goal of the course[28] and is pursued as a goal by both the tutor and the students.[29] According to these theologians of digital pedagogy, the most vital part of achieving this goal is the element of community. Some TEIs have therefore engaged in online activity to support the development of community between remote students.

The Scottish Episcopal Institute (SEI) in Edinburgh is one of the most recent TEIs to join the Common Awards program. The SEI faces a particular challenge of geography. The SEI is responsible for providing all training for those in, and those wishing to enter into, ministry in the Scottish Episcopal Church, as well as the United Reformed Church of Scotland. But the SEI is based in Edinburgh and its training must be available to ordinands across 30,000 square miles and more than 790 islands. Anyone studying part-time has to engage with the training provided in Edinburgh in some form.

To expand its reach, the SEI invested in a hybrid approach, using high quality video conferencing equipment, alongside fast, high-capacity broadband. They trained their staff well, not only in how to practically use the technology, but also in how they might do so pedagogically. However, the SEI is also deliberate in making spiritual community part of the experience for all students. O'Donnell interviewed SEI's Director of Studies, Michael Hull, to find out more about how this was achieved. Hull highlighted that when the evening class finishes at 9pm, students both on-site and online pray Night Prayer together. His explanation of SEI's approach emphasizes both hybrid and intentional community strategies:

---

[27] John Schramm, "Intentional Community and Spiritual Development," *Word and World* 8, no. 1 (1988), 48.
[28] White, "Promoting Spiritual Formation."
[29] Forrest and Lamport, "Modeling Spiritual Formation."

At SEI, we make great effort to form a community along a gathered and scattered model; that is though geographically dispersed, we use whatever means are available to bring ourselves together, for example orientation days at the beginning of the year, five residential weekends throughout the year, and common seminars with Skype and onsite learners together. Prayer is a key element to a Christian community. Providing an opportunity for prayer is important to highlight the presence of Christ among us as a community of learners according to Matthew 18.19–20.

While not necessarily undertaking anything particularly radical in the world of digital pedagogy, those engaged with Common Awards training provision are attempting to take seriously some of the theological challenges that have been levied against learning in digital contexts and its suitability for spiritually formative education. Through attention to the hybrid nature of learning, alongside intentional aims of facilitating formational communities, these TEIs are endeavoring to provide spiritually formative theological education for the digital age. It would seem clear from the work of the TEIs that the intentionality or explicit, self-reflective purpose with which spiritual formation is approached in digital spaces is essential to success in this area. Courses deliberately structured around opportunity for formation in the digital context are more likely to be considered formational by both staff and students than courses shifted wholesale from classroom to VLE with no consideration of the challenges of formation online.

3.2 *Guardians of Ancora:* children's lay formation

Our second case study focuses on a digital product aimed at children with limited experience of Christianity. *Guardians of Ancora* is a game app for smartphones and tablets, launched by the Bible-focused charity Scripture Union England and Wales in 2015 and designed for children aged 8–11. It is now available in English, Welsh, Serbian, Albanian and Brazilian Portuguese, with other language translations underway. The academic study of religion and gaming is flourishing,[30] but games produced by religious communities have received relatively little attention to date. This brief case study will explore the approach to pedagogy found in this one game, but much broader research is needed in future to compare this project to the child-focused gaming initiatives of other religious communities.

---

[30] Heidi Campbell and Gregory P. Grieve, *Playing with Religion in Digital Games* (Bloomington, IN: Indiana University Press, 2014); Vit Šisler, Kerstin Radde-Antweiler, and Xenia Zeiler, *Methods for Studying Videogames and Religion* (Abingdon: Routledge, 2018).

Guardians of Ancora invites players to become the protectors of a fantastical city. In the land of Ancora, all light comes from a tall building called the Spire, powered by stories. These stories have been lost, and the land is falling into darkness. As a Guardian, the player's task is to complete quests to rediscover the stories of Ancora and bring them back to the Spire.

The stories featured in the game are all taken from the New Testament, and each "quest" takes the player back to first-century Palestine to encounter Jesus and his disciples. The player is able to witness miracles and hear Jesus preaching, but active gameplay focuses on running, climbing, and jumping. After completing a quest, players can visit other parts of Ancora to read the text of the story from the Bible, watch a video version, answer quizzes, play a simple physics game or create pictures to share with other players. *Guardians of Ancora* can be played alone, but it has also been used as part of evangelistic missions, children's camps, church events and school clubs.[31]

To find out more about *Guardians of Ancora*, co-author Tim Hutchings interviewed the Product Developer, Maggie Barfield. Barfield was initially commissioned by Scripture Union to update its printed Bible study resources for children, but she soon decided that a more radical approach was needed: "the thing they're doing for most of their spare time is doing stuff online, or digital stuff, or playing games," she claimed, so what the charity really needed was a game of its own. Barfield was reluctant to categorize *Guardians of Ancora* as an "educational" game:

> It wasn't built to be an educational tool, it was built to be a, um, a faith environment, or . . . What I describe it as sometimes is an environment in which it's easy for faith to thrive. So it's not a place where a character will come up to you and say, "Hello Tim! Would you like to be a Christian? Here's a prayer you can say." But as Tim explores the game, he'll be stimulated and motivated and encouraged to look at stuff, think about stuff, and respond to questions, ask himself questions.

Nonetheless, *Guardians of Ancora* is still "underpinned with solid educational stuff," and Barfield drew particular attention to the game's engagement with different learning styles:

> It's a very active thing, so that's excellent for the active learning style. It's very visual, but it's also got the whole kind of, the head knowledge, the thinky stuff, because there is stuff

---

[31] Tim Hutchings, "'The Light of a Thousand Stories': Design, Play and Community in the Christian Videogame *Guardians of Ancora*," *Online: Heidelberg Journal of Religions on the Internet* 14 (2019): 159–78.

to read, there is stuff to think about... So there are different types of activity, and we'll see different children spending more time in some areas than others.

This mix of learning options is intended to help the game appeal to the widest possible audience. When I asked Barfield if she would describe *Guardians of Ancora* as "evangelism, or discipleship, or spiritual formation, or something else?," she laughed and replied "all of them.' "What we wanted," she explained, "was a game that any child could play, and that wherever they were in their faith it would give them an opportunity to kind of move towards God from having played it." For "children who knew absolutely nothing about God, didn't know what the word was, had no concept of God, it would be an opportunity for them to find out that some people do think there is a thing called God, or even a person called God" – but the game could also offer something for "the full on Christian kid who's been baptized and who's racing around telling all his friends." Above all, the simple mythology of the game is intended to encourage "a positive world view" in which the player learns to make a difference, teaching children that "the real world is a better place because you are there, and if you have God's light shining in you, that is having an impact on the world around you."

The educational institutions discussed in the previous case study used digital media to create intentional community, understanding spiritual formation as a process that required participation in shared settings. In contrast, Barfield presented the game *Guardians of Ancora* as a tool for reinvigorating group settings that already existed, but were struggling to attract and retain the interest of children in Christian learning and practice. Barfield described a range of shared gaming contexts, including play in churches, schools, and youth groups. According to Barfield, "a big area for us is after school and lunchtime clubs." School workers report that the game "attracts the non-Christian children, so at least 80% of the children who turn up for a club won't have any faith background at all." From the perspective of youth workers with an interest in proselytism, these young people with no faith background are "the children they've been desperate to get hold of forever."

In group play settings like these, the game can be augmented with other activities, drawing on the world of Ancora. In churches and schools, group leaders and children create elaborate costumes, scenery and art, sing songs and play physical games.[32] In our interview, Barfield also mentioned outdoor pursuit centers, where "you can really theme the whole holiday brilliantly as an Ancora

---

32 Hutchings, "Light of a Thousand Stories", 170

experience." An example of this kind of adventure activity was advertised by Great Wood Camp in Somerset, UK in 2019, using the tagline "You've played the game, now try the holiday."[33] Scripture Union has produced a range of free ebooks targeted at schools and churches, based on the experiences of successful groups, to suggest activities that could be developed around the game.[34] According to Barfield, introducing the game into children's groups transformed the learning environment by undermining the hierarchy of age and knowledge:

> What they report again and again is that you'll have a complete levelling within the group, so you stop having leaders and pupils and everybody comes as equals, because you sit together and the child can play the game really well and will start asking questions, or making comments, and the leaders aren't as good at playing the game, but they have those opportunities to be responding to what the children actually are asking and wanting to know. So instead of hammering them with a bible message, the message is emerging from the children.

Through this more physical layer of engagement with the game and its mythos, Ancora combines on-screen content with embodied experiences. Barfield, however, was adamant that the game itself should be understood as the central learning tool, effective even without a shared face-to-face context. I asked if the game could achieve its aim of bringing children closer to God by itself, and Barfield replied with enthusiasm: "Yes, yes, because it is doing that for plenty of children. I mean, I think the, the clubs are absolutely wonderful, a great opportunity, but there are far more children who are encountering the game as a game than are in clubs." This approach contrasts strikingly with some of the theological arguments for incarnational presence discussed above.[35] When I asked if physical activity and shared, embodied play helped to make the game more effective, Barfield disagreed: "I think it might be the other way around, because at the moment the feedback we get from people running clubs is that it's a resource that is really helping *them* to connect to the children." Churches and youth workers struggle to attract children's attention, she argued, and the appeal of the game allowed them to do their work.

---

33 Scripture Union Holidays England and Wales, "Ancora Explorers" (2019). Facebook Event, July 24–27 2019: https://en-gb.facebook.com/events/1280984602039473/
34 For example, Scripture Union, "*Guardians of Ancora*".
35 Kelsey, "Spiritual Machines", 7.

4 Concluding discussion: digital spiritual pedagogy

In our first case study, we identified two key strategies deployed by TEIs in the Common Awards program to encourage spiritual formation: hybridity and intentional community. By combining online with face-to-face resources and learning opportunities in a rich variety of contexts, TEIs hope to make their teaching accessible to the widest possible range of students. By developing opportunities for interaction and shared activity in and out of the classroom, TEIs encourage students to understand themselves as part of a community with a shared learning goal. These strategies are not centrally mandated by the Common Awards scheme, but have emerged in remarkably consistent ways across the spectrum of TEIs. These learning institutions see hybridity and community as essential foundations for spiritual formation in a digitally networked society, in which engagement with the whole life context of a student necessarily entails engagement with their digital presence.

Guardians of Ancora has a very different aim and audience, but versions of the same two strategies can be identified in our interview with Maggie Barfield. Families, churches, schools, and other youth groups found ways to combine the digital platform with face-to-face activities and interactions. Through this strategy of hybridity, adult coordinators of children's activities are trying to promote the formation of intentional community. Missional youth groups conventionally encourage children to participate in shared activities and to develop new friendships as ways to begin exploring the shared identity offered by Christian faith. According to Barfield, at least some youth leaders have welcomed the game as a way to help increase participation in and enjoyment of these more traditional group bonding strategies.

These themes of hybridity and intentional community echo the concerns summarized at the start of this chapter, in our review of Christian writing on digital pedagogy. Since at least the late 1990s, theologians interested in online learning have emphasized that formation cannot take place in a disembodied, impersonal context. Taking the Incarnation as their pedagogical model, writers like David Kelsey[36] and John Gresham[37] have called for online education to engage the physical and social context of the learner. More recently, Stephen

---

36 Kelsey, "Spiritual Machines."
37 Gresham, "Divine Pedagogy."

and Mary Lowe[38] and Ron Mercer and Mark Simpson[39] have called for digital learning to be embedded in the daily lives of students. While our interviewees did not mention these or other Christian pedagogists by name, we can see hybridity and intentional community as strategic answers to the same theological challenges. In both case studies, we see attempts at combining digital and non-digital activities, building relationships between students and promoting shared identities. In both case studies, learning draws on digital resources, but is personalized, interactive, and embedded in everyday life.

Maggie Barfield's account of the undermining of teacher–student hierarchies in *Guardians of Ancora* also echoes another long-standing observation about digital learning. Helen Cepero[40] calls for collaborative online spiritual direction, in which director and client work together to construct knowledge, and Brett Hirsch claims that the digital humanities share a distinctive emphasis on "collectivity and collaboration" in teaching and research.[41] According to Barfield, the game promotes this collaboration in a slightly different way, by establishing a digital environment in which students will inevitably outshine their teachers. Kara Kennedy[42] calls for digital humanists to help develop the digital literacy of college students, but *Guardians of Ancora* aims instead to capitalize on pre-existing expertise. Barfield is confident that young children will be more experienced and talented gamers than adults, and reports that the atmosphere of security and confidence generated by this imbalance of technique encourages students to be more open about their own spiritual questions.

In other comments, Barfield suggested an understanding of *Guardians of Ancora* much less compatible with this established tradition of Christian digital pedagogy. She celebrated the hybrid and community-building strategies of schools and youth groups, but also argued that "plenty of children" were coming closer to God by playing the game on their own without these larger shared contexts. For Barfield, hybridity and community were useful primarily to the group itself. The game was an appealing, fun, and spiritually formative tool, and groups – which struggled on their own to keep children interested – were borrowing some of that appeal to make themselves more enticing, engaging, and effective.

This argument marks a significant pedagogical distinction between the two case studies, because Common Awards continues to insist that at least some

---

38 Lowe and Lowe, "Spiritual Formation."
39 Mercer and Simpson, "What Would Kant Tweet?"
40 Cepero, "Writing Your Way Home."
41 Hirsch, "‹/Parentheses›," 16.
42 Kennedy, "Long Belated Welcome."

degree of face-to-face contact is essential for all TEIs. This difference of emphasis may be explained in part by the different histories of the institutions sponsoring each venture. Some TEIs began as wholly residential institutions and retain a strong commitment to this intensive mode of training, while Scripture Union, as a publisher, is invested in the formative impact of mediated communication. The two projects also anticipate different levels of initial commitment and final formation, and this also shapes their different expectations. Common Awards is designed to train ordinands to become ministers, capable of leading Christian communities and teaching their own faith to others. *Guardians of Ancora*, in contrast, is intended for children with little or no experience of Christianity, and its formational goals are comparatively modest. In our interview, Barfield embraced any spiritual development of the child-player as a successful outcome, however subtle or hard to measure. A game on a screen might be enough to catch a child's attention, and that momentary engagement with a Christian product is already more than many of her target audience have experienced before. We should not overstate this distinction, however, because our work on Common Awards also encountered some hesitation towards the necessity of in-person teaching. TEIs can offer different blends of online and in-person learning, from fully residential to almost fully online. In our interview, Mike Higton suggests that these approaches do not seem to correlate to measurable impacts on student formation:

> We just don't see a difference. You might expect there to be a difference. You might expect there to be differences and we don't, in terms of how our students are enabled to do their assessed work and those sorts of things. And, you know, levels of complaints and things like that... they're very minor differences and they don't seem to line up with forms of training.

In fact, he suggested, "the differences between TEIs are bigger than the differences between forms of training, where you've got more than one form in one TEI." The same appeared to be true of spiritual formation:

> People anecdotally will be more likely to talk about being formed in daily habits of prayer, if they're residential, than if they're doing evening class based, and weekend-based thing. But actually, the more I know, the smaller those differences seem to be.[43]

This would indicate that living residentially in a TEI is likely to shape routine and habit (i.e. daily habits of prayer) but that the actual impact on spiritual formation is negligible. This hesitation may indicate a future re-evaluation of digital

---

43 Interview with Mike Higton.

provision, moving over time towards a greater acceptance of spiritual formation in digital and online contexts. At this stage, it suggests at least a tension in both case studies between center and periphery, between product developers and regional implementers. In each case, a digital product is being adapted for use in churches, schools, and theological education institutes through strategies of hybridization and intentional community, and central product developers are watching these adaptations with at least a degree of ambivalence.

This chapter has analyzed two case studies which could, we argue, be considered as digital humanities projects. Neither has claimed that title explicitly, but both are attempting to understand and communicate Christian culture in new ways through digital technology. These examples are located across or outside the boundaries of university education, reminding us not to limit our attention to DH conferences and research centers. Christian churches and entrepreneurs have been pioneers in mediated communication for centuries, and these two projects build on a long history of Christian experiments, conversations and debates around the merits and dangers of online learning. Our examples are also being adapted in interesting and sometimes unpredictable ways by the groups and institutions which have adopted them, including the two strategies identified in this chapter: hybridization and intentional community. Much further research is needed to understand how these and other Christian digital pedagogy projects are impacting the learning experience and formation of their users, and this chapter has sought to establish space for this work within the field of Christian digital humanities.

5 Bibliography

Berry, David. "Introduction: Understanding the Digital Humanities." In *Understanding Digital Humanities*, edited by David Berry, 1–20. Basingstoke: Palgrave Macmillan, 2012.

Brier, Stephen. "Where's the Pedagogy? The Role of Teaching and Learning in the Digital Humanities." In *Debates in the Digital Humanities*, edited by Matthew Gold, 390–401. Minneapolis: University of Minnesota Press, 2012.

Campbell, Heidi. *When Religion Meets New Media*. Abingdon: Routledge, 2010.

Campbell, Heidi A., ed. *Digital Religion: Understanding Religious Practice in New Media Worlds*. Oxford: Routledge, 2013.

Campbell, Heidi, and Gregory P. Grieve. *Playing with Religion in Digital Games*. Bloomington, IN: Indiana University Press, 2014.

Castleman, Robbie F. "The Last Word: The Great Commission: Ecclesiology." *Themelios* 32 (2007/3): 68–70.

Church of England. "Ordination Training on Courses: The Report of the Working Party on the Structure and Finance of Theological Colleges." ACCM Occasional Paper, Second Series, no. 30, 1989.

Cepero, Helen. "Writing Your Way Home: Spiritual Direction Teaching in an Online Format." *The Covenant Quarterly* 70, no. 1/2 (2012): 60–72.

Forrest, Benjamin K., and Mark A. Lamport. "Modeling Spiritual Formation from a Distance: Paul's Formation Transactions with the Roman Christians." *Christian Education Journal Series 3* 10, no. 1 (2013): 110–24.

Gresham, John. "The Divine Pedagogy as a Model for Online Education." *Teaching Theology and Religion* 9, no. 1 (2006): 24–8.

Hess, Mary. "Attendance to Embodiedness in Online Theologically Focused Learning." Presented at Going the Distance: Theology, Religious Education, and Interactive Distance Education, University of Dayton, Ohio, November 1999. https://web.archive.org/web/20161202041436/http://meh.religioused.org/dayton.pdf.

Hirsch, Brett. "‹/Parentheses›: Digital Humanities and the Place of Pedagogy." In *Digital Humanities Pedagogy: Practices, Principles and Politics*, edited by Brett Hirsch, 3–30. Cambridge: Open Book Publishers, 2012. https://www.openbookpublishers.com/reader/161#page/24/mode/2up.

Hockridge, Diane. "'What's the Problem?' Spiritual Formation in Distance and Online Theological Education." *Journal of Christian Education* 54, no. 1 (2011): 25–38.

Hutchings, Tim. "Design and the Digital Bible: Persuasive Technology and Religious Reading." *Journal of Contemporary Religion* 32, no. 2 (2017): 205–19.

Hutchings, Tim. "'The Light of a Thousand Stories': Design, Play and Community in the Christian Videogame *Guardians of Ancora*." *Online: Heidelberg Journal of Religions on the Internet* 14 (2019): 159–78.

Kelsey, David H. "Spiritual Machines, Personal Bodies, and God: Theological Education and Theological Anthropology." *Teaching Theology and Religion* 5, no. 1 (2002): 2–9.

Kennedy, Kara. "A Long Belated Welcome: Accepting Digital Humanities Methods into Non-DH Classrooms." *Digital Humanities Quarterly* 11, no. 3 (2017). http://www.digitalhumanities.org/dhq/vol/11/3/000315/000315.html.

Lowe, Mary. "Spiritual Formation as Whole-Person Development in Online Education." In *Best Practices of Online Education: A Guide for Christian Higher Education*, edited by Mark Maddix, James Estep, and Mary Lowe, 55–64. Charlotte, NC: IAP, INC., 2012.

Lowe, Stephen D., and Mary E. Lowe. "Spiritual Formation in Theological Distance Education: An Ecosystems Model." *Christian Education Journal Series 3* 7, no. 1 (2010): 85–102.

McIntosh, Ian. "Formation in the Margins: The Holy Spirit and Living with Transitions in Part-Residential Theological Education." *Journal of Adult Theological Education* 11, no. 2 (2014): 139–49.

Mercer, Ron, and Mark Simpson. "What Would Kant Tweet? The Utilization of Online Technology in Courses Involving Formation, Meaning, and Value." *Theological Education* 49, no. 2 (2015): 1–18.

Schramm, John. "Intentional Community and Spiritual Development." *Word and World* 8, no. 1 (1988): 48–52.

Schrock, Daniel. "Using Technology in Spiritual Direction." *Vision* (2015): 19–26.

Scripture Union. "*Guardians of Ancora* for Churches," 2018. https://content.scriptureunion.org.uk/resource/guardians-ancora-churches.

Scripture Union Holidays England and Wales. "Ancora Explorers," 2019. https://en-gb.facebook.com/events/1280984602039473/

Šisler, Vit, Kerstin Radde-Antweiler, and Xenia Zeiler. *Methods for Studying Videogames and Religion*. Abingdon: Routledge, 2018.

White, Roger. "Promoting Spiritual Formation in Distance Education." *Christian Education Journal Series 3* 3, no. 2 (2006): 303–15.

Gary Slater
Nested histories: digital humanities as pedagogical laboratory for early Christian studies

> Upon this first, and in one sense this sole, rule of reason, that in order to learn you must desire to learn, and in so desiring not be satisfied with what you already incline to think, there follows one corollary which itself deserves to be inscribed upon every wall of the city of philosophy: Do not block the way of inquiry.
>
> Charles S. Peirce[1]

1 Introduction

To study ancient Christianity is to engage with a series of relationships – between allies and adversaries, text and image, church and state, and so forth. Nested Histories, which is a case study in digital humanities (DH), is a pedagogical resource to help students more effectively uncover, represent, and evaluate these relationships. I designed and led the study in 2015 in conjunction with a Teaching Innovation Fellowship at St. Edward's University in Austin, Texas. Nested Histories applies digital mind mapping and graphing technology to generate insights into early Christian history. More specifically, the project facilitates collaborative and integrative learning, enhances visual literacy, and fosters active engagement with Christian texts by allowing students to construct relationships between those texts and multiple historical contexts.

It is important to be clear from the beginning about how Nested Histories embodies DH in its pedagogy. As a DH case study, Nested Histories exists at an intersection between pedagogy, computational analysis, and experimentation. Upon reading a given primary text, students use Coggle, an open source mind mapping tool, to construct relationships between key vocabularies and the historical contexts (figure 1). Each mind map is designated by coded number sets that allow the instructor to perform a quantitative analysis on students' learning concerning key relationships within the course materials. By "course

---

[1] Charles S. Peirce, *Collected Papers of Charles Sanders Peirce, Volumes I and II: Principles of Philosophy and Elements of Logic*, ed. Charles Hartshorne and Paul Weiss (Cambridge, MA: Harvard University Press, 1931), 56.

https://doi.org/10.1515/9783110574043-014

materials," I simply mean key texts from the syllabus, plus digital artifacts generated through student searches of online databases.

To guide its experiments, Nested Histories employs the nested continua model of religious interpretation (figure 2), henceforth written as NCM, which is an interactive diagram that draws from the logic and semiotics of C.S. Peirce. Peirce (1839–1914), a foundational figure in both modern semiotics and the pragmatic philosophical tradition, is helpful for the project with regard to integrating large- and small-scale claims and exploring the nature of religious interpretation, experience, and truth.[2] Although Peirce's relevance to DH has been raised in broad terms (e.g. Clivaz 2016), Nested Histories represents the first application of Peirce's work in integrating DH, pedagogy, and Christian history.

As for the NCM, this is comprised of concentric circles representing nested frameworks of interpretation around a given historical text. The chief virtue of the NCM for the Nested Histories project is its combination of an interdisciplinary breadth that accommodates analyses of concrete religious artifacts alongside metaphysical or theological claims with a logical precision that respects social context. In purely visual terms, the concentric circles that comprise the NCM are not especially profound. When paired with the appropriate guidelines, however, the model has been shown to facilitate inquiry, reveal logical distinctions visually, and navigate among frameworks of interpretation at different levels of generality.[3] On the model's basic understanding, each circle signifies a framework of interpretation that brings into intelligible relation whatever is placed within it; a given circle can also be placed itself within other circles as a continuum nested within other continua. Here are its most relevant guidelines:

- Circles closer to center are understood as more "local," those farther away more "global," with "local" and "global" referring respectively to interpretive contexts that are particular and those that are general. A nest of circles is a trajectory of interpretation that, in moving from the center towards the edge of the nest, moves from local to global.
- Circles are not fixed: they can be switched out for other circles, layered within each other, and represented as discrete markings within other circles – that is, in a cardinal series as well as ordered.

---

2 Gary Slater, *C.S. Peirce and the Nested Continua Model of Religious Interpretation* (Oxford: Oxford University Press, 2015), 3.
3 Brandon Daniel-Hughes, *Pragmatic Inquiry and Religious Communities: Charles Peirce, Signs, and Inhabited Experiments* (London: Palgrave MacMillan, 2018), 68–76.

– Circles signify contexts of interpretation, within which a given object makes sense according to a set of norms; to put it perhaps more technically, circles are rules of reasoning within which logical distinctions take meaning.

The basic aim in employing the NCM within Nested Histories is for students to achieve a more accurate understanding regarding Christianity as an unfolding tradition, with a richer grasp of historiography as the stuff of living arguments and interpretations rather than settled facts. Far from referring all questions to a single mode of inquiry, the NCM aims to provides a vague space in which multiple modes of inquiry be playfully, tentatively, and hypothetically examined in relation to that which they explain, as well as to other modes of interpretation.[4]

One important feature of Nested Histories is that it is intended to be replicable by other instructors in other courses. This is particularly the case for courses that encompass historical and religious topics with an emphasis on primary texts. In practical terms, the demands in terms of costs and resources in implementing the project are quite minimal: basic levels for such programs as Coggle suffice, and anyone with access to a computer should have no trouble leading or participating in the program. Moreover, the more teachers try out something like Nested Histories for their courses, the better it gets as a method for enhancing student learning about religious history. That is, because the project is realized only through its being enacted by its students, there is an element of elasticity to the project that lends it the possibility of refinement through further application.

Aside from its pedagogical interest, there are at least three reasons why this project might interest a broader range of audiences. First, the project represents an extension of C.S. Peirce's thought, applying Peirce's pioneering work on iconic signification (i.e. signification through resemblance), abductive inference (i.e. hypothetical reasoning or guesswork), and the logic of relations (i.e. the study of relationships between different kinds of objects). Second, the project intersects with ongoing discussions in DH, touching on the relationship between DH and: (1) coding, (2) images drawn from electronic sources, and (3) pedagogy. Third, the project reflects the subject matter of early Christianity, modeling a contextual, unfolding nature and balance between close and distant readings that mirrors its subject of interest.

These areas of interest correspond with the different sections of this chapter. In the chapter's first section, the Peircean theoretical underpinning for the Nested Histories project is introduced and unpacked. In its second section, the prac-

---

4 Slater, *C.S. Peirce*, 13.

tices that comprise the project are described in some detail, with particular attention given to the sequence of steps that comprise the implementation of the project. In its third section, attention turns to the ways in which Nested Histories both bears on contemporary discourses within DH and facilitates learning of early Christian history.

2 DH pedagogy and C.S. Peirce

Nested Histories is inseparable from the NCM, and the NCM is inseparable from its roots in the work of the American pragmatist philosopher and semiotician C.S. Peirce. It is therefore helpful to devote some space towards explaining how Peirce's ideas inform the Nested Histories project.

In at least one area, Peirce's influence on Nested Histories has no direct bearing on the NCM, even as it shapes the approach modeled in the project. This area is pedagogy. Peirce spent a brief period in his career – 1879–1884 – as a lecturer at Johns Hopkins University. During this time, Peirce was keen to apply his burgeoning pragmatism within the classroom. As James Liszka has put it, Peirce appeared to be an "early advocate and practitioner of what we call active learning."[5] Liszka goes on to explore Peirce's action-oriented pedagogy in terms of a "community of inquiry" and a "dismissal of the old ways of force-feeding students in favor of generating curiosity, enhancing discovery, and showing students how to think for themselves."[6] The Nested Histories project shares these emphases. Liszka's depiction has been corroborated by Kathleen Hull, who recognizes that Peircean teaching "is not interested in learning as mere recapitulation of existing knowledge or as passive reception; rather, it is fascinated with learning as a process of being confronted by surprising events and originating true ideas to explain those events."[7]

As for Peirce's relevance to the project in terms of the NCM, a good description of the model's relationship both to Peirce and to the process of learning can be found in Brandon Daniel-Hughes' *Pragmatic Inquiry and Religious Communities: Charles Peirce, Signs, and Inhabited Experiments*. As Daniel-Hughes puts it:

---

[5] James Liszka, "Charles Peirce's Rhetoric and the Pedagogy of Active Learning," *Educational Philosophy and Theory* 45 (2013), 783.
[6] Liszka, "Charles Peirce's Rhetoric," 783.
[7] Kathleen Hull, "Peircean Teaching," *Transactions of the Charles S. Peirce Society* 44 (2008), 205.

> The aim of the NCM is not merely diagrammatic. It has both an explanatory function and an abductive function. It can be utilized as a tool of discovery, allowing users to render the implicit explicit and thereby discover new interpretive frameworks that support new and novel interpretations…Putting aside Peircean terminology for the moment, the foremost practical value of rendering implicit normative contexts explicit is that such renderings allows users of the model to gain critical purchase on what makes interpretive frameworks themselves better and worse.[8]

Contemporary commentators have likewise expressed resonant claims with respect to how Nested Histories uses Peirce. In "Analysis Tool or Research Methodology: Is There an Epistemology for Patterns?" Dan Dixon does more than discuss Peirce's relevance to DH; he also puts Peirce in conversation with Christopher Alexander, the author of *A Pattern Language* (1977) and an influential figure for modern coding theory. Particularly astute from Dixon is his observation that the "main benefit of using patterns as a method for system understanding is that one does not have to model the overall system in any way, or create abstract interpretations." [9] Rather, the "activity of observing, collecting, categorising, and analysing these types of pattern is not like modelling or trying to replicate the system, it is an empirical process."[10] Dixon's points express what makes Nested Histories work in using technology to elicit insights that might go otherwise unnoticed.

The key feature in what allows Peirce to shape the self-description of Nested Histories as a laboratory is the logic of abduction. Given the importance of abduction to Dixon's connection between Peirce and Alexander as well as the present project, the term "abduction" might be briefly unpacked. Here is Dixon again:

> The principle of abduction was proposed by Peirce as a formalisation of the hunches, guesses, and intuition that help the natural sciences…Abduction is the method by which hypotheses are created or discovered; induction and deduction are the methods by which they are proven. Abductive reasoning is, simply put, the spotting of patterns and relationships in sets of data.[11]

As Claire Clivaz points out in relation to Umberto Eco's *The Infinity of Lists* (2009), "when data are digitally listed and mixed-up, categorizations used in

---

8 Daniel-Hughes, *Pragmatic Inquiry*, 74.
9 Dan Dixon, "Analysis Tool or Research Methodology: Is There an Epistemology for Patterns?" in *Understanding Digital Humanities*, ed. David M. Berry (London: Palgrave MacMillan, 2012), 198.
10 Ibid., 198.
11 Ibid., 201.

the printed culture are overcome and new forms of knowledge appear."[12] Abduction is the logical form that characterizes the new forms of knowledge to which Clivaz is referring. The NCM serves as a sort of Petri dish for abductions.

Yet abduction is not the only feature of Peirce's thought that links Peirce and DH within Nested Histories. Almost as much as the logic of abduction, Peirce's work on ordinal/cardinal numbers stands out as significant, as it is this numerical distinction which facilitates within the project the transformation of individual mind maps into aggregated models. Proceeding on the understanding that cardinal numbers represent potentially infinite collections of discrete numerals and ordinal number represents potentially infinite sequence of orders, each of which contains its own infinite set of cardinal numbers, it is possible to gain some sense of how the circles on the NCM interact.

To provide an example, the terms "Roman Empire" and "third-century Carthage" represent continuous interpretive frameworks – as such, to be drawn on the graph as concentric circles – that are related *ordinally*. There is no fact of Carthaginian history during that period that is not also a feature of the history of the Roman Empire. Yet within each of these orders there is a potentially inexhaustible series of facts – e.g. "distinct theological centers emerge in Antioch and Alexandria" for the former, "Cyprian rebuilds the Church in the wake of the Decian persecutions" for the latter – that are related *cardinally*. This distinction in number types allows for relationships as well as discrete data points to be assigned numerical values.

3 Description of project

Nested Histories comprises nine course modules. Working forward from the start of the term, these are:

(1) The World of Jesus
(2) Apostolic Fathers
(3) Heretics and Apologists
(4) Alexandria, Antioch, Rome
(5) The Constantine Cataclysm
(6) From Arius to Athanasius
(7) From Cappadocia to Constantinople
(8) The Fracturing Empire
(9) The World of Augustine

Each module proceeds in three phases, each of which comprises roughly 1–2 class periods. Classes occur three times per week across 14 weeks. Phase one

---

[12] Claire Clivaz, "Digital Humanities in Ancient Jewish, Christian and Arabic Traditions: Introduction to the Special Issue," *Journal of Religion, Media and Digital Culture* 5 (2016), 9.

consists of relatively traditional pedagogy, as students first encounter their assigned readings and time in class is spent in open discussion to ensure that an appropriate initial understanding was achieved. At this point I divide students into groups corresponding to some of the key perspectives for that module: for instance, a group designated "Arian" and another designated "Nicene" for module 6. The groups are ultimately tasked with constructing models corresponding to the worldviews espoused by those holding the perspectives in question. I also provide a base set of key terms that students have to define. Although each group is free to arrange these terms however it thinks is most appropriate, all of the terms must ultimately appear on the nested continua graph.

In phase two, the focus shifts from texts and discussion towards the construction of preliminary mind maps. Although this activity is facilitated by digital technologies, the basic activity of mind mapping is not technologically demanding, nor are the concepts upon which its rules are based particularly new. In its connection to the similar notion of concept mapping, the roots of this technique are well described by D.E. Wittkower:

> Concept-mapping was developed by Joseph Novak as a method of representing student understanding in order to better guide student instruction. Novak based this process primarily on David Ausubel's theory of knowledge and learning, based on models from Piaget and Gestalt psychology, which claimed that knowledge was fundamentally hierarchical in structure, and that the process of meaningful learning is constituted primarily by the subsumption of new concepts under existing and established categories.[13]

Just prior to developing the students' mind maps, class time is spent in open speculation – guided by projected images using Coggle, which is an open source mind mapping tool – on any relevant relationships between the theological perspectives in question and the historical contexts within which the perspectives emerged.

Having witnessed an in-class demonstration as an example, each student then uses Coggle to develop his or her own mind map as preparation for the transposition in phase three of mind maps into nested continua modeling. These mind maps depict relations among the key terms, with terms arranged along a horizontal baseline representing a progression from relatively concrete and immediate realities within a given course module, towards the left, to relatively abstract and encompassing, on the right. For every step towards the right

---

[13] Dylan E. Wittkower, "Mind-Mapping Inside and Outside of the Classroom," in *Learning Through Digital Media: Experiments in Technology and Pedagogy*, ed. R. Trebor Scholz (New York: Institute for Distributed Creativity, 2011), 224.

along the baseline, terms are taken to encompass – or perhaps even explain – any terms shown to the left along that line. Terms can also be shown to deviate from the baseline, which indicates that these terms do not fit into the explanatory nest of terms, yet still occupy roughly the same level of generality and abstraction as those at the same left–right point along the baseline.

Altogether, the students' construction of these mind maps is a significant step within the project, as the patterns of relation that Coggle facilitates – cardinal and ordinal relationships – can be completely reproduced on the NCM. Moreover, each mind map can be designated by coded number sets that allow the instructor to perform a quantitative analysis on students' learning concerning key relationships within the course materials. The way this works is that each point along the baseline represents an ordinal number, and each deviation above a given point represents a cardinal number within the order represented at its base. By averaging the arrangements of ordinal and cardinal numbers for groups of students, instructors can gain insight into how some terms are prioritized over others within the imaginative construction of historical worlds that the project facilitates.

In phase three, the task is to reproduce the collections of individualized mind maps as aggregated nested continua for each respective group. As noted above, this model is an interactive diagram composed of innumerable concentric circles drawn upon a flat surface. Since Coggle's relational patterns can be encoded as number sets as well as reproduced as nested continua, it becomes possible to take the averages for each number set for all the students within a given group, then use Prezi to transpose the result in the form of nested continua. The results are skeleton structures to be filled in by the respective groups according to assigned perspectives. Prezi is ideal for this purpose, as it facilitates the creation of sets of frames, each of which corresponds to a graphed circle, which is the default shape. Prezi also offers the capacity for zooming inward and outward across a vast range of digital space, which is another congenial feature. Moreover, the circles Prezi displays allow the embedding of three different types of text: Title, Subtitle, and Body (figure 3).

This is one of the most exciting parts of the process, as the students can at this stage begin filling up their meticulously arranged imaginary spaces with vivid historical details. For the "Title" text bar, the text simply reads whatever the name of the term happens to be. For the "Subtitle" bar, students fill in the definitions that had been researched in phase one. And for the "Body" text bar, students embed URLs linking to at least five articles, images, or videos corresponding to that term. Students cite on collaborative student blogs the source for each link as it might appear in a scholarly journal.

What makes this possible is the virtually inexhaustible storehouse of digital artifacts available online. As Bernhard Rieder and Theo Röhle have observed, "digital artifacts now populate every corner of post-industrial societies," such that there has been an "explosion of material available in digital form."[14] David Michelson has commented on the impact of this explosion on the historical study of Christianity. As Michelson puts it: "For scholars in traditionally text-oriented fields, such as the history of Judaism or Christianity, this revolution in information technology has created a dramatic reversal in the material constraints that have long shaped their scholarship."[15] This challenge represents a fertile field of application for the NCM. For example, Leighton Evans and Sian Rees highlight the possibility of "zoomability" between micro and macro for large datasets, as well as the "revelation of patterns and structures which would be impossible to discern with the naked eye."[16] This echoes how Prezi facilitates the group interpretation within Nested Continua structures.

The collaborative blog for each group, in addition to displaying correct citation procedure, also provides a useful space for students to review their peers' performance and effort within the group. As for time spent in class, phase three features interactive "tours" of the findings of each group's model. For modules in which more than two groups are involved – module 4, for example – an instructive exercise involves viewing the completed models and having students guess, purely based on the configuration of circles, which group's perspective they're viewing. The ideal result is a notable-but-not-incomprehensible discrepancy between models, which facilitates a meaningful debate requiring the exchange of reasons for one interpretation over the other.

For students unfamiliar with DH as a pedagogical tool for historical analysis, the experience of Nested Histories can be jarring. For example, one student who took the course in its first semester called for "less nested continua," preferring "more talking in class about course content."[17] Another student reported: "the structure of the course didn't really lend itself to a history class that involves this many ideas." Among these initial negative reactions, the general sense

---

14 Bernhard S. Rieder and Theo Röhle, "Digital Methods: Five Challenges," in *Understanding Digital Humanities*, ed. David M. Berry (London: Palgrave MacMillan, 2012), 67.
15 David Michelson, "Syriaca.org as a Test Case for Digital Re-Sorting," in *Ancient Worlds in Digital Culture*, ed. Claire Clivaz, Paul Dilley, and David Hamidović (Leiden: Brill, 2016), 59.
16 Leighton Evans and Sian Rees, "An Interpretation of Digital Humanities," in *Understanding Digital Humanities*, ed. David M. Berry (London: Palgrave MacMillan, 2012), 23.
17 All student quotations are taken from anonymous student course evaluations for the Fall 2015 term.

seemed to be that the NCM was a focus *instead of* the course content of early Christianity, as opposed to a *means towards* engaging such content.

These comments do not, however, represent the only – or even the dominant – student response to Nested Histories. And aside from its entailing a more technology-oriented brand of pedagogy, Nested Histories can be linked with two types of learning impact:

1. Students retaining insights more effectively. They do so because of having played a more active role in creating mind maps and nested continua, and also because completed NCMs function as multi-media study guides that are both accessible and nuanced.
2. Students learning how embedding data within nested contexts represents the enactment of a comprehensive worldview, one that can be compared with others within a common visual space. They do so because of the visual metaphor that lies at the core of the NCM, in which arrangement of images and key terms within a nest of circles exist around a central point. Like the rings of a tree trunk, these circles represent chronological progressions that interact with changing environments.

Beyond these learning impacts, Nested Histories works towards debunking the false binary that exists in many academic circles between teaching and research, a binary that has taken on acute form in contemporary charges against digital humanities work as preferring research-driven projects over pedagogical ones. This has been echoed by such commentators as Brett D. Hirsch, who writes that to "bracket pedagogy in critical discussions of the digital humanities or to completely exclude it from these discussions reinforces an antagonistic distinction between teaching and research, in which the time, effort, and funding spent on the one cannibalizes the opportunities of the other."[18] Simply as the application within pedagogy of a research program originally designed for research on philosophy of history and religious history, Nested Histories works against the tendency Hirsch is identifying.

---

[18] Brett D. Hirsch, "‹/Parentheses›: Digital Humanities and the Place of Pedagogy," in *Digital Humanities Pedagogy: Practices, Principles and Politics*, ed. Brett D. Hirsch (London: Open Book Publishers, 2012), 6.

4 The call of the digital humanities

The relevance of Nested Histories to DH manifests itself in at least four constructive ways: in its use of technology to demonstrate a kind of collective intellect on the part of the students in the class, on its employment of an idiosyncratic form of coding, in its focus on images drawn from a range of electronic sources, and on its marriage of DH and pedagogy.

Before any of these specific topics can be engaged, it is worth pausing to clarify precisely what is presently understood by DH. Evans and Sian Rees articulate the digital humanities as studies that "actively engage digital methods to probe existing questions in the humanities in a qualitative manner, or propose new theories and areas of research in the humanities by accepting and making problematic the inevitable presence of computation in the world, and therefore in the humanities."[19] So understood, DH intersects with Nested Histories at an important moment in its own history. In recent years DH has undergone two pivotal developments. These are the second and third "waves" of DH scholarship.

David M. Berry has characterized these respective waves in the following terms. While first-wave digital humanities "involved the building of infrastructure in the studying of humanities texts through digital repositories, text markup and so forth," second-wave digital humanities "expands the notional limits of the archive to include digital works, and so bring to bear the humanities' own methodological toolkits to look at "born-digital" materials, such as electronic literature (e-lit), interactive fiction (IF), web-based artefacts and so forth."[20] To these two waves Berry adds a third, which is "concentrated around the underlying computationality of the forms held within a computational medium."[21]

Within Berry's framing, Nested Histories could be described as demonstrating some combination of second and third-wave DH. In its compiling of web-based artifacts, for instance, the project is clearly second wave. Yet in its employment of computational processes across its second and third phases, the project resonates with the third wave. Perhaps more helpful as schema for discussing the intersection of Nested Histories with DH are what Tim Hutchings, following Patrik Svensson, identifies as the five modes of engagement with digital technology within DH and the study of religion: as a tool, as an object of study, as an

---

19 Evans and Rees, "Interpretation of Digital Humanities," 36.
20 David M. Berry, "Introduction: Understanding the Digital Humanities," in *Understanding Digital Humanities*, ed. David M. Berry (London: Palgrave MacMillan, 2012), 4.
21 Ibid., 4.

expressive medium, as an exploratory laboratory and as an activist venue.[22] As a pedagogical laboratory, Nested Histories clearly embodies the fourth mode Hutchings names.

With this context in mind, it is possible to explore the ways in which the Nested Histories intersects with DH. As noted, there are four areas. First is its understanding of intelligence. This reflects the sense in which the digital space within Nested Histories facilitates the practice of a sort of group mind on the part of the students participating. That is, participants in Nested Histories are developing a classroom intellect with respect to designated contexts of Christian patristics. To better understand what this means, Berry offers the following instructive commentary:

> ...computer code enables new communicative processes, and, with the increasing social dimension of networked media, the possibility of new and exciting forms of collaborative thinking arises – network publics. This...is the promise of a collective intellect. The situation is reminiscent of the medieval notion of the universitatis, but recast in a digital form, as a society or association of actors who can think critically together, mediated through technology.[23]

In the case of Nested Histories, which is inescapably collaborative in its third phase, there can be little question that the activities of the students falls under the set of processes Berry is describing. What allows this to happen is the employment of an idiosyncratic form of coding. This is the second area of overlap between Nested Histories and DH.

Nested Histories employs coding with an unusual end in mind: explicating assumptions held by the students with respect to the topics the course is teaching. Scott Dexter has expressed something similar, holding that, to "study code is, indeed, to study layers, hierarchies, and the slippery meanings they imperfectly conceal and reveal."[24] This is precisely what is happening as mind maps are interpreted with respect to their ordinal and cardinal relationships between phases two and three of the project, as the numbers developed by the students in their skeleton-sets do indeed represent a set of code by which individualized mind maps can be rendered in the form of generalized nested continua. This thus represents an emergence from a kind of hiddenness, the excavation of insight through interpretation that represents the explication of the implicit. Nest-

---

22 Tim Hutchings, "Digital Humanities and the Study of Religion," in *Between Humanities and the Digital*, ed. Patrik Svensson and David Theo Goldberg (London: MIT Press, 2015), 284.
23 Berry, "Introduction," 9.
24 Scott Dexter, "The Esthetics of Hidden Things," in *Understanding Digital Humanities*, ed. David M. Berry (London: Palgrave MacMillan, 2012), 129.

ed continua models as finished conceal the coding that went into their construction. And in another way, the ability of the nested continua models within Nested Histories to reveal hidden assumptions exhibits the same movement Dexter describes, though the hiddenness in this case is in the students' imaginations rather than anything within the codes themselves.

The third area of connection between DH and Nested Histories is the prominence of images within its practices. Nested Histories is perfuse with images, from the arid geometric forms of the mind maps and nested continua models to the charmingly cluttered clumps of the digital artifacts. In its visual presentation of patterns of interpretation derived from textual analysis – in addition to links to images clustered around key terms for each module – Nested Histories offers the possibility of responding to a challenge in DH scholarship: the encounter between textual studies and visual studies.[25] There is no question that interpretive engagement with images differs from that of texts, and the scope and volume of images available through digital sources marked a significant feature of the project. As Katherine Hayles has put it: "Visualisation helps sort the information and make patterns visible. Once the patterns can be discerned, the work of interpretation can begin."[26] The Nested Histories project shares Hayles' point, albeit with one key clarification: it is not that the interpretation has to wait for the pattern to emerge; rather, the pattern *is* the interpretation.

The fourth area of relevance between DH and Nested Histories is perhaps the most basic, which is simply that the project is a pedagogical one first and foremost. There is a bit of an ambiguity in the relationship between DH and pedagogy, which has been noted by commentators such as Brett D. Hirsch:

> Do we *teach* digital humanities? Do we *profess* it? Do we *profess* to teach it? Or, do we *teach* (courses like computer-assisted text analysis and others surveyed in this collection and beyond) so that we might *profess* (our scholarly understanding of the digital humanities as the intersection of humanities and computing)?[27]

For Nested Histories, the response to Hirsch's questions is clear: DH techniques and resources have been directed in the service of teaching, not of DH itself, but of early Christian history. Although other efforts have been made to integrate DH

---

25 Clivaz, "Digital Humanities," 6.
26 Katherine Hayles, "How We Think: Transforming Power and Digital Technology," in *Understanding Digital Humanities*, ed. David M. Berry (London: Palgrave MacMillan, 2012), 51.
27 Hirsch, "‹/Parentheses›," 17.

and early Christian pedagogy[28], this project is unique in its self-understanding as a pedagogical laboratory.

With respect to its subject matter, Nested Histories has two principal aims: (1) achieving a more seamless balance between the theological and historical aspects of the pedagogy concerning early Christianity, and (2) fostering an active, collaborative role for students concerning both research and pedagogy. As such, this is a project in integrative learning, helping students work across disciplines. For instance, what relationships link Origen's *On First Principles* with, say, Augustine's *Confessions?* Such questions can be difficult to unpack without an effective history/theology balance. Moreover, the problem is compounded by the current tendency to present history as settled fact rather than living arguments, which relegates students to passive observers and fails to engage them in historiography as it is professionally practiced. This is a problem that has been noted by other instructors of religion in the ancient Mediterranean world.[29]

Aside from a more general aim of helping students become active learners or engage information visually, there are two ways in which Nested Histories resonates uniquely with its subject. The first form of resonance is a common element of fluidity among the interpretations within the modules of the course and within the interpretations of the historical period itself. The second form of resonance concerns the ability of Nested Histories to encompass – indeed, to navigate between – close and distant readings of its subject.

Regarding the shape of history itself, the essential claim here is that the meaning of early Christian history is unfinished even as it remains grounded in real events. Now of course some relationships in a given historical moment inevitably emerge as more significant than others. The *labarum* on Constantine's soldiers' shields at the Battle of the Milvian Bridge was almost certainly more significant than the temperature of the water in the river at the battle, say. But a key point here is that the significance in such relationships is only to be discerned afterwards, that is, after the relationship has played itself out as effective across a sequence of subsequent events. As such, historical interpreters participate in the refinement of meaning through their creation of meaning in an ongoing process. The events of early Christian history are not merely fluid in their meanings in an isomorphic manner to the NCM; these events are also multi-causal. Hayles has noted the influence of technology on understanding multi-causal large-scale events. As she puts it:

---

[28] For example, see Meredith Warren, "Teaching with Technology: Using Digital Humanities to Engage Student Learning," *Teaching Theology & Religion* 19 (2016): 309–19.

[29] For example, see Michael Satlow, "Narratives or Sources? Active Learning and the Teaching of Ancient Jewish History and Texts," *Teaching Theology and Religion* 15 (2012): 48–60.

> That large-scale events are multi-causal is scarcely news, but analysis of them as such was simply not possible until machines were developed capable of creating models, simulations, and correlations that play out (or make visible) the complex interactions dynamically creating and re-creating systems. ... As Alan Liu (2008) aptly observes about digital technologies (but would be equally true of print), "These are not just tools but tools that we think through." The troops march together: tools with ideas, modeling assumptions with presuppositions about the nature of events, the meaning of "reading" with the place of the human.[30]

What Hayles is describing here is an apt characterization of nested continua historiographical theory. Each layer is not merely a framework of interpretation; it is also a potential cause within which the term in question can be understood. For example, within the circles of the NCM, the visual rendering of the reception of, say, "Hagia Irene" is helpful in that it allows one to trace divergent trajectories of historical interpretation and yet retain sight of the object that initiated the trajectories. Yet there is no reason to think that the object that was the Hagia Irene is thereby inaccessible or excluded from insight because of its transmission across these potentially innumerable intervening layers; rather, the rendering of these layers explicitly allows one to gain clearer sense of the frameworks through which the objects is being interpreted. As for the resonance between early Christian history and Nested Histories through close and distant readings, the following passage from Evans and Rees is instructive:

> Instead of simply losing ourselves through our imagination, the nature of digital technology is such that we are becoming integrated with the text itself; our brain is not simply picturing a new world, it is instead developing a new world, opening up new neural pathways in reaction to the speed and expanse of interaction with digital data... The new digital readers, with hyperlinks and notes, offer a new mediated experience of "reading." What then can we define as the text itself if each person's interaction with it is completely different, following alternative links and pathways?[31]

Evans and Rees here recognize the manner in which digital technology integrates reader and text – close reading – even as it stands between reader and text – distant reading. In the following passage, Hayles draws out the implications of distant reading in a way that resonates especially with Nested Histories. As Hayles puts it:

> Franco Moretti throws down the gauntlet when he proposes "distant reading" as a mode by which one might begin to speak of a history of world literature (2007: 56–58). Literary his-

---

30 Hayles, "How We Think," 48.
31 Evans and Rees, "Interpretation of Digital Humanities," 21.

tory, he suggests, will then become "a patchwork of other people's research, without a single direct textual reading" (2007: 57). He continues, "Distant reading: where distance, let me repeat it, is a condition of knowledge: it allows you to focus on units that are much smaller or much larger than the text: devices, themes, tropes – or genres and systems" (2007: 57). In this understanding of "reading", interpretation and theorising are still part of the picture, but they happen not through a direct encounter with a text but rather as a synthetic activity that takes as its raw material the "readings" of others.[32]

Hayles here provides both a valuable insight in research and also a necessary recognition of how reception histories unfold. Within Nested Histories, there is an element of close reading that contrasts with the aforementioned "distant reading," even as it exists within the same framework. This is the sense in which the transformation of coded number sets into nested continua models cuts out mediation. In doing so, it represents the reenactment through technology of "angelic" modes of communication. As Evans and Rees put it:

> The exploration of patterns using new graphic analysis methodologies...bypass the difficulties of word signification which plagued the ideal of this early notion of communication. Such new digital approaches address the problematic interpretative nature of language use, and bring us closer, perhaps, to Augustine's idea of divine communication which transcends the problems of translation: "Angels carry dispatches that are never lost or misdelivered or garbled in transit" (Durham Peters 1999: 75).[33]

Even as it distances the interpreter from its subject, Nested Histories brings the interpreter closer. In doing so, it reenacts forms of communication indigenous to the very cultures it seeks to investigate. It also represents the possibility of marrying distant and close readings, the necessity to DH of which has been recognized in order to avoid a "stalemate" with respect to the contemporary profusion of data.[34]

---

32 Hayles, "How We Think," 46, citing Franco Moretti, *Graphs, Maps, Trees: Abstract Models for a Literary History* (New York: Verso, 2007).
33 Evans and Rees, "Interpretation of Digital Humanities," 22; citing John Durham Peters, *Speaking into the Air: A History of the Idea of Communication* (Chicago: University of Chicago Press, 1999).
34 Jan Rybicki, "Advocatus Diaboli: Lost in Distant Reading?" Presentation at 2nd European Association of Digital Humanities Symposium, 7–8 March 2016, Leipzig, Germany, http://www.dhd2016.de/abstracts/EADH_01.html.

5 Conclusion

As implemented, Nested Histories has stimulated active learning and integrative thinking among its students. It has also illuminated – in a unique way – certain features of the subject it was designed to investigate. More narrowly, the application of Peircean logic and other disciplines is of interest to scholars of Peirce and pedagogy. Still, the project remains in need of improvement in various ways. Undergraduate students do not naturally cotton to such a radical departure from their expectations in a history class like this. This is especially the case when there is so much to learn about the technical workings of the model and, to a lesser extent, the mind maps. There is also a risk that the model is conflated with the subject; that is, the device one is learning *through* becomes mistaken for the thing one is learning *about*. Avoiding either a false heuristic/object binary or the collapse of a distinction between heuristic and object is paramount in importance. Moreover, in spite of the guidelines of the model, some students report a sense of spinning out of control without a tether in the face of the vast and unfiltered digital artifacts online. Yet since mitigating and responding to this sense is one of the great virtues of DH, with the proper reflection, Nested Histories offers promise for continued refinement.

6 Bibliography

Alexander, Christopher. *A Pattern Language*. Oxford: Oxford University Press, 1977.

Berry, David M. "Introduction: Understanding the Digital Humanities." In *Understanding Digital Humanities*, edited by David M. Berry, 1–20. London: Palgrave Macmillan, 2012.

Clivaz, Claire. "Digital Humanities in Ancient Jewish, Christian and Arabic Traditions: Introduction to the Special Issue." *Journal of Religion, Media and Digital Culture* 5 (2016): 1–20.

Daniel-Hughes, Brandon. *Pragmatic Inquiry and Religious Communities: Charles Peirce, Signs, and Inhabited Experiments*. London: Palgrave Macmillan, 2018.

Dexter, Scott. "The Esthetics of Hidden Things." In *Understanding Digital Humanities*, edited by David M. Berry, 127–44. London: Palgrave Macmillan, 2012.

Dixon, Dan. "Analysis Tool or Research Methodology: Is There an Epistemology for Patterns?" In *Understanding Digital Humanities*, edited by David M. Berry, 191–209. London: Palgrave Macmillan, 2012.

Evans, Leighton, and Sian Rees. "An Interpretation of Digital Humanities." In *Understanding Digital Humanities*, edited by David M. Berry, 21–41. London: Palgrave Macmillan, 2012.

Hayles, Katherine. "How We Think: Transforming Power and Digital Technology." In *Understanding Digital Humanities*, edited by David M. Berry, 42–66. London: Palgrave Macmillan, 2012.

Hirsch, Brett D. "‹/Parentheses›: Digital Humanities and the Place of Pedagogy." In *Digital Humanities Pedagogy: Practices, Principles and Politics*, edited by Brett D. Hirsch, 3–30. London: Open Book Publishers, 2012.
Hull, Kathleen. "Peircean Teaching." *Transactions of the Charles S. Peirce Society* 44 (2008): 204–208.
Hutchings, Tim. "Digital Humanities and the Study of Religion." In *Between Humanities and the Digital*, edited by Patrik Svensson and David Theo Goldberg, 283–94. London: MIT Press, 2015.
Liszka, James. "Charles Peirce's Rhetoric and the Pedagogy of Active Learning." *Educational Philosophy and Theory* 45 (2013): 781–88.
Michelson, David. "Syriaca.org as a Test Case for Digital Re-Sorting." In *Ancient Worlds in Digital Culture*, edited by Claire Clivaz, Paul Dilley, and David Hamidović, 59–85. Leiden: Brill, 2016.
Moretti, Franco. *Graphs, Maps, Trees: Abstract Models for a Literary History*. New York: Verso, 2007.
Peirce, Charles S. *Collected Papers of Charles Sanders Peirce, Volumes I and II: Principles of Philosophy and Elements of Logic*. Edited by Charles Hartshorne and Paul Weiss. Cambridge, MA: Harvard University Press, 1931.
Peters, John Durham. *Speaking into the Air: A History of the Idea of Communication*. Chicago: University of Chicago Press, 1999.
Rieder, Bernhard, and Theo Röhle. "Digital Methods: Five Challenges." In *Understanding Digital Humanities*, edited by David M. Berry, 67–84. London: Palgrave Macmillan, 2012.
Rybicki, Jan. "Advocatus Diaboli: Lost in Distant Reading?" Presentation at 2nd European Association of Digital Humanities Symposium, 7–8 March 2016, Leipzig, Germany. http://www.dhd2016.de/abstracts/EADH_01.html.
Satlow, Michael. "Narratives or Sources? Active Learning and the Teaching of Ancient Jewish History and Texts." *Teaching Theology and Religion* 15 (2012): 48–60.
Slater, Gary. *C.S. Peirce and the Nested Continua Model of Religious Interpretation*. Oxford: Oxford University Press, 2015.
Warren, Meredith. "Teaching with Technology: Using Digital Humanities to Engage Student Learning." *Teaching Theology & Religion* 19 (2016): 309–19.
Wittkower, Dylan E. "Mind-Mapping Inside and Outside of the Classroom." In *Learning Through Digital Media: Experiments in Technology and Pedagogy*, edited by R. Trebor Scholz, 221–29. New York: Institute for Distributed Creativity, 2011.

Alexander Chow
Public theology behind the Great Firewall of China

1 Introduction

Mainland China has one of the fastest growing populations of Christians in the world today. Government documents took note of this as early as the 1980s and 1990s, describing a "Christianity fever" (*jidujiao re*) throughout all sectors of the country.[1] While accurate and official numbers for religion in China are hard to come by, the best estimates confirm this growth – from 4 million Catholics, Protestants, and Orthodox in 1949 (0.7% of China's population of 550 million), to roughly 60 million Christians in 2011 (4.6% of China's population of 1.3 billion).[2] More recently, the sociologist Yang Fenggang told a reporter from the British *Daily Telegraph*, "By my calculations China is destined to become the largest Christian country in the world very soon." He furthermore projected that the total population of Christianity – Protestantism and Catholicism combined – would exceed 247 million by 2030.[3]

This phenomenal growth is often contrasted with a sober recognition of Chinese government suppression of Christianity. This view largely comes from the

---

[1] This chapter will romanize most Chinese characters using *hanyu pinyin*, the standard system used in scholarly work today, based on Mandarin oral pronunciation. While this general practice will also be used for personal names, for those better known in alternative romanizations, these will be offered in parentheses. For discussions on "Christianity fever," see Alan Hunter and Kim-Kwong Chan, *Protestantism in Contemporary China* (Cambridge: Cambridge University Press, 1993), 1–5, 66–71; Ying Fuk-tsang, "Mainland China," in *Christianities in Asia*, ed. Peter Phan (Malden, MA: Wiley-Blackwell, 2011): 162–66.

[2] In 2011, the Institute of World Religions of the Chinese Academy of Social Sciences estimated 58 million Christians, whereas Pew Forum on Religion and Public Life estimated 67 million Christians. See Shijie zongjiao yanjiu suo, Jidujiao diaoyan keti zu [Institute of World Religions, Christian Investigative Project Team], *Zhongguo Jidujiao diaoyan baogao ji* [Reports on Investigations Concerning Protestant Christianity in China] (Beijing: Chinese Academy of Social Sciences Publishers, 2011); Pew Forum on Religion and Public Life, "Appendix C: Methodology for China," in *Global Christianity: A Report on the Size and Distribution of the World's Christian Population* (Washington, DC: Pew Research Center, 2011), 97–110.

[3] Tom Phillips, "China on course to become 'world's most Christian nation' within 15 years," *Telegraph*, 19 April 2014, http://www.telegraph.co.uk/news/worldnews/asia/china/10776023/China-on-course-to-become-worlds-most-Christian-nation-within-15-years.html. Whether this forecast will come true, we will know better in 2030.

reality that, since establishing the People's Republic of China in 1949, the Chinese Communist Party (CCP) has historically not been sympathetic to Christianity, let alone religion in general.[4] Although the suppression of religion has varied in each period, the most extreme time was during the Cultural Revolution (1966–76) when the public practice of religion effectively came to an end. While this would change as in the beginning of the 1980s, the legal practice of religion required groups to register with state-sanctioned organizations such as the Protestant Three-Self Patriotic Movement (TSPM) or the Catholic Patriotic Association (CPA).[5] Those who choose not to register with these organizations have tended to be called "house churches" (*jiating jiaohui*) or "underground churches" (*dixia jiaohui*), for Protestant and Catholic congregations respectively. The suppression of Christianity from the 1980s until the early part of the 21st century has mainly tended to affect these unregistered communities, though this seems to have begun to change since Xi Jinping became president in 2012. From 2014–16, government suppression was vividly seen in the skyline of the southeastern province of Zhejiang, wherein hundreds of registered and unregistered Protestant and Catholic churches have either had their crosses lopped off or their entire buildings razed.[6]

Against this paradoxical backdrop, this chapter offers the case study of the growth of Christian public theology[7] behind the so-called Great Firewall of

---

[4] Part of this is guided by the pessimistic view of religion as held by Marx and Lenin. The Chinese religious policy has also been guided by the so-called five characteristics of religion – that religion is complex, mass-based, long-lasting, and national–ethnic, and has international implications. Philip L. Wickeri, *Seeking the Common Ground: Protestant Christianity, the Three-Self Movement, and China's United Front* (Maryknoll, NY: Orbis Books, 1988), 75–109.

[5] Protestantism and Catholicism are treated as two separate religions in China, alongside three other religions with legal existence: Daoism, Buddhism, and Islam.

[6] According to some estimates, 1,500 to 1,800 churches have been affected by these actions. See Ying Fuk-tsang (Xing Fuzang), "Chai shizijia de zhengzhi: Zhejiang sheng 'Sangai yichai' yundong de zongjiao-zhengzhi fenxi" [The Politics of Cross Demolition: A Religio-Political Analysis of the "Three Transformations and One Demolition" Campaign in Zhejiang Province], *Logos and Pneuma*, no. 44 (January 2016): 25–61; Cao Nanlai, "Spatial Modernity, Party Building, and Local Governance: Putting the Christian Cross-Removal Campaign in Context," *The China Review* 17, no. 1 (February 2017): 29–52; Mark McLeister, "Chinese Protestant Reactions to the Zhejiang 'Three Rectifications, One Demolition' Campaign," *Review of Religion and Chinese Society* 5, no. 1 (2018): 76–100.

[7] The term "public theology" was coined by Martin Marty as a way to discuss the way Christian thinkers and communities sought to engage matters of significance to broader societies and nations. Martin E. Marty, "Reinhold Niebuhr: Public Theology and the American Experience," *The Journal of Religion* 54, no. 4 (1974): 332–59. For a good introduction to the subject, see Sebastian C. H. Kim, *Theology in the Public Sphere: Public Theology as a Catalyst for Open Debate* (London:

China,[8] one of the most restrictive Internet censorship systems in the world. The focus will be on two of the most well-known urban Protestant "house churches" – both of which have sought to engage the state and the society through public theological discourse using blogs, microblogs, and online magazines. The leaders of these churches have used these technologies to engage topics such as human rights, constitutionalism, and the civil society, and have risked arrest with their online profiles blocked or deleted by government censors. Mindful of this, this chapter argues that digital media offers unique opportunities and challenges to Chinese public theology.

2 Print culture and Chinese public discourse

Before discussing the nature of China's growing digital culture, we must first recognize the importance of print culture in China.[9] As Christopher Reed explains:

> China is now generally acknowledged to have led the world in the development of paper and printing technology through the end of the early modern period. Prior to the nineteenth century, more books were likely written and published in Chinese than in any other single published language.[10]

The significance of China's print culture – beginning with the early development of woodblock printing in the Tang dynasty (618–907) – should not be underestimated. Eight centuries later, Johannes Gutenberg revolutionized European print

---

SCM Press, 2011). For a broader discussion on Chinese public theology, see Alexander Chow, *Chinese Public Theology: Generational Shifts and Confucian Imagination in Chinese Christianity* (Oxford: Oxford University Press, 2018).

8 This term was coined in Geremie R. Barme and Sang Ye, "The Great Firewall of China," *Wired*, 1 June 1997, https://www.wired.com/1997/06/china-3/.

 Given that Hong Kong is a Special Autonomous Region of the People's Republic of China, it is presently outside the reach of the Great Firewall. While it is worthwhile to consider how digital public theology occurs within Hong Kong, especially mindful of the Umbrella movement (2014) or the protests initiated in 2019 related to the extradition bill, this is outside the scope of this chapter.

9 "Print culture" refers to the cultural, social, and political implications of print technology. For a discussion of this term compared with "print commerce" and "print capitalism," see Christopher A. Reed, *Gutenberg in Shanghai: Chinese Print Capitalism, 1876–1937* (Vancouver: UBC Press, 2011), 4–12.

10 Christopher A. Reed, "Introduction," in *From Woodblocks to the Internet: Chinese Publishing and Print Culture in Transition, circa 1800 to 2008*, ed. Cynthia Brokaw and Christopher A. Reed (Leiden: Brill, 2010), 4–5.

culture through mechanized movable-type printing. For both Europe and China, the rise of print culture was largely tied to the dominant ideology of the day. While for Gutenberg, this would include the printing of the Christian Bible, within China, a dominant form of publishing related to printing the Confucian classics. In the case of the latter, Confucianism had been considered state orthodoxy from the Han dynasty (206 BC–220 AD) until the end of the Qing dynasty (1636– 1912). The print culture around the Confucian classics was core to building and sustaining the curriculum of the imperial civil service examination system.

Protestant missionaries, arriving to the Chinese mainland in 1807, imported Western print technologies in order to produce materials related to the propagation of the faith, such as Christian Bibles and evangelistic tracts. By the late-19th century, local Chinese would likewise enthusiastically embrace these Western technologies as part of Chinese print capitalism, producing local newspapers, textbooks, and novels.[11] This was accelerated in the 1920s as a result of the New Culture movement (*xin wenhua yundong*) and the May Fourth movement (*wusi yundong*), in which reformers critiqued Confucian teachings as ideological fetters upon the Chinese mind and clamored for new ideas to seek the "national salvation" (*jiuguo*) of China through modernization.[12] Underpinning this was a literary movement that emphasized the writing of more popular literature and advocating for a written form of vernacular Chinese (*baihua*), as opposed to the conventional emphasis on classical Chinese (*wenyan wen*).[13] Reformers instrumentalized print culture to spread new ideas to the broader Chinese public space.[14] One of the most significant periodicals of this period was *Xin Qingnian*

---

11 Reed, *Gutenberg in Shanghai*.
12 The New Culture and May Fourth movements are quite connected and often blur together. The first often finds its starting point in 1915, whereas the latter was inaugurated by protests in China on 4 May 1919 ahead of the signing of the Treaty of Versailles in Paris that same year. See Tse-Tsung Chow, *The May 4th Movement: Intellectual Revolution in Modern China* (Cambridge, MA: Harvard University Press, 1960); Vera Schwarcz, *The Chinese Enlightenment: Intellectuals and the Legacy of the May Fourth Movement of 1919* (Berkeley: University of California Press, 1986).
13 Due to these literary developments, scholars such as Hu Shi would describe this as a "literature revolution" and a "Chinese Renaissance." Hu Shih, *The Chinese Renaissance: The Haskell Lectures, 1933* (Chicago: University of Chicago Press, 1934). See also Leo Ou-Fan Lee, "Literary Trends I: The Quest for Modernity, 1895–1927," in *The Cambridge History of China, Vol. 12: Republican China 1912–1949, Pt. 1*, ed. John K. Fairbank (Cambridge: Cambridge University Press, 1983): 451–504.
14 Timothy Cheek, *The Intellectual in Modern Chinese History* (Cambridge: Cambridge University Press, 2015), 35–39. I use the term "public space" to denote the fluid arena between the state and the family in which intellectuals and others attempt to engage. This has rough parallels with Jürgen Habermas' "public sphere" and Richard John Neuhaus' "public square." My choice

(also known in French as *La Jeunesse* or in English as *New Youth*). From its first issue in 1915, *Xin Qingnian* attacked Confucian teachings and promoted Western ideas such as science, democracy, and modern literature, all using written vernacular Chinese. Its editor was the public intellectual Chen Duxiu (1879–1942) who, for a time, worked as lecturer in Chinese Literature and dean of the famous Peking University. Significantly, Chen used *Xin Qingnian* to promote Marxism from 1919 until it was shut down in 1926 by the Nationalist Party of China, the Kuomingtang (KMT; also known as the Guomingdang).[15]

Chinese Christian public intellectuals during this period would likewise capitalize on this print culture to produce Christian books and periodicals. For them, Christianity was wrongly lumped together with Confucianism as feudalistic and unscientific, and therefore seen as counterproductive for the progress of China's modernization. Christian literature would serve an apologetic function, presenting Christian theology in ways which engaged in politics and various social issues. Some of the most significant Protestant intellectuals formed a group in the elite Yenching University known as Life Fellowship, included figures such as Wu Leichuan (1870–1944), Liu Tingfang (Timothy T. Lew, 1892–1947), and Zhao Zichen (T. C. Chao, 1888–1979). Like Chen Duxiu, these were public intellectuals, and they produced periodicals such as *Zhenli yu Shengming* (*Truth and Life*) to engage the broader Christian and non-Christian public using written vernacular Chinese from 1919 until 1937.[16] Theologically, they were informed by the American social gospel and argued for Christianity's role in China's progress and national salvation.

---

in using "public space" is an attempt to counter the contextual issues related to the rise of these alternative terms in German and American discourse. See Chow, *Chinese Public Theology*, 4–7.
15 *New Youth*'s emphasis on Marxism began with the May 1919 issue, which was dedicated to the subject of Karl Marx himself. Wen-hsin Yeh, *Provincial Passages: Culture, Space, and the Origins of Chinese Communism* (Berkeley: University of California Press, 1996), 205–6. In 1921, Chen Duxiu became one of the cofounders of the Communist Party of China, serving as its first general secretary until 1927.
16 Liu Tingfang and the Life Fellowship launched a journal in 1919 known as *Shengming yuekan* (*Life Monthly*), which included Chinese and Western authors. After 1922, Wu Leichuan became critical of the foreignness of Christianity and withdrew from the Life Fellowship. He established his own periodical in 1923, *Zhenli zhuokan* (*Truth Weekly*), which included only Chinese authors. By 1926, the two periodicals merged into one and was renamed *Zhenli yu Shengming* (*Truth and Life*). Samuel D. Ling, "The Other May Fourth Movement: The Chinese 'Christian Renaissance,' 1919–1937" (PhD diss., Temple University, 1980), 62–65, 71; John Barwick, "Liu Tingfang: Christian Minister and Activist Intellectual," in *Salt and Light 3: More Lives of Faith That Shaped Modern China*, ed. Carol Lee Hamrin with Stacey Bieler (Eugene, OR: Pickwick Publishers, 2011): 69–70.

For Catholicism, the periodical *Shengjiao zazhi* (*Revue Catholique* or *Catholic Review*) established in 1911 would likewise be an important periodical of this time. *Shengjiao zazhi* published articles which emphasized the neo-scholastic theology officially favored in the Catholic Church before Vatican II. Like *Zhenli yu Shengming*, *Shengjiao zazhi* also had apologetic importance. The Jesuit Xu Zongze (P. Joseph Zi, 1886–1947), its editor for many years, complemented these articles with his own articles which built upon papal encyclicals and offered a Chinese Catholic response to the pressing social issues of the time, engaging a range of social topics including education, politics, women's issues, and the Sino-Japanese War.[17] Both the Republic of China under the KMT and the People's Republic of China under the CCP leveraged print culture to expand their official propaganda. Timothy Cheek explains:

> China's propaganda state used the propaganda system as this "directed public sphere" in which the Party directly managed the public arena and controlled public associations of "civil society."... The propaganda system in China under the CCP came to include the arts and universities, as well as the media. Writers, professors, researchers, as well as journalists – indeed, all *professions* – were incorporated into the propaganda and education system under the direct management of the Propaganda Department of the CCP. In Mao's China there was no other public space for intellectuals.[18]

Indeed, religion was also included in this "directed" public space. In the 1950s, Protestants needed to show their allegiance to the CCP and ally themselves through the TSPM.[19] Like the shift in the print culture of the time towards a kind of "print communism,"[20] the TSPM produced its own periodical *Tian Feng* (*Heavenly Wind*) to promote views which supported the CCP. However, such efforts appeared for a time to be in vain. By the start of the Cultural Revolution in 1966, all public religious activity was closed.

---

17 Chloë F. Starr, *Chinese Theology: Text and Context* (New Haven, CT: Yale University Press, 2016), 100–27; Lai Pan-chiu and Li Lili, "Chinese Catholic Responses to Sino-Japanese War: A Study of Xu Zongze's Public Theology of War and Peace," in *Yearbook of Chinese Theology, 2017*, ed. Paulos Z. Huang (Leiden: Brill, 2017): 166–86.
18 Cheek, *The Intellectual in Modern Chinese History*, 129.
19 The TSPM officially held its first National Christian Council in 1954. Many of the key figures in this movement signed the so-called Christian Manifesto (*sanzi xuanyan*), penned in 1950 in collaboration with Zhou Enlai.
20 See Christopher Reed, "Advancing the (Gutenberg) Revolution: The Origins and Development of Chinese Print Communism, 1921–1947," in *From Woodblocks to the Internet: Chinese Publishing and Print Culture in Transition, circa 1800 to 2008*, ed. Cynthia Brokaw and Christopher A. Reed (Leiden: Brill, 2010): 275–311; Cheek, *The Intellectual in Modern Chinese History*, 126–9.

After Mao Zedong's death and Deng Xiaoping's rise to power, the late-1970s and 1980s began to experience an openness to new ideas once again. As mentioned in the outset of this chapter, this period would experience a Christianity fever. Yet many government documents, drawing from Marxist assumptions of religious belief, rationalized that this phenomenal growth was mainly among the so-called four manys (*si duo*; many old, many women, many illiterate, and many ill) – that is, "rice Christians" coming from the margins of society.[21] However, what we see in the late-1980s and 1990s is a growing number of "cultural Christians" (*wenhua jidutu*) – intellectuals interested in Christianity's possibilities in transforming China's future but not very interested in participating in any local Christian community.[22] Figures such as Liu Xiaofeng (b. 1956) and He Guanghu (b. 1950) promoted their ideas about Christianity through periodicals such as *Dushu* (*Reading*) and *Jidujiao wenhua pinglun* (*Christian Culture Review*). While the latter had an explicitly Christian focus, the former periodical was and still is one of the leading periodicals for China's elite intellectuals. Like Christian intellectuals of the May Fourth period, these cultural Christians would once again harness the power of print culture to engage the Chinese public space.

3 The advent of the Chinese internet

The discussion so far has emphasized the print culture of China. This is quite important for understanding the role of text in contemporary Chinese public theology – or Chinese public intellectualism, more generally. The Gutenberg revolution and the publication of the Bible facilitated the Protestant Reformation and its emphasis on the written Word of God. Likewise, Chinese print culture is tied to the printing of and education in the Confucian classics. But the intellectual history of China has emphasized learning not for the sake of knowledge itself, but to transform society.

The contemporary Confucian scholar Tu Weiming makes this point when he explains that early antecedents of "public intellectualism" cannot be found in Hindu, Buddhist, Jewish, Greek, Christian, or Islamic traditions – all of which

---

21 See Ryan Dunch, "Chinese Christianity," in *The Wiley-Blackwell Companion to Chinese Religions*, ed. Randall L. Nadeau (Malden, MA: Blackwell, 2012), 272–4.
22 The Sinophone usage of the term "cultural Christian" is quite different from its usage in English. In China, it refers to those who have no background in Christianity but are drawn to Christian culture, seeing its value in the advancement of Chinese society and culture. See Fredrik Fällman, *Salvation and Modernity: Intellectuals and Faith in Contemporary China*, rev. ed. (Lanham, MD: University Press of America, 2008); Chow, *Chinese Public Theology*, 70–91.

have emphasized a soteriological aspiration in a spiritual realm separate from the mundane world. According to Tu,

> The minimum requirement for an intellectual – politically concerned, socially engaged, and culturally sensitive – is fundamentally at odds with a person passionately devoted to the service of a higher reality beyond the mundane concerns of the secular world.... In all of the aforementioned religions the rupture of the chain of being by privileging the "Pure Land" or the "Kingdom of God" outside of the daily routine of human existence is undeniable....
>
> By making the existential decision to be an integral part of the world in order to transform it from within, Confucius opted for a form of life unique among the axial-age civilizations. Confucian followers were primarily action intellectuals, deeply immersed in "managing the world" (*jingshi*) of economics, politics, and society. [23]

The Confucian scholar–official was educated in the Confucian classics in order to effect change in the management of the world. Print was understood as the medium for communicating change in the society, opening the space for public discourse. This would be the accepted norm of Chinese public intellectuals. The question then arises about what happens with the advent of digital media – how does digital culture change the approach of public engagement?

Within China, as well as elsewhere in the world, the 1990s would see the growing use of the Internet spreading throughout the country. With over 700 million Internet users in the country in 2017 (more than half of the Chinese population) and about 95% accessing it through mobile phones, China is one of the most important countries for Internet usage in the world. However, it also has one of the most restrictive approaches to the technology as well. The "Great Firewall of China" notoriously blocks many Western news outlets and social media sites, such as Facebook and Twitter, and the Chinese government has underwritten the production of Chinese alternatives. Many netizens in China who wish to *fanqiang* – literally, to climb over the wall – turn to VPN technologies, but these are often blocked as well. Furthermore, within the bounds of the firewall, Chinese censors are known to filter unwelcome content as it arises and evolves. For instance, in spring 2018 when the Xi Jinping administration discussed repealing the limits on presidential terms, the popular Chinese microblog Weibo witnessed a surge of discussion around Xi Jinping as an emperor. Yet as

---

[23] Tu Weiming, "Intellectuals in a World Made of Knowledge," *The Canadian Journal of Sociology* 30, no. 2 (Spring 2005), 219–20.

soon as Chinese censors noticed these terms, the content was swiftly blocked.[24] For Chinese Internet users and content producers, this results in a constant cat-and-mouse chase where netizens use Chinese homophones[25] or other memes to convey their ideas before they get blocked and users are forced to create new ones.

4 Mixing print and digital cultures

In terms of Chinese public theology, today's public intellectuals likewise underscore the role of texts but now seek means of digital communication within a strongly controlled and directed virtual space for public discourse. Perhaps the most prominent approach has been to simply translate the print culture into digital culture through the hybrid production of periodicals which are both printed and distributed online. Online magazines are an easy means of disseminating ideas which were once limited by the traditional postal system. Being digital, their content can also be easily copy-and-pasted and, therefore, redistributed in multiple digital platforms – PDF, forums, blogs, microblogs, and instant messaging. Contrastingly, digital publication is also limited in that it can be quickly detected by automated systems and blocked or taken down. Hence, a number of groups have employed a hybrid approach, combing various print and digital formats.

One of the most prominent examples of a hybrid periodical can be found in *Xinhua (Almond Flowers)*, produced by Shouwang Church (Shouwang jiaohui) in Beijing.[26] Shouwang is one of the largest unregistered Protestant churches, boasting approximately 1,000 parishioners before it was clamped down by the government in 2011. The foreword to the first issue of *Xinhua* in 2007 set the stage for the church and the periodical based on Jeremiah 1:11–12.[27] In this passage, the prophet Jeremiah sees the vision of an almond tree branch, but God

---

24 Josh Rudolph, "Sensitive Words: Xi to Ascend His Throne (Updated)," *China Digital Times*, 26 February 2018, https://chinadigitaltimes.net/2018/02/sensitive-words-emperor-xi-jinping-ascend-throne/.
25 Different words in Chinese often have the same sound but different meanings. As is found in the Hebrew or Greek Bibles, homophones in Chinese have been used to play with sounds to offer multiple meanings.
26 The articles of the periodical can still be found in PDF and blog formats on the church's website, https://www.shwchurch.org. At the time of this chapter's writing, the website is still available.
27 Editors, "Juan shou yu" [Foreword], *Xinhua* (2007): 1–2.

responds through a Hebrew pun that this is a message about needing to pay attention. The editors explain that the periodical is therefore a metaphor for the church, with a name "Shouwang" that conveys a meaning of keeping watch for the works of God.

The foreword continues to outline *Xinhua*'s three main purposes: (1) to construct and propagate a biblically based theology for the church, (2) to be a witness of truth for the encouragement of Christian brothers and sisters to grow, and (3) to offer a cultural perspective to the broader Chinese society. Of these three purposes, the second is perhaps most consistent with what one may find in any Christian periodical, in China or elsewhere: to encourage fellow Christians. But when seen from the vantage point of the other two purposes, there appears to be a greater meaning. The senior pastor of the church, Jin Tianming (b. 1968), studied chemical engineering at Tsinghua University in Beijing, one of the top universities in China, from 1986–91. Many of the elders and parishioners of Shouwang likewise are students, graduates, and professors of some of the leading universities of Beijing. Like earlier print periodicals such as *Zhenli yu shengming*, *Shengjiao zazhi*, or *Jidujiao wenhua pinglun*, *Xinhua* was meant to be a periodical for Christian intellectuals to propagate Christian ideas to the broader public space. However, unlike the earlier generation of "cultural Christians," this generation of Christian intellectuals see much more value in the role of the local Christian community. Shouwang would be prototypical of other urban churches that wished to develop a theology for building the institution of the church that would be a vehicle of witness to the broader Chinese society.[28]

The second year of *Xinhua*'s production in 2008 would be quite key for Shouwang's vision. The Spring and Summer 2008 issues of *Xinhua* focused on themes related to the theological rationale behind churches registering with the state and God's purposes for Christian marriage – two matters commonly debated among China's urban churches. The next two issues were themed around topics related to social care (*shehui guanhuai*) and the Dutch Neo-Calvinist notion of the cultural mandate (*wenhua sheming*). May 2008 was in many ways a *kairos* moment, a divine opportunity, for many urban churches, when the great Wenchuan earthquake hit Sichuan province with a magnitude of 8.0 and aftershocks of 6.0, killing over 69,000 and leaving 4.8 million homeless. The last two issues of *Xinhua* in 2008 reflect a conscious decision by its editors to use the Wenchuan earthquake as a way to underscore the role and the responsibility of the church for the broader society.

---

28 See Chow, *Chinese Public Theology*, 105–11; Carsten T. Vala, *The Politics of Protestant Churches and the Party-State in China: God Above Party?* (New York: Routledge, 2018), 171–97.

This change in 2008 was an important shift, given the history of Protestantism in China. For most of the twentieth century, the vast majority of Chinese Protestants – especially later in unregistered churches – had tended to emphasize a more conservative form of Christianity, largely shaped by American fundamentalism. Contrastingly, the Life Fellowship of the 1920s and 1930s and the TSPM beginning in the 1950s are often described as embracing more progressive theologies.[29] Generally speaking, conservative Chinese Protestants have tended to withdraw from the world and see any engagement with the society or the state as being an expression of theological liberalism. But this would change for a number of urban churches, especially after 2008. Increasingly, conservative Christians realized the church could not simply uphold a separatist approach with the world, but needed to actively respond to the concerns of its day in hopes to transform it.

For Shouwang, part of this required them to create a physical and public presence.[30] Since the early 1990s, the church existed primarily as a network of smaller groups of 30 to 50 members each. Desiring to meet as a single congregation, they raised funds and purchased office space for holding church meetings, but the property manager refused to give them the keys to the premises due to pressure from government officials. In response, Shouwang leaders chose to initiate public worship services outdoors in 2011. However, the pastors and elders of Shouwang were put on house arrest and would-be parishioners who gathered for outdoor services were likewise rounded up by the police. For a number of subsequent Sundays, parishioners still gathered for outdoor church services while being fully aware that they would be arrested.

Sun Yi (b. 1961), one of the elders of Shouwang and an associate professor in philosophy at Renmin University of China, explained in an article in *Xinhua* the next year that churches need to pursue a goal of "openness and integrity" (*gongkai zhengti xing*), seeking legal existence, in order to act as a non-governmental organization (NGO) and work towards building a civil society.[31] This was a remarkable statement to make, given that it was published the year following a government clampdown on Shouwang which put Jin Tianming, Sun Yi, and other leaders of the church under house arrest.

---

[29] For the latter, this view is more of a characterization than a statement of truth. Many of the TSPM leadership and most of its congregation's members would self-describe as evangelicals.
[30] Carsten Vala explains these developments as an approach to institutionalization which underscored the public vision of the church. Vala, *Politics of Protestant Churches*, 173–6.
[31] Sun Yi, "Jidujiao jiuguo qingjie dui jiaohui guan de yingxiang" [The Influence of Christian National Salvation Complex upon Ecclesiology], *Xinghua* (Winter 2012): 37–40.

This also suggests a different understanding of the church. Jin Tianming explains that there has historically been an impasse in China between a clandestine and illegal existence through the house church movement and an open position through the "adulterous" TSPM.[32] Instead, a number of Christian intellectuals argue there needs to be a "third way" (*disan daolu*) or a "third church" (*disan jiaohui*) – a new ecclesiology, if you will, which is open yet maintains Christ at its head. In effect, the church has become a public body which collectively engages the state and the society.[33]

The editors of *Xinhua* continued to produce the periodical for a few years after these events, eventually ending after three final issues in 2013. PDF copies and blog posting versions of *Xinhua* are still available on its website shwchurch.org, which is hosted outside of China and often requires VPN to access. Despite the setbacks from government pressure, the church began to upload onto its website PDFs of a new online-only periodical, first named *@Shouwang* before being renamed *Shouwang wangluo qikan* (*Shouwang Online Journal*). In the first issue of the new periodical in 2011, Jin Tianming begins with an article entitled "Now if we died with Christ, we believe that we will also live with him," based on Romans 6:8.[34] While Jin Tianming himself was on house arrest, the article offered his views about why church members should continue to gather for outdoor meetings in spite of government opposition. Along with this new periodical, since 2012, Shouwang has also been uploading audio recordings of sermons – preached by various individuals without a physical congregation – and selections of hymns every week. In essence, the public nature of Shouwang Church has gone entirely online.

5 Public discourse on blogs and microblogs

Another important figure in contemporary Chinese public theology is Wang Yi (b. 1973) in Chengdu, founder and senior pastor of the Early Rain Reformed Church (Qiuyu zhi fu guizheng jiaohui), later renamed Early Rain Covenant Church (Qiuyu shengyue jiaohui). From 1996 to 2008, Wang Yi was a law professor at Chengdu University. He was also known as an outspoken advocate of political liberalism and a lawyer engaged in the so-called rights defense movement (*weiquan yundong*). In 2004, he was invited by his friend Yu Jie (b. 1973) to de-

---

32 Jin Tianming, "Tuidong jiaohui dengji dao jintian" [The Promotion of Church Registration], *Xinghua* (Spring 2008): 40–1.
33 See Chow, *Chinese Public Theology*, 146–59.
34 Jin Tianming, "Women ruoshi yu Jidu tong si, jiu xin bi yu ta tong huo" [Now if we died with Christ, we believe that we will also live with him], *@Shouwang* no. 1 (2011): 4–10.

fend the religious freedom of house churches through the Chinese Christian Rights Lawyers Group. The next year, he converted to Christianity and started Early Rain as a fellowship in his home, eventually resigning from the University to take up full-time pastoral work.

Beginning in 2006, Yu Jie and Wang Yi produced a print-only periodical known as *Fangzhou* (*Ark*), later renamed *Ganlanzhi* (*Olive Branch*). At the time, Yu Jie was an elder of Ark Church (Fangzhou jiaohui) in Beijing, another important unregistered urban church.[35] Ark Church and its periodical *Fangzhou* saw part of its purpose as establishing a Chinese Geneva, whereby Christians can Christianize Chinese society and culture. The church attracted a number of well-known human rights activists, as well as poets, literary critics, and other artists.[36] *Fangzhou* also became a platform for public discourse between Christians and non-Christians, including writings by Liu Xiaobo (1955–2017), who was later arrested in 2009 and awarded the Nobel Peace Prize in 2010.

While both Shouwang Church and Ark Church in Beijing were forcefully closed down by government authorities, Wang Yi's Early Rain Church was allowed for many years to continue meeting. It was only in December 2018 when the church was finally closed down by authorities, with Wang Yi and his wife Jiang Rong arrested.[37] While there are regional variations in how local government authorities treat religious groups, it is unclear why Early Rain had such liberties for so long. Nevertheless, until his arrest, Wang Yi continued to be quite vocal through his weekly pastoral letters to Early Rain, as well as through various blog and microblog platforms, engaging a range of topics related to theology, law, and politics.

His Weibo account had over 11,000 followers and has been blocked or temporarily shut down multiple times – including after his arrest in December 2018.[38] In a series of posts and responses to interlocutors in April 2013, Wang Yi debated differences between nationalism (*minzu zhuyi*) and patriotism

---

35 Since 2012, Yu Jie has been living in exile in the United States. See Gerda Wielander, *Christian Values in Communist China* (New York: Routledge, 2013), 118.
36 Fredrik Fällman, "Calvin, Culture and Christ? Developments of Faith Among Chinese Intellectuals," in *Christianity in Contemporary China: Socio-cultural Perspectives*, ed. Francis Khek Gee Lim (New York: Routledge, 2013): 160–2.
37 Given the very current nature of these events, some of the observations in this chapter may have to be taken as preliminary. See Ian Johnson, "Pastor Charged with 'Inciting Subversion' as China Cracks Down on Churches," *New York Times*, 13 December 2018, https://www.nytimes.com/2018/12/13/world/asia/china-religion-crackdown.html.
38 As of the writing of this chapter, information about the church can still be found outside of China, hosted on their Facebook page: https://www.facebook.com/earlyraincovenantchurch.

(*aiguo zhuyi*). While these terms are fairly related in English, both were invented within Chinese political discourse in the last century. Philip Wickeri explains, "More than the love of an old civilization, more than simple nationalism, patriotism meant the love for New China [after 1949], and with it, loyalty to the People's Government under the leadership of the [Chinese Communist Party].'[39] This is why the Three-Self Patriotic Movement (est. 1954) and the Catholic Patriotic Association (est. 1957) have in their names the word "patriotic' – literally in Chinese, "love of country." But for Wang Yi, true Christian patriotism can be found in house churches which love their neighbors and seek the welfare of the city (Jeremiah 29:7). Nationalism, in contrast, is a war of aggression that is keen to destroy its enemies. For Wang Yi, the government-sanctioned TSPM rallies behind nationalism – not patriotism, as its name may indicate. As such, the TSPM upholds a form of totalitarianism and is unwilling to underscore the transcendence of the Christian faith.[40]

In another example, Wang Yi posted online in August 2015 his version of Martin Luther's 95 theses entitled, "Reaffirming our Stance on the House Churches."[41] Clearly, he was drawing on particular imaginary of the Reformation in his public engagement.[42] However, instead of simply commemorating Luther's 1517 disputation posted in Wittenberg, the 95th of the Chinese theses explains that his document was penned for the sixtieth anniversary of the arrest of Wang Mingdao (1900–1991) in August 1955. Often described as the "dean of the house churches," Wang Mingdao was a fundamentalist pastor who was imprisoned for refusing to join the TSPM after it was initiated. Early Rain took this opportunity to reaffirm the sovereignty and headship of Christ over the church, attacking

---

39 Wickeri, *Seeking the Common Ground*, 94. See Lydia H. Liu, *Translingual Practice: Literature, National Culture, and Translated Modernity – China, 1900–1937* (Stanford: Stanford University Press, 1995), 189.
40 Carsten T. Vala and Huang Jianbo, "Three High-Profile Protestant Microbloggers in Contemporary China: Expanding Public Discourse or Burrowing into Religious Niches on Weibo?" in *Religion and Media in China: Insights and Case Studies from the Mainland, Taiwan and Hong Kong*, ed. Stefania Travagnin (New York: Routledge, 2017): 176–81. For a discussion about the Chinese Christian discourse around transcendence or transcendental values, see Wielander, *Christian Values in Communist China*, 130–50; Chow, *Chinese Public Theology*, 131–45.
41 The original Chinese has been posted on a number of sites, though also deleted. As of this writing, it is still available on Early Rain's Weixin page (https://mp.weixin.qq.com/s/DvI QU6xSjldN5sNTEZnb9 A) and is archived at https://perma.cc/VZF9-JYQM. It has also been translated into English by China Partnership at http://www.chinapartnership.org/blog/2015/08/95-theses-the-reaffirmation-of-our-stance-on-the-house-church.
42 See Chloë F. Starr, "Wang Yi and the 95 Theses of the Chinese Reformed Church," *Religions* 7 (2016/12): 1–15.

attempts to submit the church to the state (as has been done with the TSPM), and asserting the two kingdoms theology of Luther and Augustine. It concludes:

> Up until this day, the Church of our Lord Jesus Christ in China has been under continuous political persecution for sixty years. Because of this, our church decided to publish these ninety-five theses, for the purpose of reaffirming the Chinese House Church's position on our faith, and before the government and society at large, with a fearful but humble heart, defend the Church.[43]

Signed by Early Rain's pastors and elders, the document testifies to a view that this church continues the legacy of older house churches. While churches like Shouwang consider themselves as part of the "third church," Wang Yi and Liu Tongsu, a Chinese American pastor in Northern California, have argued that such terminology misrepresents the situation of Chinese Christianity and breaks the continuity that exists between traditional house churches and the growth in urban Christianity outside of the TSPM.[44] In many ways, this is consistent with Wang Yi's other writings which compares Jin Tianming with Wang Mingdao – both of whom he sees as correctly opposing the state-sanctioned TSPM.[45]

6 Conclusion

At the time of this writing, new issues of Shouwang's online-only periodical *Shouwang wangluo qikan* and audio recordings of sermons and hymns continue to be uploaded to the church's website. Due to years of government pressure, Shouwang Church is only able to meet virtually, if that. It is hard to know how many of Shouwang's former church members check the website on a weekly basis to read the online periodical or listens to sermons and sings along to hymns. But this shift to an entirely online existence also opens more of its content to the public space than ever before. While Wang Yi and Early Rain Church have had more freedom, they have ceased to meet as of December 2018. Up until that date, Wang Yi had been quite vocal on various blogging and microblogging technologies, both in producing and debating his ideas. Expecting these liberties

---

[43] Early Rain Reformed Church, "95 Theses: The Reaffirmation of our Stance on the House Church," 18 August 2015, trans. China Partnership, http://www.chinapartnership.org/blog/2015/08/95-theses-the-reaffirmation-of-our-stance-on-the-house-church.
[44] Liu Tongsu and Wang Yi, *Guankan Zhongguo chengshi jiating jiaohui* [Observation on China's House Churches in Cities] (Taipei: Christian Arts Press, 2012), 45.
[45] Wang Yi, "Jin Tianming shi ni shenme ren?" [Who is Jin Tianming to You?], *Meizhou mu han* [Weekly Pastoral Letter], 3 February 2013.

would soon come to an end, Wang penned a public letter which was circulated 48 hours after his arrest.[46] Members of the church continue to use online platforms such as Facebook and Github, both hosted outside of China, to share updates about the church and its members.[47] While Facebook is readily blocked in China, the government has been reluctant to block Github due to its importance for the country's tech industry. Ironically, some in China use this source code management website as a vehicle for free speech.[48]

For several millennia, Chinese intellectuals primarily leveraged Chinese print culture to engage the public space. With the advent of the Internet, new digital technologies now offer a new space for public discourse of these Christian intellectuals, akin to the coffee houses, salons, and table societies discussed by Jürgen Habermas.[49] But, as explained earlier in this chapter, the print and digital media are both *directed* public spaces, given the censorship of print materials and the restrictions of the Great Firewall of China. Interestingly, while Shouwang has shifted from a hybrid approach of print and digital periodicals to a fully online church, Wang Yi has also adopted a hybrid approach whereby he has collected a number of his online essays and published them through a press based in Taiwan which is outside the reach of communist censors. It seems as though these church leaders see digital technologies as essential for their public engagement, but print technologies are likewise important for participating in wider debates, inside and outside of China.

Finally, this chapter has suggested shifting understandings in the nature of the church. Due to the rapid urbanization and modernization experienced by contemporary China, the traditional structure of the Chinese family has broken down. In one respect, the church has become a surrogate family which is a key vehicle for public engagement. But the church's online presence offers a virtual dimension which extends beyond physical boundaries. This is quite important given that Chinese religiosity has traditionally prioritized physical religious space, particularly around the family home and the ancestral hall. The urban

---

46 Wang Yi, "My Declaration of Faithful Disobedience," 4 October 2018, trans. China Partnership, http://www.chinapartnership.org/blog/2018/12/my-declaration-of-faithful-disobedience.
47 See https://www.facebook.com/earlyraincovenantchurch and https://github.com/chengduqiuyu/-/issues.
48 See Zhou Youyou, "Four of the Top 25 Github Projects Are Written in Chinese, Six Containing No Code," *Quartz*, 17 May 2018, https://qz.com/1280215/four-of-the-top-25-github-projects-are-written-in-chinese-six-contain-no-code/. Elliott Zaagman, "Github Gives Chinese Developers Censor-Proof Forum," *TechNode*, 16 April 2019, https://technode.com/2019/04/16/github-gives-chinese-developers-censor-proof-forum/.
49 Jürgen Habermas, *The Structural Transformation of the Public Sphere: An Inquiry into a Category of Bourgeois Society*, trans. Thomas Burger (Cambridge: Polity Press, 1989), 27–56.

church as a surrogate family outside of one's ancestral home, and now with a virtual dimension, radically reorganizes understandings of religious space and ecclesiology. Moreover, their online presence allows both Shouwang and Early Rain to engage a wider social network of Christians and non-Christians. Chinese public theologians, in their utilization of digital media behind and beyond the Great Firewall of China, produce new theological questions around how the Christian, the public theologian, and the church can engage the state and the society.

7 Bibliography

Barme, Geremie R., and Sang Ye. "The Great Firewall of China." *Wired*, 1 June 1997. https://www.wired.com/1997/06/china-3/.

Barwick, John. "Liu Tingfang: Christian Minister and Activist Intellectual." In *Salt and Light 3: More Lives of Faith that Shaped Modern China*, edited by Carol Lee Hamrin with Stacey Bieler, 59–80. Eugene, OR: Pickwick Publishers, 2011.

Brokaw, Cynthia, and Christopher A. Reed, eds. *From Woodblocks to the Internet: Chinese Publishing and Print Culture in Transition, circa 1800 to 2008*. Leiden: Brill, 2010.

Cao Nanlai. "Spatial Modernity, Party Building, and Local Governance: Putting the Christian Cross-Removal Campaign in Context." *The China Review* 17, no. 1 (February 2017): 29–52.

Cheek, Timothy. *The Intellectual in Modern Chinese History*. Cambridge: Cambridge University Press, 2015.

Chow, Alexander. *Chinese Public Theology: Generational Shifts and Confucian Imagination in Chinese Christianity*. Oxford: Oxford University Press, 2018.

Chow, Tse-Tsung. *The May 4th Movement: Intellectual Revolution in Modern China*. Cambridge, MA: Harvard University Press, 1960.

Dunch, Ryan. "Chinese Christianity." In *The Wiley-Blackwell Companion to Chinese Religions*, edited by Randall L. Nadeau, 261–82. Malden, MA: Blackwell, 2012.

Early Rain Reformed Church. "95 Theses: The Reaffirmation of our Stance on the House Church," 18 August 2015. Translated by China Partnership. http://www.chinapartnership.org/blog/2015/08/95-theses-the-reaffirmation-of-our-stance-on-the-house-church.

Editors. "Juan shou yu" [Foreword]. *Xinhua* (2007): 1–2.

Fällman, Fredrik. *Salvation and Modernity: Intellectuals and Faith in Contemporary China*. Rev. ed. Lanham, MD: University Press of America, 2008.

Fällman, Fredrik. "Calvin, Culture and Christ? Developments of Faith Among Chinese Intellectuals." In *Christianity in Contemporary China: Socio-cultural Perspectives*, edited by Francis Khek Gee Lim, 153–68. New York: Routledge, 2013.

Habermas, Jürgen. *The Structural Transformation of the Public Sphere: An Inquiry Into a Category of Bourgeois Society*, trans. Thomas Burger. Cambridge: Polity Press, 1989.

Hu Shih. *The Chinese Renaissance: The Haskell Lectures, 1933*. Chicago: University of Chicago Press, 1934.

Hunter, Alan, and Kim-Kwong Chan. *Protestantism in Contemporary China*. Cambridge: Cambridge University Press, 1993.
Jin Tianming. "Tuidong jiaohui dengji dao jintian" [The Promotion of Church Registration]. *Xinghua* (Spring 2008): 40–1.
Jin Tianming. "Women ruoshi yu Jidu tong si, jiu xin bi yu ta tong huo" [Now If We Died with Christ, We Believe that We Will Also Live with Him]. *@Shouwang* no. 1 (2011): 4–10.
Johnson, Ian. "Pastor Charged with 'Inciting Subversion' as China Cracks Down on Churches," *New York Times*, 13 December 2018. https://www.nytimes.com/2018/12/13/world/asia/china-religion-crackdown.html.
Kim, Sebastian C. H. *Theology in the Public Sphere: Public Theology as a Catalyst for Open Debate*. London: SCM Press, 2011.
Lai Pan-chiu, and Li Lili. "Chinese Catholic Responses to Sino-Japanese War: A Study of Xu Zongze's Public Theology of War and Peace." In *Yearbook of Chinese Theology, 2017*, edited by Paulos Z. Huang, 166–86. Leiden: Brill, 2017.
Lee, Leo Ou-Fan. "Literary Trends I: The Quest for Modernity, 1895–1927." In *The Cambridge History of China, Vol. 12: Republican China 1912–1949, Pt. 1*, edited by John K. Fairbank, 451–504. Cambridge: Cambridge University Press, 1983.
Ling, Samuel D. "The Other May Fourth Movement: The Chinese 'Christian Renaissance,' 1919–1937." PhD diss., Temple University, 1980.
Liu Tongsu and Wang Yi. *Guankan Zhongguo chengshi jiating jiaohui* [Observation on China's House Churches in Cities]. Taipei: Christian Arts Press, 2012.
Liu, Lydia H. *Translingual Practice: Literature, National Culture, and Translated Modernity – China, 1900–1937*. Stanford: Stanford University Press, 1995.
Marty, Martin E. "Reinhold Niebuhr: Public Theology and the American Experience." *The Journal of Religion* 54, no. 4 (1974): 332–59.
McLeister, Mark. "Chinese Protestant Reactions to the Zhejiang 'Three Rectifications, One Demolition' Campaign." *Review of Religion and Chinese Society* 5, no. 1 (2018): 76–100.
Pew Forum on Religion and Public Life. *Global Christianity: A Report on the Size and Distribution of the World's Christian Population*. Washington, DC: Pew Research Center, 2011.
Phillips, Tom. "China on Course to Become 'World's Most Christian Nation' within 15 Years." *Telegraph*, 19 April 2014. http://www.telegraph.co.uk/news/worldnews/asia/china/10776023/China-on-course-to-become-worlds-most-Christian-nation-within-15-years.html.
Reed, Christopher A. "Introduction." In *From Woodblocks to the Internet: Chinese Publishing and Print Culture in Transition, circa 1800 to 2008*, edited by Cynthia Brokaw and Christopher A. Reed. Leiden: Brill, 2010.
Reed, Christopher A. *Gutenberg in Shanghai: Chinese Print Capitalism, 1876–1937*. Vancouver: UBC Press, 2011.
Rudolph, Josh. "Sensitive Words: Xi to Ascend His Throne (Updated)." *China Digital Times*, 26 February 2018. https://chinadigitaltimes.net/2018/02/sensitive-words-emperor-xi-jinping-ascend-throne/.
Schwarcz, Vera. *The Chinese Enlightenment: Intellectuals and the Legacy of the May Fourth Movement of 1919*. Berkeley: University of California Press, 1986.
Shijie zongjiao yanjiu suo, Jidujiao diaoyan keti zu [Institute of World Religions, Christian Investigative Project Team]. *Zhongguo Jidujiao diaoyan baogao ji* [Reports on

Investigations Concerning Protestant Christianity in China]. Beijing: Chinese Academy of Social Sciences Publishers, 2011.
Starr, Chloë F. *Chinese Theology: Text and Context*. New Haven, CT: Yale University Press, 2016.
Starr, Chloë F. "Wang Yi and the 95 Theses of the Chinese Reformed Church." *Religions* 7 (2016/12): 1–15.
Sun Yi. "Jidujiao jiuguo qingjie dui jiaohui guan de yingxiang" [The Influence of Christian National Salvation Complex upon Ecclesiology]. *Xinghua* (Winter 2012): 37–40.
Tu Weiming. "Intellectuals in a World Made of Knowledge." *The Canadian Journal of Sociology* 30, no. 2 (Spring 2005): 219–26.
Vala, Carsten T. *The Politics of Protestant Churches and the Party-State in China: God Above Party?* New York: Routledge, 2018.
Vala, Carsten, and Huang Jianbo. "Three High-Profile Protestant Microbloggers in Contemporary China: Expanding Public Discourse or Burrowing into Religious Niches on Weibo?" In *Religion and Media in China: Insights and Case Studies from the Mainland, Taiwan and Hong Kong*, edited by Stefania Travagnin, 176–81. New York: Routledge, 2017.
Wang Yi. "Jin Tianming shi ni shenme ren?" [Who is Jin Tianming to You?]. *Meizhou mu han* [Weekly Pastoral Letter] 3 February 2013.
Wang Yi. "My Declaration of Faithful Disobedience," 4 October 2018. Translated by China Partnership. http://www.chinapartnership.org/blog/2018/12/my-declaration-of-faithful-disobedience.
Wickeri, Philip L. *Seeking the Common Ground: Protestant Christianity, the Three-Self Movement, and China's United Front*. Maryknoll, NY: Orbis Books, 1988.
Wielander, Gerda. *Christian Values in Communist China*. New York: Routledge, 2013.
Yeh, Wen-hsin. *Provincial Passages: Culture, Space, and the Origins of Chinese Communism*. Berkeley: University of California Press, 1996.
Ying Fuk-tsang. "Mainland China." In *Christianities in Asia*, edited by Peter C. Phan, 149–70. Malden, MA: Wiley-Blackwell, 2011.
Ying Fuk-tsang (Xing Fuzang). "Chai shizijia de zhengzhi: Zhejiang sheng 'Sangai yichai' yundong de zongjiao-zhengzhi fenxi" [The Politics of Cross Demolition: A Religio-Political Analysis of the "Three Transformations and One Demolition" Campaign in Zhejiang Province]. *Logos and Pneuma*, no. 44 (January 2016): 25–61.
Zaagman, Elliott. "Github Gives Chinese Developers Censor-Proof Forum." *TechNode*, 16 April 2019. https://technode.com/2019/04/16/github-gives-chinese-developers-censor-proof-forum/.
Zhou Youyou. "Four of the Top 25 Github Projects Are Written in Chinese, Six Containing No Code." *Quartz*, 17 May 2018. https://qz.com/1280215/four-of-the-top-25-github-projects-are-written-in-chinese-six-contain-no-code/.

Index

Albanian   140, 291
algorithm   151, 166, 174
analysis
– computational   12, 13, 38, 117, 198, 223, 266f., 275f., 301, 309
– graph and visual   69, 223, 313, 316
– linguistic   12, 63, 117, 175, 177, 182f., 188, 190, 227
– of digital culture   1, 7, 34, 283
– postcolonial   8
– quantitative   157, 209, 301, 308
– textual   2, 10, 47, 68, 84, 135, 261, 263f., 272, 274, 313
– *see also* social network analysis
Anglicanism   see Church of England
annotation   62, 65, 68, 116–118, 132, 272
anthropology   196, 285
application programming interface (API)   61–63. 91, 97, 129
Aquinas, Thomas   30, 55f., 69
Arabic
– Bible in   25, 34f.
– Christian texts   103, 105–108, 127, 139–141, 265
– learning   131
– translation 34, 136f., 143f.
archives   11–13, 28f., 47, 53, 67, 87, 132f., 140f., 144f., 199, 213, 216, 218–220, 222–224, 226, 232f., 264, 311
Armenian   103, 106–108, 127, 139, 141, 262
Augustine of Hippo   70, 97, 218, 257, 306, 333
autobiography   214, 216, 218–220, 223, 233

Barnabas (Epistle of)   105–107, 120
Barth, Karl   24, 37, 41
Bible
– as text   1, 8, 28, 56, 138, 152f., 155f., 158, 160, 162, 165, 214, 238, 245f., 256f., 322, 325, 327
– Bible app *see* YouVersion

– citations of   56, 71, 78–81, 87, 95f., 253f., 266
– computer analysis of   4–6, 10, 30, 134,
– in digital age   21–25, 36, 39f., 283, 291f., 294
Bonaventure   49
Book of Common Prayer   238, 240, 242f., 245, 247
Busa, Roberto   4, 29f., 38
Bush, Vannevar   38

Calvin   237, 243, 328
canon   9–11, 24f., 36, 41, 77–85, 88f., 94–99, 106, 138, 158, 246, 253f., 261f.
Casanowicz, Immanuel   155f., 159
catalogue   37, 55f., 64, 98, 112, 114f., 134, 138, 139f., 221, 264, 271
Catholicism   29, 47, 213, 251–254, 257, 319f., 324, 332
children   186, 217, 242, 291–297
China   14, 319–335
Church of England   14, 238, 242f., 245, 247, 251–253, 258, 283, 288f.
classification   37, 119, 130, 156f., 159, 170, 185, 199, 209, 263, 266
Clement of Alexandria 79, 103–105, 111, 113f.
clustering   172, 229, 231, 313
Codex Sinaiticus   37, 80, 87, 119, 134, 144
collaboration   1, 12, 14, 33–35, 38, 73, 98, 103, 111, 114f., 134, 136f., 247, 250, 261, 266–268, 273, 275, 281f., 287, 296, 301, 308f., 312, 324
commentary   11, 47–49, 55, 64, 69, 71, 83, 103, 111, 158, 283
communities
– academic   24–28, 34f., 37, 47–49, 53–60, 67, 72f., 77, 84, 88, 90f., 97–99, 133, 136, 304
– religious   13, 24, 39–41, 157, 165, 198, 204f., 207, 214f., 217f., 219–221, 223, 228–231, 238, 247, 249, 252–254, 257,

267f., 283f., 287, 289–293, 295–298, 320, 325, 328
computer language   28, 128f.
computing   10, 28, 131
– see also humanities computing
concordance   4f., 138, 266, 275
Confucianism   322f., 326
Coptic   103–110, 113f., 116–118, 127, 130, 135–137, 139, 141f., 144, 262, 268
corpora   6, 11, 52, 110, 118, 127, 133, 161f., 164f., 170f., 173, 223
Cranmer, Thomas   245f.

databases
– interaction between   54, 60, 63, 112, 129, 134f., 274
– lexical   110, 115, 118, 159
– primary sources   12f., 65, 81, 96, 127, 131, 138f., 143–145, 221, 228, 233, 263f., 266–270, 275, 302
– structure and making of   8, 128f., 136, 198, 224, 226, 268, 271
data mining   110, 117
Didache   105, 113
Digital Humanities,
– and biblical studies   5, 22, 40
– and collaboration   134, 296
– and pedagogy   282, 310, 313
– history of   29f., 311
– definition of   1, 3, 8, 38, 151, 198, 209, 223, 281f., 311
digital religion   5
digital revolution   2, 5f., 13f., 51, 261
digitization   1, 7, 96, 103, 110f., 112f., 120, 134, 137f., 213, 222f., 226, 233, 275, 283
digitized humanities   3f., 7, 38
Donne, John   237f., 240f., 243f., 247–259

ecclesiology   214, 218, 220, 281, 329f., 335
editing tools   39, 54, 59, 115, 132, 135, 226, 264, 271f.
edition
– citations of   78f., 87–89, 99, 266
– digital   9, 13, 38, 50–52, 58, 65, 77f., 82–85, 90, 93, 96, 114f., 265, 272–275

– print   55, 59, 116, 137, 243
– scholarly or critical   11, 22, 31–37, 47, 49, 82–85, 103–109, 111, 135, 271
encoding   9f., 28, 52, 59f., 69, 84, 94, 118, 128f., 132, 138, 140, 159, 265, 271–273
– see also Text Encoding Initiative (TEI)
Ethiopic   103, 105–107, 109f., 116–118, 127, 139, 141f.
Eusebius of Caesarea   80, 108, 134
extensible markup language (XML)   55, 93, 116, 128f., 134, 137, 139f., 226, 271–273, 275

Facebook   25, 289, 326, 334
flesh (in Greek: sarx)   169, 177–179, 183f., 191, 284f.

game   283, 291–297
Georgian   103, 105, 109, 113, 127, 141f.
Google   31, 52
Greek
– ancient   118, 133, 151f.
– and other languages   136f
– Bible in   25, 31–37, 41, 114, 134, 137f., 169, 174, 327
– Christian texts   11, 103, 105, 107, 111, 114f., 117, 119, 127, 130, 137f., 265
– learning   131–133, 135, 143–145
Gui, Bernard (Book of Sentences)   197, 201, 206
Gutenberg, Johannes   23, 321f., 324f.

hapax legomena   12, 151–166
Hebrew   12, 131, 141, 152–154, 158, 163, 165f., 176, 265, 327f.
Hermas (Shepherd of)   103f., 109f., 113
history
– ancient and early Christian   14, 110, 127, 135, 143, 157, 262, 301–304, 306, 313–317
– medieval and modern Christian   90, 197, 200, 213–216, 218, 223f., 227f., 233, 238f., 258, 268, 298
– of China   14, 321–325, 329
– of DH see Digital Humanities, history of
– of liturgy   261f., 265, 267, 269, 275f.

– of textual studies 11 f., 81, 85, 108, 134, 137, 140, 158, 309
humanities computing 1, 4, 29 f., 37 f., 313
hypertext markup language (HTML) 88–94, 116, 128

Ignatius of Antioch 106 f., 117
inquisition 12, 195, 197, 199, 202–204, 208 f.
– and inquisitorial procedures 195, 197, 198, 202–205, 209 f.
– and inquisitors' manuals 195, 198, 201, 204
– sampling methods 205–209
– sources and registers 197, 199 f., 206, 208 f.
interface 10, 93, 118, 136, 224, 226, 238
– see also API
interpretation, history of 21–45, 47–75, 77–102, 103–123, 127–149, 152–165, 195–202, 215–222
International Image Interoperability Framework (IIIF) 62, 65, 90 f.
internet 3, 33 f., 38, 68, 72, 77, 85, 96, 98, 116, 135, 144, 213, 285, 292, 321, 324–327, 334
interoperability 53, 58 f., 272
– see also International Image Interoperability Framework (IIIF)

Jesus 34, 36, 79, 158, 188, 190, 231, 241, 244, 281, 283, 285, 292, 306, 333

languages
– ancient 11, 103, 112, 127, 131 f., 136, 141–143
– evolution of 154, 164 f., 223
– learning of 131–133, 170 f., 286
– vernacular 200, 246, 322 f.
– see also Albanian; Arabic; Coptic; Ethiopic; Georgian; Greek; Hebrew; Latin; Syriac
Latin
– Bible in 35, 80
– learning 130–132, 136, 142–144
– nonbiblical texts in 50, 82–84, 97 f., 103–111, 113 f., 117 f., 120, 127, 133 f., 140 f., 200 f., 252, 265, 270

lexicography 12, 131–133, 169, 174, 265
libraries 5 f., 9, 35, 40, 55, 62, 65, 90 f., 104–107, 111–113, 130–140, 197, 222, 263, 275
liturgy 13, 85, 138, 142, 238 f., 241, 245, 261–275
Lombard, Peter 49, 55
Luther, Martin 243, 332 f.

machine learning 166
manuscripts
– Biblical 10, 33–37, 80, 134
– digitized 9, 62, 65, 82, 91, 112–120, 127, 131, 134, 137–145, 222, 226, 233, 263–267, 269–276
– historical 10 f., 24, 71, 81–84, 104–114, 120, 135, 195, 197, 216, 218, 220, 244
mapping 13, 56, 58, 131, 162
– map visualization 255
– mind maps 14, 301, 306–308, 312 f.
markup 38, 128, 226, 271, 311
– see also extensible markup language (XML)
Masoretes 152 f., 159
medieval literature 47–75, 77–102, 151–168, 195–212
memoirs 13, 213 f., 216–224, 226–228, 231–234
metadata 53, 70, 83, 94, 99, 115, 129 f., 134, 213, 222, 224–226, 233
methodology 8, 173, 177, 196, 206, 213, 305, 319
ministry 39, 281, 283, 285, 288, 290
missionary 82, 227–229, 233, 322
Mirador 65, 67, 91
models and modelling 13, 14, 55 f., 58, 85, 97, 110, 130, 158, 196, 198, 204, 207, 209, 218, 223, 237–241, 243, 248–252, 258, 266, 285, 302–309, 312–317
Moravian Lives 213, 215, 222, 224, 233
multimodality 1, 5, 7, 9 f., 13, 21 f., 25, 37–40

n-grams 151–168, 169–192

Optical character recognition (OCR) 117
ontology 166

Open Access   33, 37, 51, 112, 114, 116, 118, 129 f., 135–137, 267
orality   9 f., 40, 220, 238, 243, 245 f., 319

painting   38, 239
Papias   108
Patrick of Ireland   82
patristic literature   9, 52, 106–108, 143
pattern   12, 71, 95, 158, 165, 171, 184, 187 f., 198, 202, 217, 222 f., 226, 253, 267, 269, 275, 305, 308 f., 313, 316
pedagogy   10, 13, 132 f., 142 f., 281–285, 287–291, 295 f., 298, 301–304, 306 f., 310 f., 313, 317
Peirce, Charles Sanders   301–306, 316
permalink   86–89, 95, 98 f.
persistent identifier (PID)   81, 85–87, 98
philology   30, 48, 133, 157
power
– supernatural   185, 187 f.
– political   202–204, 206 f., 251, 325
– of language   7, 254 f., 292, 325
preservation   28, 51, 59, 77, 92, 94, 98, 116, 133, 153, 199, 209, 219
printing and print culture   9, 81, 96, 214, 283, 321 f., 324 f.
Protestantism   14, 21, 23 f., 31, 40, 48–50, 214 f., 242, 251 f., 257, 319 f., 329
– See also Reformation, Protestant
Prudentius   134
publishing, digital
– approaches to   11 f., 21, 27, 31, 35, 38 f., 52 f., 56 f., 61, 85, 88–90, 93, 113, 129 f., 132 f., 266
– as challenge to traditional models   1 f., 5 f., 11, 47, 50 f., 77, 98 f., 261, 282, 334

Reformation, Protestant   21, 23 f., 48 f., 71, 207, 213–215, 237 f., 242 f., 245 f., 250–252, 257, 325, 332
Resource Description Framework (RDF)   59 f., 63–65, 70, 129 f.

scholasticism   11, 47–53, 55 f., 64 f., 68, 72 f., 324
Scottish Episcopal Church   284, 288

Scripture   5, 21, 24, 36, 37, 40 f., 70, 241, 244, 257, 267
– see Bible
segmentation   116
semantics   129, 154, 158, 166, 169 f., 173 f., 176 f., 187 f., 190 f.
– semantic codes and identifiers   69, 81 f., 84 f., 87, 95, 98, 223
– semantic data   12, 169, 174
– semantic domain   158, 161, 169, 173–175, 184
– semantic structure   53, 81
– semantic web   47, 129 f.
Septuagint   138, 153, 158, 160 f., 171 f.
sermon   13, 237 f., 240 f., 244–252, 254–259, 262, 330, 333
social network analysis   12, 195–198, 204, 213, 215, 223
sociology   2, 33 f., 195–197, 198 f., 202 f., 205 f., 214 f., 319
sources   1 f., 10, 12 f., 50, 63–65, 78, 133 f., 137, 145, 195, 197–202, 206, 208–210, 218, 222, 234, 259, 261–263, 265 f., 268–272, 274 f., 303, 311, 313 f.
spirit (in Greek: *pneuma*, *daimon*)   179 f., 183 f., 187, 220, 243, 281, 284
standard query language (SPARQL)   60–63, 129
standards   1, 11, 47, 53–55, 61, 69, 72 f., 79, 89, 95, 103, 111, 114, 139, 207, 226
statistics   12, 151–153, 155–158, 160–163, 165 f., 170–174
stemma   112–115
St Paul's Cathedral, London   13, 237–260
structured query language (MySQL)   198, 224
Syriac
– early Christian writings   103–111, 113
– digital transcriptions and collections   114, 117, 130, 135 f., 138–141, 143–145, 265.
– learning   131, 133, 142

tagging   110, 114–117
teaching *see* pedagogy
Text Encoding Initiative (TEI)   38, 55, 58 f., 65, 82 f., 91–95, 99, 129, 134, 271 f., 284

textual criticism   9 f., 32 – 34, 36
theology, Christian
– academic study of   1, 9 f., 13, 281, 283, 314
– digital   3 f., 6, 21, 41, 214, 285
– early   127, 143
– historical   10, 31, 50, 68, 233, 242, 323 f., 333
– public   14, 320 f., 325, 327 f., 328 – 331
ThéoTeX 31
tradition
– linguistic and cultural   127, 131, 139, 334
– religious   9, 22, 47 – 49, 51 – 53, 68 f., 73, 80, 105, 143, 206, 208, 215 f., 221, 233, 244, 250, 263, 267, 284, 286, 303, 333
– traditional humanities scholarship   1 f., 9, 11 f., 47 – 49, 89, 96, 98, 151, 232, 272, 287 f., 295 f., 302, 306, 309, 325
transcription   11, 34, 55 – 60, 65, 82 – 84, 106, 110, 114 – 120, 127, 132, 134, 222, 224, 226 f., 233, 252

translation   200, 291
transliteration   34, 117, 136
travel   216, 225 6, 283

Uniform Resource Locator (URL)   86 – 90, 96 – 98
Unix   28

versioning   88 f.
viewer   35, 62, 65, 84, 91, 96, 272
virtual   9, 34, 114, 237 – 239, 242, 247, 252, 258 f., 286, 288, 327, 334 f.
visualization   6, 9, 13, 39, 60 f., 64 f., 112 f., 116 – 120, 129, 131, 198, 213, 215, 223 – 232, 237, 313

Wikipedia   88 f., 96
WorldCat   62

YouVersion Bible app   5, 25, 39 f., 40

www.ingramcontent.com/pod-product-compliance
Lightning Source LLC
Chambersburg PA
CBHW070808300426
44111CB00014B/2449